Nazi Looting

Nazi Looting

The Plunder of Dutch Jewry During the Second World War

Gerard Aalders

Translated by
Arnold Pomerans with Erica Pomerans

Oxford • New York

Translation © 2004 Berg Publishers
Editorial offices:
1st Floor, Angel Court, 81 St Clements Street, Oxford OX4 1AW, UK
838 Broadway, Third Floor, New York NY 10003-4812, USA

Original Dutch language title: *Roof: De ontvreemding van joods bezit tijdens de Tweede Wereldoorlog*, by Gerard Aalders, 1999. All rights reserved. Published in arrangement with the original publishers, SDU Uitgeverij, Den Haag, Netherlands

All rights reserved.
No part of this publication may be reproduced in any form
or by any means without the written permission of Berg.

Berg is an imprint of Oxford International Publishers Ltd.

Library of Congress Cataloging-in-Publication Data

Aalders, Gerard.
 [Roof. English]
 Nazi looting : the plunder of Dutch Jewry during the Second World War / Gerard Aalders ; translated by Arnold Pomerans and Erica Pomerans.
  p. cm.
Original Dutch language title: Roof: De ontvreemding van joods bezit tijdens de Tweede Wereldoorlog.
  ISBN 1-85973-722-6 — ISBN 1-85973-727-7 (pbk.)
 1. Jews—Persecutions—Netherlands. 2. World War, 1939–1945—Confiscations and contributions—Netherlands. 3. Jewish property—Netherlands. 4. Holocaust, Jewish (1939–1945)—Netherlands. 5. Netherlands—Ethnic relations. I. Title.

DS135.N4A2313 2004
940.53'18132'09492—dc22

2003022156

British Library Cataloguing-in-Publication Data
A catalogue record for this book is available from the British Library.

ISBN 1 85973 722 6 (Cloth)
 1 85973 727 7 (Paper)

Typeset by JS Typesetting Ltd, Wellingborough, Northants.
Printed in the United Kingdom by Biddles Ltd, Guildford and King's Lynn.

www.bergpublishers.com

For all the victims of the anti-Jewish decrees

Contents

Preface xi

Acknowledgements xix

List of abbreviations xxi

Introduction 1

Part 1 Looting in the Netherlands during the Second World War

1   The Many Forms of Looting 11
   Introduction 11
   The abolition of the currency border 12
   Levying occupation costs 15
   Contributions to the cost of the war against the Soviet Union 16
   Occupation expenses 16
   Foreign bonds 16
   Looting by purchase 18
   Looting by compulsory charity 20
   Looting by confiscation 23
   Looting by forced surrender or by requisition 23
   Looting by fining 26
   Looting by the liquidation of associations and foundations 26
   Looting by *Kapitalverflechtung* 28
   Looting by individuals 33
   The looting of gold 35
   Monetary gold 35
   Non-monetary gold 37
   The Devisenschutzkommando 37
   The Four-Year Plan 39
   Bühler and Rebholz 40

2   The Looting of Cultural Property 43
   Introduction 43

	The Einsatzstab Reichsleiter Rosenberg	48
	The Kümmel report	49
	Hereditary enemies of Nazi ideology	50
	Competition between the ERR and the RHSA	52
	The ERR in France	54
	The ERR in the Netherlands	56
	The Bibliotheca Rosenthaliana and other libraries	59
	Ants and flies	62
	The Dienststelle Mühlmann	62
	The Dutch art market	66
	The Chabot Collection	68
	The Lugt Collection	70
	The Gutmann and Koenigs Collections	71
	Kröller-Müller	72
	The Lanz and von Pannwitz Collections	73
	N. V. Kunsthandel J. Goudstikker	75
	The leading Nazis' love of art	78
	Hitler's and Göring's financial resources	80
3	**The Allies and the Loot**	85
4	**The Destination of the Loot**	91

Part II The Looting of Jewish Property

5	**The Looting of Jewish Property**	99
	The prelude	99
	The flight of Jewish capital	101
	Preparations for the total seizure of Jewish possessions in the Netherlands	104
	Enemy property	109
	Non-profit-making societies and foundations	111
	Aryanization	114
	The Aryanization of the Jacob Stodel Fine Arts Company	119
	The Aryanization of the diamond industry	120
	Agricultural property	122
	Non-agricultural property	123
6	**The Robber Bank in Sarphatistraat, Amsterdam: Lippmann, Rosenthal & Co. (Liro)**	127
	Introduction	127

Contents

	The establishment of Liro Sarphatistraat	131
	The Liro board of directors	132
	Von Karger and Witscher	134
	The Liro staff	135
	The structure of Liro	136
	Fire and theft insurance	138
	Internal fraud and theft	139
	The *Sammelkonto*	141
	Payments to Jews from Liro funds	142
	Liro's administrative problems	143
7	**The First Liro Decree in Practice**	**147**
	Introduction	147
	The surrender of assets	148
	The price of the surrendered shares	150
	The administrative handling of the shares	151
	Liro Sarphatistraat as accredited stockbroker	152
	Liro securities and normal Stock Exchange transactions	153
	Sales through the Stock Exchange	157
	American shares	159
	Rebholz's discount	162
	How much did members of the Stock Exchange know?	163
	Moral, legal and economic considerations	165
	Sales outside the Stock Exchange	166
	Securities and banks	169
8	**The Second Liro Decree in Practice**	**175**
	Claims	178
	Claims by Aryans against Jews	179
	Claims abroad	179
	Insurance policies	180
9	**The Looting of Cultural Property from Jews**	**185**
	Introduction	185
	The Liro sale of cultural property	186
	Jewish art on loan to museums	195
	Purchases by Dutch museums from Liro	197
	The Rijksmuseum	199
10	**The Looting of Household Effects: The M-Aktion**	**203**

Contents

11	***Sperrstempel*, emigration and tax**	211
	Sperrstempel and emigration	211
	Liro and tax	218
Conclusion		221
	The state of affairs at the Liberation	221
	The looting of Jewish property 1940–45	223
	The selling-off of Dutch cultural property	224
	Discrepancies	224
	The tactics of the looting process	225
	Traceability	227
	To close	228
Notes		229
Exchange Rates and Price Index		283
The Main Anti-Jewish Property Decrees		285
Archives		287
Bibliography		289
Index		301

Preface

In the autumn of 1989, the publication of *Affärer till varje Pris: Wallenbergs hemliga stöd till nazisterna*, a study by Cees Wiebes and myself, caused a great stir in Sweden. Among other things, the English version, entitled *The Art of Cloaking Ownership. The Secret Collaboration and Protection of the German War Industry by the Neutrals: the Case of Sweden*, Amsterdam University Press, 1996, described the close relationship between the Swedish bankers Marcus and Jacob Wallenberg and German concerns during the Second World War. The Wallenberg brothers were certainly no Nazis; their sole motive was profit. To the Wallenbergs, war meant 'business as usual', even though their conduct of affairs during the war differed from their peacetime practice.

For the sake of appearances, the Wallenbergs acquired German subsidiaries in the United States, 'buying' them for the duration of the war. The Americans could not confiscate businesses run by bankers from neutral Sweden as enemy property. Nor did the Swedish tycoons confine themselves to this form of aiding and abetting the Germans; they also bought stolen securities. The furore caused by these disclosures in Sweden was due not so much to indignation at the lax business morals of the two brothers as to sheer amazement: Sweden's most powerful, most influential and frequently idolized family was surely not capable of doing such things. The Swedes simply refused to believe it, and so it could not be true.

The trade in looted Jewish possessions described in *Affärer till varje Pris* was the direct cause of my writing the present book. When the Dutch translation, entitled *Zaken doen tot elke prijs: De economische steun van neutrale staten aan Nazi Duitsland*, was published in 1990, some Jewish circles in Amsterdam concluded that it was time to take a closer look at the looting of Jewish property in the Netherlands during the Second World War. A close study of the post-war restitution policy of the Dutch government would follow naturally from such a scrutiny.

It is largely thanks to Jaap Soesan and Chaïm Natkiel that the investigation was launched in December 1990. During the initial phase, I confined my research mainly to the Ministry of Justice, which, so to speak, became my second home. I owe a large debt to Jaap van Doorn, who in addition to being a very knowledgeable representative of the Ministry, also proved to be a most inspiring and stimulating colleague.

The polite concern ('how very interesting') the outside world had originally shown in my work turned into a sensation in the summer of 1995, when the question of Jewish assets in Switzerland was taken up by the Dutch media and politicians. It did not take long for the concern to spill over from 'fugitive' Jewish capital in Switzerland to all aspects of German looting and to the post-war restoration of rights (a more fitting term than 'restitution'). The press, radio and television wallowed in the fate of stolen art, securities, 'Jewish gold', insurance policies, the Goudstikker case and, last but not least, the Liro affair. That affair, in particular, caused unusually wide interest, not only in the Netherlands, but also in Europe and the United States. At the end of the twentieth century, almost sixty years after the event, looting turned out to be not only a historical fact but a burning topical issue.

The sudden interest in the subject had marked repercussions on the progress of my investigation, because from the middle of 1995 quiet research had to make way for a spell in which there was enormous public interest in my work, a rather bizarre situation for any historian.

The many interviews, requests for information from home and abroad, and speaking engagements at symposia and conferences meant that my original schedule inevitably came to grief. I had originally set aside three days a week for my research. In 1993 this turned into a full-time occupation, thanks to my job at the State Institute for War Documentation (Rijksinstituut voor Oorlogsdocumentatie), which added to the pressure significantly. The international attention paid to the subject as well as my appointment to what had meanwhile been renamed the Netherlands Institute for War Documentation (Nederlands Instituut voor Oorlogsdocumentatie, or Niod) did, however, have a positive effect on my work, which at first had been focused entirely on the looting of Jewish securities. Almost as a matter of course, my research was no longer confined to this one aspect, but spread to the looting of Jewish property at large. Besides my schedule, I also had to revise the planned length of the work.

This volume deals solely with looting in the Kingdom of the Netherlands in Europe. Any comparable events in the Dutch East Indies (now Indonesia) have been ignored; they would have rendered my research, which already embraces a multiplicity of aspects, far too unwieldy.

The varied types of looting, the many government departments involved in it, the complex bureaucratic machinery of the looting process, the special position of stolen cultural objects, and the many decrees and prohibitions connected with the thefts – which, moreover, were often in conflict with or overlapped one another – have made it virtually impossible to present the events in strict chronological order.

A relatively large amount of attention has been devoted to the looting of Jewish and non-Jewish cultural possessions, because of the great interest in this subject, although minor overlaps in this field have clearly been unavoidable. It has also been impossible to avoid the summary treatment of a number of measures passed by the Dutch government in exile and by the Allies, who were aware at an early stage of the vast scale of the looting perpetrated in Europe.

Preface

The anti-looting measures (for instance the Decrees A1, A6, and E 100, passed by the Dutch government, the Allied Declaration and the freeze imposed by President Roosevelt), although important, particularly in the framework of the post-war restoration of legal rights, have been summarized where appropriate. In a number of other cases, it also seemed desirable for the sake of greater clarity to deal in slightly greater detail with the post-war restoration of legal rights and the agencies involved in it. All these subjects will naturally be covered at greater length in the next two volumes.

The looting took various forms. These are reviewed in the introduction and in Chapter 1 of this book, and the meaning of the term 'theft' or 'looting' is defined in terms of the Hague Convention on Land Warfare (1907), which remained in force during the Second World War and had been signed by Germany. The Hitler regime appeared to be fully conversant with this document, and Germany performed prodigious legal feats to act in accordance with it, at least *pro forma*. But apart from their legal aspect, theft and robbery naturally have a moral aspect. I felt that I had to pay particular attention to the legal aspect, but I realized only too well that the very acceptance of the Hague Convention was based on a moral standard. The Convention gave rise to a host of discussions about theft and looting during the Second World War, and in that sense the Convention may be considered a yardstick used throughout this book. In Chapter 1, the reader is presented with a discussion of the many forms of looting that took place and with a summary of the relevant German regulations, which, in principle, affected every Dutch citizen and not merely Dutch Jewry.

Non-Jewish Netherlanders, too, fell victim to a number of compulsory expropriation measures, although their nature and ferocity was hardly comparable to that of the measures to which the Jewish section of the population was subjected. Jews, together with Gypsies, fared by far the worst under the German occupation, both as population groups and also as individuals.

The account of the looting of Dutch Jewry is preceded by a short survey of comparable events in Germany from the moment Hitler seized power in 1933, placing the looting of the Netherlands in a broader historical perspective. In both countries the expropriation of Jewish property was ultimately almost completed.

Much attention is paid to the existence and activities of Lippmann, Rosenthal & Co., Sarphatistraat, Amsterdam (the 'robber bank') and to two of the most important anti-Jewish property decrees (*Verordnungen*), the so-called Liro Decrees. By virtue of the First and Second Liro Decrees, Jews were forced to hand over their real estate and all other assets. Before that happened, however, the expropriation ('Aryanization') of Jewish businesses and the winding up of non-profit-making Jewish associations and foundations had already taken place. Where clarity demands it, special attention has been paid to particular looting organizations such

Preface

as the Einsatzstab Reichsleiter Rosenberg (Reich Leader Rosenberg's Special Task Force).

The theft of Jewish securities has also been examined at length, as has the manner in which the 'tainted shares' found their way to the new shareholders. I estimate that Dutch Jews were robbed of a total of at least one billion guilders (14 billion guilders, or more than six billion US dollars at 1997 rates), and that the theft of securities accounted for about one third of that amount.

I deliberately use the term 'new shareholders' instead of 'new owners'. J. W. Kersten, a member of the editorial committee responsible for the publication of the Dutch edition of this book, has repeatedly drawn my attention to the difference between 'possession' and 'ownership'. Somebody can be in *possession* of a stolen painting, but the mere fact that the canvas hangs on his wall does not make him its *owner*. It is important to keep this distinction in mind. A word of thanks is also due to the other members of the committee, Professor Dr J. de Vries and Dr A. J. van der Leeuw, whom I repeatedly consulted during this study. The committee members saved me from numerous legal, economic and other pitfalls on this 'thieves' road', and I am greatly indebted to them for their extremely helpful observations and comments.

I have been asked many times what I found worst, most memorable, most harrowing or most abhorrent about 'this whole looting business'. I have always had difficulty answering. During my years of detective work in various archives, I regularly came across bizarre cases and complex intrigues. In the long run, that leads to a sort of professional numbness, to one's ability to be surprised being reduced to a minimum. But even though genuine surprise was rare, I was far from immune to dismay and revulsion.

There was one aspect of this whole looting business that struck me as being particularly perverse. I am referring to the Amsterdam 'diamond Jews', who were released from Westerbork camp because the Germans had come to suspect that they must have secreted significant quantities of diamonds and a temporary reprieve seemed the only way of getting hold of the gems. The realization that this particular group had not yet been robbed to the hilt did not filter through to the Germans until the 'diamond Jews' were waiting in the antechamber of death for their final deportation to the east. They were released (after having been stripped of the rest of their possessions) only to be arrested again. This time for good.

What I have tried to demonstrate above all in this study is the thoroughness and systematic nature of the looting. Another striking aspect I shall be stressing repeatedly is the veneer of legality with which the Nazis almost always covered their plundering campaign. With the help of special decrees, Jews were declared liable by law to surrender their property. The question of whether Hitler set to work in the other occupied parts of Europe in a similar way cannot yet be answered for lack of literature in this field. However, in the wake of the recent disclosures,

Preface

investigations have been started, the results of which may be expected within the foreseeable future.

The historian is always dependent on his sources. Chance discoveries sometimes play an important role. The various Dutch ministries, the General State Archives in The Hague and the Netherlands Institute for War Documentation have amassed a vast quantity of material, but the whole story cannot be reconstructed from that alone. Research in the National Archives in Washington has yielded a further quantity of essential material, and so have studies in many other archives.

As the list of the archives consulted shows, these institutions are scattered over a large number of places. Sometimes files turn up that were thought to have been destroyed or that ought to have destroyed in accordance with specific instructions (for instance, in the case of Liro). The discovery of the Liro archives in December 1997 attracted enormous attention, but the overall view of the looting, reconstructed from earlier documents, did not change as a result. Moreover, only a small section of the Liro archives was discovered. The view of the looting may not have been altered by the uncovering of the Liro archives, but there is no question that the discovery made a great emotional impact on those concerned. For them the recovered index cards served as a tangible reminder of the past, and frequently of a murdered member of their family.

Here we touch upon a sensitive, emotional component. The loss of a house, a business or a parcel of shares can be drastic when viewed from the financial angle, but the house, the business and the securities may perhaps be replaced. A silver locket, however, to which intense, very personal memories of a loved one, now dead, are attached, is simply irreplaceable.

Seen in that light, it is pointless to make pronouncements about the value of surrendered or vanished objects. 'Valuable' in that case, at best, tells us something about the material from which these objects were wrought (silver, gold, and so on), but nothing about the emotional value, which, by definition, can neither be determined nor restored. In material terms the theft of gold, silver, art and other collections was relatively small (six million guilders), certainly in comparison with the total value of the loot of at least one billion guilders. That does not detract from the fact that, in emotional terms, the most severe blows were probably struck in this particular area. Restitution is the only acceptable answer, but it proved impossible in most cases, because the objects in question had disappeared without a trace.

The choice and evaluation of the source material is and will always remain a personal matter. I have tried to give the broadest possible sketch of the history of the looting, without allowing myself to be distracted by the countless examples found in the archives. My aim was to throw as much light as possible on the looting process itself, including the bureaucratic procedures bound up with it.

Preface

The historian looks back and knows, with some certainty, the outcome of the historical process. That makes his work easy on the one hand, but on the other hand it can give rise to a form of ill-concealed cynicism. Thus we know today that 'emigration' (*Auswanderung*) was a German euphemism for deportation, and that it meant an almost certain death. However, did the Dutch revenue official, who in 1942 tried to collect the unpaid taxes of 'emigrants' through Liro, realize the gruesome implication of a word that has, no doubt rightly, been called the most euphemistic understatement of the twentieth century? What every one of us knows today is something that that official could not have suspected in his wildest dreams. Or could he? For by no means everybody was blind to what was going on. There were moments when it was difficult to suppress a gibe, although I have done my best. After all, the historian is expected to present his text as clearly and impersonally as possible.

The source material used may be considered extensive but is, in fact, no more than a small selection from the huge quantity of material that has been piling up in my archive over the years. Much of it comes from the period before I joined the Netherlands Institute for War Documentation. From the estimated 80,000 pages that I have amassed in the form of photocopies (which in turn result from vast quantities of archive material) and the many hundreds of metres of relevant archive material found in the Netherlands Institute for War Documentation (on which I can draw directly without having to resort to photocopiers), only a fraction could be included in this book.

The reader will repeatedly be faced with the words 'robbery', 'theft' and 'looting' in combination with other words. This evokes Willem Klaas Elsschot's book *Cheese*. Elsschot uses such odd compounds as 'cheese dream', 'cheese dragon', and 'cheese trial'. In this book too, the reader will find such unusual compounds as 'robber bank', 'robber's universe' or 'robber's kitty'. I am personally less happy with the term 'robbery' because it conjures up associations with such often reported events as train robberies or bank robberies. The words 'plundering', 'booty' or 'pillage' do not quite meet the bill either.

Dutch and English provide few alternatives: 'theft' sounds too vague, 'expropriation' sounds too friendly in the circumstances, and a word such as 'confiscation' is inappropriate because it implies a legal basis, which was only present in camouflaged form. On the other hand, the word 'loot' is perhaps too mild for the circumstances, because those who have not fallen under the wheels of the German looting machine can scarcely have any idea what it means to be forced to surrender literally everything, including the most personal items. But 'loot' and 'looting' are perhaps the most appropriate terms.

Most of the sums and figures mentioned in this book are based on the prevailing rates at the time. The 1997 exchange rate may easily be computed by using the key included at the end.

Preface

This work would have been impossible without the help of the many archivists, recorders, librarians, fellow historians, associates of the Netherlands Institute for War Documentation and a variety of institutions, departments and agencies at home and abroad. All of them have been assured by word of mouth and in writing of how much I value their collaboration and counsel. I remember with great satisfaction and gratitude the many occasions when the discussions were continued informally after the end of the official working day.

Last but not least, I would like to thank Marleen for her patience.

Gerard Aalders
Netherlands Institute for War Documentation
Amsterdam, March 1999.

Acknowledgements

Publication of this translation has been made possible with financial support from the Foundation for the Production and Translation of Dutch Literature. Berg Publishers would also like to thank Centraal Joods Overleg and Prins Bernhard Cultuurfonds for their financial assistance.

Abbreviations

AEZ	Archief ministerie van Economische Zaken
AGA	Amsterdams Gemeente Archief
AGD	Archiefdienst van de Gerechtelijke Diensten
AMF	Archief ministerie van Financiën
AMJ	Archief ministerie van Justitie
ANBO	Algemeen Nederlands Beheer van Onroerende Goederen
ARA	Algemeen Rijksarchief
AZ	Archief ministerie van Algemene Zaken
BdS	Befehlshaber der Sicherheitspolizei und des SD
BEG	Bundesentschädigungsgesetz
Belga	N.V. Beleggings- en Garantie Maatschappij voor Duplicaten van Buitenlandse Effecten
BiZa	Archief ministerie van Binnenlandse Zaken
Brüg	Bundesrückerstattungsgesetz
BuZa	Archief ministerie van Buitenlandse Zaken
BVD	Archief Binnenlandse Veiligheids Dienst
BWEH	Bank voor West Europeeschen Handel
CABR	Centraal Archief Bijzondere Rechtspleging
CGNEB	Commissariaat Generaal voor de Nederlandsche Economische Belangen
CGR	Commissaris Generaal Recuperatie
CORVO	Commissie Rechtsverkeer
CRBE	Commissie Rechtsherstel Buitenlandse Effecten
CVO	Centrale Vermogens Opsporingsdienst
Dego	Deutsche Golddiskontbank
DRT	Deutsche Revisions- und Treuhand AG
DSK	Devisenschutzkommando
ERR	Einsatzstab Reichsleiter Rosenberg
FiWi	General-Kommissariat für Finanz und Wirtschaft
FRUS	Foreign Relations of the United States

Abbreviations

Gestapo	Geheime Staatspolizei
HKB	Hollandsche Koopmansbank
HSSW	Hamburger Stiftung für Sozial- und Wirtschaftsgeschichte
HTW	Handelstrust-West
IARA	Interallied Reparation Agency
IISG	Internationaal Instituut voor Sociale Geschiedenis
IMTN	International Military Trials Nuremberg
JOKOS	Stichting van Joodse Kerkgenootschappen en Sociale Organisaties voor Schadevergoedingsaangelegenheden
KB	Koninklijke Bibliotheek
Krip	Kriminalpolizei
Liro	Lippmann, Rosenthal & Co. Sarphatistraat
LVVS	Liquidatie Vermögens-Verwaltung Sarphatistraat
M-Aktion	Möbelaktion
MFA & A	Monuments Fine Arts and Archives Section
NA	National Archives, Washington DC, USA
NAGU	Niederländische Aktiengesellschaft für die Abwicklung von Unternehmungen
NBI	Nederlandse Beheersinstituut
NedBank	Archief Nederlandsche Bank
NGV	Niederländische Grundstücksverwaltung
Niod	Nederlands Instituut voor Oorlogsdocumentatie (previously Riod)
OKH	Oberkommando des Heeres
OKW	Oberkommando der Wehrmacht
OWC	Departement van Opvoeding, Wetenschap en Cultuurbescherming
POD	Politieke Opsporingsdienst
PRO	Public Record Office, London
RG	Record Group
Riod	Rijksinstituut voor Oorlogsdocumentatie
Robaver	Rotterdamsche Bankvereeniging
Roges	Rohstoff-Handelsgesellschaft mbH

Abbreviations

RSHA	Reichssicherheitshauptamt
RWM	Reichswirtschaftsministerium
SA	Sturmabteilung
SD	Sicherheitsdienst
SNK	Stichting Nederlands Kunstbezit
SP	Sicherheitspolizei
SS	Schutz Staffel
TGC	Tripartite Commission for Restitution of Monetary Gold
URO	United Restitution Organization
V-männer	Vertrauungsmänner
VO	Verordnung
VvdE	Vereniging voor de Effectenhandel
VVRA	Vermögens- und Rentenanstalt
W-Aktion	Weihnachtsaktion
WNRC	Washington National Records Center, Washington DC, USA
WOL	Hague Convention Respecting the Laws and Customs of War on Land
WPS	Wirtschaftsprüfstelle

Introduction

The greatest looting in Dutch history took place during the Second World War.[1] Art treasures, gold, silver, precious stones, jewellery, machinery and transport, valuable ritual objects, manuscripts, complete libraries and archives – to take a few random examples – were stolen by the occupiers, taken to Germany and sold there. This large-scale looting was not, however, confined to the Netherlands: all territories occupied by the Nazis were ravaged by the brutal acquisition of property.

In ancient, and also in more recent times, many cases of serious depredation took place. Napoleon's men also excelled in this field. His Grande Armée dragged national treasures as spoils of war to Paris and lodged them in the brand new Musée Napoléon, now the Louvre. Precious manuscripts, plundered in all parts of the world, were taken to France and placed in the French National Library. During the Congress of Vienna (1814–15), the victors tried to reach some agreement about the return of stolen cultural treasure, but they were no more than partly successful. Much of the loot was left in France.

The British Museum in London, which cynics have called the 'greatest robbers' den in the world', also assembled its inventory in an anything but irreproachable manner – the British Empire was not at all fussy about property rights in colonial territories. But compared with the rapacity of Hitler's Third Reich, these examples fade into insignificance. They were what cat burglary is to a spectacular bank robbery.

Estimates of the total value of the loot are to some extent irrelevant, seeing that the value of a unique painting, statue, manuscript or collection of rare books, in short, of art and cultural treasures in general, is hard to express in monetary terms. That does not mean that no attempts have been made to arrive at approximate figures. However, these have had to be regularly adjusted.

A good example of the arbitrary nature of estimates is the Dutch claim for stolen paintings, which was put at 200 million guilders in 1948. On closer examination it appeared that the term 'paintings' was used to cover all forms of cultural property – not only Rembrandts and Van Goghs but also carpets, sculptures and porcelain.[2]

Much the same applies to the overall value of the loot arrived at by the United States Economic Warfare Department. The department eventually arrived at a figure of $144 million, while Francis H. Tailor, the director of the New York Metropolitan Museum of Art, set the figure at between $2,000 million and $2,500 million, more than the total value of all works of art found in the United States.

Introduction

Finally a report compiled in Paris on 1 June 1945 claimed that the Nazis had stolen approximately one-fifth of all the world's works of art.[3] At the International Military Tribunal in Nuremberg, where the leaders of the Third Reich were put on trial, one of the United States prosecutors summed up the looting of art treasures as follows:

> I doubt that any museum in the world, whether the Metropolitan in New York, the British Museum in London, the Louvre in Paris, or the Tretiakov Gallery in Moscow, could present such a catalogue as this; in fact should they pool their treasures the result would certainly fall far short of the art collection that Germany amassed for itself at the expense of the other nations of Europe. Never in history has a collection so great been amassed with so little scruple.[4]

There is thus anything but unanimity on the subject; the extremely subjective nature of determining the value of works of art renders this impossible.

Things are different when it comes to the value of the precious metals, merchandise and foreign currency stolen by the Germans. But even here the picture is thoroughly muddled by deflation and inflation, revaluation and devaluation, political and economic changes, variations in classification systems, and not least by the time factor. According to a rough estimate by the Dutch Ministry of Economic Affairs, articles worth 3.4 billion guilders were stolen from the Netherlands. That estimate admittedly includes the value of missing paintings (200 million guilders), but the 300 million to 400 million guilders in stolen securities have not been taken into account.[5]

Only towards the end of the war did the Allies, although fully aware of Hitler's rapacity, begin to gain a clearer idea of the full range of this gigantic theft, not least because of the discovery of enormous hoards of loot in southern Germany and Austria.

On 6 April 1945, the advancing American army reached the mines near Merkers in the central German state of Thuringia and came upon a fabulous hoard of cultural treasures. Part of it was German national property that had been taken to safety in this potash mine from Allied air raids and other attacks, but the major share of the art treasures, stocked in piles many metres high, had been pilfered in territories occupied by the Nazis.

At the same time, it became clear what colossal quantities of gold Hitler had misappropriated, remnants of which were discovered in the vaults of the Reichsbank in Frankfurt and in several of its branches.

Yet this was no more than a fraction of the German loot. The greater part had been used to buy goods abroad and had found its way to the vaults of a number of Swiss, Spanish and Portuguese banks. Further gold was found on, or rather in, the soil of the Third Reich. Thus Allied investigation teams discovered gold worth many millions buried near Mittenwald and Garmisch Partenkirchen, there to await

Introduction

more propitious times. Some of this loot came to light during the first post-war summer, but a considerable part remained the property of those who had entrusted it to the earth. A fair amount was discovered and then stolen by American soldiers, often after being told by, and working hand-in-glove with, those who had buried the gold at the end of the war. Nothing has been heard since of these dishonest gold diggers. They disappeared without a trace, just like their loot.

This gold robbery was so embarrassing for the American authorities that they drew a veil over it for many years. It was felt that the disclosure would detract from the heroic character of American army. Not until 1984 was the affair brought into the open, thanks to the stubborn detective work of two Britons, who called it the biggest robbery in history.[6] As an example of 'private' robbery this theft undoubtedly holds pride of place, but compared with what the Nazis misappropriated during their European plunder campaigns it fades into insignificance.

The extent to which the post-war recovery or restitution of stolen property in Europe to its original owners was successful can only be guessed at.[7] In many cases it was hard to provide conclusive legal proof of theft, while in other cases the victims had the greatest possible difficulty in establishing that they had genuinely fallen prey to German rapacity. In this area, the ingenuity and ability of legal counsel proved of paramount importance. Often the country in which the case was brought to court proved to be the essential factor, for there was certainly no uniform approach to the restitution problem, despite international agreements on the subject.

Particularly harrowing are the cases of breaches of confidence to which the Jews, forced by the German decrees to hand over their money, valuables, art objects and paintings to Lippmann, Rosenthal & Co. (Liro) in Sarphatistraat, Amsterdam, fell ready victims. Some Jews tried to elude the decrees by entrusting their property to others, without demanding a written receipt. That seemed, after all, quite unnecessary, for the custodians were generally acquaintances, neighbours and friends. The possession of receipts was, moreover, dangerous because it constituted proof of evasion of the German decrees.

Comparable cases are the businesses and homes registered by notarial act in the name of someone thought to be trustworthy. Secret clauses, specifying that the contract was a sham drawn up for the sole purpose of hoodwinking the Germans and that the *status quo ante* would be restored after the war, could not, of course, be written into the contracts. In a number of cases all went well, but in others the confidence bestowed in the nominee proved badly misplaced. To what extent these *bewariërs* misappropriated possessions entrusted to them will probably never be fully determined because the whole affair was conducted in secret and nothing could be proved against the culprits. In many cases nothing more was heard of the

Introduction

matter for the simple reason that the real (Jewish) owner had perished in a concentration camp, and his heirs, at least those who had survived the camps, very often had no knowledge of the portion that was theirs by right. And how often was documentary evidence not destroyed by fire or by acts of war? We owe our knowledge of these practices to the testimony of the victims. And once these have gone, we are left with no more than stories and suspicions.

Incidentally, the term *bewariër* was perfectly respectable until about 1942–3, and did not to acquire its pejorative connotation – someone who refused to return property entrusted to him – until after the war.

The most unpalatable fact is that those who handed their possessions over to Lippmann, Rosenthal & Co. in accordance with the German decrees had the best chance of restitution or 'rehabilitation', as the return of property to the real owners was called officially after the war. Those Jews who had heeded the decrees, and hence surrendered all their possessions to the Germans, were in possession of written evidence, unlike those who had entrusted their money or goods to trusted fellow citizens. Yet, despite having such administrative proof, they, too, faced a number of problems. Sums of money can be scrupulously accounted for down to the last cent, securities have numbers or are made out in the name of an individual, just like insurance policies, but when it comes to the valuation of silver cutlery, of a gold ring without a hallmark or of precious stones, problems inevitably appear, and confusion is rife. For what price are we to put on 'a silver cutlery canteen', 'a gold ring' or 'a precious stone'? These descriptions apply to many thousands of articles handed over. Worse still, after the Liberation, many of the goods handed in had disappeared, simply because they had been sold long ago – often abroad.

The 'robber bank' in Sarphatistraat – the term was coined by Dr Louis de Jong – administered the surrendered goods, valuables and securities with scrupulous care. Almost the entire bookkeeping apparatus could be reconstructed after the war, albeit with great difficulty.

This book is primarily concerned with the looting of Jewish property, and the many methods the Germans used in the process. The scale of the thefts was immense and ranged from the activities of specially created looting agencies to unorganized plunder by individuals. The last form was ubiquitous and occurred at all times. The first was less widespread and, thanks to its institutionalized form, a typical product of the twentieth century, with its far-reaching organization of companies, its government agencies and its striving after efficiency. Even looting was, so to speak, being run on an 'industrial' scale.

Before we go more deeply into this matter, we must specify what we mean by the term 'loot' (in Dutch, *roof*). In this specific context, *roof* comprises much more than the definition given in Van Dale's *Groot Woordenboek der Nederlandse Taal*

Introduction

(*Great Dictionary of the Dutch Language*), namely, 'the violent seizure of what belongs to others'. Violence may have been one aspect, but it was certainly not a prerequisite; the Germans preferred more subtle methods and often went to a great deal of trouble to lend their depredations the semblance of legality. They did this by 'justifying' them with the help of various decrees (the *Verordnungen* or VOs) by which they assumed the right to confiscate goods at will. According to the British historian Allan Bullock, Hitler would invoke law whenever it suited him to do so. The Führer was greatly attracted to constitutional façades. That was one of the reasons why he did not immediately abolish the Reichstag, which was rendered impotent after the Nazi seizure of power, but used it – whenever it suited him to do so – to, for instance, have the anti-Jewish Nuremberg laws legally adopted.[8]

Throughout this history of the German looting campaign, mention will be made of the Convention Respecting the Laws and Customs of War on Land (WOL), adopted in 1899 at the first Peace Conference in The Hague and revised in 1907. It is also referred to as the Hague Convention. One of its objectives is to protect the civilian population in regions ravaged by war, and it was also meant to afford a certain form of protection to the population of occupied territories. Germany, like the Netherlands, was one of the signatories of the Convention. The Nazis generally rode roughshod over WOL and in many cases it was, in fact, no more than a piece of paper. But on the other hand, Hitler was clearly aware of its existence, although he did not base his actions upon it. In fact, WOL is (apart from the moral viewpoint, which could vary from one individual to the next) the only instrument by which we can gauge the scope of robberies committed in 1940–5.[9]

The use of so many distinct looting methods was to cause a number of specific problems after the war, all hinging on the question of whether it was possible to prove that particular possessions had actually been stolen. The main problem was whether or not the original owner had surrendered his property under direct or indirect threats or extortion.

In order to highlight that difference during the post-war negotiations on restitution, the Dutch authorities made a distinction between 'straight looting' and 'technical looting'. Their definition of looting or theft is found in the 'Dutch Government Memorandum on German Restitution':

All goods by their nature fit for restitution, which the enemy, his agents or his subjects, by the favour of the occupation of the whole part of the Netherlands, have removed from the country's national patrimony as it existed before the occupation, either directly by acts of transfer or dispossession or indirectly by purchases or by transactions effected by means of payment which were created, imposed or extorted by the enemy due to the occupation.[10]

Introduction

The Memorandum treats 'theft' or 'looting' as acts involving different countries. Whether anything was rendered in return was of no importance according to this definition, in view of the fact that the goods had been paid for in worthless or potentially worthless cash, had been obtained by extortion or had been forcibly removed from Dutch ownership in some other way. The value of the loot was put at 3.64 billion guilders.[11]

There is no doubt that the Jewish section of the population suffered most from the war, both materially and psychologically. That does not mean that the rest of the Netherlands had a lucky escape; far from it. The Nazi looting machine was a many-headed monster that menaced the whole of society in occupied territories. The great difference between Jews and Gentiles was that the Jews were the victims of special expropriation measures.

A group comparable to the Jews, and like them the victims of Nazi race delusions, were the Gypsies, a group far smaller in number. The Nazis detested European Gypsies because they did not meet the Nazi criteria of racial purity and national cohesion. They were looked upon as common criminals and treated as such. From 1936 onwards, Gypsies were locked up in German concentration camps and robbed of their possessions, almost as a matter of course.

In the Netherlands, measures against Gypsies were not taken until relatively late in the war (1944). Which persons were covered by the term 'Gypsy' was not, however, clearly defined. According to the Nazis, Gypsies were people who, on the basis of their 'looks', 'customs' and 'habits' could be described as such, or 'who roamed about like Gypsies'. In the middle of May 1944 the Germans started to round them up. Like the Jews, the Gypsies were first taken to Westerbork, a transit camp in Drenthe province. Here, 309 Gypsies were registered, sixty-four of whom were later released. On 19 May 1944, 245 Gypsies were deported to Auschwitz-Birkenau. As far as is known, no more than thirty of them survived.

The property they 'left behind' was confiscated on the orders of the Befehlshaber der Sicherheitzpolizei und des SD (the BdS, or the Commander of the Security Police and the Security Service of the SS), and 'earmarked for . . . removal pending the compilation of inventories'. The items involved were caravans, musical instruments, household effects, clothing, bedding, and the like. Horses were taken to a central depot where they were at the disposal of 'people of good name and reputation'. Jewellery and other valuables had to be sent by registered post to the BdS. Cash was paid into the giro (post office) account of the BdS, and marked 'Gypsy Registration'.[12]

The persecution of the Gypsies was directed by the German Kriminalpolizei (Kripo). What the Kripo did with the confiscated items can no longer be established. All we can say with certainty is that they were kept separate from the list of confiscated Jewish possessions.

Introduction

In additon to Jews and Gypsies, other Netherlanders suffered from German rapacity. To convey some idea of the systematic looting process we shall first look at a range of looting methods not directed specifically at the Jewish population.

At an early stage (on 3 June 1940) Seyss-Inquart ordered an inventory of Dutch property by issuing a special decree to that effect. It covered virtually every field, both in the private and in the state sector.[13] The collated data would later be used to force citizens, authorities and industries to hand in goods or to have their possessions confiscated.

Most forms of looting in the Netherlands were explicitly based on some German decree, order or measure. In addition, however, the Germans were also masters at 'camouflaged' or indirect robbery. In principle, most of the German 'looting decrees' applied to all Dutch citizens. Only two, the so-called Liro Decrees passed in 1941 and 1942, were explicitly directed at the Jewish population. It did not prove practicable to distinguish Jewish property – the main theme of this study – from non-Jewish property in every case, hard though the author tried to apply such a distinction. Too sharp a distinction would moreover have detracted from the clarity of the argument and would have split up the text unnecessarily. By eschewing this approach, it was possible to keep the number of unavoidable overlaps to a minimum.

Part I
Looting in the Netherlands during the Second World War

–1–

The Many Forms of Looting[1]

Introduction

Looting is the oldest form of robbery by soldiers. Through the centuries, it has been considered a normal supplement to their generally meagre pay. In practice, it was a reward for victory, a bonus mercenaries could collect in person as soon as they had defeated the enemy. Even under Roman law, cultural possessions were treated as *res nullius* – ownerless property – as soon as war was begun. The victor was entitled to seize them in accordance with the ancient right of *ius praedae*, the accepted custom of confiscating enemy property. It went so far as to preclude the original owner from the automatic restoration of his rights should he succeed in recovering his property after the war. Only in the Middle Ages, with the emergence of the idea of 'just wars', did a change occur. The underlying idea was that the side waging a just war had the right to seize as much war booty as it could lay its hands on. In the course of time, the distinction between just and unjust wars became increasingly blurred and the legitimacy of seizing spoils of war was no longer taken for granted. However, it was not until the promulgation of the Convention Respecting the Laws and Customs of War on Land (WOL) in 1907 that looting was expressly proscribed.

As far as can be established, the Germans engaged in robbery in all the occupied territories. The civil administration set up in the Netherlands almost immediately after the capitulation appeared especially malignant in its welcome of the chance to implement all the German looting measures passed by the Reichskommissar. When participating in these looting operations, Seyss-Inquart naturally made use of the Netherlands administration, then under Nazi control.

At first the Dutch industrial machinery was left largely intact – although it, too, was placed under strict German control – and Seyss-Inquart did his best to integrate Dutch industry as far as possible with German war aims. Originally, the looting was confined to the confiscation of supplies, radios and means of transport such as ships, bicycles and motorcars, but as the war continued, the rapacity of the *Herrenvolk* assumed increasingly unbridled forms and the Germans increasingly rode roughshod over the WOL convention. After the Allied airborne landings at Arnhem in September 1944, all looting restrictions – insofar as they were still in place – were dropped.

With the approaching end in sight, the Germans began to dismantle a significant part of Dutch industry and removed it to Germany. Only in April 1945, when transport to the Fatherland had become virtually impossible, did the big grab come to an end. Seventy per cent of the looting of the Netherlands took place between September 1944 and April 1945.

A striking difference from earlier times was the radical change in plundering methods. In some ways, these methods may be said to have become more subtle. The Hitler regime looted directly as well as indirectly, that is, not merely by straight coercion but also by camouflaged or implicit extortion: 'If you refuse to sell at the price we are offering, we are entitled to confiscate the articles in question and you will get nothing at all.' Anyone selling under such pressure is in fact no less a victim of robbery than someone who surrenders the contents of his safe under the threat of violence. The form may differ, the approach may change, but for the owner the result is the same.

In addition to direct and implicit coercion, the Nazis also looted by the deliberate misreading of a number of articles of the WOL convention and hence breached the Hague Convention even in that respect. Sometimes the Wehrmacht served as a cover because WOL stipulates that requisitions in kind by an occupying army are permissible. The Germans proved particularly inventive in the interpretation of the WOL articles sanctioning requisitions, systematically ignoring the restrictions stipulated in these articles.

To sum up, a clear distinction must be made between 'direct' and 'indirect' robbery. With 'direct' robbery, the removal of goods under coercion, there can be little argument, although it is possible to differ about the degree of force involved. 'Indirect' robbery (technical looting), by contrast, being far less blatant, is often not even recognized as robbery.[2]

Many examples of indirect robbery will be given below. These involve decrees and measures by the Third Reich imposed on the Dutch state and its citizens:

- the abolition of the currency border between the two countries;
- the levying of 'occupation costs';
- contributions to meet the cost of the war against the Soviet Union;
- costs arising directly from the occupation that could not legitimately be treated as 'occupation costs', but were nevertheless extracted from the occupied country.

All in all these measures yielded the Germans 18,000 billion guilders.

The Abolition of the Currency Border

Before the invasion in 1940, transactions between the Netherlands and Germany were controlled by the Nederlandse Clearinginstituut, which ensured that the imports and exports of various countries were in accordance with bilateral trade agreements. The traffic of goods between Germany and the Netherlands had been subject to a number of regulations before the invasion, and these were enforced by the customs authorities of both countries. Permits for imports and exports were needed and involved the payment of import and export duties. A Dutch supplier was not paid directly by his German client, but by the Clearinginstituut, which, in turn, worked in collaboration with its German counterpart, the Deutsche Verrechnungskasse. These two institutions adjusted mutual debts and claims.

Until 1 January 1940, the Netherlands almost continuously had claims on Germany, although rarely for more than two million guilders. The Netherlands held a considerable amount of foreign currency and enjoyed a favourable balance of payments. Currency controls – that is, control of foreign currency transactions by the Dutch government – were therefore not needed.

With the invasion, the situation changed dramatically. To prevent capital flight and unbridled speculation in foreign currency, gold and securities, state intervention had become imperative. The Amsterdam Stock Exchange was closed, the banks were given instructions to freeze payments to foreign countries, and currency regulations were introduced. This 'emergency currency control measure' by the Dutch government,[3] which was, moreover, meant to use the foreign currency reserves for financing the war and for laying in food supplies, was replaced by the German occupiers on 24 June 1940 with a foreign currency decree bringing financial dealings with the outside world under strict control. VO 27/1940, 'concerning foreign currency transactions', replaced the emergency measures of 10 May, which had simply frozen such transactions. The German decree was to all intents and purposes the same as a law already drafted by the Dutch government for keeping the country solvent in case of war. The establishment of a foreign exchange institute, which issued the necessary permits and ensured the implementation of the new measures, served much the same purpose.

Germany had been familiar with foreign currency controls since 1931, and had set up the necessary control agency. A number of its officials were despatched to the Netherlands as the Devisenschutzkommando (the exchange control commando, or the DSK). The original intention had been to restore the balance of payments, which had been badly disrupted by the economic crisis, but under the Nazis the DSK was used mainly as an instrument of general economic policy.

Immediately after the invasion of the Netherlands, the Germans passed a number of measures intended to 'liberalize' currency exchanges between the two countries in three phases. During the first phase (9 May–1 November 1940), currency exchanges were subjected to strict rules. The second phase (1 November 1940–1 April 1941) saw the abolition of currency restrictions, although that step was still a far cry from total freedom from exchange controls – there were only a few breaches of the currency border. For that reason the period is often referred to as the *durchlöcherte Devisengrenze* (perforated currency border).

Dutch financial circles were strongly opposed to these measures, but on 1 April 1941 they were silenced by the complete abolition of the currency border between the Netherlands and Germany under VO 65/1941, which marked the beginning of the third phase. The regulations governing internal monetary exchanges inside Germany thenceforth applied to the Netherlands as well, although some restrictions were imposed in the case of certain securities. The abolition of the currency border spelled the economic annexation of the Netherlands.

From 1 April 1941 until the Liberation in May 1945 the Nederlandsche Bank was compelled to convert all cash into German Reichsmarks at a (disadvantageous) rate set by the Germans.[4] As a consequence, enormous quantities of marks poured into the Netherlands. The bargain sale of Dutch assets was about to begin.

The Nazis intended to integrate the Netherlands economically into Germany so that Germany might enjoy unhampered control of the goods, raw materials and in some cases means of production (see below); in addition such integration would help to harness Dutch industry to the German military machine. In fact, these measures helped to render 'indirect robbery' as smooth as possible. Even so, the Germans went to great lengths to keep up the appearance of legality and rectitude.

The Dutch economy was robbed systematically by the abolition of the currency border, something that Dutch citizens did not feel directly affected them. After all, they were being paid in guilders for the goods they supplied, and they failed to realize that most of these guilders were nothing but camouflaged marks. The President of the Nederlandsche Bank, the lawyer L. J. A. Trip, observed that German purchases from, and payments to, the Netherlands were 'conducted on the back of the Dutch State, which had to procure the necessary guilders in exchange for any claims against Germany'.[5] His fear that the marks claimed back could not be converted into hard currency proved justified.

The measures that rendered this indirect robbery possible could only be implemented thanks to coercion by the German authorities. Trip did not want to assume responsibility for the consequences and resigned. He was succeeded by another lawyer, M. M. Rost van Tonningen, a member of the NSB (the Nationaal-socialistische Beweging, the Dutch National Socialist Movement), who did as the Germans asked.

This complex of measures had considerable repercussions on the currencies of both countries. The German marks found their way to the Nederlandsche Bank and lay there for the rest of the war, with the result that at the Liberation the Reichsmark claims of the Nederlandsche Bank ran to about six billion marks. After the abolition of the currency border, shares and bonds disappeared into Germany without any real *quid pro quo*.

Some of the German issuing institutions made grateful use of the abolished exchange border by redeeming loans prematurely. Such transactions were highly advantageous to them, thanks to the favourable rate of exchange. Many German agencies seized this opportunity to liquidate their foreign obligations on the cheap.

Levying Occupation Costs

Another form of indirect robbery involved burdening the Netherlands with exorbitant occupation costs (more than 6.3 billion guilders). The money was paid straight to the Wehrmacht. In April 1941, after nearly a year of occupation, the Germans decided that the Netherlands would have to make a supplementary payment. Thus, on 1 April, together with the abolition of exchange controls, Berlin levied a retrospective tax of 376.8 million guilders, as an afterthought so to speak, to cover 'costs incurred by the German Reich within Germany for the occupation of the Netherlands'. Seventy-seven million had to be paid in gold; the rest was offset against Dutch claims on Germany.[6]

Article 52 of WOL laid down that requisitions in kind and services could be imposed for the benefit of the army of occupation. They had to be in proportion to the resources of the occupied country. In practice, such requisitions were often marked 'on behalf of the Wehrmacht'. The Germans continued to go to great lengths to lend their measures a veneer of legality, as may be gathered from the accompanying VO 49 (16 July 1940), which refers to 'regular tasks' performed on behalf of the Wehrmacht. These tasks included the supply of goods, but not 'the provision of land or buildings'. It was not until September 1940 that the confiscation of 'cultivated or uncultivated grounds' on behalf of the German army was sanctioned by VO 144.

At the same time the Netherlands was saddled with the costs of the German civil administration, which amounted to 173.8 million guilders. When that amount is added to the occupation costs, it is found that the Third Reich collected more than seven billion guilders in occupation costs.[7]

By a special decree (18 May 1940), a Reichskommisar was appointed and the entire Dutch administrative machinery placed in German hands. The same thing happened in Luxembourg and Norway, while in France and Belgium the Germans made do with military occupation, leaving it to the Befehlshaber (military commanders) to decide how to allocate the funds that flowed into the German coffers. Nor were exchange controls abolished in these countries. One of the consequences was that marks smuggled in and used to pay for unauthorized purchases of goods could not be changed into French or Belgian francs and found their way illegally into the Netherlands.

Under the leadership of Reichskommissar Dr Arthur Seyss-Inquart, four general commissars, experts and other officials were appointed and settled themselves into every nook and cranny of the Dutch economy. As a result, the Commissioner

General for Finance and Economic Affairs, H. Fischböck, and his colleagues gained a stranglehold on the entire financial and economic system.[8]

Contributions to the Cost of the War against the Soviet Union

The Netherlands was also made to bear part of the cost of the war against the Soviet Union. The first 'instalment' was demanded in 1942 but was applied retrospectively to the beginning of the war in the east, that is, to June 1941. The Netherlands had to contribute 37.5 million guilders a month. Part (7.5 million guilders) had to be paid in gold, while another part was used to offset Dutch claims against Germany. The Germans used this method to enrich themselves by a total of 1.69 billion guilders. The Netherlands thus helped to pay for a war that had nothing to do with it, although the Germans, of course, thought otherwise. If we consider this sum, too, a direct consequence of, and hence part of, the occupation costs, then the Netherlands paid out more than 8.7 billion guilders at the rate prevailing at the time.

According to WOL[9] the occupying force was entitled to recover the costs of the occupation within reasonable limits, but these limits had to be based on the resources of the occupied country and 'this shall only be for the needs of the army or of the administration of the territory in question' (Article 49). Hence the total amount of nearly nine billion guilders cannot be treated as unmitigated robbery, certainly not when 'occupation costs' were involved, because a charge for these could be levied legitimately. Even so, it is clear that the levies foisted upon the Netherlands were absurdly high and bore no relation to the costs actually incurred. Only half of the costs of the eighteen billion guilders claimed for the occupation can be accounted for in this way.

Occupation Expenses

Credits obtained under German pressure and the costs of evacuating citizens and institutions account for the other half. In any case, the major part of these costs (approximately 8.5 billion guilders) arose from extra government expenditure due to German insistence that the Dutch civil administration be run on German lines. The resulting changes and adaptations cost on average 1.7 billion guilders a year.[10]

Foreign Bonds

Auslandbonds were foreign bonds issued by the German state and by German institutions and industries in *non*-German currency, together with foreign share

The Many Forms of Looting

certificates issued in the Netherlands. They appeared mainly in 1924–31, when Germany contracted large foreign debts. A post-war investigation by the Netherlands Ministry of Finance estimated that the total value of these bonds was just on 200 million guilders. Another 100 million had to be added for interest. The occupying force treated *Auslandbonds* as foreign securities, which meant that trading in them required a special permit from the exchange control institute.

The Dutch board of the foreign-exchange control institute was extremely parsimonious in issuing permits, but in the long run it was unable to stand up to German pressure. Repeated refusals generally resulted in threats that the Germans would take the issue of permits into their own hands, and this, the board feared, would be the thin end of the wedge.[11]

The German trade in these foreign bonds was reserved for the Deutsche Golddiskontobank (the German Gold Discount Bank, or Dego). Since 1933–4, Dego had been buying foreign bonds on behalf of the Konversionskasse für Deutsche Auslandsschulden (Conversion Bank for German Foreign Debts). The purpose of buying up these foreign bonds was to repay Germany's foreign debt *below* market value. Since the *Stillhalte* or standstill of 1931, the blocking of all bank accounts held by foreigners in Germany, and the stopping of repayments of short-term foreign credits, the price of *Auslandbonds* had declined markedly. Two years later, interest transfers were also stopped (*Transfer-moratorium*), to the considerable financial disadvantage of long-term credit providers and particularly of the foreign owners of *Auslandbonds*. The curbs on interest payments exerted a strong downward pressure on the value of these securities, which was precisely what Hjalmar Schacht, Hitler's Minister of Economic Affairs, intended to achieve. It did not take long before *Auslandbonds* dropped to half of their nominal value.[12]

The background for these measures was that, in 1931, Germany's balance of payments had been badly upset – something she was unable to remedy with a permanent export of gold. Nor did the German government want to leave the rate of exchange, and hence the values of the mark, to the supply-and-demand fluctuations of the free market. Germany preferred a more drastic solution: government control of all foreign-currency transactions. The first step was the proclamation of a *Stillhalte* on 15 July 1931 (see above).

As a result, free marks came to exist side by side with *Sperrmarken* (blocked marks). Although originally intended as an emergency measure to prevent a drastic drain of foreign bank balances, it turned into a permanent German currency control mechanism, which, moreover, became more and more complex with the passage of time.

However, capital transactions with foreign countries were not confined to the transfer of bank balances, and the ever-increasing difficulties of transferring foreign debts forced the German government to pass a transfer moratorium on 15 June 1933.[13] Between September 1941 and September 1944, three Amsterdam stockbroking companies with close German connections, namely Rebholz's Bankierskantoor, Hollandsche Koopmansbank (HKB) and Wodan Handelsmaatschappij (from 9 March 1942 amalgamated with Kol & Co.) were given permission by the Deviezeninstituut to buy *Auslandsbonds.* The purchases of this so-called 'Konto Trio' – after the addition of Kol & Co, it operated as the Konto Quarto – were conducted on the orders of Seyss-Inquart, who sold the bonds, in turn, to Dego in Berlin. That bank was forced to reduce its foreign debt annually by a fixed amount. Thanks to the war, the Netherlands was one of the few countries that could still be considered as markets for *Auslandsbonds*.

The sales to Germany helped Seyss-Inquart to make an exchange profit of five million guilders. With that money he 'bought' the Mannheimer Collection, one of the best-known private art collections in the Netherlands, and offered it to Adolf Hitler, who, in his turn, earmarked it for the Führermuseum to be built in Linz, Austria.[14] At first sight, this may look like a generous gesture, but on closer examination it proves more selfish than one might have believed. To begin with, the exchange windfall dropped into Seyss-Inquart's lap as a result of the foreign exchange regulations, and secondly, the Reichskommissar paid less than two-thirds of the true value of the famous collection, which was valued at eight million guilders in 1940.[15] Alois Miedl, a German businessman, banker and acquaintance of Reichsmarschall Hermann Göring, had offered 7.5 million guilders, but due to the intervention of Dr Kajetan Mühlmann, a close collaborator of Seyss-Inquart, whose task it was to 'take works of art to places of safety', the sale was called off. Protests by Miedl were of no avail; the Reichskommissar acquired the collection for 5.5 million guilders.[16]

Looting by Purchase

In the autumn of 1945, the Reparation Conference opened in Paris. The countries occupied by Germany had gathered in France to discuss the damage they had suffered and to press claims against the defeated Third Reich. At this conference, the Netherlands presented a claim of 26 billion guilders. That amount was a rough estimate of the economic damages suffered by the Netherlands during the war. It included not only looting but also every conceivable German measure and activity that had damaged the Netherlands. The claim was deliberately kept on the high side in the belief that the higher the opening bid the greater the chance of being paid. In the event, it looked most unlikely that a great deal could be recovered from a defeated Germany.

In the 'Memorandum by the Dutch Government on its Compensation Claims against Germany', on which The Hague based its claims, stolen goods were defined as objects that the Germans had misappropriated directly by forced transfer

The Many Forms of Looting

and expropriation, or indirectly by sham purchase or other means whereby, as the occupying power, they forced the legitimate owners to surrender their possessions. Whether anything was tendered in exchange was irrelevant in this connection, since the owners were often paid in money that though it had some officially set value, was in practice virtually worthless after the war.

That was also true of the *Reichskreditkassenscheine* introduced directly after the Dutch capitulation. These were paper marks that, though issued by the Reichsbank, were not valid in Germany but were intended exclusively for use in the occupied territories. This unlimited supply of paper money provided the Germans with what Trip, the president of the Nederlandsche Bank, called 'total financial control'.[17] *Reichskreditkassen* (Reich credit offices) were opened in various Dutch cities to speed the circulation of the new currency. The notes in question did not enjoy a long life, because the Nederlandsche Bank took them over on behalf of the Dutch state and converted them into Dutch means of exchange. *Reichskreditkassenscheine* played hardly any role in exchange transactions.

The underlying idea was to render the circulation of money as smooth as possible. All in all this operation involved 133.6 million guilders. Originally the money had been earmarked for financing the cost of the German occupation, but it was not long before it was used for buying up consumer goods for use in the Reich. The available supplies of goods had previously been catalogued by the Germans as best they could. For understandable reasons Dutch enthusiasm for this measure was not very great. As a result many goods were not reported to the Germans or were only partially reported. Naturally this did not go unnoticed, but even the prospect of severe punishment was unable to persuade a good many people to submit correct records. Nor was this always a case of early national resistance. Self-interest probably played a greater role, which is also borne out by the fact that many goods turned up on the black market and found their way to the consumer at usurious rates.

The Germans did not fail to realize this, of course. But it did not lead, as one might have expected, to a co-ordinated campaign against the black market. On the one hand, the Germans admittedly took increasingly severe steps against black marketeers but, on the other hand, they themselves used the black market to buy goods.[18]

The German authorities probably realized that buying on the black market was more practical in the long run than handing out fines or confiscating black-market goods. An increasingly repressive regime would have driven the market even further underground, thus cutting off a source of essential goods. Paying for merchandise was not a great problem, because the Germans paid for it, as they did for other 'purchases', with guilders bought with grossly overvalued marks. A considerable advantage of this approach was that it encouraged the black market to provide goods. Another consideration was undoubtedly that the eradication of the black market was a hopeless task.

The indirect theft of merchandise from the occupied territories was organized centrally by the Rohstoff-Handelsgesellschaft (Roges), set up in December 1940 in The Hague. One of the most notable feats of this firm was the *Weihnachtsaktion* (Christmas campaign) of 1942, during which Roges, acting on direct orders from Göring, bought up in occupied territories anything with which the rather bare windows of German shops could be brightened up at Christmas time: from trinkets, silver and gold to furniture and toothpaste. These Christmas acquisitions cost in total about 176 million Reichsmarks and were offered to the German public at reduced prices.[19]

Numerous German agencies and individuals were active in the black market, not only in the Netherlands but in all occupied territories. An army of 'official' buyers, mostly specialists in a particular field, would comb the black market and make sure of a steady flow of merchandise to Germany.

Even a number of Jews worked in this line of business. They were experts, with a good knowledge of the market and of its traders. Because of their difficult circumstances, they were often paid with promises and proved easy to manipulate. Jews engaged in the purchase of metals were sometimes known as 'oxide-Jews'.

The Wehrmacht, too, was most active in the black market, though they were almost exclusively after the finished products. The first to realize that there was much more to be had than end products was Colonel Josef Veltjens, a comrade-in-arms of Hermann Göring from the First World War.

Veltjens, incidentally, denied that he had been guilty of large-scale black marketeering. In a somewhat grotesque attempt to refute that charge, laid against him by one of his enemies, he pointed out that the merchandise served exclusively to help the German war economy, so that his organization could not really be accused of black marketeering. He himself thought up an alternative name: *Blau-Aktion* or 'blue trading'. It would be vain to look for any logic in this argument, but it is another example of the attempt to lend a semblance of legality to actions that did not pass muster in international law.

In the period from 1940 to 1944, Dutch industry supplied goods with an approximate value of one billion guilders to Germany. The share of the black market in these transactions was, incidentally, no more than a few per cent, which raises the question of why the Germans took so much trouble with it, certainly when one considers the negative influence this policy had on the population, a policy that moreover 'attacked the economic roots of the German occupation of the Netherlands'.[20]

Looting by Compulsory Charity

'Looting by compulsory charity' was delegated to the Stichting Winterhulp Nederland (the Dutch Winter Aid Foundation),[21] which German propaganda presented as a neutral, non-party organization for providing material aid to needy Dutch people. It was a copy of the Winterhilfswerk des Deutschen Volkes (Winter Aid for the German People), which had been collecting money and goods even before the war, sometimes under pressure, for subsequent distribution to the population. The Dutch Winterhulp was simply an appendage of the German sister organization and was shunned by many people for that very reason.

The establishment of a national steering committee, including eleven provincial commissioners (formerly queen's commissioners), brought few changes, and the support of the German-sanctioned 'Nederlandsche Unie' (Netherlands Union) under a 'triumvirate' (J. E. de Quay, L. Einthoven and J. Linthorst Homan) was unable to earn Winterhulp the reputation of honesty and reliability that it so desired. The presence of Rost van Tonningen on the committee added to the bad impression, while the choice of Carel Piek (renowned for his pro-German views and, moreover, a member of the NSB from 1933 to 1940) as the first director-general of Winterhulp helped Netherlanders to indulge in their favourite sport of mockery: *'Geen piek voor Piek'* – no pennies for Piek.

At the end of August 1940, a decree made all collections for charitable institutions dependant on possession of a permit. In fact, Winterhulp was granted a monopoly for holding collections on 22 October 1940 – again by decree. During the last week of October, Permanent Secretary of Justice J. C. Tenkink and the five procurators-general of the Netherlands, who were responsible for all charitable collections, were instructed to licence Winterhulp collections only. At the beginning of November, the press was ordered not to publish any further reports about charitable institutions.

These measures, which were meant to popularize Winterhulp, had precisely the opposite effect. Its monopoly in running collections, its creation by Seyss-Inquart and the presence of NSB members in the 'honourable' steering committee, lent the organization the taint of Nazi complicity. The lavish contributions by NSB members and by Seyss-Inquart also made a negative impression.

However, most of the money came from the 'voluntary' contributions of businesses and the 'spontaneous' wage contributions of workers. In time, formerly Jewish businesses made the most generous contributions. Particularly active in this field were companies placed under German control, or sold to German or pro-German individuals. The *Verwalter* (administrators) generally copied the methods used by Winterhilfe in Germany, namely a deduction of 5 per cent from wages or profits. Dutch companies which were dependent on German orders, or considered it unwise not to play their part, contributed as well – a quiet hint was usually enough to persuade them to hand over 5 per cent of their profits.

On 25 October 1941, Dutch dailies reported that the Nederlandsche Bank had agreed to make a contribution of 50,000 guilders for the winter of 1941–2. That amount, too, was not handed over voluntarily – the majority present at a joint meeting of directors and commissioners wanted to contribute no more than half that figure but, thanks to the personal intervention of Rost van Tonningen, the full amount was eventually handed over.[22]

'Wage donations' for Winterhulp were generally about 1 per cent of the wages, which seemed to be a kind of official norm. 'Spontaneous' wage donations seemed to happen less spontaneously than the word suggests. Thus the acting mayor of Oldenzaal told his officials in an address that he absolutely refused to force them to 'offer' 1 per cent of their salaries to Winterhulp. However, they would do well to remember that when it came to 'a possible appointment, permanent position, et cetera, in the municipal service' he might be guided by their compliance with the 1 per cent norm.[23]

The yield from street collections was disappointing, probably because the contributions were given anonymously. Things were quite different with house-to-house collections when the collectors entered the names, addresses and amounts given on special lists. Many people thought it judicious to participate. After all, their response could be checked and used against them. There was thus no direct coercion but certainly a good measure of intimidation. However, the fact that Winterhulp lotteries, in contrast to other forms of collection, did elicit a good public response puts a different complexion on the widespread opposition to it.

The so-called 'Wheels of Adventure' could be found at busy points in many Dutch cities. Here citizens who liked a gamble could buy five, ten or twenty Winterhulp tickets for an insignificant sum, and if they drew a prize, it was paid out on the spot. Whether the gambling instinct won out over the reluctance to contribute to Winterhulp, or whether other factors were at work is not entirely clear. What is certain, and the public knew that as well of course, is that the money from collections as well as from lotteries ended up in the same coffers.

In fact Winterhulp did help poor families and was paid out both in cash (in the form of vouchers) and also in kind (food, fuel, clothing, and so forth).[24] It is a misconception to believe that most of the proceeds of Winterhulp collections went to Germany or to soldiers fighting on the eastern front.[25] No doubt the wish to see nothing but perfidy in anything the Germans did played a part in this mistaken view.

That does not detract from the fact that the Germans did not benefit from donations obtained from the Dutch population partly by coercion or at least by a subtle form of intimidation. Winterhulp was probably the best-disguised form of indirect looting.

Looting by Confiscation

On 4 July 1940, within two months of the invasion, Reichskommissar Seyss-Inquart, Hitler's deputy in the Netherlands, issued VO 33. With it, the Germans gave themselves *carte blanche* to confiscate the money and property of individuals and institutions that had somehow displeased them. Among other things, the decree stipulated that those societies and persons 'guilty of having encouraged, of encouraging or being likely to encourage in the future, any attempt to harm the German people or the Reich, may have their property confiscated entirely or in part.'

The reference to possible future activity is striking. Actions that had not yet been performed but might be expected in the future became the basis for a completely arbitrary confiscation procedure. The Sicherheitspolizei (German Security Police, or SP) could seize any goods or funds earmarked for confiscation. The SP were obliged to make the confiscation publicly known or at least to notify the owner in writing of the impending confiscation, but in practice this made little difference to the victims.

It is clear that on the basis of VO 33 the Germans could do as they pleased and that the door was opened wide to purely arbitrary measures. The legal basis Seyss-Inquart attempted to give to this form of looting by decree was not contrary to international law in principle, although in this particular form it flew in the face of it. Article 46 of WOL stated expressly that private property could not be confiscated.

By the 'metal requisition' decree of 21 July 1942, the Germans assumed the right to confiscate metal objects. This term covered a wide spectrum of items and installations, including church bells, 'parts and components of buildings', the fittings of cafés, brewery vats and beer pipes, milk churns, rollers, music presses, and 'parts of filling stations no longer in service'. The owners of metal objects were expected, as soon as they had been given notice, to hand over their property at a specified place. Objects of special artistic value did not have to be handed in, but had to be entered on a special list, to be inspected by experts.

On demand, the metal value (which differed radically from the actual value) of the surrendered material would be paid, but that did not mean a great deal to those whose businesses could no longer function, or function normally, for lack of the items they were forced to surrender. Failure to comply with VO 33 was considered a crime against the German Reich and severely punished.

Looting by Forced Surrender or by Requisition

Closely related to confiscation and partly overlapping with it was the decree on 'surrender' or 'requisition'. VO 108 (18 June 1941) laid down that 'the disposal of objects found in the occupied Netherlands and consisting wholly or largely of copper, nickel, tin, lead or alloys thereof' was forbidden and that these objects had to be surrendered. The metals and alloys were in the first place earmarked for the German arms industry, although they were clearly not used exclusively by the army of occupation in the Netherlands as stipulated by WOL.

At other periods the surrender of bicycles, boats, radios, textiles and household goods including plates, spoons and gravy boats became obligatory. Livestock, machinery, means of transport (cars, trains, ships), and every conceivable raw material were all covered by the German surrender decree. Practically everything surrendered was placed at the disposal of the Wehrmacht, of German citizens and of German industry.[26] For the items surrendered the owner was generally paid compensation and issued with a certificate to the effect that he had done his duty. But with the prevailing scarcity of goods, the money he was paid was of little worth.

Even labour[27] (*Arbeitseinsatz*) was requisitioned. In the beginning there was no law directing Dutch citizens to undertake labour in Germany, although a refusal to work in the Fatherland had dire financial consequences. In February 1941, the Germans tried, under threat of deportation to concentration camps, to recruit thousands of workers for the German metal industry. However, after a protest strike in Amsterdam and serious labour disturbances in Rotterdam, the plan was shelved. Pressure on Dutch workers, and coercive measures directed at them, were stepped up as the tide of war turned against Germany.

In terms of Article 52 of WOL, personal services could only be demanded to cover the needs of the army of occupation. Labour conscription for Germany was no part of that definition. It might be added that the conscripts were not paid adequate wages for their work, which was, moreover, performed under duress. What capped it all, however, was the work prisoners were forced to do for the *Arbeitseinsatz* in a number of special camps. The I. G. Farben concern, for instance, ran its own concentration camp at Monowitz near Auschwitz, where slave labour, especially by Jews, was introduced in 1942. The victims were selected in Auschwitz by the SS and put to work in wretched conditions either in Monowitz itself or else in one of the I. G. mines in the immediate vicinity: Fürstengrube, Janinagrube or Gunthergrube. There was no kind of financial compensation, and the working days were long and exceptionally hard. Food was far from sufficient, the clothing inadequate and the accommodation deplorable. I.G. Farben looked upon its labour force as a kind of raw material that had to be worked as efficiently as possible. As a result the physical power of the Monowitz prisoners was completely exhausted within an average of four months. Life expectancy in the mines was at one point reduced to no more than about five weeks. Those who could no longer work were packed off to the gas chambers.

The motivation of I. G. Farben was not anti-Semitic in principle, but purely economic: the employment of new slaves rounded up en masse all over Europe proved to be even cheaper than providing those already employed with adequate food, clothing and accommodation.[28]

Buildings, including private homes and hotels, did not escape the requisition system either, but were taken over by the Wehrmacht on a large scale. The owners were paid no more than two thirds of the rental value.

In about November 1944, the Wehrmacht announced that all families and single men had to hand in a woollen blanket, a man's shirt, a man's pullover, a man's winter coat, and a number of other articles of clothing. For these the German army paid a fixed fee. Thus a woollen blanket fetched 25 guilders and a winter coat 50 guilders. Whether the Wehrmacht made these payments in guilders exchanged for Reichsmarks is not clear – in some cases they certainly did.

In any event, the sums paid were not enough to enable citizens to buy replacements, even if replacements had been available. It was not without reason that the Germans made do with second-hand clothing. They had little alternative because all supplies of new clothing had been confiscated.

Moreover, the purchasing power of the guilder was to decrease dramatically during what became known as the Hunger Winter of 1944–5. During the last phase of the war, barter was the most important means of getting hold of absolute necessities, certainly in the west of the Netherlands. The role of paper money was temporarily suspended.

Some of the goods handed over to the Germans may perhaps be considered as occupation costs, in which case they do not fall under the heading of 'loot'. However, that interpretation is at variance with the fact that WOL states explicitly that private property must be respected (Article 46). Incidentally, WOL is not consistent, because Article 52 specifies that requisitions in kind or services shall not be demanded from the inhabitants except for the needs of the army, and shall only be demanded on the authority of the commander in the locality occupied.

After *Dolle Dinsdag*, 'Mad Tuesday' (5 September 1944), when premature celebrations of the Liberation began across the Netherlands, looting by confiscation was unbridled. Everything not yet requisitioned, confiscated or otherwise grabbed by the occupying forces, now fell prey to them. The Germans were particularly after cattle, the remaining supplies of raw materials, industrial machinery and means of transport. Virtually all of these vanished to Germany. However, many of the goods never arrived because traffic became increasingly chaotic following incessant Allied air raids on roads, railways and bridges. Formalities such as the issue of requisition slips became rare.

Even the Allies who liberated the Netherlands made use of the right to claim occupation costs. That was, however, carried out through consultations between Eisenhower as the Supreme Commander of the Allied Expeditionary Forces and the Dutch government, on the basis of the 'procurement agreement'. By virtue of that agreement, all the country's resources were to be put at the disposal of the

Allies in emergencies. Beyond that, all requisitions (and compensation payments) were subject to strict rules,[29] which helped to define what may be considered 'reasonable' during occupations.

Looting by Fining

The Germans were never short of imagination and invention, at least not when it came to decrees whose purpose it was to gain them material advantage. 'Expiation' (*Sühneleistung*) is a case in point. Citizens who deliberately harmed German interests could be forced to make good the damage and had to pay 'expiation money' in addition. These fines were thus a form of vindictive damages to ease the pain inflicted upon the occupiers.

This measure came into force as early as 25 May 1940 and was primarily aimed at persons, associations and foundations 'that approve or encourage such actions [the deliberate harming of German interests] or of whom it can be supposed that they do so'. In addition, municipalities within whose borders such actions took place could be forced to pay expiation money. In fact it all came down to the Germans fining people at random for actions with which they had nothing to do but that the occupiers believed they might condone. The promulgation of VO 7/1941 was meant to remove the appearance of arbitrariness attaching to these penalties, and lend the measure a legal basis, at least in form. Article 50 of WOL, however, stipulates that no penalty shall be inflicted upon the population on account of the acts of individuals for which they cannot be regarded as jointly and severally responsible.

The strike in February 1941 cost the Amsterdam municipality 15 million guilders in expiation money. Even before the strike started, Leeuwarden, The Hague, Groesbeek, Gennep and Heerlen had been forced to pay fines for sabotage committed within their boundaries, sharing out the fines between the highest taxpayers, unless these happened to be NSB members, Germans or pro-German elements. Heerlen municipality was fined 100,000 guilders, not only because of the 'undisciplined behaviour' of certain inhabitants, but also because of anti-German provocation. Bussum was presented with a bill for 300,000 guilders for cutting down four Wehrmacht telephone cables – the fine to be paid within a week. Here too the fine was divided among taxpayers, pro-German groups being exempted.[30] This was probably the only form of looting that could in part be made good by fiscal means after the war, to those citizens who paid capital gains tax.[31]

Looting by the Liquidation of Associations and Foundations

VO 145 of 20 September 1940 had a dual purpose: the registration of the members and also of the financial resources of non-profit-making institutions. The directors of these institutions were instructed to report in writing to the procurator-general of the nearest court within twenty days. The response to VO 145 was overwhelming – in no time at all some 130,000 registrations had been received. The administrators preferred to be on the safe side: in the case of 40,000 registrations it turned out on closer examination that they did have a subsidiary economic objective. That left 90,000 registrations, and these provided the Germans with a sweeping survey, on the basis of which they were able to plan robberies of, and assaults on, all sorts of associations and foundations. The results did not take long to come. Just over half a year later Masonic lodges, rotary clubs and the Rosicrucians had ceased to exist.[32]

German fears of voluntary associations was perfectly understandable: the members would meet and take the opportunity to exchange ideas on such occasions. The chance that resistance groups would then spring up was anything but imaginary. Voluntary associations were potential foci of resistance and had to be kept under strict control. On the other hand, associations also lent themselves to the propagation of Nazi ideas, but even in that case control seemed desirable. All voluntary associations were placed under German supervision and their financial freedom curtailed to a minimum – just enough to enable them to keep their heads above water.

Registration was no more than the first phase. The second phase began on 28 February 1941 with VO 41/1941 concerning the 'reconstruction of non-profit-making associations and foundations'. The German-born Dutch businessman Hans Werner Müller-Lehning was appointed 'Commissioner for Non-Profit-Making Associations and Foundations'. He was authorized to take what organizational and financial measures he thought fit. Müller-Lehning could change articles of association, wind up societies, suspend or dismiss committee members, but above all deploy their financial resources in the 'general interest', a term that covered, for instance, Winterhulp and the Nederlands Arbeidsfront (Dutch Labour Front). The administrative costs incurred by this commissariat were charged to the various associations and foundations, and could run up to 10 per cent of their assets.

As a corollary of the *Verordnungen* that covered associations and foundations, the old political parties were liquidated. The Roman Catholic National Party, the Anti-Revolutionary Party, the Social Democratic Workers Party, the Christian Democratic Union, the Reformed Party, the Christian Historical Union and the Liberal Democratic Union were all dissolved. If their funds included *Auslandsbonds*, these were sold through Otto Rebholz to Dego.[33]

Numerous different associations and foundations were also closed down. Within eight months of the introduction of obligatory registrations some 7,700 institutions had been liquidated. These included the Netherlands Scouts, the Catholic Scouts, the Christian Metal Workers Union, the White-and-Yellow Cross, the Royal Institute of Engineers, the De Witte literary society, and the Association of Dutch Housewives.

The Bible-Kiosk Society, which was banned in March 1942, explained in a circular to its members that they had been liquidated because they were alleged to subvert national life. Seyss-Inquart, as appears from a circular signed by him, found this allegation so serious that he also ordered the destruction of all the society's publications. Bibles and biblical illustrations were burned and money and goods of value confiscated.[34]

Müller-Lehning's office set to work rather arbitrarily, and was guided in its work above all by directions from the Sicherheitsdienst (the Security Service, or SD) and by complaints from NSB members or other pro-German individuals. How much booty he carried off has never been clearly established (large sections of the archives were burned and Müller-Lehning committed suicide before he could be questioned), but it is clear that the major part of the loot came from liquidated Jewish associations and foundations.[35]

Looting by *Kapitalverflechtung*

Kapitalverflechtung involved the integration of the Dutch economy into the German planned economy. As early as May 1940, Hitler gave orders to 'merge' the Dutch and German economies. In concrete terms that meant that German concerns acquired an interest in Dutch companies through the purchase of shares. The ultimate aim was to place Dutch industrial life under German control.

Admittedly, Dutch capital was also offered a chance of investment in Germany, but it was clear from the outset that the players were not evenly matched. After all, German capital was not only much larger than Dutch capital, but the German enthusiasm for investing in the Low Countries was many times greater than the opposite trend. The Permanent Secretary for Economic Affairs, Dr H. M. Hirschfeld, supported by the Permanent Secretary for Finance, L. J. A. Trip, who was also President of the Nederlandsche Bank, protested against the *Kapitalverflechtung* for that very reason; they feared it would put an end to independent Dutch industrial activity, which was under considerable threat as it was. With the negative experiences they had had in Germany after the First World War, Dutch investors were loath to invest in the Third Reich, particularly under such unpredictable conditions. Hirschfeld made it clear to Fischböck that there was little chance of any Dutch influence being wielded on German industry, and that for that reason too, Dutch people had little incentive to invest in Germany.

Of course, the government in Berlin, and particularly Hitler, Göring and Walther Funk (the German Minister of Economic Affairs and President of the Reichsbank) were not deterred by such considerations. The boards of the Dresdner Bank and of the Deutsche Bank, together with a number of large concerns, including I. G. Farben, saw the way as wide open for expanding their influence and profits in the Netherlands. As part of *Kapitalverflechtung,* Germany invested approximately 50 million guilders in nearly 4,000 concerns in the Netherlands. After 1941, however, interest shifted increasingly to Jewish concerns that were about to be 'Aryanized' and that, moreover, constituted a much easier form of prey.[36]

A major role in *Kapitalverflechtung* was played by 'Bureau Mojert'. Its leading figures were Dr P. Mojert, an associate of the Deutsche Bank, H. Amstmann of the Dresdner Bank, Dr Holz of the Reichskreditgesellschaft and Dr Pfeffer of the Commerz Bank. All the major German banks were represented in the bureau. Its central task was to inform the Reichswirtschaftsministerium (the ministry of economics, or RWM) in Berlin about the financial standing of Dutch businesses. It was the Bureau Mojert that gave Liro instructions to sell selected securities to selected German banks. In all such cases, F. H. Schifferstein, head of the Liro banking division, made contact with the interested banks in Germany in order to agree the sale price.[37]

In *Kapitalverflechtung*, just as in the case of *Auslandbonds*, the ability to exchange marks for guilders played a crucial role. Attempts to merge the two economies had occurred chiefly before the Aryanization measures made an impact in the course of 1941, that is, during the period of the 'perforated' foreign currency border.

Another problem raised by the sale of shares in Dutch concerns – but also by *Auslandbonds* – is the degree of collaboration involved. In other words, was this a case of Dutch collusion with the German authorities beyond what in practice was unavoidable pragmatic collaboration with the occupiers?[38] In this connection, an interesting question was put to the post-war general secretary of the Nederlandsche Bank, Prof. A. M. de Jong. Did he know of any Dutch bankers who, on their own initiative, had sought out German colleagues for the express purpose of offering them shares in Dutch companies, and who had not applied to the foreign currency institute for permits until after the event? Were the bankers concerned right to claim that they had merely acted in response to German pressure, that they had been forced to make such sales, or had they themselves taken the initiative? De Jong replied that they had indeed taken the initiative, but that he was unable to prove it.[39]

Coercion or free choice? On the answer to this question depends the justification of the charge that Dutch banks collaborated with the Germans. While there is no written proof of German pressure on Dutch financial institutions, all the indications are that by and large the initiative seems to have been taken by the Dutch side: 'the more so as Dr Bühler has stated that he did not make things difficult for anyone who refused to sell foreign securities to Germany.'[40]

Whether this declaration by Dr Anton Bühler, the German *Beauftragte* (administrator) in the Nederlandsche Bank, is entirely true cannot be established with any degree of certainty either. It all depends on the pressure his superiors in Berlin brought to bear on him.

With the sale of securities in general, it must be remembered that they were paid for in German marks. The Germans were primarily interested in the shares of such large companies as Shell, Unilever, Philips and Algemene Kunstzijde Unie (the General Rayon Union, or AKU). Even when shares were subsequently sold on to other countries, the foreign currency was invariably paid to Germany, the owner at the time of the sale. After all, the Netherlands had been paid in full, albeit in marks. That is the crux of the matter when it comes to deciding whether these transactions served to 'aid and abet the enemy', and goes hand in hand with the question of whether or not those concerned acted under compulsion. Germany was able to sell the shares on to such formally neutral countries as Switzerland, Sweden, Spain and Portugal, and to make purchases there with the proceeds. For even if securities were sold to, say, the Dresdner Bank, it was nevertheless the German government that was indirectly enabled to acquire foreign currency for use in the war.

The handover to German banks of so-called 'qualifying minority holdings' (large parcels of shares), thanks to which the buyers acquired a sizeable share of if not a majority interest in Dutch concerns, can also be considered a form of collaboration, inasmuch as there was no German coercion to sell these holdings. As an excuse, the sellers often argued that securities, unlike goods, would be returned after the war, because all of them had been registered. That view is at best questionable, certainly if the sale took place at the beginning of the war, when no one could predict the outcome and the prospects of the occupied countries did not look promising.

The success of *Kapitalverflechtung* was anything but overwhelming. True, the German authorities could state with some satisfaction that the placing of commissioners in Dutch concerns ensured that these concerns worked for the benefit of the German war economy. That the increase in influence by the acquisition of shares in Dutch companies was negligible was above all due to the extremely complicated relations between these concerns and foreign businesses, whose shares they owned completely or in part. Their actual market position was extremely difficult to establish by virtue of these impenetrable relationships and also because of the uncertain size and spread of the capital involved. At Shell and Unilever the results of *Kapitalverflechtung* were insignificant. That was also true of Koninklijk Nederlandsche Hoogovens (Royal Dutch Blast Furnaces), which outwitted the Germans by quickly handing over more than 50 per cent of their shares to an accounts office.

The board of Shell had left for London during the first days of the war, while the registered offices of the main Shell subsidiaries were moved out of Europe. Thus the registered offices of Royal and Batavian Shell were transferred to Curaçao and those of the Nederlandsch–Indische Aardoliemaatschappij (Dutch East Indies Mineral Oil Company) to Batavia. The shares in the parent company could no longer be traded, although the Germans appointed a *Verwalter* immediately after the invasion.[41] That was done for purely economic reasons. A German report stressed the 'particularly important role in the war economy' that Shell could play. It was referring to oil extraction in Romania, which Shell largely controlled by participation in the Astra Romana Oil Company. The second reason given was that Shell had started drilling for oil in the Netherlands after the occupation.[42]

The commissioners appointed for Philips were Dr O. Bormann and O. Merkel, who served as administrators in Eindhoven from 5 July 1940 to 20 July 1942. They were succeeded by L. Nolte, an engineer, as 'trustee of all Philips concerns'. According to Philips it is an open question to what extent the company was involved in the German war economy. Speaking of 'total involvement' is probably going too far, but it is certain that from 1942 the occupier increasingly imposed his will on the company. *Kapitalverflechtung* played no part of any importance in Philips' case, although the board seems to have been afraid of moves by AEG and Telefunken in that direction.[43]

From June 1941 to the end of the war, Unilever had just one supervisor in the person of Dr W. Modest (Reichsbeauftragter des Reichskommissars für den Unilever Konzern in den Niederlanden). The Reichskommissar at Unilever was Dr Posse. As might be expected, Unilever was called in to assist German food production but, as with Philips, German companies failed utterly in their efforts at *Kapitalverflechtung*.[44]

In the case of AKU, however, with its close links to Germany, the Germans were able to acquire a majority share of the share capital, something that was kept a strict secret because of the interests of AKU in foreign countries.[45]

The Dresdner Bank in particular played a pioneering role in attempts to bring Dutch industry under German control. To that end the bank worked in tandem with the Reichswirtschaftsministerium (the Reich ministry of economics). Nor did the Dresdner Bank confine itself to the Netherlands; it considered all occupied territories as its legitimate stamping ground. One of its directors, Dr Karl Rasche, had a particularly dubious reputation:

> Wer marschiert hinter dem ersten Tank?
> Das ist der Dr. Rasche von der Dresdner Bank!
> (Who's that marching behind the first tank?
> It's Dr Rasche from the Dresdner Bank!)

This jingle, incidentally, was thought to be very flattering (*sehr schmeichelhaft*) by the bank's board. They were obviously unaware that these lines had served as the refrain of a satirical song in Czechoslovakia four years earlier.[46]

In 1939 the Dresdner Bank founded the 'Handelstrust West' (the Commercial Trust West, or HTW) in Amsterdam, which made unrivalled profits from the war.[47] Its purchasing methods, certainly when used outside the Amsterdam Stock Exchange, were extremely simple, as the following copy of a (standard) note from HTW to the Generalkommissar für Finanz und Wirtschaft (Commissioner General for Finance and Economic Affairs) in The Hague shows:

> We would ask you to instruct the bankers Lippmann, Rosenthal & Co., 55, Sarphatistraat, Amsterdam, to offer us the shares in N.V. Heemaf Hengelo accrued from Jewish property for the account of the prospective German buyer, Brown, Boveri & Cie, A.G., Mannheim...[48]

The name Heemaf can easily be changed for hundreds of other names of Dutch companies that attracted the interest of German business. In the case of Heemaf and Brown Boveri, the shares were stolen Jewish securities that proved attractive because they went relatively cheaply, the lower price being due to the extra risks attaching to these shares. At a very early stage, the Dutch government-in-exile had let it be known from London, through its mouthpiece, Radio Oranje, that after the war, the shares would be returned to their original and rightful owners. However, at the time when their sale took place, buying them seemed a justifiable risk. Germany appeared omnipotent and the Allies were yet to set foot on the European continent.

With the help of Dutch banks, HTW also bought shares through the Stock Exchange. As part of *Kapitalverflechtung*, these banks were entitled to deal with Germany directly. Apart from HTW, only seven other banks were permitted to do so, all of them closely linked, in one way or another, to German banks or companies.[49]

In addition to the Dresdner Bank, the Commerz Bank and the Bank der Deutschen Arbeit opened new branches to support their activities in the Netherlands. The Deutsche Bank had enjoyed Dutch support even earlier, thanks to Handelsmaatschappij Albert de Bary & Co., a bank in Amsterdam.[50]

The success of *Kapitalverflechtung* was largely confined to a number of medium-sized and relatively small concerns, over which the Germans were able to exert control, thanks to the planned acquisition of shares. Thus the Vereinigte Stahlwerke saw a chance of acquiring a 40 per cent interest in Koninklijke Nederlandsche Hoogovens, while Rheinmetall Borsig AG acquired a 30 per cent share in NV Werkspoor (Railway Track). Fokker, the aircraft company, also fell into German hands – the Fokker shares reached the Reichsluftfahrtsministerium (the German Ministry of Aviation) through front men in the Bank der Deutschen Luftfahrt (German Aviation Bank).

In Belgium, on the other hand, the Germans were less successful than in the Netherlands. German concerns were able to buy shares in that country to the value of no more than 13–15 million marks. In addition the penetration by German banks in Belgium was insignificant; only the Dresdner Bank could boast a branch in Belgium.[51]

Looting by Individuals

'Pillage is formally forbidden', as the WOL convention put it tersely in Section III, Article 47. 'Pillage' holds a special place in this succinct description of looting methods because it was the sole form of dispossession that the occupying power did not, in one way or another, try to sanction or legitimize and actually opposed. Pillage sapped discipline, and could therefore not be tolerated. It was not so much forbidden because it ran counter to international law but because it flouted the interests and discipline of the German army. Goods handed in on the basis of a *Verordnung* were considered the property of the German Reich and stealing such property was a felony.

In practice, there is of course little difference between pillage and robbery by sham sales, confiscation or dispossession. In the last three cases the original owner was admittedly furnished with documentary proof or received payment in some form or another, but given the prevailing scarcities he could do very little with such compensation.

Pillage during the Second World War was not a German prerogative. The Allies, too, were guilty of it,[52] and the looting of gold by American troops mentioned earlier is just one of many such examples, although the one that appeals most to the imagination.

During house searches, individual Germans would occasionally, if the opportunity arose, steal jewels or money – things that a soldier could easily and unobtrusively stuff into his pocket. In the street, bicycles were a favourite booty.

Until *Dolle Dinsdag*, plundering remained within limits, chiefly because the military authorities frowned upon it for disciplinary reasons. But in the chaos that set in after September 1944 many soldiers saw their chance and seized it. A host of bicycles, provisions, money, jewels and other valuables, clothing and household effects changed owners illegally.

Arnhem suffered worst from this form of pillage. After the Allied air landings on 17 September 1944, the population was forced to evacuate the town and the German soldiers stationed there did not let the chance to loot pass them by. Virtually no house was spared. Cupboards and floor were ripped apart in the hunt for loot, walls broken for secret hiding places and gardens dug over. The haul was enormous, the rapacity extraordinary, and there was a great deal of pointless destruction. What remained or could not be carried off there and then fell prey to a form of organized pillage after the Allied defeat. Because the population was likely to support the Allies, the town was impounded and then robbed of everything. The booty was transported to Germany. The damage in household effects is estimated at 350 million guilders; goods to the value of 30 million guilders disappeared from businesses. The looting in Arnhem was so serious that Kreisleiter (District Officer) Kenrath suggested burning down the remains of the town, so that it might never leak out how the German army had behaved there.[53]

Personal possessions deposited in bank safe-deposit boxes, too, did not seem safe from the avarice of the German military. Thus American shares worth half a million dollars were stolen, and German engineers forced their way into the Arnhem branch of the Amsterdamsche Bank with the help of explosives.[54] The looted diamonds vanished to Berlin. Gold from the Nederlandsche Bank handed to the Amsterdamsche Bank for safekeeping and worth five million guilders was another part of the booty. The gold that was taken to safety in Meppel (2 million guilders) suffered the same fate in the spring of 1945. On 22 November, the Devisenschutzkommando, one of whose tasks it was to control the implementation of various foreign-exchange regulations, moved in. They misappropriated just under 28 million guilders in the form of banknotes and coins, including gold ten-guilder and five-guilder pieces, from the Arnhem branch of the Nederlandsche Bank. That money was transferred to branches of the Nederlandsche Bank in Deventer. The German Security Police, Task Force Almelo, took more than 3.5 million guilders in the form of gold coin 'into custody'.[55]

The use of dynamite was a favourite tactic for cracking and emptying safes in other banks as well. In the middle of March 1945 it was the turn of Tiel. The inhabitants of this small town with a relatively large number of affluent citizens were evacuated, and German troops used the opportunity to blow open the vaults of the Amsterdamsche and Rotterdamsche Banks, the Nederlandsche Handelsmaatschappij and the Nutsspaarbank (Public Savings Bank). The haul came to roughly 150 million guilders and consisted of securities, cash and valuables. The cash disappeared for good, but after the war Dutch investigation agencies managed to recover a large part of the rest of the loot in the Netherlands and in Germany. The missing American shares, the so-called *Amerikaantjes*, had however vanished without a trace. The suspicion is that they ended up in French and Belgian criminal circles as a means of payment in the flourishing post-war smuggling trade.[56]

After the war, a number of affairs involving illegal transactions and smuggling of equities attracted wide public attention. The mysterious death of Friedrich Schallenberg in a shallow lake off Groothertoginnelaan in The Hague, the vanished 'poet' of Dr F.A. Mucke and the 'shady practices' of the Rotterdam business man P. L. Henssen, can all be traced back to the theft of equities during the war.[57]

The Looting of Gold[58]

The gold held by the national banks, but also by private individuals in the occupied territories, helped Hitler to buy goods and raw materials in neutral countries. It mitigated the acute shortage of foreign currency, at least in part. A large proportion of the stolen gold found its way to Switzerland. Throughout the war, the Swiss supplied Hitler with munitions, arms, detonators, precision instruments, radio and aircraft parts, raw materials, chemicals and various services. But though relations between the two countries were close, the Swiss refused to accept payment in Reichsmarks. The explanation was obvious – if Germany should lose the war, Switzerland would be stuck with piles of worthless currency. However the Swiss had no objection to being paid in gold – far from it. The Allies reproached the Swiss for accepting payment in gold they knew was not above suspicion, because as early as 1943 the Swiss National Bank accepted more gold from the Reichsbank than the country had owned before the outbreak of war, a situation of which the Swiss were well aware. Throughout the war, the British and American intelligence services kept an eagle eye on the flow of gold from Germany to neutral countries, constantly alerting these countries to the fact that the Germans were settling their debts with stolen gold and stolen goods. Besides Switzerland, Sweden, Spain, Portugal, Turkey and a number of South American countries also accepted tainted German gold.

During the Second World War, the Nazis stole gold to the tune of about ten billion marks from the national banks of occupied Europe. This so-called 'monetary gold' was kept in the Reichsbank. Non-monetary gold came from private sources. In the Netherlands, all citizens were forced to surrender their gold through the Nederlandsche Bank.[59]

Monetary Gold

The Germans stole approximately 110,174 kg of gold coin from the Nederlandsche Bank.[60] The gold was generally used for the purchase of strategically important material. The greater part of the gold finished up in Switzerland, although some ended up in countries that had been able to maintain their neutrality throughout the war, namely Sweden, Spain, Portugal and Turkey. After the war, Dutch gold was also discovered in Italy.

Switzerland served as a kind of 'gold exchange': gold stolen by Germany was changed into Swiss francs in Switzerland, enabling Hitler to able to pay for his imports from neutral countries that refused to be paid in Reichsmarks. Central banks in neutral countries (for instance the Swedish Riksbank) changed these francs back in Switzerland for the same gold with which Berlin had bought them.

Switzerland thus served as both as middle man and also as scapegoat for countries exporting to Germany, for these countries could convincingly claim that they had acquired the gold from Switzerland through the normal international channels.

The Germans claimed part of the Dutch gold as a contribution to the occupation costs. They were entitled, as we have seen, to claim maintenance costs for the army of occupation within reasonable bounds, the costs being mainly to cover provisions, housing, clothing and transport. However, German claims were excessive and bore no relation to the actual costs, as specified in WOL. As usual, the Germans went to a great deal of trouble to lend their gold thefts a semblance of legality. The most blatant case was the *Aufschlagszahlung Äussere Besatzungskosten* (surcharge for external occupation costs), which was applied to the costs incurred by Germany before the outbreak of war for the mobilization and training of the troops to be used in the occupation of the Netherlands.

Article 46 of the Hague Convention prohibits the confiscation of private property. This posed a problem for the occupying power because the Nederlandsche Bank was a limited company and hence a private concern. The dilemma was solved by handing the bill to the Ministry of Finance, which was then forced to buy the necessary gold from the Nederlandsche Bank. As a result, the gold passed into state ownership. According to WOL, nothing now stood in the way of confiscation, and the gold quickly disappeared in Germany.

Another part of the gold was, in conflict with WOL, claimed as the Dutch contribution to Operation Barbarossa, the war against the Soviet Union. The Netherlands was presented with a bill for 50 million Reichsmarks per month, 20 per cent of which had to be paid in gold. Once again the Ministry of Finance paid the bill and instructed the Nederlandsche Bank to transfer the money to the Reichsbank in Berlin. The relevant instruction by Seyss-Inquart calling for a further war contribution was dated 25 April 1942. On the preceding 30 March, Rost van Tonningen, the permanent secretary at the Dutch Ministry of Finance, had, acting on the orders of the Reichskommissar, already presented an account for 450 million Reichsmarks. The explanation given was that the monthly payments of 50 million Reichsmarks had been owed since 1 July 1941 (Barbarossa had been launched on 22 June). Hence there was 'good reason' to demand a retrospective contribution for nine months at fifty million Reichsmarks.[61]

During the night of the German invasion of the Netherlands, two ships managed to escape with gold from the head office of the Nederlandsche Bank in Amsterdam to London. A third ship, carrying 11,012 kg of gold from the Rotterdam branch office ran into a mine even before it could reach the North Sea in its flight to England, and sank.

The Germans managed to retrieve 9,571 kg of the sunken gold. The Prize Court in Hamburg ruled that the gold was war booty and assigned it to the Reichsbank. The rest of the sunken gold was salvaged after the war.[62] Finally, 2,500 kg of gold was looted from the branch offices of the Nederlandsche Bank in Arnhem and Meppel.[63]

Non-monetary Gold

By virtue of *Devisenverordnung* (foreign exchange decree) VO 27/1940, issued on 27 June 1940, and foreign exchange decree VO 63/1041 of 1941, all inhabitants of the occupied Netherlands were obliged to surrender their gold bars and gold coins (Dutch as well as foreign) to the Nederlandsche Bank, if the bank asked them to do so, and to exchange the gold for guilders. This measure, incidentally, applied not only to gold and other precious metals, but also to 'foreign bills of exchange' and 'foreign securities'.

The Reichsbank purchased 28,837 kg of the 35,476 kg of gold that was handed in and removed it to Germany.[64] All these transactions were clearly conducted under duress, although the Germans considered them perfectly normal, so much so that they did not even bother to come up with excuses. The Dutch authorities protested to Berlin, but, as was only to be expected, their complaints fell on deaf ears.

After the war, the Netherlands submitted a claim for 145,649 kg of monetary and non-monetary gold.[65] Private Dutch citizens were unable to demand the return of the gold they had handed in, because they had been paid in guilders for it. The Nederlandsche Bank bore most of the loss because it had been paid off in Reichsmarks.

The Devisenschutzkommando

The Devisenschutzkommando (the Foreign Exchange Protection Commando, the DSK) nominally ensured the implementation of all the foreign exchange regulations introduced almost immediately after the occupation. By his foreign exchange decree of 5 June 1940 ('concerning transitional measures in the field of foreign currency protection'), Seyss-Inquart required that the implementation of these regulations would be vested in Dutch and German officials of the DSK. Seyss-Inquart's original promise that the foreign exchange controls would benefit the Netherlands was broken from the very start; everything seemed geared exclusively to the needs of the German war economy. That must have been the intention from the outset, for there could be no other reason for deploying a German investigation team in addition to the Dutch inspectorate.

German 'collaboration' with the Dutch customs inspectorate was nothing but a sham, intended to gain the confidence of the Dutch public. Here, too, the Germans' aim was to maintain a show of integrity and fair play.

It quickly transpired that the concept 'foreign currency' (used to purchase goods and services in foreign countries) was being interpreted so broadly that it covered anything of value. In practice, the Germans confiscated whatever they thought might prove useful to them.

The Devisenschutzkommando set to work with a will. As early as 17 and 18 May 1940, banks in Maastricht, Roermond, Sittard, Venlo, Nijmegen and Arnhem were banned from disposing freely of foreign currency, gold and Reichsmarks. A few days later, banks in Amsterdam and its surroundings were subjected to the same ban, and the rest of the country quickly followed suit.

Almost immediately, the inspection of private safe deposits, in the presence of the owner and a bank employee, was also introduced. What foreign currency and gold were found in them was not confiscated at once, but placed in a special account. Dutch money was credited to the owner's account, so that it was no longer kept out of circulation and could therefore be more easily controlled. The Germans left it at that for the first few months.[66]

One year later, the inspection of the safes was completed. The yield was considerable, for the Dutch seemed to keep a whole spectrum of valuable property in their safe-deposits: gold (9,645 kg), silver (12 kg), gold coin (ranging from dollars and Swiss francs to Swedish crowns), banknotes, foreign securities and precious stones. Even so, it had not been possible to inspect everything during that first year. In a letter to the Nederlandsche Bank written more than half a year later, the DSK demanded a list of the names of the owners of safe-deposits that had slipped through the net. Should the owners refuse to cooperate, their safes would be opened by force at their expense.[67]

The DSK was solely concerned with the search and not with the administration of the loot. Gold and silver were deposited with the Nederlandsche Bank, which, as we mentioned earlier, had been placed under German control. However, the DSK also had the task of ensuring compliance with the so-called First and Second Liro Decrees, promulgated in 1941 and 1942 respectively. Jewish property confiscated by virtue of these decrees was transferred to, or registered with, Lippmann, Rosenthal & Co. in Sarphatristraat, Amsterdam, or the Vermögensverwaltungs- und Rentenanstalt (Property Administration and Pensions Institute) which, just like the 'robber bank', controlled and administered Jewish property.

Oberzollinspektor (Chief Customs Inspector) Guth, head of the DSK, informed Liro in August 1942 that staff expansion had enabled him to take stronger steps against anyone in breach of the two Liro decrees. He accordingly asked the bank to report as many incidents as possible 'in which punishable actions were performed or suspected. These include the retention of assets or objects in safe deposits held by Jews, since it will usually transpire that that these assets have been unlawfully retained.' Guth strongly advised that all suspected cases be left for him to deal with, so that the Jews concerned were given as little chance as possible to hide their possessions.

The duties of the DSK included tracing 'enemy property', that is, property owned by citizens of countries at war with Germany and resident in the Netherlands. Special *Verwalter* (administrators) were appointed to deal with their property. The Wirtschaftsprüfstelle (Economic Investigation Bureau) of the General-Kommissariat für Finanz und Wirtschaft (General Commission for Finance and Economic Affairs, the FiWi), under Seyss-Inquart's direct control, was responsible for the appointment of these administrators.

The DSK employed a small army of informers, traitors and tipsters, the so-called *Vertrauensmänner* or *V-männer*. The closer the German defeat approached, the more brutal the DSK became, confiscating anything that might serve the German war machine. Not even an appearance of legality was now kept up: 'What is right is what is good for Germany'.[68]

The Four-Year Plan

In August 1936, Hitler wrote a memorandum in which he declared that Germany was too small to feed its own population. The only solution, according to him, was to expand German *Lebensraum*, thus providing the German Reich with more ample sources of food and raw materials.

To that end economic and military mobilization had to be speeded up, and Hitler decreed that the rebuilding of the German army was to be completed within four years. The German economy was similarly given four years to be transformed into a war economy.[69] Hitler's memorandum became the starting point of the *Vierjahresplan*, the four-year plan that during the war played a major role in the looting of foreign currency, gold, diamonds and other valuables needed to buy goods and raw materials abroad.

The central task of the planning authority was to ensure that the German war industry did not suffer a shortage of raw material and manpower. The supply of raw material, in particular, caused the regime grave concern, the main obstacle being an acute lack of foreign currency for the purchases outside the occupied territories. The shortage of raw materials and the lack of foreign currency were inseparably linked.

In 1936, Göring was appointed Beauftragter für den Vierjahresplan (Administrator of the Four-Year Plan). At first he tried to solve the foreign currency shortage by stepping up German exports, but this proved no real solution, certainly not after the outbreak of war.

The Four-Year Plan proved unable to attain its original objective: the rebuilding of the German economy into a largely self-sufficient war economy within four years. The foreign exchange question continued to pose Göring's planning bureau an insoluble problem. Other objectives, for instance the launching of a comprehensive industrialization programme and the bringing of the armed forces up to war strength, proved more successful, but not completely so. The plans were too ambitious to be implemented in full.

Because the foreign exchange problem could not be solved decisively, the supply of raw materials from foreign countries caused bottlenecks throughout the war. Part of the problem was solved by the levy of exorbitant occupation costs. The national gold reserves of the occupied countries, inasmuch as they had not been taken to safety abroad in time, were confiscated and used to pay suppliers in neutral countries. Confiscated foreign currency was placed at the disposal of industries dependent on the free flow of imported raw materials.

During the Nuremberg trials (1946–9), when the leaders of the Third Reich were arraigned, it became crystal clear that in preparing for a war of aggression Germany had expressly counted on the capture of raw materials. German supplies were, just as during the First World War, sufficient for waging a short conflict only. As early as the winter of 1939, an acute shortage of basic raw materials made itself felt. Hitler then had to choose between rationing the available supplies in the expectation of a long war, or throwing everything into the battle in the hope of a quick solution. According to Göring, Hitler opted for the second alternative.[70]

Bühler and Rebholz

Two names keep cropping up in the account of the German looting of Jewish and non-Jewish property in the Netherlands. The name of Rebholz has already been mentioned in connection with *Auslandbonds*, the trade in securities, and his role in indirect looting. He was also to play an important role in the sale of shares of Jewish provenance in the Amsterdam Stock Exchange. Anton Bühler's name turns up thanks to his central position as 'administrator' of the Nederlandsche Bank. Both men worked closely together during the occupation, and were in regular contact about their stock-exchange dealings.

Dr Otto Rebholz, an Amsterdam banker of German origin, had come to the Netherlands in 1924 to work in the office of F. Leeser, a (Jewish) stockbroker. That same year he was appointed deputy manager, and five years later senior partner. After the death of F. Leeser, Rebholz continued to run the office with K .J. Leeser as a silent partner. In September 1940, under pressure of the new circumstances, the firm started to trade under the name of Rebholz' Bankierskantoor (Rebholz's Banking

Office). In 1932, Rebholz, then thirty-two years old and resident in the Netherlands for eight years, acquired Dutch nationality.

Rebholz can hardly be accused of anti-Semitism: he had a Jewish partner, many Jewish clients (thanks largely to Leeser) and came to the aid of many Jewish citizens during the war. In January 1941, admittedly, he joined the NSB and six months later he even became a patron member of the Dutch SS. He probably did this for business reasons, although this cannot be definitely established.

After the war, Rebholz was accused of having played a central role in the trade in stolen Jewish property and of having had a share in the 'indirect looting'. In particular, he was blamed for having bought securities for Dego and for Reichskommissar Seyss-Inquart.

Otto Rebholz, acting on behalf of Knauth, Nachod & Kühne (Leipzig), was also involved in the trading of Dutch and foreign funds. That firm was a front for the Otto Wolff Konzern, a steel company in Cologne, which sold the shares in neutral countries and used the proceeds to buy stores and raw materials for the German war machine.

The post-war charge against Rebholz, put briefly, was that his activities helped to provide Germany with foreign currency, thus enabling Hitler to buy essential war materials. In addition, he was charged with having played a key role in the sale of looted Jewish securities.

After the outbreak of war, a business associate brought Rebholz to the attention of the Reichsbank in Berlin, which introduced him to Dr A. J. Bühler, the German Beauftragte in the Nederlandsche Bank, a post he had taken over from H. C. H Wohltat in 1941.

Bühler had arrived in the Netherlands as early as May 1940, but for a year had worked under his predecessor Wohltat. Wohltat's immediate superior in the Netherlands was Dr Hans Fischböck, General-Kommissar für Finanz und Wirtschaft, with whom Wohltat did not get on. They were so often at loggerheads that Wohltat decided to resign his post.

Like his predecessor, Bühler was sceptical about a German victory, although needless to say neither expressed this view in public. Quite early on, Bühler was said to have become convinced that Germany had as good as lost the war and that it could only been won if all Europe had been 'pacified' in 1940.[71] The conviction that Hitler was bound to lose the war probably accounts for his lack of fanaticism during the occupation.

Bühler's main task was to supervise the running of the Nederlandsche Bank. He also served as a link to the Reichsbank and supervised banking and credit affairs and the trade in securities in general. Finally, he served as advisor to Seyss-Inquart, who was beginning to take a growing interest in financial matters. Bühler also held a supervisory position at Liro.

The Beauftragte was no dominant or driving force, but rather the typical good German doing his duty, albeit quite often reluctantly. He was admittedly a member of the German Nazi Party, the NSDAP, but certainly no fervent follower of Nazi ideology. Bühler felt responsible for the good of the Nederlandsche Bank entrusted to him as Beauftragte, and as such he did his best. Under the circumstances, that attitude often led to conflict because the instructions he received from his superiors in Berlin were designed to further German interests and were accordingly in conflict, at least in part, with Bühler's perceived duty to promote the interests of the Nederlandsche Bank..

In the end, he carried out the orders from Berlin, albeit half-heartedly.[72] Originally, Bühler had been opposed to the abolition of the currency border. In a detailed summary, he laid his objections before the responsible ministries in Berlin, but under pressure from Reichsmarschall Hermann Göring the measure was nevertheless introduced. Göring's plans to 'buy' works of art in the Netherlands undoubtedly played a crucial role in this decision. Bühler's opposition was due to his conviction that the guilder must be 'kept intact in view of its international importance'.[73] According to Rebholz, Bühler was a man with no more than a superficial understanding of the banking trade, more of a diplomat then a financier, and had been appointed by the Reichsbank mainly because of his negotiating skills.

Bühler disliked Rost van Tonningen, Trip's successor as President of the Nederlandsche Bank, but had excellent relations with Seyss-Inquart, who was always glad to receive him. Bühler called Rost van Tonningen a 'bucking horse', someone who looked at everything from a political angle and was, moreover, responsible for placing him under constant SD supervision. 'He treated me abominably,' Bühler complained, and 'was unable to keep a single friend'.[74] Bühler himself had a poor grasp of Dutch economic affairs; in that sphere, he relied heavily on Otto Rebholz.[75]

–2–

The Looting of Cultural Property

Introduction

A number of German government agencies specialized in the confiscation and removal of cultural property of all kinds, ranging from carpets and libraries of rare books and valuable manuscripts to archives, antiques and art collections – all of which appealed to the avarice of the Nazis. Part of the loot came from liquidated Jewish property and from societies and organizations dissolved by decree. However, furniture belonging to the Dutch royal family and items from the royal archives, to give two examples, were also removed and carried off to Germany. Almost all the royal property was returned after the war.[1]

The possessions of individuals who, according to German law, had been classified as enemy subjects, were confiscated as well, and those in breach of certain regulations (for instance by helping people who had gone into hiding) were sometimes stripped of their possessions. In these cases, not all the confiscated items were, of course, cultural property.

A large part of what the Germans misappropriated was 'purchased' with guilders bought with Reichsmarks, a form of technical looting. Sometimes the transactions were entered into voluntarily, but as often as not there was explicit or implicit coercion or the blatant use of threats.

Reichsleiter Dr Alfred Rosenberg and the operational staff named after him (Einsatzstab Reichsleiter Rosenberg, or ERR), as well as the Dienststelle Mühlmann, an administrative department led by Dr Kajetan Mühlmann, were notorious in art circles, their names being synonymous with looting. The ERR was at its worst in France and in Eastern Europe. Mühlmann himself concentrated on Poland and the Netherlands.

Cultural property holds a special place and must be distinguished from 'ordinary' objects of everyday use. This is particularly true of items considered to be of national importance, including the contents of museums and art galleries, but also famous national collections. Cultural property has an historical or artistic 'surplus value' and often both. Frequently, sentimental and chauvinist factors also come into play. Another special feature is that the value of cultural property does not decrease with the passage of time, but actually increases, which rarely happens with non-cultural items. Not surprisingly, therefore, cultural property plays a special role in WOL (Article 56). The cultural heritage of occupied countries was considered to be so important that special safeguards were deemed necessary, especially in time of war.

While claims for stolen machinery or means of transport cease to be worth pursuing after a time because these items become obsolete or inefficient, claims for stolen cultural property are far more long-lived. Nowadays, there are even special treaties subjecting the trade in cultural property to very strict rules.[2]

Keen interest in cultural property of historical importance first surfaced during the eighteenth century, and is particularly associated with the writings of Empheric de Vattel, a leading jurist of his day. His *The Law of Nations* (1758) lays down the following basic principle:

> For whatever cause a country is ravaged, we ought to spare those edifices which do honour to human society, and do not contribute to increase the enemy's strength – such as temples, tombs, public buildings, and all works of remarkable beauty. It is declaring one's self an enemy to mankind, thus wantonly to deprive them of these monuments of art.[3]

In the nineteenth century, concern about cultural property increased significantly, and De Vattel's principle was accepted as part of international law.

During the Second Peace of Paris (1815), attended by the victors over Napoleon, the principle was first placed in an international context. France was ordered to return to their countries of origin all the national treasures carried off by the Grande Armée. That applied not only to cultural property acquired under duress, or to put it more bluntly, looted, but also to cultural treasures transferred to France by treaty – and clearly with a degree of coercion. The Duke of Wellington spoke for all the Allies when he said that the systematic looting of cultural property by Napoleon in Europe was in conflict with both accepted legal principles and also with the rules of modern warfare.

The earliest attempt to codify the basic principles safeguarding cultural property was made by Dr Francis Lieber, a professor of constitutional history and public law in New York. Abraham Lincoln passed the Lieber Code in 1863 during the American Civil War (1861–5). Lieber had postulated among other things that though an invading army had the right to confiscate cultural property, it was obliged to protect it against damage. Cultural property had to be kept safe until a final decision about its ultimate ownership was taken. That decision had to be part of the final peace treaty.

The effect of the Lieber Code on international law was considerable; it became the basis of the declaration issued by the Brussels Conference in 1874. That declaration was never ratified but was the first international attempt to codify the rules underpinning the protection of cultural property. Lieber's idea was incorporated into the Hague Convention (1907), ratified by some forty countries.[4]

This special interest in man's cultural heritage explains why cultural property can still be reclaimed more than fifty years after the last war. The famous Koenigs Collection is a case in point, but many more examples can be mentioned.

During the Second World War, German 'purchases' of cultural property went initially to Adolf Hitler's Führermuseum in Linz, and to the personal collections of Hermann Göring and other party heavyweights somewhat lower in the Nazi hierarchy. Other clients included museums and art galleries in Berlin, Breslau, Bonn, Cologne, Dresden and Hamburg. The remaining cultural booty ended up with the German art trade. Hitler's and Göring's craving for art was to have far-reaching effects on the Dutch art market during the war.

For obvious reasons, the Führermuseum had first refusal; the rest could only choose after Linz had picked the best pieces. After all, Hitler had spent his youth in this small Austrian town. The fact that Vienna was not considered the more logical home for these treasures probably reflected its failure to appreciate the Führer's artistic gifts: Vienna had refused to admit him to the academy of art.

Even before the outbreak of war, Hitler had instructed Dr Hans Posse, the long-serving director of the Dresden art gallery, to take charge of a new art gallery to be built in Linz. 'All Party and Government departments are enjoined to support Dr Posse in the performance of his task.'[5] And so Posse became the director of Sonderauftrag Linz (the Special Linz Project), intended to transform the town in which Hitler had spent his youth into the cultural Mecca of Europe. Hitler's architect, Albert Speer, was commissioned to design the building.

Until his death in 1942 Posse pursued an active acquisition policy. In a letter to Reichsleiter Martin Bormann he wrote that before the end of 1940 paintings with a value of eight million guilders had been 'exported' from the Netherlands to Germany. That figure did not cover his last purchase, the Koenigs Collection, valued at 1.4 million guilders. Posse's own share in these acquisitions was worth more than 1.5 million guilders.

Göring spent approximately the same amount. Art dealers put up the remaining five million. The list of purchases and the artists' names associated with them is impressive.[6]

The sums involved may look striking if converted into their present-day equivalents but in fact they were no more than a weak reflection of the true value of the paintings, which was rarely or never paid. But then, who dared to refuse an offer, made under threat of all sorts of reprisals, by Hitler, Göring and other top Nazis? In many cases, the threat of confiscation – used for instance in the case of the Mannheimer Collection – or even the mere suggestion of such means, was not even needed to 'persuade' the owners to proceed with the sale, certainly not when the Führer's name was bandied about. The sums paid in these circumstances can therefore give us no more than a feeble indication of the true market value. The sales had been made under pressure, after all, and such pressure always resulted in low – and never in high – prices. After Posse's death, Dr Hermann Voss, director of the Wiesbaden museum, was handed responsibility for the Linz project.

Voss too was up to every trick. From 1943 to 1944, the Linz Collection was – according to Voss's own estimate – extended by about 3,000 paintings, which he had bought for a total sum of 150 million Reichsmarks. Most of his acquisitions were nineteenth-century German paintings. Hitler, unlike Göring, was more concerned with quantity than with quality.[7]

Besides Posse and Voss, Heinrich Hoffmann, Hitler's official photographer, played a leading part in assembling the Linz Collection. Even before the war, Hoffmann, who had known Hitler since 1922, had acted as the Führer's art adviser. He was present when Hitler 'acquired' his first purchase for Linz, the collection of Alphonse de Rothschild in Vienna, which had been confiscated after the Anschluss. Hoffmann, an NSDAP member from the very beginning – he held Party membership number 59 – stated emphatically that Hitler had banned the purchase of works of art from the hoard of the Einsatzstab Reichsleiter Rosenberg.

Once a month or so, all works of art that had come in (that is, confiscated as well as purchased items) and offers by dealers made through the architect Hans Reger, were assembled in the Führerbau in Munich. Hitler, flanked by Posse, and after Posse's death by Voss or a museum director and sometimes also by Hoffmann, would point to the paintings of which he approved, whereupon they were handed over to the staff of the Führermuseum. Hoffmann's contribution was largely confined to the selection of photographs of the paintings Hitler been offered by his art agents or by private individuals. He usually forwarded his selections and recommendations to Hitler.[8]

According to Miedl, Hoffman did not confine his activities to advising the Führer; he also acted as Hitler's agent. Miedl, banker and art expert rolled into one, called Hoffmann an 'honest and decent person', one, moreover, who went out of his way to protect his Jewish friends.[9]

Like Hitler, Göring, too, was busily amassing an enormous art collection. To secure the very best items, he had the whole of occupied Europe combed by 'art agents'. One of these was Andreas Hofer, and Alois Miedl may also be counted amongst Göring's scouts.

Both had been active in the Netherlands even before the war, Hofer as a Berlin art dealer who paid regular visits to the Netherlands, and Alois Miedl as a banker and businessman. Miedl had been living in the Netherlands for some considerable time and had a Jewish wife, which seemed in no way to mar his good relations with Göring.

The Looting of Cultural Property

Another art supplier to Göring was E. Gritzbach, his principal private secretary, who was regularly sent on tours for the express purpose of expanding his chief's art collection. Sometimes Dr Bruno Lohse, Göring's special representative with the ERR in Paris, would also visit the Netherlands or in Belgium on special missions.[10] Kajetan Mühlmann was a regular supplier of works of art to Karinhall, Göring's country estate outside Berlin. Karinhall, named after Karin von Fock, Göring's Swedish wife who had died in 1931, had grown into an impressive temple of art over the years. What the Führermuseum was to Hitler, Karinhall was to Göring.

In addition to such 'official' looting agencies as the ERR and Hitler's and Göring's art scouts, independent dealers and representatives of the German art trade and museums were active buyers of paintings in Paris, Brussels and Amsterdam. Most of the works of art they bought found their way to Germany, whence some were sold on to such neutral countries as Spain, Portugal, Sweden and Switzerland. Many works of art went to various sources in Germany after having passed through the hands of dealers acting as Hitler's and Göring's agents. These dealers generally paid for their purchases, but almost never the full price – most owners were afraid to refuse the often scandalously low offers they were made. The psychology of coercion by the exercise of power was in full sway.

Before America entered the war in 1941, many attempts were made to sell looted works of art to the United States and Latin America via Spain and Portugal. The American vessel *Excalibur* was found, during an inspection outside Lisbon harbour, to be carrying a collection of five hundred paintings, including works by Renoir, Cézanne, Gauguin, Degas, Manet, Monet and Picasso, and also a case of rare books.[11] Throughout the war, stolen works of art were smuggled to all corners of the world on a large scale. Often, the smuggling was done by diplomatic post, which, by international agreement, was not subject to searches.[12]

It is likely that the Nazis traded in looted works of art even before the outbreak of the Second World War. This applied particularly to the art they called *entartet*, degenerate – art that did not satisfy the Nazi aesthetic criteria. Cases in point were impressionist and modernist paintings, and 'Bolshevik art'. *Entartete Kunst* had been banned in Germany since 1937 and removed by order of the authorities from private collections and galleries. Some of it found its way onto the international market.[13] After the war, Alfred Rosenberg – born in Estonia in 1893 and the leading Nazi ideologist – vented his views on 'corrupt' art once more at his trial:

The European peoples had definite aesthetic conceptions. In contrast to these conceptions, there arose in various metropoles a completely alien, artificial concoction of various tendencies. This gradually became the glorification of the neurotic, the loathsome, the unscrupulous, and finally attempts were made to disguise this actual lack of

– 47 –

ability by all sorts of wild sensations, all the way to tacking on tin, or newspaper; they called these trends by something new every other year in order to make a splash. Fundamentally, this was no longer art but simply a business in sensationalism in lieu of art.[14]

The Einsatzstab Reichsleiter Rosenberg

Apart from being active in Eastern Europe, Alfred Rosenberg also busied himself in the West. In July 1940, the military commanders in France, Belgium, Luxemburg and the Netherlands were instructed to offer their full assistance to the Einsastzstab Reichsleiter Rosenberg (ERR). Hitler was personally involved. The ERR, whose different sections covered practically every aspect of cultural life – there was for instance a Sonderstab Bildende Kunst (Special Fine Arts Staff), a Sonderstab Kirchen (Special Churches Staff), a Sonderstab Musik (Special Staff for Music) and a Sonderstab Bibliotheken (Special Staff for Libraries) – employed a team of specialists whose duty it was to ensure that as much valuable cultural property as possible was transferred to Germany.[15]

The Einsatzstab was particularly active in France, which boasted the richest art centres in Europe. The spoils were removed to the Fatherland by the wagonload. The fact that part of the loot consisted of German property forcibly removed, especially in Napoleon's day, was used as a justification, because the Germans frowned on undisguised 'looting'. There had to be a legal justification for seizing goods, and if one did not exist, it had to be invented.

The Einsaztstab Rosenberg was generally paid by the recipients of the loot. They included such top Nazis as Hermann Göring, who even opened special bank accounts for the purpose. Payments, however, were generally a pure formality, because realistic prices were rarely asked or paid. Those who can see through the cover-up techniques will find that nothing at all was paid in a great many cases..

Göring's camouflage went so far that he instructed Professor Jacques Beltrand, one of his art experts, to hand in estimates of the value of the works of art selected. But no actual payments were ever made, as Göring had to admit at his Nuremberg trial.[16]

After the war, Rosenberg was asked whether he really expected Göring to pay for the works of art. He said that this had been a bone of contention. He had not insisted on payment, because in that case the works of art would formally have changed hands. He personally preferred confiscation by the German authorities, coupled to a proper inventory and satisfactory storage. In order to keep track of the relevant works of art and to be able to lay his hands on them whenever he felt like it he would have liked to have all the confiscated articles photographed. What this party ideologist was actually advocating was the incorporation of the loot into the

German national stock of art treasures. But of course it was up to the Führer to decide what to do with the spoils. Rosenberg, moreover, considered looted art as a possible bargaining point during future peace talks.

Asked to define the precise difference between his activities and outright looting, the head of the ERR replied that the confiscations of works of art had been state policy. Had he personally appropriated works of art, then that would have been looting. In Rosenberg's view the work his staff had done was to act as custodians of enemy property; in corroboration he – mistakenly – mentioned as precedent what had been done in 1914–18 to the population of the German colonies.[17]

The Kümmel Report

Joseph Goebbels, Hitler's minister of propaganda, started preparations for the repatriation or 'return' of German cultural property as early as 1931. With the Napoleonic wars at the back of his mind, he instructed Professor Otto Kümmel, director of the Berlin museums, to draw up a report on 'works of art and objects of historical importance that since 1500 have fallen into foreign hands, without our consent or on the basis of dubious legal arguments.'

In 1940, Kümmel produced an interim report, in which he summed up the cultural losses suffered by the various German states as a result of the Thirty Years' War, the Napoleonic wars and the Treaty of Versailles. In his conclusion, the professor wrote that, if France wished to repay Germany for art and cultural treasures looted through the centuries, it was very much an open question whether all French possessions put together would suffice to make good the injustices inflicted on Germany.[18] The Kümmel report was not, of course, the cause, but only one of the pretexts used by Hitler to drag art treasures from the cultural centres of Europe to Germany.

In a secret military order dated 5 November 1940, Hermann Göring laid down how to distribute works of art of Jewish provenance. The official term was *Sicherstellung*, to put into safekeeping. The Führer had first choice, then it was the turn of Göring himself (who, whenever he saw a chance of getting away with it, would snap up objects earmarked for Hitler), and only then could Rosenberg have his pick for the 'High School for the Overall Intellectual and Philosophical Education of the NSDAP', the Hohe Schule founded by Rosenberg on Hitler's instructions in 1940. What that trio left was in principle allocated for distribution to German museums. Finally, art considered to be too decadent or too modernistic in Nazi eyes was put up for auction on the French market.[19]

Gerhard Utikal, Rosenberg's right-hand man, wrote a remarkable pamphlet in 1941 in which he set out the 'motives' for the confiscation of Jewish property. This paper, steeped in racial delusions, casts an illuminating light on Nazi thinking. It dealt primarily with France but, as Utikal stressed several times, it also applied to other European countries. After duly referring to Hitler's confiscation orders, Utikal accused the Jews, and the Freemasons too for good measure, of having instigated the war. This was the usual opening gambit. Building on that idea, Utikal went on to argue that the Nazi occupation of Europe must be seen not merely as a blessing but also as a liberation from the baneful influence of international Jewry. The armistice provisions did not extend to French Jewry, seeing that 'according to the legal and political standards of the Greater German Reich', Jews could in no way be considered Frenchmen. Worse than that, they constituted a state within a state.

According to Utikal, Jews had been able to corner so many works of art (and other riches) because, using their wide political influence, they had been able to prevent Germans from claiming their rightful share. Had Jewish emigrants not made sure that Germany was stripped of her cultural treasures? According to Utikal, all Jewish cultural property was demonstrably of German origin. By confiscating it, Germany was simply making sure of a 'relatively small compensation' for the injustice she had suffered.

Moreover, the confiscation of Jewish property could be justified in international law: 'It is an acknowledged principle of international law that, in war, it is permissible to apply the same means and outlook and to exact the same retribution as was first used by the enemy.'

According to Jewish law, as allegedly laid down in the Talmud and elsewhere, Gentiles were on a par with 'cattle'; in other words, they had no rights and were not entitled to own property. In addition, Utikal argued, no one else had been able to enjoy the cultural treasures in Jewish possession because the owners jealously kept them to themselves. No one else even had a chance to view them.

Nor did Utikal think that the Hague Convention, which (as was noted above) prohibited the confiscation of private property, applied to Jews. According to Utikal's simplistic arguments, Jews themselves had placed themselves outside the law by their misconduct: for thousands of years they had treated Gentiles as outlaws and they were at long last being paid back in their own coin.[20]

Hereditary Enemies of Nazi Ideology

Rosenberg's Hohe Schule was intended to serve as a National Socialist study centre, with the aim of laying a 'scientific' foundation for Nazi ideas. The heart of this Nazi university was to be a cluster of some ten institutes, each with its specialist field of study. Thus there were institutes for the study of Judaism, of Freemasonry, of communism and of German folklore. The chief function of the associated

Institute for Race Studies was to bestow a scientific status upon the German race ideology. Although the Hohe Schule was not due to be opened before the end of the war, Rosenberg was given special permission by Hitler in January 1941 to start collecting books for its library.

Hence it was not part of Rosenberg's original task to take an active part in the theft of cultural property. However, Hitler's order of 5 July 1940 changed matters. The archives and libraries of declared Nazi opponents – which at that time consisted primarily of Jews and Freemasons – were ordered to be confiscated.[21] The fact that they, together with the communists – although the latter were not mentioned after the signing of the Molotov-Ribbentrop pact in September 1939 up to the invasion of the Soviet Union in June 1941 – were Germany's declared mortal enemies was a Nazi dogma.

Nevertheless, the theft of their possessions was thought to need a 'legal' basis, at least in the West. This came on 24 January 1941. Since Germany's victory over France, Rosenberg had racked his brain over the question and also discussed it with the Führer. The result can be summed up as follows:

> The war of 1939, being a struggle for German *Lebensraum*, is part of the major struggle conducted by our enemies for the destruction of the national-socialist philosophy of the German people. A victory in battle is by no means a philosophical victory. Philosophical enemies do not fight like soldiers and do not confine themselves to military means. Their aim is the destruction of the German Reich. Since time immemorial, they have been:
>
> 1. Anonymous and secret wire-pullers,
> 2. constant saboteurs of international understanding,
> 3. fanatical enemies.
>
> They wage war without regard for the people, that is, without regard for the interests of their respective host nation. All they are concerned with is the subjection of Germany.[22]

There could be no doubt about the identity of the ideological opponents and the nature of their crimes, of which there was no shortage of examples. Everything pointed to the fact that these ideological enemies were the true instigators of the Second World War.

According to this reasoning, the murder of Franz Ferdinand in Sarajevo, which had signalled the beginning of the First World War, had been organized by the Freemasons. The idea of the League of Nations, which Germany joined in 1926 but from which it later resigned, was born during a meeting of Freemasons in Paris on 28 June 1917. Several of these Freemasons had been Jews, Karl Liebknecht and Walter Rathenau amongst them. The first, murdered in 1919, was one of the founders of the revolutionary Spartacus League, which was later to become the German Communist Party. Rathenau, murdered three years later, was, as Germany's Foreign

Minister, partly responsible for the Treaty of Locarno signed with the Soviet Union in 1922, the year of his death. But he was above all associated with the Weimar Republic, loathed by the Nazis.

And finally the monument in Compiègne – a scandalous symbol in Nazi eyes – had been paid for by the Jew Rothschild and by several American Jews. Germany had signed the armistice on 11 November 1918 in the Forest of Compiègne, and had thus become the acknowledged loser of the Great War.[23]

The Nazis believed that any means was justified in the fight against Germany's opponents; the 'study' of their books and archives was a part of that struggle. Familiarity with their writings and ideas might help to analyse their pernicious mentality and hence assist Germany in ousting these hereditary enemies.

Competition between the ERR and the RSHA

After Hitler had approved the founding of the Hohe Schule, Rosenberg's acquisition of libraries and archives made a slow start. At the time there was already a collection of Judaica and Hebraica in Frankfurt. Rosenberg was authorized to take this over from the municipality, and to found the Institut zur Erforschung der Judenfrage (Institute for Research into the Jewish Question) in Frankfurt. In addition, he picked up several foreign libraries, including a Danish one. However, until the German invasion of France, Rosenberg's acquisitions remained limited. All this was to change with the war.

Many Jews and Freemasons, Germany's arch-enemies, had taken flight, leaving behind almost everything that might hamper their getaway. Many libraries and archives were abandoned, particularly in Paris.

Rosenberg was quick to act. On 18 June 1940, he wrote a letter to Martin Bormann, Reichsleiter and Hitler's confidant, in which he mooted the possibility of confiscating various French private collections. At the same time he proposed the setting up of the ERR. Just then, excited reports were pouring into Berlin originating from collaborators of Rosenberg as well as from members of the Reichssicherheitshauptamt (the Central Security Department of the Reich, or the RSHA), mentioning the large number of works of art and valuables abandoned in their homes and chateaux by families, such as the immensely rich Rothschilds, who had fled France.[24]

The reports by Rosenberg's colleague, Reichsstellenleiter (deputy leader) Georg Ebert, a member of the NSDAP Department of Foreign Affairs under Rosenberg's direct control, persuaded Rosenberg to plead with the Führer to sanction the creation of a team of specialists working hand-in-hand with the Wehrmacht in a comprehensive search for the cultural and artistic treasures left behind by fugitive Jews and Freemasons. According to Rosenberg, the material was of the highest importance for the political, ideological and scientific work of both the NSDAP and also of the Hohe Schule. Hitler, who had himself given orders for the setting up of the Hohe Schule and who was known to be particularly interested in paintings for the Führermuseum, agreed.[25]

On 5 July 1940, the Chief of the Oberkommando der Wehrmacht (the High Command of the Armed Forces, the OKW) issued the following order:

> To the Commander-in-Chief of the Army, the Commander of the Armed Forces in the Netherlands.
> Reichsleiter Rosenberg has petitioned the Führer to make searches of
>
> 1. national libraries and archives for writings of value to Germany,
> 2. the offices of the major church authorities and Masonic lodges for political material directed against us and to have such material confiscated.
>
> The Führer has given orders that these proposals be acted upon and that the Geheime Staatspolizei [Gestapo] – supported by Reichsleiter Rosenberg's archivists – be put in charge of these investigations. The chief of the Security Police, SS Gruppenführer Heydrich, has been notified; he will contact the responsible military commanders with a view to implementing these orders.
> This measure is to be applied in all parts of the Netherlands, Belgium, Luxembourg and France occupied by us.
> You are requested to notify subsidiary offices.[26]

Art was not yet mentioned at this stage. It should be noted that the Gestapo was assigned a leading role in these investigations, supported by archivists of the ERR.

The interest taken by the Gestapo, the secret political police, which was part of Reinhard Heydrich's Central Security Department, in archives was self-evident; archive material, particularly from foreign security services with their often political briefs, helped to trace acknowledged ideological enemies of the Reich, such as Jews, communists, social democrats, Freemasons and trade unionists, and to have them arrested.

The confiscated material could, after examination by the SD (Security Service), be handed over to the ERR. This caused a great deal of friction between these two rivals. But Heydrich had the upper hand and knew that he did; Hitler's order, the *Führerbefehl*, had assigned no more than a supportive role to the ERR; Heydrich's department had first refusal and the chief of the RHSA tried to take full advantage of this state of affairs. Even so, in quantitative terms, the ERR probably collected the lion's share of the material in Western Europe, and this thanks largely to the fact that Heydrich's intelligence service had had its fill of material – after all, the RHSA had been able to loot unhampered by competition, not only in Germany itself but also in the protectorates of Bohemia and Moravia, and in Poland. What with this rich booty, Heydrich was generous enough to leave something over for the ERR. For that reason, the Rosenberg units were able to reap their richest harvest in France, working in close collaboration with the military authorities. Hundreds of libraries and archives were 'secured'.

The ERR in France

The Nazi plans to confiscate works of art as well as archives and libraries took shape fairly quickly. The situation in France, where many houses, chateaux and other buildings had been abandoned by their owners, helped to open up veritable treasure troves, with the loot lying ready for the taking. The Oberkommando des Heeres (the Army High Command, the OKH), responsible for occupied France, did its best to prevent cultural property from being removed, and to leave it where it belonged. But Graf Wolff Metternich's *Kunstschutz* (art protection) campaign had little chance of stemming the Führer's rapacity. On 30 June, Hitler issued orders for the expropriation of Jewish art. Because these orders were not put in writing, Metternich continued to oppose them. However, he was fighting a losing battle.

On 17 September, the issue was settled when Rosenberg, on Hitler's explicit instructions, was authorized to confiscate all abandoned (*herrenlose*) art collections, including those that on the outbreak of war on 1 September 1939 had been placed in the custody of the French state by various opponents of National Socialism. This was a slap in the face of Rosenberg's rivals, for the Reichsleiter had, as if by magic, been promoted from second to first place in the thieves' hierarchy. Heydrich's apparatus, no less than Göring's Devisenschutzstelle, slipped back to second place. Rosenberg set to work with a will. Göring, like Hitler a lover of fine art, realized that the chances of expanding his own collection in a simple and above all in a cheap way had decreased significantly, and he accordingly sought an alliance with Rosenberg, collaboration with whom now seemed the obvious solution.

The Nazi ideologist, for his part, saw major advantages in an alliance with Göring, for he was faced with two problems:

- a lack of support in his attempts to keep up with the various agencies competing in a battle that continued to rage under the surface; and
- opposition from the German army command in France to the transport to Germany of the stolen cultural treasures.

Göring could help in the solution of both problems: he had an unassailable position in the Nazi hierarchy, and he also had control of railway traffic. Rosenberg was thus able to solve his logistic problems while Göring could expand his art collection without too many financial headaches. At the beginning of the war, the Party ideologist and the Reichsmarschall thus constituted an effective looting duet, in which Göring in fact ran the show. Rosenberg had no option but to accept the situation, because Göring happened to outrank him. In addition, Rosenberg was not held in high regard by the Nazi top brass or by the army high command.[27]

Characteristic of Göring's power was the decree he issued on 1 May 1941 to all Party, government and army departments. In it he ordered that every possible assistance be rendered to the ERR. Even so, he stipulated that all reports on the progress of the looting campaign, certainly if there were any problems, be sent to his office in the first instance.[28]

The Sonderstab Bildende Kunst (Special Fine Arts Staff), a section of the ERR, confiscated numerous Jewish art collections, often of international renown (for instance the Rothschild collection). In the Netherlands, this Sonderstab did not seize much more than about a thousand works of art. The Sonderstäbe Musik, Kirchen, Osten, Bibliothekenaufbau der Hohen Schule and Rassenpolitische Fragen (Special Staffs for Music, Churches, the East, the High School Library, and Race-Political Questions), each fought its own corner. By 1942, no fewer than 3,500 collections, libraries and archives had been 'secured' by the Hauptarbeitsgruppe Frankreich (Main Working Group France) of the ERR – France having been divided into five districts.[29]

Rosenberg declared himself satisfied with the course of events, as appears from a letter and report he sent to Hitler:

> In my wish to please you, my Führer, on your birthday, I take the liberty of sending you an album of photographs of some of the most valuable paintings my Einsatzstab has confiscated on your orders from abandoned Jewish art collections in the occupied territories in the west. These paintings are an addition to the 53 very valuable works of art that have previously been added to your collection. However, this album conveys no more than a feeble impression of the enormous value and scale of the works of art taken to safety on behalf of the Reich by my Dienststelle in France.

Rosenberg went on to express the hope that he might soon be able to tell the Führer about his work in person, and set out, in what he called an interim report, the results of his labours. In that report he missed no opportunity to stress the difficulties his men encountered in bringing art collections 'to safety', but which, thanks to their ingenuity, thoroughness and enthusiasm, they continued to overcome.

> Everything possible is being done to trace and to confiscate works of art hidden by Jews in Parisian houses, in provincial chateaux, in forwarding depots and in other warehouses. In general the campaign has been most onerous and time-consuming and has also not yet been fully brought to a conclusion . . .

> The Jewish fugitives have been very skilful in disguising the depositories in which their works of art were being hidden ... The Einsatzstab, assisted by the Devisenschutzkommando, have nevertheless succeeded in bringing most of the works of art left behind by Jewish refugees in France to safety and in having them sent to Germany.

The report goes on to summarize the type of property that had been expropriated, the sorting and packing activities, and the transport to and storage in Germany. A special transport carrying fifty-three major items had been delivered to the Führerbau in Munich, and 594 works of art had been despatched directly to Hermann Göring in Berlin. Rosenberg had also been able to lay his hands on the valuable collections belonging to the Rothschild family, divided between various houses in Paris and Bordeaux and chateaux on the Loire, although 'it took hard detective work to find them'.[30]

The ERR in the Netherlands

In the Netherlands, Rosenberg's looting teams set to work with considerably less energy than it had in France. There were no Jewish art collections of the same calibre, and officially only art treasures belonging to fugitive Jews were subject to confiscation as enemy property. At first, therefore, most of the confiscated art came from Masonic lodges, which had been wound up on the orders of Seyss-Inquart. After a time, however, the library of the Spinoza House, the Dutch Scientific Humanitarian Committee, the International Archive of the Women's Movement, the Portuguese-Israelitic Seminary Ets Haim, the Beth Hamidrash Library, the library of the Nederlandsch-Israelitic Seminary, the Valkenburg Monastery Library and the Dutch Economic and Historical Archive fell into the occupier's hands. In October and November 1943 it was the turn of the Amsterdam Ashkenazi archive and of several smaller Jewish archives in the provinces. The high point was of course the famous library (of about 160,000 volumes) of the International Institute for Social History (IISG) in Amsterdam, which was confiscated within two months of the invasion.[31]

The reason why Rosenberg's looters in the Netherlands – at work since the middle of September – were so much less successful than they had been in France, was not simply that the Dutch collections of art and cultural property were significantly smaller. In France, the ERR had had to contend with the RSHA and an uncooperative Wehrmacht, in the Netherlands it came up against the Dienststelle Mühlmann and the Feindvermögensverwaltung (Administration of Enemy Property), two agencies under the direct control of the Reichskommissar.[32] Hence art collections in the Netherlands were not the ERR's first priority.

Rosenberg admittedly had a mandate to proceed against the 'enemies of National Socialism' in the Netherlands and in Belgium as well, but the approach in the Low

Countries was somewhat less drastic than in France. Interest was mainly focused – at least in the beginning – on the archives of Jews and Freemasons. Confiscations in the Netherlands in the cultural sphere were primarily conducted by the Feindvermögensverwaltung, and secondly by the Devisenschutzkommando.

The Security Police (SD) were also involved in the confiscation of works of art. Once confiscation had been decided upon, the Dienststelle Mühlmann swung into action and decided whether the booty should go to Hitler, to Göring or some other top Nazi, or perhaps to a German museum.

What was left, and by definition the remainder was always of lesser quality, was sold by Van Marle & Bignell in The Hague or by Frederik Müller and Mak van Waay in Amsterdam. The last of these auction houses worked in close collaboration with Lippmann, Rosenthal & Co., whose offices also offered storage facilities to the Devisenschutz.[33] According to Mühlmann, works of art confiscated in the Netherlands were never exchanged for other items, Seyss-Inquart having expressly forbidden it on the grounds that 'all trade must comply with the precepts of law and justice'.[34] On at least one occasion this rule was broken, in the case of the Kröller Müller Museum.[35]

In France, exchanges were common, as can be seen from an enthusiastic letter from Andreas Hofer to Göring. In it Hofer, who acted as 'art agent' for the Reichsmarschall, suggested exchanging confiscated items from the Paul Rosenberg collection for other works of art.[36]

On 15 September 1940, the ERR set to work in the Netherlands, following the *Führererlass* (Führer decree) of 5 July 1940. Freemasons were the first victims. The Nazis considered them international plotters against the Germanic idea. The brotherhood – which had sprung from mediaeval English guilds and had crossed into the Netherlands in 1743 – was a close society wrapped in a shroud of secrecy. According to Rosenberg, Masons were the natural enemies of the national and racial ideas propounded by the Nazis. Freemasonry was proscribed in Germany as early as 1933, and the same fate awaited Dutch Masons. Meetings were banned almost immediately after the invasion in May 1940, to be followed on 3 September by a total ban of all Masonic activity.

From an (undated) report, it transpires that all the 'useful' material from seventy-six lodges, mainly in Amsterdam, but also in The Hague, Amersfoort, Bussum, Delft, Groningen, Den Helder, Hilversum, Rotterdam, Nijmegen, Utrecht, Zaandam and Alkmaar, was taken to Germany. Part of the inventory and a number of ritual articles, such as the Master's Gavel, also disappeared to Germany. The report mentions proudly that American Masons had offered five million dollars in 1930 for the Biblioteca Klossiana of the Great Eastern Order of the Netherlands in The Hague, with its many precious volumes.

The paper treasures of fifteen Rotary Clubs and of the Rosicrucians soon went the same way. The Germans looked upon the Rotary Clubs with their widespread international contacts as a modern form of Freemasonry.[37] The Independent Order of Odd Fellows, an international body with humanitarian objectives and in many ways related to the Freemasons (although there were no official links between the two), was also placed on the list of suspect organizations, and the libraries and archives of thirty-six Odd Fellow lodges were confiscated by the Security Police.[38]

The libraries of the Societas Spinoza in The Hague and the Spinoza House in Rijnsburg were packed into eighteen chests and sent to Germany for closer study. The books of the Alliance Française in The Hague, and the German-language writings (the 'emigré literature' of authors who had fled Germany) published, inter alia, by Allert de Lange and Querido, were also impounded, just like a number of private collections by declared Nazi opponents and by Dutch citizens who had fled abroad upon the outbreak of war. The stock of such communist bookshops as Pegasus and Kultura suffered the same fate. A large quantity of books and household utensils from the homes of Jewish refugees was confiscated as enemy property and handed over to the ERR. The list of confiscated libraries can easily be expanded: it included those of the Theosophical Society (with valuable works in Sanskrit), of the Spiritualists, of the Esperanto movement and of the Bellamy groups, together with the archives and libraries of small pacifist, anarchist and anthroposophic organizations.

These libraries were seized before the invaders turned their attention to collections of Jewish books. Jewish libraries were considered to be of particular interest for students of West European history. August Schirmer, leader of the Arbeitsgruppe Niederlande (Working Group Netherlands) of the ERR, judged that they might well contain new data about the Cromwellian period and the Glorious Revolution of 1688, and the ensuing Personal Union between England and the Netherlands. Most particularly he hoped that that he might gain further insights into Cromwell's attitude to the Jews, and 'possibly even into the Jewish influence on the development of the [British] Secret Service'.

The Arbeitsgruppe did not have an easy job; Schirmer could not refrain from pointing out that his team had been putting in overtime for weeks, and that they even worked on Sundays 'just like the men on the battlefields'. He added proudly that the libraries were worth at least thirty to forty million Reichsmarks.[39] The ERR had turned the offices of the IISG at 264 Keizersgracht, Amsterdam, into its headquarters. Special depots had been opened at various addresses in the Dutch capital; here the material was sorted and packed for despatch to Germany.

In the summer of 1942, the ERR was to launch a spate of new activities as part of its so-called M-Aktion. M stood for *Möbel* (furniture), though in fact the ERR seized household effects of all kinds looted from the homes of deported Jews.

The Bibliotheca Rosenthaliana and Other Libraries

The Bibliotheca Rosenthaliana was a special case because it belonged to the Amsterdam municipality and not to a private individual. However, because the library was of Jewish origin, the occupiers thought it more convenient to treat it as a private concern, and ignore the fact that it was part of the Amsterdam University Library. The collection was said to have a 'clear Jewish character' and that was enough for the Germans, Jewish character, rather than ownership, being a crucial consideration when dealing with Judaica.

In October 1941, the Security Police locked and sealed the library on ERR instructions. For a time, that was how they left it and the library staff made grateful use of the opportunity – after breaking the seal – of rescuing valuable manuscripts and incunabula. A significant part of the collection in the store of the Amsterdam University Library was rendered 'untraceable' by the staff, but they nevertheless failed to prevent the removal of 153 cases (about 60,000 books) to the Hohe Schule in Frankfurt.

After the war, Seyss-Inquart was to declare in Nuremberg that he had opposed the confiscations on the grounds that the Bibliotheca Rosenthaliana was not Jewish and therefore not subject to the Führer decree. The ERR had nevertheless emptied the library behind his back. The same was true of the IISG library. The Rosenberg team had merely had permission to examine the material on the spot. If libraries and collections were not expressly covered by Hitler's decree, the Reichskommissar considered them his personal responsibility. In this connection it is remarkable that the comment that the 'nature of the proprietor' does not matter in the case of Judaica should have come from Dr F. Wimmer, one of Seyss-Inquart's closest lawyer colleagues.

Dutch university and public libraries did not escape the attention of the overworked ERR either, although they were hardly if ever earmarked for confiscation. Books that displeased the Nazis were simply withheld from borrowers, who were thus guarded against unwholesome influences.[40]

This was also the case in the Royal Library (the Koninklijke Bibliotheek, or KB) in The Hague. Having been ordered on 8 August 1940 to change its name to the National Library, an edict followed on 28 August demanding it to remove all publications of a subversive or anti-German tenor from the list of books available for loans.[41]

Libraries were combed for manuscripts, especially in the field of German and Dutch mysticism, which 'have not hitherto been available for research and in which Master Eckhart, among many others, may well be included.'

Moreover, large and 'efficiently run antiquarian bookshops, too, facilitate the acquisition of large quantities of valuable writings, and not only of Dutch origin. It is important to seize all the opportunities available in the Netherlands.'

The search of libraries and antiquarian bookshops began in August 1941 and was directed by Dr W. Grothe and F. Brethauer. The Amsterdam University Library topped the list because it contained the largest collection of manuscripts in the Netherlands (60,000 items). From the middle of September, Parteigenosse (Nazi Party Comrade) Paul Ruhbaum, who had won his spurs in Paris, also joined the hunt for old manuscripts. After Amsterdam, it was the turn of the Utrecht, Leiden and Groningen university libraries, but the Haarlem and Rotterdam municipal libraries, the Fries Genootschap, the Meermanno-Westreenianum (The Hague), the Nijmegen Municipal Museum and the archive of the Haarlem bishopric also received the attentions of the manuscript hunters. The relevant document does not state whether the contents were actually confiscated, but it does mention that 1,421 pages of seventy-five manuscripts were copied.[42]

All the existing *Erlasse* and *Verordnungen* clearly failed to legalize confiscations of library items whose owners could not be labelled ideological enemies of the Third Reich – at the very least, these items had to have a 'clear Jewish character', as did, for instance, the Bibliotheca Rosenthaliana.

A closer look at the libraries and archives mentioned above does not always provide decisive answers about the activities of the ERR, but that is of course no proof that they were spared its attentions. Many ERR interventions were not recorded on paper, or possibly the records were destroyed or can no longer be found. However it seems most unlikely that the ERR should have falsified reports about copies, purchases and exchanges of manuscripts.

As far as can be established, no books were 'purchased' from the Royal Library in The Hague but German manuscripts in it were exchanged for items of interest to the Netherlands. These 'exchanges' were co-ordinated by Dr Vollmer, General-Kommissar für Verwaltung und Justiz des Reichskommissar für die besetzten niederländischen Gebiete (General Commissioner for Administration and Justice under the Reichskommissar for the Occupied Netherlands). Like works of art, archival documents had to be returned to the archives from which they originated in accordance with the 'provenance principle'. Vollmer asked the Royal Library to exchange one of its manuscripts with the Reichsarchiv in Vienna and three manuscripts with the Staatsarchiv in Munster. The Royal Library deliberately delayed the exchanges to such an extent that very little became of the whole business. Admittedly, two German manuscripts were exchanged for three from the Royal Library, of which one was certainly, and two were probably, of Dutch origin. The Royal Library itself was satisfied with these 'swaps', seeing that the German manuscripts were of small value, while at least two of the Dutch manuscripts handed over in return were considered welcome additions to their collection.[43]

As far as can be established, no manuscripts were stolen or 'bought' from Leiden University Library either, although some were copied (against payment). The invoice (87.90 guilders for '153 large and 89 small photographic reproductions') issued by the Rijksuniversiteit Leiden to Dr Grothe of the Sonderstab Bibliothekenaufbau (Special Library Reconstruction Staff) in Berlin and the receipt have been preserved.[44] If articles were not covered by the valid confiscation rules, the ERR resorted to copying. The invoice to Dr Grothe is yet further proof that the Germans felt the need to place their confiscations on a 'legal' basis.

In Leiden, too, the idea of exchanges was mooted, albeit on a very modest scale: a chronicle of Egmond owned by the city of Breslau against 'a splendid piece, a survey of the monastic properties in and around Breslau'. In this case, too, the Dutch institution did not seem adverse to the exchange, which, however, never took place, because it was stipulated that the exchange would not be made until after the war.[45] Not mentioned, but obvious enough, is the fact that a final German victory was taken for granted. Groningen University, too, expressed its approval of an exchange with the Aurich State Archive.[46]

Although in the three cases mentioned there was some enthusiasm for the exchanges (which were considered advantageous to the Dutch side) in principle, the balance was of course weighted in favour of Germany, the exchanges being not unlike forced sales.

According to the account of Dr J. H. Kernkamp, curator of the Meermanno-Westreenianum in The Hague, the visit by the ERR in November 1944 to that museum with its famous collection of books and paintings was fruitless. Although in possession of a valid *Ausweis*, Kernkamp played it doubly safe when the Germans came to inspect his collection: he hid in a display case, 'taking the place of an Egyptian mummy which, in its turn, had been moved to a bomb-proof shelter in the Zandvoort dunes'. Inside his hiding place, he listened to a 'most remarkable conversation'. When the ERR representative asked whether the museum contained German works of art or artefacts that were 'indisputably older than Dutch contributions in the same field', he was told by a 'quick-witted' member of the museum staff that 'a significant part of the museum property consisted of Egyptian art treasures, of which it cannot be said that they were of more recent date than the few German exhibits found in the collection.'[47]

According to the ERR report, the Germans also bought books from Dutch libraries:

> A whole series of works that the [German] Central Library has wanted for a long time and which constitutes the basic stock of any scientific library, could be acquired here. Most of the works in question are serial and reference works, journals and publications by scientific societies in those branches of science for which the Central Library is anxious to assemble the most comprehensive possible collection of basic material. The sum of 70,000 RM has been approved for the purchases . . . Up to 1 April 1942, the book inflow amounted to 3,860 volumes. Nearly all paper-bound journals and volumes have been sent to the binders.[48]

No traces of these items could be recovered in the institutions mentioned above. The report also mentions visits to antiquarian booksellers.[49]

In October 1941, the stock of Jewish antiquarian booksellers fell into the hands of the ERR,[50] probably as a result of the 'Aryanization' of Jewish concerns. In 1941, Jewish antiquarian bookshops were given the choice of going into voluntary liquidation or handing their businesses over to a *Verwalter* (administrator).[51]

Books that were of no interest to the Hohe Schule or the RHSA were placed at the disposal of the Wehrmacht and of German schools and institutes, on condition that their Jewish origins were not obvious and that the owners' names had been removed from the books.[52]

Ants and Flies

In some reported cases the Germans were either not very particular about observing the confiscation regulations or else gave them a decidedly flexible interpretation. The confiscation of the collections of Wasmann and Schmitz, two Jesuits born in Germany, was a case in point.

In 1875, E. Wasman took up residence in Exaeten Castle, between Roermond and Weert. He was an expert on ants, in which field he had done major research and built up a world-famous collection of specimens. In 1899 he moved to Luxemburg, but in 1911 he returned to Exaeten, where he died in 1931.

Hermann Schmitz lived in Limburg from 1894 to 1942, with two short interruptions. Schmitz's special field was flies and his collection of Phoridae enjoyed no less international fame than Wasmann's collection of ants.

According to Dr F. Plutzar of the Hauptabteilung Wissenschaft, Volksbildung und Kulturpflege des Reischskommissariat (Central Division for Science, National Education and Culture of the Reichskommissariat), both men were of German origin and hence not Netherlanders, so that their collections could not possibly be treated as Dutch cultural property. In other words, they were German cultural possessions and belonged in Germany. In March 1943, Plutzar let it be known that henceforth both collections would be taken care of by the Zoological Museum of the University of Berlin.[53]

Both cases should probably be seen in the context of the Kümmel report, according to which German cultural property had to be kept in Germany. Characteristically, the actual confiscation was preceded by an extensive exchange of letters.[54]

The Dienststelle Mühlmann

Dr Kajetan Mühlmann[55] had been part of the circle of Seyss-Inquart's friends for some time before he came to the Netherlands. He was given instructions by the

The Looting of Cultural Property

Reichskommissar to organize the looting of art, although, of course, that term was not used officially. Mühlmann could boast of ample experience in Poland, but the methods he had used there could not be applied in the Netherlands, which, at least at the beginning, was considered a fraternal country. Because it was Hitler's aim to integrate the Netherlands into the German Reich, there was no point in confiscating Dutch collections and transporting them to Germany.

In place of *Sicherstellung* (safekeeping), as the looting of Polish cultural possessions was euphemistically called, Mühlmann's colleagues had the necessary funds to buy up works of art, often on the regular Dutch art market. Eduard Plietzsch and Dr Franz Kieslinger, both associated with the Dienststelle Mühlmann, had known most Dutch art dealers from before the war, especially Plietzsch, an art historian and specialist on Dutch art. It is not entirely clear where the Dienststelle obtained its resources, though it was probably from a *Sonderfond* (special fund) made available by Seyss-Inquart. The sources of that fund are obscure.[56]

The Dienststelle Mühlmann did not have much to do with confiscated property from sources other than the Abteilung Feindvermögen (Enemy Property Section) and later also from Lippmann Rosenthal & Co. The Reichskommissar appointed Kieslinger of the Dienststelle Mühlmann as Sammelverwalter (collective administrator) of all works of art confiscated from enemy sources.[57]

All in all, the Dienststelle confiscated no more than a few collections as enemy property: the Hamburger Collection in Laren, the Hartog Collection in Wassenaar, the Nienhuys Collection in Bloemendaal, the Polak Collection in Amersfoort, and the remains of the Lugt Collection. Several items from these collections were earmarked for the Linz museum. Compared with outright purchases, confiscations accounted for no more than a small part of Mühlmann's activities.[58] The possibility that works of art on loan to Dutch museums might fall under the heading of enemy property was also taken into consideration. To that end, the Ministry of Education, Science and Culture wrote to all the directors, asking for notification by return of post of all the relevant items held by them.

The Rijksmuseum in Amsterdam came up with a list within a few days: one carpet, two sculptures and one painting met the criteria of enemy property on loan. Three other items on loan were difficult to classify, since it was not known whether the German owners had meanwhile changed their German nationality for another.[59]

Every *Verwalter* of works of art had instructions from Seyss-Inquart to make them available to the Dienststelle if asked to do so. Mühlmann's only rival was Dr Hans Posse, who bought works of art for the Führermuseum in Linz. Mühlmann himself would sometimes act on Posse's instructions. On 20 December 1940 and on another occasion, precisely one week later, the Dienststelle sent twenty-seven paintings to Linz, including work by Rubens, Dou, Van Ostade, Steen, Van Ruysdael and Rembrandt.[60]

On the list Mühlmann sent Posse on 20 and 27 August in response to Sonderauftrag Linz (Special Linz Order), several of the same names shine out: Rembrandt, Brueghel, Rubens, Dou, Van Goyen, Van Ostade, Van Mieris, Steen and Van Ruysdael.

The list Mühlmann handed to Posse between December 1940 and March 1941 also included the names of many painters whose work regularly fetched large sums, although the recorded purchase prices would not lead one to suspect that fact.[61]

Mühlmann also drew on the collections of antique dealers placed under a *Verwalter*. The *Verwalter* would draw up a list of the works of the available works of art and submit it to the Dienststelle, which could then make a selection. The most valuable items went to Hitler and other top Nazis 'against payment'. Two paintings by Cornelis Troost finished up in this way with the art-loving Führer.

What these gentlemen did not want went largely to two auction houses: Weinmüller in Vienna and Lange in Berlin. Payment was generally made to the *Anderkonto* (other account) of the Dienststelle Mühlmann at the Handelsmaatschappij H. Albert de Bary & Co. The accounts were then settled through Omnia Treuhand, appointed by the *Verwalter*.[62]

As noted above, the Netherlands could boast few art collections of international renown belonging to Jews or non-Jews. However, the Dutch population at large did own a relatively large number of works of art, including paintings of outstanding quality.[63] From one of Plietsch's reports to Mühlmann it appears that Mühlmann had sought expert opinions about the background and current state of the Dutch art market. Mühlmann knew fairly accurately where private collections – including those of Netherlanders abroad – were to be found. Nor did he forget to order searches of collections on loan to museums.[64] These searches were conducted in close collaboration with Lippmann, Rosenthal & Co. – one representative of that 'robber bank' and one of the Dienststelle would jointly visit the museums in question and inspect the works of art they held on loan.[65]

Mühlmann's 'art intelligence service' left very little to chance. With some satisfaction German art experts noted that England had ceased to be a competitor on the Dutch art market. Instead there was now a threat of a form of inflation, for: 'paintings often command the same sum in guilders as they fetch in marks in Germany, that is, the mark has the same purchasing power on the German art market as the guilder has in Holland.'[66]

The largest Dutch collection in private hands was that of the Royal Family. Although Seyss-Inquart had confiscated all possessions of the House of Orange on 10 September 1941, almost the entire collection survived the war unharmed, because a Dutch commission managed time after time to delay its final removal.

However, many thousands of paintings and other works of art did find their way to Germany through the Dienststelle Mühlmann, to be sold there to leading Nazis,

The Looting of Cultural Property

museums and art dealers. The regular clients included Hitler, Göring, Baldur von Schirach (then Reichsstatthalter and Gauleiter in Vienna), and last but not least Hans Frank, the Governor-General of Poland. The Dienststelle usually took a commission of 10 to 15 per cent, although in some cases, for instance that of Göring, the surcharge was waived. For works of art destined for Linz, the commission was often waived as well. The most important direct source of our knowledge of these activities is the *Geschäftsbuch der Dienststelle Mühlmann* (Dienststelle Mühlmann account book), in which 114 works of art are listed, most of them paintings. The account book is, however, far from exhaustive. The titles of smaller works of art (listed separately in a ledger that could not be recovered) are almost entirely missing, as are the names of the buyers. After the war, only about a third of these works could be returned to the Netherlands.[67]

Mühlmann was mainly active on the open market and – unlike other German looting agents – worked as a more-or-less ordinary art dealer. Nor was he exclusively after art owned by Jews. That does not alter the fact that he put potential sellers under pressure with threats if he thought that the best way of attaining his objective. Thus he would insinuate unmistakably that he was able to 'annihilate' not only the art business concerned, but also its owner.

Mühlmann's most important purchase was a Vermeer, *The Man in the Top Hat*, from the Ten Cate Collection in Twente. In 1940, Ten Cate sold that canvas to Miedl. Göring took an option on it, but dropped the matter because Baldur von Schirach wanted the painting for Vienna, as a replacement for *The Painter's Studio*, which had been chosen for the Führermuseum in Linz. Mühlmann then bought the painting in Seyss-Inquart's name for 750,000 guilders. The Reichskommissar had the famous work transferred to the capital of the country of his birth, in accordance with von Schirach's wishes.[68]

The fact that the Dienststelle Mühlmann had a freer hand in the Netherlands than the ERR, which had set to work in France almost unimpeded, was undoubtedly connected with Seyss-Inquart's central role. Both the Dienststelle Mühlmann and the Feindvermögensverwaltung (Administration of Enemy Property) fell under his jurisdiction. The two agencies worked in tandem and the collections confiscated as enemy property found their way to Germany via the Dienststelle. Mühlmann also worked hand in glove with the Devisenschutzkommando (Foreign Exchange Protection Commando) and the Gestapo, two bodies that intervened whenever Jews proved uncooperative in handing in their possessions. The staff of the Dienststelle Mühlmann consisted of five members in addition to Mühlmann himself, namely Mühlmann's brother Josef, two Viennese art historians, a bookkeeper, and the senior assistant, the art historian Eduard Plietzsch, who, as was noted earlier, was a specialist on Dutch art. This team continued almost unchanged throughout the war.

Thanks to its small staff and the large 'market' in which it operated, the Dienststelle, whose clients included leading Nazis as well as such famous auction houses as the Dorotheum in Vienna, Adolf Weinmüller in Munich and Hans Lange in Berlin, was able pay its own way.[69] In addition, the Dienststelle had the right to impose a levy of 10 to 15 per cent on all confiscated goods sold at auctions.[70]

The Dutch Art Market

The German invasion brought great prosperity to the Dutch art market. The crisis during the 1930s had helped to depress the art trade, as had the outbreak of war in 1939. Dutch art dealers had been swamped with supplies, while there had been practically no sales. Germany (traditionally the most important trading partner in this field as well) had ceased to be an export market in the wake of Hitler's monetary measures.

These factors helped to produce rock-bottom prices. At the beginning of the German occupation of the Netherlands in the spring of 1940, the art trade was in the doldrums. One glance at a catalogue of the Amsterdam auction house Frederik Müller from April 1940 shows that prices had sunk to an all-time low. Needless to say, one cannot be careful enough when making price comparisons. It is hard to imagine today that most seventeenth-century masters did not really come into vogue until the beginning of the First World War, and then largely thanks to German interest. Nor did impressionist paintings fetch anything like the astronomical prices to which we have become accustomed.

Almost immediately after the invasion of the Netherlands the depression in the art market lifted. Trade picked up rapidly, and prices soared. This development is represented in Table 2.1 (with 100 as the index price in 1940).

The horde of German dealers, including Hitler's and Göring's 'art agents', museum directors and private buyers, who poured into the Netherlands, was largely responsible for lifting the market. The competition among the top Nazis to acquire the best pieces, with Hitler and Göring leading the way, provided a strong stimulus, and in the wake of the trade depression of the thirties, the Dutch art trade profited with gratitude.[71]

In 1940 and 1941 the supply of Dutch works of art offered by Matthias Lempertz in Cologne increased markedly not only in quantity but also in quality. Auctions during the first half of 1941 were dominated by Dutch canvases, including work by Bol, Rembrandt, Cuyp, Van der Helst, Van Ruysdael, Potter, Dou, Van Ostade and Jan Steen. In addition, works by Di Cosimo, Goya and Brueghel came under the hammer. Most of these paintings were bought by collectors from Cologne. However, in Hamburg (Arcana), Munich (Weinmüller), Berlin (Lange) and Vienna (Dorotheum) the trade in Dutch art and other works of art from the Netherlands

Table 2.1 Changes in the price of artworks

	1940	*1943*	*1947*
Old masters (to ca.1750)	100	600	180
Romantic School (1750 to ca.1860)	100	800	240
Modern masters (Hague School)	100	300	180

Source: Ministerie van Justitie, Centraal Archief Bijzondere Rechtspleging, J. Dik, jr., dossier: 'De kunsthandel in Nederland' compiled by Douwes Bros, art dealers in Rokin, Amsterdam. The report on price fluctuations at art auctions and so forth was published in October 1947 on the orders of the Council for the Restoration of Legal Rights, Administration of Justice Division. The compilers were N. Beets, Dr A. van Schendel and the compiler of 'De Kunsthandel in Nederland', a member of the board of Douwes Bros whose signature is illegible.

also increased by leaps and bounds. The Galerie Fischer in Lucerne (Switzerland) offered almost 2,000 items for sale between 25 and 29 May 1941, most of them the work of seventeenth-century Dutch masters. With the exception of the canvases offered by Fischer, most of the works of art mentioned had not been looted, but were being offered for sale on the free market.[72]

On their arrival in the Netherlands, the German art buyers had found a dead market, but thanks to their avid buying activities prices quickly spiralled upwards, and that spurred Dutch buyers to join in the chase. They preferred to buy in a rising market; a falling market – with the prospect of a further decline in prices – encouraged a cautious attitude.

The factors that drove Dutch buyers into the art market were various. Some collectors had found that as the old sources of their income were cut off (in the Dutch East Indies and elsewhere), they were forced to sell part of their art collections; others used these very circumstances to improve the quality of their own collections or to extend them. Many museums were offering items from their stores for sale, and a number of private individuals 'did likewise with pieces they did not consider of good enough quality'. Items of lesser quality were thus replaced with better ones.[73]

Art auctions sprang up like mushrooms. When the best pieces, mostly by seventeenth-century masters, had been creamed off, items of the 'second rank' were increasingly being offered, although lovers of the Dutch Romantics could still satisfy their passion. The flourishing market was also an open invitation to art forgers, and quite a few 'old masters' turned out to be contemporary works.

Many businesses and auction houses threw in their lot with German dealers and agents, and took little notice of the proclamations by the Dutch government in exile. After years of rock-bottom prices in a depressed market, they rejoiced in the fact that there was money to be made again.

> The various agents competed against each another, and were as a rule played off one against the other by art dealers and collectors when they sought to make ostensibly legitimate purchases. It should also be noted that the wiser dealers and collectors avoided giving any bills of sale or receipts for purchases of art objects to German customers, and many owners frankly stated that they expected to get their artistic possessions back after the war.[74]

It would seem that the warning by the Dutch government in London had filtered through to some people at home, and that many of them were counting on having their works of art restored to them after the war – for nothing, or at the worst for a song. The paintings would again hang in their old places, and financially the whole thing would have proved extremely lucrative.[75]

The Chabot Collection

Private collections, too, such as that of J. J. M. Chabot, which had been on loan for some fifteen years to the Centraal Museum in Utrecht and included an early Rembrandt, *The Clemency of Titus,* a Van Ostade, a Hobbema and a Van de Velde the Younger, were put on sale by the Hague auction house Van Marle & Bignell on 1 September 1942.[76] The Rembrandt was bought for 300,000 guilders by Dr B. Mensing of the Frederik Müller auction house. From there, the painting found its way to Linz.[77]

While in the Chabot case there seem to have been free negotiations between the museum and Chabot, the Germans later exerted pressure to proceed with the sale. The loan consisted of more than fifty paintings, temporarily entrusted to the museum between 1925 and 1931. Eight of the paintings, all by Utrecht masters, were of particular interest to the museum. For that reason, Chabot stipulated that, after his death, the museum could buy the paintings for the price he himself had paid for them. When Chabot's health deteriorated in 1942, it was decided to act on that stipulation and the eight works came into the possession of the Centraal Museum for the price of 16,300 guilders.

A. B. C. D. Chabot and G. Rog acted as J. J. M. Chabot's authorized agents. Fifteen paintings had been returned to their owner before the war; the remainder (thirty-one paintings) was put on auction in The Hague and fetched 587,000 guilders. Nine paintings were acquired for 138,000 guilders by Goudstikker, an art-dealing concern administered by Miedl.[78]

The Looting of Cultural Property

The crowning items in the Chabot Collection were two Rembrandts: *The Clemency of Tito*, mentioned above, and the still-life *Peacocks*, which at the time of the negotiations had been on loan to the Amsterdam Rijksmuseum for twenty years. The Germans were very keen on acquiring these two paintings (and possibly others from the Chabot Collection as well), as witness the funds they transferred to the special Linz account in The Hague. No less a sum than 47,000 guilders was set aside for information, research, possible leads and advice. The authorized agent, G. Rog, was paid the relatively small sum of 500 guilders for his 'support' – others netted 1,000 guilders, 5,000 guilders, 7,500 guilders and even 20,000 guilders each.

Chabot was put under pressure at an early stage to sell *Peacocks* and later that pressure was stepped up even further. It is probable that Chabot did not too badly because, according to A. van Schendel, the director of the Rijksmuseum, he was keen on 'realizing' this painting, which he was prepared to let the Rijksmuseum have at cost price (about 350,000 guilders). Chabot let the museum know that two German 'gentlemen' had put him 'under strong pressure' to sell the painting, and when he told the Germans that he had already entered into negotiations with the Rijksmuseum, the Germans uttered threats in that direction as well.

However, Dr Erhard Göpel, a buyer for Linz and a resident in the Netherlands for some time, told the director quite a different story, namely that he had been pursued for a while by the two authorized agents, Rog and Chabot, who had pressed him to make an offer, and that they were trying to play him off against the Rijksmuseum. Göpel, who was not badly disposed towards the Dutch art world, even declared that he was willing to warn the Rijksmseum whenever the German authorities showed interest in works of art of Dutch origin.[79]

Soon after that, Göpel again turned up at the Rijksmusum, this time accompanied by F. I. Goyvaerts, a picture restorer. Goyvaerts, a member of the NSB who had connections with the Reichskommissariat, had been assigned to Göpel with instructions to keep an eye on him. It was he who had uttered the threats and urged the sale of the paintings, if necessary 'by force'.

The Ministry of Education, Science and Culture (OWC), which was responsible for the Rijksmuseum, was also visited by the two gentlemen with the result that the minister of state at the OWC instructed the Rijksmuseum to desist from further negotiations.

Goyvaerts was paid 20,000 guilders for his help and mediation. W. M. A. Weitjens, a member of the Dutch Supreme Court at the time Goyvaerts acted as mediator, received 7,500 guilders for his tip that the Chabot Collection was up for sale. Weitjens was also actively involved in the sale of art and antiques to German museums. Nor was his interest confined to the art and antiques sector; he was also instrumental in the sale of a large consignment of condoms to the Wehrmacht.[80]

The Lugt Collection

One of the collections on which the Dienststelle was able to lay its hands was the collection of the (non-Jewish) art historian F. J. Lugt in The Hague. Frits Lugt had left the Netherlands as a precaution as early as 1939, and had gone by way of Switzerland to the United States, where he remained throughout the war. Lugt had sent part of his valuable collection of drawings by registered post to Switzerland; the remainder fell into Mühlmann's hands. The reason given for the confiscation was Lugt's alleged anti-German attitude (as laid down in VO 33/1940 governing the confiscation of property).[81] The administrator, whom Lugt himself had appointed because he trusted him, informed Mühlmann that his employer had ordered him to hide the collection with friends. The Lugt Collection was confiscated at the beginning of 1941. Mühlmann chose about twenty-five items for the Führermuseum in Linz, and all these items were bought by the Sonderbeauftragte and sent to Germany on 31 July 1941.

When it eventually transpired that the administrator had invented the story of Lugt's anti-German attitude because he hoped to get into the Germans' good books and to be offered a position by them, the invaders were forced to rescind the measures (in part). Moreover, Frits Lugt's authorized agent, supported by officials of the Netherlands State Bureau for Art-Historical Documentation and of the OCW, had protested against the confiscation. All the officials concerned belonged to Lugt's circle of friends.

The Reichskommissariat had meanwhile realized that even a more-than-broad interpretation of VO 33/1940 provided inadequate grounds for confiscating Lugt's collection. However, for obvious reasons, it seemed impossible to bring the paintings back from Linz. The war with the United States, which started in December 1941, provided a welcome solution, since at a stroke Lugt had become an *Aufenthaltsfeind* (residential enemy).

A complicating factor was that Mühlmann had omitted to hand over the sum paid by Sonderauftrag Linz to the Sicherheitspolizei. Seyss-Inquart probably used the money to make the Führer a present of several paintings. Driven into a corner, Seyss-Inquart was forced to apply VO 33/1940 all the same; in any case it provided a temporary solution of his financial problems. Everything would be put right after the war.[82] Dr Erhard Göpel, not only 'buyer' for Linz but also an old friend of Lugt, declared after the war that part of the Lugt Collection was deliberately sold to leading figures in the Third Reich so that their personal involvement would lead to their support for the confiscation order, and hence their opposition to a repeal of the decree.[83]

The 'legal basis' (VO 33/1940) of the confiscation was questionable, something Seyss-Inquart realized perfectly well, but in this case avarice prevailed over German love of legality for there was no concrete evidence against Lugt. On the contrary, he had never displayed anti-German sentiments, and had given German art historians every possible help. Lugt employed German assistants and he was an enthusiastic contributor to German-language publications. Frits Lugt may have had his faults, but no one could say that he was anti-German. Moreover his choice of Switzerland, where he had moved before the outbreak of war, could not be used against him because Switzerland was a neutral country, and so was the United States when he landed there in December 1940 – the war between the United States and Germany was still a year away. In short, Lugt could not be said to have escaped from the occupied Netherlands since he lived abroad before the outbreak of the war.[84]

The Gutmann and Koenigs Collections

In 1941, Posse was able, with the help of a Berlin art dealer and Karl Haberstock, a prominent member of the e*ntartete Kunst* (degenerate art) committee of appraisal, to lay his hands on four paintings from the Gutmann Collection in Heemstede. Haberstock was one of Hitler's leading suppliers of paintings. The rest of the collection was carried off by Walter Andreas Hofer, Göring's agent. Friedrich and Louise Gutmann were deported. Louise died in the gas chambers in Auschwitz; her husband was beaten to death in Theresienstadt concentration camp.

Their heirs, Nick and Simon Goodman[85] and Lily Gutmann, have been trying to this day to recover the paintings. In 1997, a confidential financial settlement was reached with these three concerning a painting by Sandro Botticelli, *Portrait of a Young Man in a Red Cap*, which was sold by Sotheby's in New York for $650,000 and appeared to come from the Gutmann Collection. The Goodmans heard of the sale before its new owner collected the painting.

A second painting from the Gutmann Collection, *Landscape with Smokestacks* by Degas, was bought in 1987 by Daniel Searle, a multimillionaire from Chicago. In August 1998, a fifty-fifty agreement was reached between Searle and the Gutmann heirs. Searle donated his half to the Art Institute of Chicago; the other half was bought by the Art Institute from the Goodmans. Because of the high legal fees involved, the Goodmans had no option but to sell their share. The Degas is now on permanent display in the Art Institute of Chicago, with a note that it comes from the collection of the late Friedrich and Louise Gutmann and that it was donated by Daniel C. Searle. In their search for other canvases from the parental collection, the family has since also been able to locate Renoir's *Pear Tree*.[86]

One of Posse's greatest successes was the purchase of part of the famous Koenigs Collection, which consisted largely of drawings by the great masters. Due to the economic crisis, Franz W. Koenigs, a naturalized Dutch banker of German origin, found himself forced in 1933 to deposit more than 2,600 drawings as security for a loan with the Jewish bank of Lisser & Rosencranz. It was agreed that the bank would not hide the drawings away in its vaults but exhibit them in the Rotterdam Boymans Museum.

When Koenigs was unable to meet his financial obligations shortly before the German invasion, the board of Lisser & Rosencranz suggested to Dr D. Hannema, the director of the Boymans Museum, that he buy the drawings. The alternative was that they would have to go to America. It never came to that, however. The Rotterdam shipping magnate and art lover D. G. van Beuningen bought the entire collection in April 1940.

Six weeks after the German invasion, Posse managed to acquire 527 of the drawings for Linz. The rest of the collection remained in the Boymans Museum. In 1945, Soviet troops seized the drawings sold to Linz and they have been kept as 'war trophies' in St Petersburg ever since. For years, the rights to them have been disputed between the Dutch and the Russian authorities, The Hague claiming the drawings because Van Beuningen sold them voluntarily to Posse, so that the transaction is covered by the terms of the Allied Declaration of 1943, of which Moscow was one of the signatories.[87]

Franz Koenigs, whose financial difficulties were not solved by the sale of his securities lodged with Lisser & Rosencranz, sold about twenty-eight paintings to Alois Miedl, almost all of them by Rubens. Koenigs asked 800,000 guilders for them, but accepted 700,000 in the end. After the war, Miedl told an American investigation team that the transaction had been a stroke of luck for him. Koenigs had had little choice in the matter because he had to meet various financial obligations and because the banks refused to take works of art as securities. Miedl presented one of the paintings – a bathing Diana, goddess of the hunt, by Rubens – to Göring. Koenigs is said to have been very pleased with Miedl's action, believing that the Reichsmarschall was then in his debt and that he might be able to take advantage of that in the future.[88]

Among his many other activities, Göring was able to arrange for an important exchange of works of art with the Kröller-Müller Museum in the Hoge Veluwe National Park.

Kröller-Müller

Immediately after the First World War, Helene Kröller-Müller and her husband Anthony George Müller came into possession of three old German masters: a Hans Baldung Grien, a Lucas Cranach the Elder and a Barthel Bruijn. However, Göring felt that the three masters did not belong in the Veluwe but in his own gallery. The collection of the Kröller-Müller couple had been kept from 1938 onwards in a museum named after them in recognition of their generous contributions.

Cranach was one of Göring's favourite painters. One reason for the proposed repatriation of the paintings to Germany given by the Reichsmarschall was that, at the time of the original sale, 'unreasonably' low prices had been paid for them, so that Germany had been stripped of them unfairly.

The initial offer through Mühlmann, acting as agent, of 600,000 guilders for the three canvases was turned down, but the two parties eventually reached an understanding. The museum was offered a choice of impressionist works worth 600,000 guilders, needless to say through the Dienststelle Mühlmann. In addition, property rights to the Hoge Veluwe National Park – in which the museum was located – were thrown in. Mühlmann conducted the negotiations in the name of Seyss-Inquart, who was anxious to remain in the Reichsmarschall's good books

A commission made up of Dr D. Hannema (director of the Boymans Museum in Rotterdam), S. van Deventer (director of the Kröller-Müller Museum) and A. Plietzsch (on Mühlmann's staff) was charged with determining the value of the paintings for which the old German masters were to be exchanged.

As we know, the Nazis considered the impressionists and related schools as 'degenerate', and were therefore only too pleased to include a Pissarro, a Degas, a Corot, a Renoir, a Fantin Latour, a Van Gogh and a Breitner, not least because two of the paintings had been confiscated in Paris. Göring was delighted about the exchange. He could get rid of several 'degenerate' works, and although the Lucas Cranach and the Barthel Bruijn were earmarked for Linz, he nevertheless managed to corner all three works for his own collection.

After the war, the three German masters returned to the Hoge Veluwe. The impressionists – apart from the two stolen in Paris – have hung in the Kröller-Müller Museum ever since.[89]

The Lanz and von Pannwitz Collections

Another feat by Posse, acting as the Führer's art agent, was the purchase of the Otto Lanz Collection, which consisted mainly of Italian paintings, sculptures and Renaissance furniture. Otto Lanz's widow, who lived in Switzerland, seemed willing to sell part of the collection. Posse had first seen the works in the Rijksmuseum, where some of them were exhibited on loan. The Lanz affair is another example of how thoroughly the Germans set to work when stripping the Dutch art market. The correspondence between Posse and Bormann and other high-up Nazis about the purchase of the Lanz Collection – which was paid for partly in Swiss francs and partly in Dutch guilders – also shows how complicated this kind of sale could be, not least because of the procurement of the necessary foreign currency. Even if it was a purchase for the Führer himself, all the bureaucratic procedures involved in the release of foreign currency still had to be observed.

It certainly needed more than a simple telephone call to the Reichsbank. Göring, who also showed keen interest in the collection, was unable to obtain the necessary two million Swiss francs. Posse, with his more-or-less direct line to Hitler through Bormann, did manage to do just that, although it probably also helped that Reichsmarschall Göring was loath to put a spoke in the Führer's wheel too conspicuously. In addition to the two million francs, a Swiss visa had to be procured for Nathan Katz of D. Katz & Co. in Dieren, one of the leading art dealers in the Netherlands.

Nathan Katz, of Jewish origin, was closely involved in the acquisition of the Lanz Collection, because Mrs Lanz insisted on dealing with Posse exclusively through him. Moreover, part of the eagerly sought-after collection was in Switzerland, and that meant providing Katz with an exit visa. Now issuing such visas was no simple matter in the bureaucratic Third Reich, but with the help of Bormann, who in turn made contact with Heydrich, Posse did manage to get hold of one for the art dealer from Dieren. Nathan Katz probably owes his life to the Lanz Collection, for after having left the Netherlands late in 1941, he remained in Switzerland, and hence out of Nazi reach, for the rest of the war.

Twenty-five members of Nathan Katz's family also owe their life to the Nazis' love of fine art. In exchange for a Rembrandt – *Portrait of a Man: a Member of the Raman Family* – owned by the art dealer, twenty-five visas were issued: one Rembrandt for twenty-five visas. That was one side of the deal. The other side was that Nathan, thanks to his excellent contacts, would try to buy as many seventeenth- and eighteenth-century Dutch masters as possible for his German principals before his departure from the Netherlands.

Posse, who was determined to acquire this particular Rembrandt because he had failed so far to lay his hands on any important work for his masters, had little choice but to let Nathan Katz go to Switzerland: the coveted *Portrait of a Man* was in Basel. This was fortunate for Katz, but unfortunate for Posse, because, had the canvas been in the Netherlands, its acquisition would have caused few if any problems.

Remarkably, Nathan Katz continued, even while in Switzerland, to negotiate the sale of works of art to German buyers. Even before leaving the Netherlands, he had done business with the invaders, voluntarily and on a large scale.[90] One of his best customers was Alois Miedl, to whom Katz sold about 150 paintings to the tune of more than two million guilders, including Vermeer's *Man in a Top Hat*.[91]

After the war, Katz's firm – which now claimed it had acted under duress – became involved in a major scandal. In its wake, B. Katz, one of the partners, and Dr A. B. de Vries, a director of the Netherlands Art-Collection Foundation – whose tasks included the return of Dutch art treasures discovered in Germany to their rightful owners – were arrested for suspected fraud.[92]

That an exit visa to Switzerland could be the object of a business transaction also emerged in the case of Catarina von Pannwitz. Hofer had received a tip from the banker and art collector Fritz Gutmann that Mrs von Pannwitz wanted to meet him. Catarina von Pannwitz, German by birth but carrying an Argentine passport, was anxious to emigrate to Switzerland, and wanted Hofer to tell her how best to set about it. Hofer suggested the sale of a number of paintings to Göring. Apart from money, she would then also receive an exit visa. Shortly afterwards Göring turned up in person at the von Pannwitz home in Heemstede, made his choice and clinched the deal in the way Hofer had suggested.[93]

After the war, during questioning about the von Pannwitz transaction, it was put to Göring that he had abused his position, because ultimately only he and no one else could procure the exit visa. He had clearly placed Catarina von Pannwitz under pressure: no sale, no visa; but Göring insisted that there had been no pressure whatsoever, and that he had simply helped Frau von Pannwitz to solve her problems. Apart from a visa, she had also lacked the money to pay for her move to Switzerland, because during the war it was impossible to draw money from her Argentinian bank. Asked whether he would have confiscated the five paintings had Argentina been at war with Germany, he wisely refused to commit himself, saying that the question was speculative.[94]

N. V. Kunsthandel J. Goudstikker

The most notorious transaction in the art sector was undoubtedly the takeover of the art dealers N. V. Kunsthandel J. Goudstikker by Alois Miedl and Hermann Göring. Miedl, a German, had been living in the Netherlands since 1932, in order, as he said, to ensure the safety of his Jewish wife. The Goudstikker case was a blatant example of 'robbery by purchase', when it would have been much simpler to confiscate the business as enemy property.

On 14 May 1940, Jacques Goudstikker set out to flee to England with his wife and small son. The Jewish art dealer came to a most unfortunate end: he fell into the ship's hold and broke his neck. Apart from his wife and child, he left his art business at 458 Herengracht, Amsterdam, a country estate, Huize Oostermeer near Ouderkerk on the Amstel, and Nijenroode castle in Breukelen. Goudstikker fled Holland without signing a power of attorney, not because of negligence but due to *force majeure*: his authorized representative, the lawyer D. A. Sternheim, had died of heart failure on the day of the German invasion, four days before Goudstikker's hasty departure.[95]

Alois Miedl immediately showed great interest in Goudstikker's business. In this he was not alone, for Göring, too, had his eye on the company's art treasures. Both knew that there was much to their taste to be had.

As already stated, it would have been simpler to liquidate the company as enemy property. However, that did not suit Göring, for it would have meant losing any control over this fine collection. Enemy property fell under the jurisdiction of Reichskommissar Seyss-Inquart, who was due to be installed on 29 May. Confiscation would inevitably have meant that Hitler would have had first refusal. In other words, before Göring could step in, the cream of the collection would have been taken and he would have been left with the dross.

When interrogated after the war, Seyss-Inquart declared that he had tried to look into the background of the sale of Goudstikker's company, but that Göring had intervened with 'unmistakable threats'. All investigations were banned, and Miedl, who had been detained for twenty-four hours in connection with Seyss-Inquart's enquiries, was released on Göring's personal intercession.[96]

In short, the purchase of the Goudstikker business had been conducted in a great hurry. But there was yet another reason for speed. Almost immediately after the Dutch capitulation, the art market soared, which meant that the price for the Goudstikker business was bound to rise. In great haste, even before the end of May, a new director, A. A. ten Broek, was appointed. The legality of that appointment was extremely questionable, but the purchase of the business simply had to be concluded without delay. And not only as quickly as possible but as cheaply as possible. There is good evidence that Miedl spread the rumour that the business was in serious financial difficulties, that the fiscal authorities had confiscated large parts of the stock and that liquidation due to bankruptcy was a real possibility. The older Jan Dik, Jan Dik junior and the newly appointed director Ten Broek helped to spread these rumours, whose sole purpose was to undermine confidence in the firm and hence to depress the purchase price as far as possible.

From an analysis of the firm's books (which, incidentally, proved exceptionally complicated) and a glance at the assets, it appears that there were no financial difficulties of any kind. Goudstikker's debts to Incasso Bank N. V. (less than 200,000 guilders) and a few outstanding credits of 85,000 guilders gave not the least cause for concern, certainly not when seen against the background of the valuable stock of thousands of paintings (including great masterpieces), and the completely unencumbered Nijenrode, Ostermeer and Herengracht properties.

Although the widow, Desi Goudstikker-von Halban-Kurz, had let it be known via Switzerland that she would not agree to the sale of the business under any circumstances, it was sold all the same. The smear campaign of the Diks was successful. By suggesting that a speedy sale was the only way of preventing the imminent liquidation of the business, they were able to convince all concerned that a sale could not be avoided. The firm was accordingly sold to Miedl and then on to Göring, who, after having picked the best canvases, sold the rest back to Miedl. Miedl had been unable to put up the purchase price of 2,555,000 guilders (estimated to be one third of the real value) and Göring, who had got wind of Miedl's plans (and was afraid of missing the boat), sent Hofer to close the deal. Göring paid two million guilders for the stock, while Miedl came away with 458 Herengracht,

Ostermeer, Nijenrode and a few minor effects, and also with the name and goodwill of the firm, for 550,000 guilders. Miedl had probably not only been short of the necessary funds, but had also been loath to lock horns with the powerful Reichsmarschall.

Miedl paid the people whose gossip had facilitated the sale a generous commission of 400,000 guilders. Walter Hofer came away with 50,000 Reichsmarks. Two other closely involved accomplices even received 180,000 guilders each, to which an extra 'pension bonus' of 30,000 guilders was added later. The story that Goudstikker owed the Treasury a great deal of money was, incidentally, not pure invention, though it had happened in the early 1930s. According to a pledge lodged by N. V. Kunsthandel J. Goudstikker with the Receiver of Revenue, the company had designated a number of paintings as security until its debt to the tax office was paid.

In August 1933, fourteen paintings, including a Jan Steen, a Jan van Goyen and a Tintoretto had been temporarily handed over to the Rijksmuseum as a pledge. As early as 22 February 1934 the first three paintings were returned. Ten further paintings followed in 1937. The last painting, a Jacob van Ruysdael, was released on 29 October 1938.

Alois Miedl continued the business under the name of Kunsthandel voorheen J. Goudstikker (the former J. Goudstikker Art-Dealing Company). He bought the rest of the collection back when Göring (and the Führer) had taken their pick. Miedl left the proceeds of the company sale untouched throughout the war and assigned them to the widow of Jacques Goudstikker with the express promise that they would not be confiscated. In this way, Miedl was trying to maintain the myth of a voluntary sale.[97]

Miedl had never believed in a German victory. Like many other Nazis, he probably realized that a German defeat would mean that the transactions would be declared null and void after the war. He had taken that into account when he made his purchase. When he was told during his interrogation in Spain (where he had fled towards the end of the war) that the Goudstikker Collection was considered to have been looted, he was utterly dismayed. Clearly his plans had misfired.[98]

The explanation of the German urge to lend their purchases a veneer of legality was presumably rooted in the fear that, should they lose the war, their 'purchases' would be taken from them. That must also have been the reason why Miedl went to so much trouble in putting this purchase on a contractual basis. An American investigation team has given an excellent account of the German method of looting works of art:

The legal protection of the loot was assured in many ways . . . The Nazis knew that abolition of their laws by the victorious allies would automatically deprive them of the right to their booty. Thus no art collection or single work of art was seized, requisitioned or robbed by them without their 'legalizing' these crimes by some sort of sales certificate or exchange paper duly signed by their victims through force. Moreover, during the temporary conquest of Europe by the Nazis, most of the looted works of art were made the object of a series of successive transactions to disguise their origin.[99]

As director of the 'former J. Goudstikker Art-Dealing Company', Miedl was extremely active in the art market. He was in contact with both Hitler's and Göring's agents as well as with various German and Dutch art dealers. He himself never acted as Göring's agent (his Jewish wife stood in the way of that), but he nevertheless did do a great deal of business with the Reichsmarschall, and had, moreover, known him for many years. Miedl was on friendly terms with Göring's brother-in-law, whose wife, Göring's sister, used to stay regularly with the Miedls in Amsterdam.[100] The Goudstikker case was to have a long epilogue after the war.

The Leading Nazis' Love of Art

There seems little doubt that there were many passionate art collectors among the highest ranking in the Third Reich, but one wonders where their love of art really sprang from. Normally one would not ask such a question, and normally speaking it is in fact hardly relevant, and yet it forces itself upon our attention here because Hitler and Göring are among the last we would associate with beauty and the love of art.

Adolf Hitler first showed a special liking for art and architecture at an early age. His own artistic ambitions had ended in failure, but that had not caused him to lose interest. Hitler's love of art, provided it was 'Aryan', set an example to the other Nazis, although their collecting passion did not manifest itself before the 1930s.

For Hitler, art was a means of making sure the great German past was driven home to his compatriots. In many of his speeches he referred to the fine arts and that, too, made a direct impact on his closest collaborators. Like their Führer, they began to build up art collections.

The seizure of power in 1933 meant a considerable improvement in the standard of living of most men at the top of the Nazi hierarchy. Their homes became appreciably more luxurious and there were more generous financial resources available to embellish their new environment with paintings, sculptures and other objets d'art. After his accession to power, Hitler himself boasted several impressive residences, and hence many square metres of wall space, all crying out for artistic decoration.

During the twelve years of Nazi rule, the taste of the Nazi elite developed from being rather homespun, rural and populist – reflecting the party programme – to an appreciation of the old Dutch, Flemish, Italian and of course German masters. Their preferences changed from the Biedermeier style to the sixteenth- and seventeenth-century masters.

Hitler's Berghof in Obersalzberg is a striking example of his originally petit-bourgeois style, and Göring's Karinhall, which with the passage of time was to contain a dazzling collection of old masterpieces, originally had the appearance and the layout of a luxurious hunting lodge: the floors strewn with the skins of the game he had bagged and the walls extravagantly hung with antlers.

In the mid-1930s or thereabouts, Hitler's Berghof was adapted to the changing taste. In the prevailing climate, with its chauvinism, traditionalism and love of the glorious German past, there was no room for modern art – which was proscribed as degenerate or depraved in 1937.[101] Living painters (both Jewish and non-Jewish) whose work did not fit in with reigning Nazi aesthetics, were made to suffer, prevented both from buying materials and from exhibiting their work. A special committee kept an eye on the German galleries and arbitrarily – the taste of the committee members being the decisive factor – ordered the removal of everything considered to be degenerate. Thus the work of Edvard Munch, applauded less than a year earlier by Josef Goebbels as one of the greatest geniuses of the Nordic race, was banned. The confiscation of 'degenerate' art, facilitated by a special law, extended to paintings on loan to museums by private persons. Most of these works were sold at auction in Switzerland; the proceeds were used for the acquisition of paintings that did appeal to the Nazis. As has been mentioned earlier, there were also some direct exchanges.

All German museums were cleared of 'degenerate works'; as replacements, the directors were encouraged to make a selection from German works that passed Nazi muster. There was no question of financial compensation, which would have facilitated the purchase of replacements on the free market.[102]

After the war, Seyss-Inquart declared that he had considered the degenerate art policy to be 'nonsense', while Hermann Göring contended that it had all gone too far. He had found that calling Van Gogh too *entartet* (degenerate) was pure 'nonsense'. According to the Reichsmarschall, Goebbels had been the instigator of that policy, or at least the first to raise the subject. 'None of us wanted it,' Göring claimed. According to Rosenberg, Nazi opinion on Van Gogh ranged from 'extreme enthusiasm' to pronounced 'disgust'. Like Seyss-Inquart, he thought it 'nonsense' to call Van Gogh degenerate.[103]

One factor that shaped the Nazis' artistic taste and the character of their collections was the desire to be considered part of the cultural and political elite of Europe. In this context, the predilection for old masters meant playing it safe. With their art collections, the Nazis not only believed they could gain social respect, but also that they could enhance their political position. Besides being a display of power, art was also a means of copying the old elite; you could tell a man's status from his art collection.

Hitler owned the largest collection of all (6,775 paintings, including 5,350 old masters); Hermann Göring, second in the Nazi hierarchy, could boast a collection of between 1,700 and 2,000 works of art. The collections of Goebbels, von Ribbentrop, Himmler and other top Nazis, all reflected the importance of their position.[104]

Göring declared more than once that he would hand over his art collection to the state on his sixty-fifth birthday. That would have been on 12 January 1958, but it is highly questionable that he ever seriously entertained the idea because he was extremely proud to be the owner of the largest private art collection in Europe.[105]

Hitler's and Göring's Financial Resources

Where did they get their money? Both Hitler and Göring spent enormous amounts of money on art; their coffers seemed inexhaustible. The Führer put more than 163 million Reichsmarks into works of art, which, in his day, made him the greatest art buyer of all time. Apart from looting and actually buying works of art, he received many paintings as outright gifts. It had become a custom for those in Nazi circles to offer presents to their leaders. In that way, hundreds of paintings fell into Hitler's lap. Not only his closest collaborators used his birthdays as occasions for presenting works of art to their Führer. Leading industrialists too, such as Alfred Krupp von Bohlen und Halbach, would, when the occasion arose, present the leader of the German nation with a masterpiece. Göring also received a host of such 'perks'. In many organizations under Göring's control, a small part of the staff wage packet was withheld and diverted into the Göring Art Fund, for the purchase of works of art.[106]

Some of Hitler's acquisitions were paid for with the royalties from his book *Mein Kampf*, which sold an extremely large number of copies. According to H. Hoffmann, Hitler's official photographer, additional revenue came from a special surcharge on postage stamps (of six, eight, twelve and twenty pfennigs) bearing the Führer's likeness and based on Hoffmann's photographs. The extra revenue was channelled into an arts fund – created by Hoffmann – which at one point is said to have run to no less than fifty million Reichsmarks.[107]

In most cases, Hitler paid for the paintings he acquired from the Netherlands. During a post-war examination Mühlmann claimed that he made no profit from his sales to Linz, but the relevant documents show that he was not averse to charging even the Führer a commission of approximately 15 per cent. Hitler raised no objections, for like Göring he was anxious to present these purchases as normal trading practice.

A special 'Linz account' was opened with the Rotterdamsche Bankvereniging in The Hague. Between February 1941 and August 1944, the account received deposits amounting to 15,164,477.21 guilders. By September 1944 that amount, with the exception of 1,604.75 guilders, had been spent.[108]

Göring had his own 'arts fund'. During one of the post-war hearings he refused to say how that fund had been obtained because it was 'an internal German affair'. He did however say that he had bought part of his collection with his own money, that he had inherited another part and that 'a large part' had been presented to him even before the war.[109]

Göring's art fund (also called *Sonderkonto* or special account) was under the strict supervision of the Reichsmarschall himself who, as many sources have testified, watched over every least detail, always trying beat prices down, always after a bargain, and always making certain that the transactions looked honest, at least on paper.

> Göring was essentially a hard-headed, acquisitive businessman. He wanted to buy everything, but when bought it had to be at the lowest prices. In spite of the enormous sums of money at his disposal, he never failed to bargain, no matter how small the sum concerned, and he frequently bought second-rate objects because of their low price . . . However, when he himself made a sale, his price was among the highest; as, for example, in the case of MIEDL, who paid RM 750,000 for six pictures, five of which had cost Göring nothing . . . True to the precepts of National Socialism, Göring was scrupulous in his efforts to cloak his shadiest dealings in the appearance of normal business practice. He insisted that bills be presented, receipts signed, and everything recorded with characteristic German thoroughness.[110]

The same principle also applied to the works of art the ERR seized in Paris. Alfred Rosenberg and his staff regularly received inquiries from Göring about how they wanted him to settle his account. He never received a straight answer, however, and ultimately he never paid anything for the paintings. He demonstratively refused to accept presents from Jews grateful for his protection from the anti-Semitic laws, or whom he had helped to obtain exit visas to neutral countries. However if the proposed present was particularly tempting, he generally ensured that it came into his possession by way of one exchange or another.

It is therefore not clear precisely where Göring obtained the money for his art purchases. Hofer, Göring's agent, thought that it came partly from state funds, in accordance with an agreement between Hitler and Göring. What is certain is that millions of marks were involved and that some came from donations by German business concerns. In this connection, the names of the industrialist Kurt Hermann, the Hamburg tobacco factory owner Reemstma, and the Kali Syndikat (potash syndicate) have been mentioned. In addition Göring received a large number of 'birthday presents'.

These presents, above all, were an inventive method of art acquisition. Göring was particularly keen on presents in the form of paintings. But he was very choosy and did not want to be flooded with presents he did not like or that did not fit into his art collection. To get over this problem, he devised an ingenious system.

When he visited art dealers in various countries, he first chose the items he was keen to add directly to his collection, and next the pieces that might be considered a kind of 'reserve', but for which he nevertheless paid. He did not incorporate these immediately into his collection but left them temporarily in the hands of Hofer or his other agents. If someone then wanted to send him a present, he was referred to Göring's principal private secretary, who would put the generous donor in touch with Göring's art agents. From them they would then buy a painting of which they knew for certain that it would be to Göring's taste; after all, he had picked it himself. The money was paid into the arts fund, Göring received his present and the circle was closed. In the final analysis these presents were simply payments into Göring's arts fund.[111]

Göring's 'honesty' remains a curious phenomenon. If a painting was partly the property of an enemy subject, he insisted on settling that part, as enemy property, with the Feindvermögensverwaltung, the custodians of enemy property. In the Goudstikker case, thirteen paintings could be considered to be enemy property. These were canvases of which not only Goudstikker but also 'enemies of the Reich' and in some cases even Germans were co-proprietors. With the German owners, Göring himself settled up immediately. The enemy share he settled through Fischböck, whose jurisdiction extended to Feindvermögen.[112]

However, Göring's payments were certainly not very high, as appears from the purchase of a number of paintings from the Amsterdam dealer D. A. Hoogendijk and the London firm of Asscher & Welcker. Both were half-owners of paintings Göring bought. In a letter, once again to Fischböck, Göring let it be known that he would pay the English share over to the Feindvermögensverwaltung.

That letter conveys a clear picture of Göring's characteristic method. What strikes one above all is that he wanted the best for the lowest possible price, and that his payments to Fischböck were primarily intended to go through the motions of complying with the international law governing the control of enemy property. For although the English firm and Hoogendijk each owned precisely half the paintings and Hoogendijk was paid 140,250 guilders, Göring considered a payment of 22,500 guilders adequate compensation for the English partner.[113] His explanation was that the price paid to Hoogendijk was much too high, because, according to Göring, the Amsterdam dealer had made an excessive profit. Göring would have had to put up with that, but he had no wish to contribute to Asscher & Welcker's profit as well.

In my view, there is absolutely no reason for paying the profit to the English gentlemen as well, but at most the value of the paintings to these people at the time that they bought them. With some of these paintings, the Dutchman told me quite clearly that he had included an extra charge of 100 per cent as his profit, that is, that these paintings must have cost the Englishmen only one half [of their claim], and in several cases even less.

According to Göring, a valuation of the paintings was the only way of arriving at an acceptable figure and, since the paintings had already been sent to Berlin, he felt that his agent Hofer was the right person to perform that task. Finally he asked when Fischböck wished to be paid, 'so that the paintings may pass completely into my rightful possession.'[114]

–3–

The Allies and the Loot

As early as 1940, the Dutch government-in-exile in London broadcast a warning on Radio Oranje against the purchase of goods and securities likely to have been stolen by the Germans from fellow Dutch citizens. The belief that the Nazis would keep to the War on Land Convention was obviously not very great.

In modern wars, economic factors play an increasingly important role beside military considerations. Britain and America even set up ministries of economic warfare and passed appropriate legislation.

The Allies had come to know early on about German looting practices in the occupied territories. As such, these practices were not all that surprising, and in fact they were predictable. The Nazis' behaviour differed in no way from that of all conquerors since time immemorial. They plundered whatever they could lay their hands on, although the efficiency and the spirit with which the Nazis set to work was different, not least in their unremitting efforts to justify their thefts and to lend them a semblance of legality.

The idea of economic warfare had emerged during the First World War, and although that conflict had passed the Netherlands by, its implications and particularly the restitution and reparation clauses embodied in the Treaty of Versailles had not escaped The Hague. The Dutch government had even foreseen the possibility of the country being drawn into some future war and for that reason had drafted a law intended to regulate judicial matters in wartime.

Before the draft could become law, however, the Germans had occupied the Netherlands. Since the definitive text was practically ready, the Besluit Rechtsverkeer in Oorlogstijd (A6) (Decree on Judicial Matters in Wartime) was promulgated in London as early as 7 June 1940.[1] Decree A6 ('containing a provision to prevent judicial damage to the interests of the Kingdom of the Netherlands in time of war') was one of the so-called London emergency decrees (*wetsbesluiten*) aiming to protect the interests of the Kingdom.[2] Among other things it proscribed any agreement with the enemy unless prior consent by the Legal Affairs Committee (Commissie Rechtsverkeer, or Corvo) had been obtained. All agreements entered into without the consent of that committee were declared to be invalid in law.[3]

Decree A1, published on 24 May 1940 ('covering special provisions in respect of demands, claims and possessions of persons resident in the Kingdom [of the

Netherlands] on the European mainland'), was intended to protect the private interests of Dutch citizens. The Dutch state was given the right to act as fiduciary proprietor, the better to protect these claims, demands and possessions. By virtue of A1, the government in London, in fact, assumed the property rights of its citizens for the duration of the war, with the intention of providing protection for citizens in the occupied Netherlands, should the Germans, for instance, put them under pressure to 'sell' their investments in the United States to the German Reich. Such transactions, camouflaged as genuine sales, posed a real threat. Thus, if the Germans used intermediaries in a neutral country such as Switzerland, it would be practically impossible to produce proof of sale under duress – the transaction would look like a normal deal between a Dutch and a Swiss citizen, with Germany remaining completely out of the picture. Under A1, however, not the owner himself but the Dutch government in exile had control of all his possessions out of Hitler's reach. In short, A1 made it difficult, or even impossible, for Germany to confiscate Dutch property (especially securities) in neutral countries.

The Americans, too, took measures to prevent Hitler from laying his hands on assets invested by citizens from the occupied territories in the United States. Duress did not have to be obvious, because it was quite possible that Swiss or Swedish banks had been used as intermediaries in the sales. On the surface, it then looked like a sale to a neutral country, when, in fact, Berlin was behind it all. Immediately after the attack on Norway and Denmark on 10 April 1940, President Roosevelt reacted with his Executive Order 8389 freezing Norwegian and Danish assets in the United States, lest Hitler turn them into cash for his war machine. In the wake of subsequent acts of German aggression, the Order was extended to all countries that had fallen to the Nazis.

The Netherlands, together with the United Kingdom, Switzerland and France was among the biggest foreign investors in the America – in the middle of 1937, Dutch investments in the United States ran to about 970 million dollars. Upon the invasion of the Netherlands, Washington froze more than 1,600 million dollars in Dutch 'long-term investments'. Supervision of the frozen funds was vested in the Foreign Funds Control, which eventually controlled just under 13,000 million dollars invested by non-American citizens in shares, companies, real estate and many other possessions.[4]

In a broadcast on 3 June 1942, over Radio Oranje, the Dutch government-in-exile warned listeners against the purchase of stolen property:

> The occupier is cunning. He has NSB members say, 'Netherlanders, buy Jewish property lest it fall into German hands.' Our answer to them has been, and we repeat it once more: 'Whatever the Germans could and can carry off, they will carry off in any case. But whatever there is in the form of securities, land and other registered property and to

which the legitimate owner, be he Jewish or Gentile, can later prove his rights, that the Germans and other thieves and receivers will not enjoy for long. It will be taken from them just as swiftly as they have acquired it. And this process of remedying abused property relations will be the easier and the quicker the fewer Dutch interests are involved.'[5]

Of course, London could do little in practice beyond cautioning buyers and pointing out the likely post-war consequences. The government-in-exile had no direct means of coercion at that time.

Apart from buyers in the occupied territories, neutral countries were also being warned off. On 5 January 1943 Allied broadcasting stations transmitted the Allied Joint Declaration, also known as the Allied Declaration, the Declaration of St James, the Declaration of London, or the Déclaration Solennelle.

In it, the governments of the United States of America, Australia, Belgium, British India, Canada, the Czechoslovak Republic, the United Kingdom of Great Britain and Northern Ireland, Greece, Luxemburg, the Netherlands, Norway, Poland, the Union of Soviet Socialist Republics, Yugoslavia, the Union of South Africa and the French Comité National issued

> a formal warning to all concerned, especially to persons in neutral countries, that they intend to do their utmost to thwart the methods of dispossession practised by the governments with which they are at war against the countries and people who have been so wantonly assaulted and robbed.
>
> Accordingly, the governments making this declaration and the French National Committee reserve the right to declare invalid any transfers of, or dealings in, property, rights and interests of any description whatsoever found in the territories that have fallen under the occupation or control, direct or indirect, of the governments with which they are at war or that belong or have belonged to persons, including juridical persons, resident in such territories. This warning applies regardless of whether such transfers or dealings have taken the form of open looting or plunder, or of transactions apparently legal in form, even when they purport to be voluntarily effected. The governments making this declaration and the French National Committee solemnly record their solidarity in this matter.[6]

As might have been expected, the Germans were not deterred by this warning, and simply kept on looting. Nor did the neutral countries cease to make profitable purchases of stolen property. And yet the Allied Declaration did have a positive effect, and was decidedly more than an idle warning. It was to exert a marked influence on post-war decisions in restitution matters and also made its influence felt in international law. The fact that restitution nevertheless made little headway in most areas had other causes. What was completely new was that the Allies reserved the right to declare illegal all property transactions by citizens in the occupied territories, even though the WOL convention allowed 'special provisions for the needs of the army of occupation', although these were subject to strict rules. Actions permitted under WOL could be declared illegal on the basis of the Allied Declaration.

The Declaration was aimed against all acts of dispossession, and proposed measures annulling direct as well as indirect thefts. Post-war restitution measures were based directly on the Declaration. Because the signatories to it had declared their common agreement, they were forced to take restitution measures if stolen property turned up on their own territory. That also applied to the parts of Germany occupied by France, Great Britain, the Soviet Union and the United States.

In July 1944, the Allied Declaration was supplemented by Resolution VI of the United Nations Monetary and Financial Conference held in Bretton Woods in the United States. Once more the Allies declared that they would take all necessary steps to undo the German robberies. 'Bretton Woods' was directed chiefly at neutral countries that had unscrupulously bought stolen property or had helped the Germans through puppets to protect their ill-gotten gains after the war, wheresoever

> enemy countries and their nationals have taken the property of occupied countries and their nationals by open looting and plunder, by forcing transfers under duress, as well as by subtle and complex devices, often operated through the agency of their puppet governments, to give the cloak of legality to their robbery and to secure the ownership and control of enterprises in the post-war period . . .[7]

In October 1944, the United States asked neutral countries in Europe to take steps under Bretton Woods Resolution VI. Not much later, London and Moscow followed suit. The response of neutral capitals was far from satisfactory, the neutral countries seeming disinclined to forego their role as receivers.

A very special place in the measures against German plunder is held by the Gold Declaration. For a number of understandable reasons, gold played a special part in the German robberies: it had a high and fixed value, it could easily be exchanged for any foreign currency and, importantly, its origins could rarely be traced, or only with great difficulty.

The looting of gold had assumed such proportions that the US Secretary of the Treasury, Henry Morgenthau, saw fit to issue a special warning on 22 February 1944 to neutral countries, declaring that the United States would not recognize German sales of gold to neutral countries and would declare them null and void after the war. He further declared that Washington would ban the possession of gold originating from countries maintaining relations with Germany and her allies. The most important result of Morgenthau's warning was that buyers as well as sellers of gold – that is, in Allied eyes, the thieves as well as the receivers – went to (even greater) trouble to disguise the real origins of their gold holdings.

The Allies and the Loot

The government of the Netherlands, too, did not idly sit by but continued to prepare for the restoration of legal rights after the war. On 17 September 1944 the Decree for the Restoration of the Rule of Law (Besluit Herstel Rechtsverkeer), generally referred to as E 100, was promulgated in London.[8] Its aim was to restore the rights of the original owners. The actual restoration of these rights was a well-organized operation delegated to the Raad voor het Rechtsherstel (Council for the Restoration of Rights).

That Council was a co-ordinating body, to which a number of departments were assigned in the wake of the Besluit Herstel Rechtsverkeer, among them justice, share registration, administration, provision for absentees, and provision for juridical persons. After the war, a real-estate department was added.[9]

Another important decree to be promulgated in London was E 133 of 20 October 1944 (Enemy Property Decree), which laid down that the property of enemy states and enemy subjects would pass into the hands of the Netherlands state.[10] The Netherlands Beheersinstituut (Netherlands Administrative Institute), as laid down in Article 151 of E 100 and Article 33 of E 133, was to play a leading role in the post-war restoration of rights. As a first step, it was able to place the 'robber bank' Liro and the Vermögensverwaltungs- und Rentenanstalt (Institute of Property Administration and Pensions), together with their German or NSB clients, under administrative control.

A third legal decision with a direct bearing on the post-war restoration of rights was E 93, the Occupation-Measures Decree.[11] It includes a list of 423 German decrees due to be revoked, including all anti-Jewish measures. This decree (and others, some of which were changed several times after the war) provided the Dutch authorities with the legal basis for the post-war restoration of rights.

In other words, the Dutch government-in-exile knew what had to be done after the war, and the receivers of Jewish property were aware of what lay waiting for them.

–4–

The Destination of the Loot

It is impossible to say where the Nazis' enormous loot ended up. By and large, we do know the destination of the looted cultural property, certainly of the most important works of art, but that does not alter the fact that countless items vanished after the war without the slightest trace. Were they stolen, burned, destroyed or hidden away? To this day, 20 per cent of the most valuable paintings have not been recovered, and many works of lesser importance have disappeared. Tracing the masterpieces was relatively easy because they were concentrated in a small number of places (Linz, Karinhall, various German museums, and so on) and because detailed descriptions were available.

However, the loot did not consist of cultural property alone. The Nazis stole an enormous variety of goods and sent them to as many different destinations. Many of these were easy to discover. Machinery was usually taken to locations where it was needed; steel-making equipment turned up in German steel plants; road-building equipment was used to build German roads; clothing went to soldiers or to specific sections of the population, and furniture and household utensils finished up with German families as replacements for the items they had lost to Allied bombs. However, the greatest part of the loot was used in German war industries, which was forced to rely in part on foreign countries for their raw materials and had to pay for them in hard currency, precious metals or the proceeds of sales of the loot. A relatively small proportion is believed to have finished up in the pockets of top Nazis – originally in order to raise their standard of living, but towards the end of the war increasingly as starting capital for a new life.

Various countries in South America, Switzerland, Spain and Portugal came high on the list of new domiciles for the Nazi top brass. Sweden, too, provided political asylum after the war for Germans suspected of war crimes, on condition that they did no harm to Sweden's good name. That generally meant that as a condition for their political asylum they could not play an active part in politics, could not live in the main cities, and could not work in the Swedish state archives.[1]

Switzerland was an extremely popular sanctuary. An American memorandum dated 5 September 1945 contained a detailed report on the large sums in money or securities that were turning up in Davos. In addition, a great many Nazis took refuge in the various German sanatoria opened in Davos during the First World War for the treatment of tubercular German soldiers. On top of that, a great many hotels, apparently Swiss but in fact German property, served as sanctuaries for Nazis on the run; Davos is also said to have been home to a host of German industries, officially registered as Swiss-owned.[2] All in all, every country where Nazis could take refuge with false papers, or if necessary anonymously, served as a possible hiding place.

Allied searches for securities, foreign currency, precious metals or jewels siphoned off into foreign countries by such Nazi leaders as Hitler, Göring, Reichsführer SS Heinrich Himmler, Foreign Minister J. von Ribbentropp and SS-Obergruppenführer und General der Polizei Ernst Kaltenbrunner, produced few spectacular revelations. However, that is no proof that such transfers did not take place. It is not too far-fetched to assume that those Nazis who owned capital or valuable movable property must have tried to take it to safety in Sweden, Switzerland and above all in South America.

Rumours about secret caches of treasure tucked away by Nazi leaders are persistent and crop up with great regularity. This is not surprising because the ingredients of such rumours abound: the theft of unimaginable riches, war criminals, chaos, and a far-flung empire in a state of dissolution. There could hardly be a better basis for the wildest fantasies. So far, however, few treasures have actually turned up, despite extensive searches by special American task forces that set to work immediately after the war.[3]

Number one on the list of sites of hidden treasures is undoubtedly Lake Toplitz near Salzburg, in Austria. In the autumn of 1959, the German magazine *Stern* organized a spectacular expedition 'to the treasure in Lake Toplitz'. Reports of this expedition can be found in a series of major reports under the title of 'Geld wie Heu' ('Money to burn'). The magazine engaged divers to search the bottom of the lake, but the only treasure they came up with were chests of forged British pound notes. The forgeries were so perfect that even the Bank of England found it hard to tell them from legal tender. The forged money with a (pseudo) value of some £5 million was incinerated under the supervision of a handful of employees of the Bank of England.

The forged notes were part of a plan by Himmler and SS-Gruppenführer Reinhard Heydrich, head of the SP and the SD, to damage the British economy. Engravers and printers held in Oranienburg concentration camp, which became the biggest forgery plant in the world for a time, produced the best possible forgeries under the supervision of the SS. Towards the end of the war, the plant was transferred to the Mauthausen 'branch' in Austria. As the Allied armies approached, Bernhard Krüger, the commanding SS officer (the plan of swamping Britain with forged notes owed its code name 'Operation Bernhard' to this man) was given orders to execute the 'forgers'. The plan was to be kept strictly secret but Krüger refused to carry it out. Most of the commandeered forgers were able to escape with a large quantity of forged money, although it is impossible to tell how much of it

The Destination of the Loot

they managed to put into circulation. What is certain is that the SS used it to pay their agents all over the world. Eliezar Bazna, the notorious spy who worked for the British ambassador in Turkey as a valet under the code name of 'Cicero', did not realize until after his escape to South America that the £150,000 he had been paid for his intelligence work had been forged.

Friedrich Schwend, one of the men behind the forgeries, was able to start a new career in Peru. 'Master forger' Schwend was arrested in 1945 in Munich and examined by two agents of the Counter-Intelligence Corps, but released soon afterwards. It emerged later that the intelligence agents examining him had been generously paid, so much so that they were able to open profitable businesses in Paris and Michigan respectively.

By contrast, no gold from Lake Toplitz has been raised to the surface so far. According to unconfirmed rumours, gold and jewellery to the tune of several million guilders were dug up in Linz. The treasure was allegedly buried there by SS-General Karl Wolff, and SS-trooper Sepp Dietrich, with the aim of using it to finance 'Odessa', the secret SS escape organization.[4]

The fact that the various investigations did not produce sensational results does not necessarily mean that top and middle-ranking Nazis did not try to get away with fortunes. There are a number of possible explanations:

- No capital was actually funnelled abroad;
- the capital was never found and no one knows where it is;
- the capital *was* funnelled abroad but deployed so cleverly by front men that it has never been discovered;
- the capital ended up in the hands of third parties who, out of self-interest, shunned any form of publicity.

In ideological respects, the top echelons of the Third Reich may have been united, but when it came to personal possessions there were marked differences between them. Hitler himself does not seem to have bothered to take his capital abroad, although well before the outbreak of the war he had some of the royalties of *Mein Kampf* paid into a Swiss bank account. Psychologically, he was probably quite unprepared for the end of his Reich and continued to believe in a final German victory almost to the bitter end.

Göring was different. According to rumours amongst his closest associates, he dipped deep into funds connected with the Four-Year Plan. Thus Walther Funk, the Minister of Economic Affairs and also president of the Reichsbank, confirmed that Göring had lined his own pockets. According to a different source, Göring's fortune was taken to safety in Spain by Alois Miedl. General Erhard Milch claimed that the Reich Air Marshal had spirited away between thirteen and fourteen million Reichsmarks to Switzerland. The steel magnate Fritz Thyssen, too, had heard about

Göring's financial manipulations; according to Thyssen, one of Göring's confidential agents crossed into Switzerland at regular intervals with large amounts of money. Göring's top courier was apparently Josef Angerer, who is alleged to have visited Switzerland frequently for the express purpose of transferring securities. There is, however, no hard proof for any of these allegations. Another source claims that Göring invested millions in Argentina, where he is said to have sold stolen works of art for that express purpose.

Göring himself always denied siphoning off money for private purposes; his family and confidantes declared that smuggling money out of Germany was not in his character. The Allied investigators treated these claims with some reservation, pointing out that Göring was renowned for his tricks. In principle, he trusted no one; it was certainly not out of character that he should have put everyone on the wrong trail.

Göring did admit, however, that he had hidden away treasure in the Soviet zone (as it was later called). In addition, there are indications that he hid sizeable amounts of money in Southern Germany and Austria, in the expectation of better times. He was never to see these. On the eve of his planned execution, on 16 October 1946, the Reichsmarschall committed suicide in his cell in Nuremberg.

In 1981, a 122-piece service, which was alleged to have been part of Göring's buried treasure, was dug up in the German Democratic Republic. A West German who gave his name as 'Weber' handed over four sketches to the East German authorities on which the hiding place of the treasure was marked. On the basis of one of the drawings, it was indeed possible to locate the porcelain service, but any further spadework was vitiated by the insistence of the East German authorities on paying Weber's 'finder's reward' in practically worthless GDR marks. Because the actions of the East German authorities were disappointing in other respects as well, Weber refused to return to the GDR, and the matter ended there. However, it is not clear if a compromise was reached later; vast sums of money seem to have been involved.[5]

It is impossible to establish whether Himmler smuggled goods or money to foreign countries. From the interrogation of his masseur, Felix Kirsten, among others, we gain the impression that he was a fanatic, with little or no interest in personal wealth; he was certainly not the type to stash money or goods away. This picture is, however, in conflict with the report that American investigators dug up treasure worth one million dollars belonging to Himmler, consisting of various forms of foreign currency, underneath a barn in the vicinity of Berchtesgaden.[6]

Joachim von Ribbentrop – incidentally a great admirer of Himmler – certainly had the intention, the knowledge and, as Minister of Foreign Affairs, the opportunity to take money to safety abroad. According to Walter Schellenberg, head of counter-intelligence of the Reichssicherheitshauptamt (the RSHA), von Ribbentrop

The Destination of the Loot

had secreted assets abroad, through German embassies holding large amounts of foreign currency. The American investigation team concluded that he had hidden five million gold Reichsmarks somewhere in Germany. Schellenberg himself was suspected of having smuggled money across the border. The same is true of Ernst Kaltenbrunner, who is said to have hidden ample funds abroad, while the RSHA also secreted sizeable funds outside Germany.

As far as we know, none of these funds ever reappeared. Like Göring, Himmler committed suicide. Von Ribbentrop and Kaltenbrunner were hanged in Nuremberg on 16 October 1946 and Schellenberg died a few years after the war. For the remainder of his life he did not give the impression of being a man of means.

Part II
The Looting of Jewish Property

–5–

The Looting of Jewish Property

The Prelude

When Adolf Hitler came to power on 30 January 1933, anti-Semitism was given free rein in the young Third Reich. The new ruler had never made a secret of his hatred of the Jews. On the contrary, anti-Semitism played a central role in his political career from the start. As early as 1920, the NSDAP manifesto stated quite clearly that only *Volksgenossen*, ethnic Germans, could be considered citizens of the German Reich. That debarred all Jews from German nationality. 'Non-citizens are guests in Germany and shall be treated as aliens.'[1] In April 1928, the future Führer declared that the article of his party manifesto governing the expropriation of private property was exclusively aimed at Jews.[2] Almost immediately after Hitler's seizure of power in 1933, a stream of anti-Jewish measures was let loose, a process that continued until February 1945, that is, until a few months before the end of the Second World War. Four distinct periods can be distinguished in Hitler's *Judengesetzgebung* (Jewish legislation):

1. From Hitler's seizure of power to the 'Nuremberg Laws' (31 January 1933 to 15 September 1935).
2. From the 'Nuremberg Laws' to the so-called Reichskristallnacht (15 September 1935 to 9 November 1938).
3. From Kristallnacht to the outbreak of the Second World War (10 November 1938 to 1 September 1939).
4. From the outbreak of the Second World War to the destruction of European Jewry (1 September 1939 to 16 February 1945, after which no further anit-Jewish measures were published).

During the first period, 637 laws, bans, decrees, regulations, guidelines and similar measures were passed; during the second period the figure was 582; during the third it was 229, and during the last it was 525.

To implement the NSDAP programme and all the race hatred it enshrined, a gigantic apparatus was created and extended to all parts of the Third Reich immediately upon Hitler's appointment as chancellor. The Nuremberg race law (*Gesetz zum Schutze des deutschen Blutes und der deutschen Ehre* – law for the protection of German blood and honour) gave anti-Semitism an extra impetus; Kristallnacht, which saw the destruction of Jewish shops, businesses and synagogues throughout Germany, raised Jewish misery to a new peak. After December 1941, when the transport of Jews from Berlin to the extermination camps began, the anti-Jewish apparatus was transformed into a murder machine.[3]

The attempt – which was also conspicuous during the occupation of the Netherlands – to justify all crimes against Jews by pseudo-legal measures, was a striking feature of Nazi rule from the outset. As long as the Nazis could shelter behind one law or another, they considered themselves not guilty of murder and other crimes, especially robbery with murder, many of the measures making it clear that the Nazis had designs not only on the lives but also on the possessions of Jews.

On 14 July 1933, the *Gesetz über Widerruf von Einbürgerungen und die Aberkennung der deutschen Staatsangehörigkeit* (Law revoking naturalizations and the abrogation of German citizenship) was passed, involving not only the forfeiture of German nationality but also the confiscation of assets. On 10 November 1938, Reichskristallnacht, scores of synagogues were burned down, Jewish businesses and stores were looted and destroyed, thousands of Jews were arrested and packed off to concentration camps, and thirty-five Jews lost their lives, all by order of the authorities. The occasion was seized upon on 12 November as a pretext for imposing an 'expiation' levy on Jews as punishment 'for their hostile attitude to the German people and the German Reich'. German Jews were collectively made to pay one thousand million Reichsmarks. Senseless acts of destruction such as Kristallnacht were not repeated. Thenceforward everything was done to confiscate as much undamaged Jewish property as possible.

On 3 December 1938, the *Verordnung über den Einsatz des jüdischen Vermögens* (Decree on the use of Jewish assets) called for the 'Aryanization' of Jewish businesses. Jewish-owned land could be sold off without the owners' consent, and Jews were banned from disposing freely of their gold, silver, platinum, jewels and works of art. In addition they were ordered to deposit their securities in a bank.

The measures to rob Jews of their possessions culminated in the *Verordnung zum Reichsbürgergesetz* (Decree on Reich citizenship) passed on 25 November 1941. One month later came the first mass transports of Jews from Germany to the extermination camps in the East. With them the confiscation of Jewish possessions on behalf of the Third Reich reached its logical end phase. This was because the *Verordnung* laid it down that the possessions of all Jews domiciled abroad – voluntarily or otherwise – had become the property of the German Reich. By that time, a great many German Jews had fled their homeland, the first batch as early as the first year of the Hitler regime. Most of those who had not opted for this kind of 'voluntary' exile were destined for death in Poland. In both cases, their property fell into the hands of the German Reich by virtue of the owners' loss of German citizenship, unless they had lost all their belongings earlier, not least thanks to one of the many decrees passed since 1933.[4] All these Nazi measures persuaded Jews to take their money and valuables to safety across the German border, and hence out of the reach of the Nazis.

The Flight of Jewish Capital

The question of precisely how much money and how many shares and valuables were taken to safety in banks abroad by far-sighted Jews after the advent of Hitler seems likely to remain unanswered for all time. All we can do is guess at the figures.

Originally, it would seem, a great many Jews found a safe haven for their possessions in Switzerland, not least because of the special protection afforded them by the Swiss secrecy laws. After the war, paradoxically, that secrecy turned against Jewish bank-account holders: many had lost their papers during the war and their heirs were often quite unable to produce legal proof of ownership.

From American sources it appears that the German surprise attack on Norway and Denmark on 9 April 1940 caused another flight of capital, this time not *to* but *from* Switzerland to the United States and Great Britain.[5] People had come to believe that because such traditionally neutral countries had been overrun there was good reason to fear that Switzerland was likely to suffer the same fate. In any case, a growing stream of capital from Europe had started to flow to America. That tendency had begun as early as 1933, the year Hitler came to power. The flow of capital from Europe ran first of all from Germany to the United States, but with the increase in political tensions and the threat of war it increasingly spread to neighbouring countries.

Ironically, the notorious anonymous numbered accounts owe their existence to the Nazi regime in Germany, which introduced severe penalties in 1934 to stem the flight of capital and took punitive measures against all who failed to observe the strict foreign-currency regulations. By allowing the flow of capital into anonymous accounts, the Swiss were hoping to circumvent the draconian Nazi measures. That was, of course, a godsend for those who wanted to take their fortunes to safety, and coincidentally for the Swiss banks.

Under normal circumstances, the anonymity of Swiss bank accounts was totally reliable and indeed part of the Swiss image, but Hitler's intelligence services had penetrated the banks, with the result that opening an account in one's own name could be perilous. By introducing numbered and other forms of anonymous accounts, the Swiss banks hoped not only to regain the confidence of their clients, but also to strengthen their reputation.

And indeed, many of these clients, and we may take it tens of thousands of Jews were amongst them, made ready use of these covert measures to transfer their money and valuables to safety in Switzerland (often with the help of intermediaries). Frequently the owners would not even tell their nearest relatives about these transactions; it was a time in which the head of the family was virtually the only person to deal with the family's finances. The obvious disadvantages of this situation only came to light after the war: with no more than the vaguest suspicions about this form of capital tourism, the heirs knocked vainly at the doors of Swiss banks, with no legal backing for their claims.

More than fifty years after the end of the Second World War, on 23 July and 29 October 1997, the Swiss Bankers' Union published a list of 'dormant accounts'. 'Dormant' in this connection referred to accounts in existence since 10 May 1945, but not used during the past ten years for deposits or withdrawals. In practice this was tantamount to assuming that the owner had been, or could be presumed to have been, dead for at least ten years.

The list published in July comprised more than 2,250 account holders; the second list comprised about 14,000, with credit balances of approximately 12.4 million dollars. The total amount discovered by searches of more than 120 Swiss banks and financial institutions came to 54 million dollars. On the basis of the information obtained, it seemed practically impossible to determine whether or not the account holders were Jewish. In short, the lists comprised the names of *all* depositors, not just of Jews, and even the names of notorious Nazis were apparently included.

The first list included nine private individuals and two businesses from the Netherlands. The total value of these eleven Dutch accounts has never been made public. Moreover, the October list gives absolutely no reason for supposing that many Netherlanders had taken their capital to safety in Switzerland before the war. The amounts on the October list were all relatively modest, what with the large number of names on the list and total deposits of no more than 12.4 million dollars. The average amount was about 1,800 guilders, at the 1998 value.

The search went a long way back in time, as we can tell, for example, from the inclusion of the name of Vladimir Ulyanov, an account holder in Zurich. Ulyanov was the real name of V. I. Lenin, the founder of the Soviet Union, the man who travelled back to his homeland from Switzerland in 1917 to launch the revolution. Incidentally, the father of the Russian Revolution had less than seventy dollars in his account.

In fact, the total of the accounts rescued from oblivion came to far less than the many hundreds of million dollars the World Jewish Congress claimed from Swiss banks. The attempt in 1962 to trace dormant accounts also produced scant results. As far as the Netherlands was concerned, the investigation yielded no more than nine names, four with credit balances of no more than a thousand Swiss francs each.

The Looting of Jewish Property

There is no doubt that many Jews, Dutch citizens included, took their fortunes abroad for safety, but the question of where and how much they removed is very difficult to determine. Many Jews, often entire families, lost their lives in Hitler's horror camps, and with their deaths, hard information about their bank accounts was, in most cases, lost as well. As a result many claims now presented necessarily rest on vague hints, feelings or suspicions that can rarely serve as hard evidence.

There are countless indications that money and valuables were not entrusted directly to a bank, but went first to intermediaries, agents, confidantes and the like. Because accounts could be opened in Switzerland under a pseudonym, it is extremely hard to determine under which particular name assets were lodged with banks.

If money or valuables were entrusted to a bank in the name of a front man or confidante, no trace of the transaction can generally be found. There may have been some verbal or written agreement, but if the real owner was murdered in a concentration camp, knowledge of the verbal agreement disappeared with him. Written evidence, too, vanished in most cases, because Jews were systematically stripped of all their possessions, papers included. In such cases, the intermediary acting as 'owner' had presumably asserted his illegitimate rights to the possessions long ago, without anyone being the wiser.

Quite often money and valuables were left with, invested with, or entrusted to lawyers, investment funds or other financial institutions. And whether or not that was done under a fictitious name, it is quite certain that in these cases, too, the person to whom the assets were entrusted, is (or was) the only one to know what really happened. Here, too, the chance of restitution is next to nothing. Most of the people concerned – we are talking, after all, about transactions of which most took place before the summer 1940 – have meanwhile died.

Other countries serving as hosts to fugitive capital were the United States, Great Britain and Cuba, a country in which many American banks had subsidiaries.

The Swiss 'Independent Committee of Eminent Persons', led by Paul Volcker, a prominent US banker, looked among other things into the pre-war possessions of Jews in European countries occupied by Hitler. The creation of this so-called Volcker Committee was a joint initiative of the Swiss Bankers' Association and the World Jewish Congress.

One of its tasks was to produce an estimate of the overall Jewish wealth in the Netherlands on the eve of the Second World War. With the help of that estimate, the committee hoped to gain some idea of how much Dutch fugitive capital might have been channelled to Switzerland. In the Netherlands, the investigation was led by the economist Helen B. Junz, who, with the help of data from the Netherlands tax authorities and of other archive material, put the overall assets of Dutch Jews at approximately two billion guilders. According to my own calculations, Dutch Jews were robbed of at least one billion guilders during the war.[6]

The difference of one billion guilders between what the Nazis looted (one billion) and the size of the estimated total Jewish wealth in about 1939 (two billion) is not easily explained. If we may take it that both sets of figures are more or less correct (the figure of at least one billion stolen possessions was confirmed by the Junz report, which came up with 1 to 1.2 billion guilders), then the explanation must be sought, among other things, in untraced dormant accounts, the activities of those whom the Jews had entrusted with their money and posessions, black assets, and assets of unknown value lost due to the war, or capital invested abroad without the knowledge of the Dutch authorities.[7]

The latter did not, in fact, have the slightest idea of the size of the flight of capital, which emerged when the subject was brought up after the war as part of the measures to trace wartime black-market profiteers and to deal with them:

> It would seem that large Dutch fortunes were taken to safety abroad before the war, especially to Britain and the United States of America. These still have to be reported, if they have not yet been registered by virtue of the instructions issued by the Dutch government in London. Without international co-operation it will not be easy to check the information and to call for appropriate sanctions in cases of failure to report.[8]

On the basis of the archives of, for instance, the US Treasury, the Economic Warfare Department, the Alien Property Custodian and especially the Foreign Funds Control, it is, to be sure, possible to gain an idea of the scale of Dutch assets invested in the United States shortly before and during the war, and also of the manner in which this was done; however, it is practically impossible to distinguish assets of Jewish origin from the rest. According to the United States Trading with the Enemy Act, heirless Jewish property of Dutch origin in the United States had to be transferred to the Jewish Restitution Successor Organization. For poor Netherlanders the flight of capital to foreign havens was, of course, not a subject that weighed heavily on their minds. More prosperous Jews, who had failed to take their capital abroad before 10 May 1940, quickly finished up in a situation that differed little from that of their less affluent companions in misfortune. All of them, rich and poor alike, faced the total loss of their possessions

Preparations for the Total Seizure of Jewish Possessions in the Netherlands

Like their brethren in Germany, Dutch Jews were faced with a series of regulations issued by the invaders, all aimed at robbing them of their possessions. The looting was a phase of the *Endlösung*, the Final Solution, a phase implemented as conscientiously, as thoroughly and as deliberately as the genocide itself. The occupying forces invented various euphemisms for the looting: they 'transferred', 'remitted', 'managed', 'controlled', and 'administered', but at all times they took good care not be demonstrably guilty of stealing from their victims. Words such as loot, plunder or booty were never used, and were, in fact, taboo. At most, assets were seized or confiscated, but only if there were good reasons for doing so. This form of camouflage, the concealment of the real motives – the plundering and mass murder of the Jewish people – was honed to perfection during the invasion.

The looting of Dutch Jewry was carried out systematically, mostly on the basis of some *Verordnung*, a decree treated as law. Apart from *Verordnungen*, the Germans also used 'measures', 'instructions' and 'orders' by the Security Police. In the last case, the measures largely covered the compulsory surrender of bicycles, radios or household utensils. In other cases, the Devisenschutzkommando played a leading role. The *Verordnungen* were published simultaneously in German and Dutch in the *Verordeningenblad voor het Bezette Nederlandsche Gebied*, which appeared from 1940 to 1945.

The highest authority in the Netherlands was vested in Dr Seyss-Inquart, who also had the final say about the looting campaign. This Austrian governor derived his authority from the *Führererlass* (Führer decree) of 18 May 1940, which covered the exercise of government power in the Netherlands. The first section of the *Führererlass* laid down that

> the occupied Netherlands falls under the jurisdiction of the 'Reichskommissar for the Occupied Netherlands Territories'. His seat is in The Hague. The Reichskommissar is the protector of the interests of the Reich and holds ultimate government power in the civil sector. He is directly responsible to me and takes his directives and instructions from me.[9]

Hitler further decreed that Dutch law would remain in force 'inasmuch as it can be reconciled with the occupation' and that the Reichskommissar (Seyss-Inquart's appointment was announced in Section 6) was authorized to pass *Verordnungen* having the force of law.

Once Seyss-Inquart, or in some cases Hans Fischböck, General-Kommissar für Finanz und Wirtschaft, had taken a decision about Jewish property, the relevant instructions were drafted by the Generalreferat (general desk) of the General-Kommissariat für Finanz und Wirtschaft. Seyss-Inquart's *Verordnungen* were translated by the 'general desk' into workable instructions that were passed on by internal circulars to the staff of the robber bank of Lippmann, Rosenthal & Co (Liro). The most important instructions, however, were personally approved and signed by the Reichskommissar or by Fischböck. The influence of the robber bank on the instructions it had to carry out was slight, even though some form of consultation was common practice. In effect, Liro was little more than a rubber stamp.

The number of instructions was enormous, largely because of the distinction the Germans made between various types of property. Securities, jewellery, money, bank accounts, post-office deposits, mortgages, bills of exchange and many more, all posed special problems and had to be covered by separate instructions. Matters were complicated further by the intricate rules for the release of funds for living expenses (a task that was later taken over by the Jewish Council) and the return of property or parts thereof to half-Jewish or non-Jewish heirs, while yet other rules applied to 'de-starred' persons (persons exempted from wearing the yellow star) and to the so-called 'Calmeyer cases'. 'Destarred' persons, although still Jewish under the prevailing rules, were spared because they were still important to the Germans; 'Calmeyer cases' were officially declared to be non-Jewish.

But things could be more complicated still; it often happened that certain exceptions and regulations applied in practice to one and the same case. Week after week, cases had to be examined in the Reichskommissariat involving issues that had been overlooked during the preparatory work, or that could not possibly have been foreseen.[10] These complications slowed down the administrative work of Liro, and inevitably led to chaos.

To implement his *Verordnungen,* Seyss-Inquart was able to call on the help of the German police. Quite clearly, the *Führererlass* was issued with the WOL convention in mind. If, however, we place Hitler's limiting clause ('inasmuch as it can be reconciled with the occupation') side by side with Article 43 ('unless absolutely prevented') of the WOL convention, we are bound to conclude that the Führer left himself considerable elbow room.[11]

The *Verordnungen* never failed to make reference to the basis of Seyss-Inquart's power, namely, Article 5 of the Führer decree of 18 May 1940 concerning the exercise of government authority in the Netherlands. The *Verordnungsblatt* (*Verordnung* Gazette) also served to publish changes in and revocations of existing laws, thus effectively replacing the Dutch *Staatsblad* (Government Gazette).

The first pseudo-legal step in the looting campaign was thus taken: the Reichskommissar could, in the Führer's name, pass whatever *Verordnungen* he saw fit to introduce, including those covering the confiscation of property.

The second essential step towards the complete expropriation of Jewish property was the definition of 'Jew'. That definition was needed to enable the Germans to set to work adequately and 'legally'. On 22 October 1940 there appeared, as part of *Verordnung* 189/1940 'concerning the registration of enterprises', a detailed definition of a Jew. Article 4 laid down that:

1. A Jew is a person with at least three grandparents who are full-blooded Jews by race.
2. A Jew is also a person with at least two grandparents who are full-blooded Jews and who (1) was either a member of the Jewish religious community on 9 May 1940 or who subsequently became a member, or (2) was married to a Jew on 9 May 1940 or subsequently married a Jew.

3. A grandparent shall be a full-blooded Jew if he or she was a member of the Jewish religious community.

However clear this set of definitions may seem to be, in practice Article 4 of VO 189/1940 did not cover all cases. Mixed marriages, in particular, caused the Germans considerable administrative problems and necessitated a flood of regulations, exemptions, and special measures.[12]

The complications caused by the definitions may have impeded the looting process, but they certainly did not stop it. *Verordnungen* were the chosen tool by which the Nazis legitimized their programme of plunder; the dagger had, so to speak, been replaced with the bureaucrat's pen, but that worked, if anything, even more efficiently, certainly during the initial phase, when it helped to conceal the Germans' true objectives. The great advantage was that it caused neither agitation nor panic. The expropriation of Jewish citizens by means of *Verdordnungen* was comprehensive and covered everything that is normally understood as 'property': from post office (giro) accounts to art collections and businesses.

While the German definition of who was a Jew was fairly clear, in practice it did not cover all Jewish citizens. But that, too, was taken care of. On 1 July 1942, the Netherlands Census Office published a 'List of Surnames of Persons of Jewish Blood.' On the cover it stated that all names followed by a G (for *gemengdbloedigen*) belonged exclusively to people of mixed blood. All other names were those of full Jews.

Once the definition of who was a Jew and a list of all Jewish names had been made known, the third logical phase could follow, namely the obligatory registration of all Jewish citizens. Registration was governed by VO 6/1941 'concerning the registration of persons fully or partly of Jewish blood'. According to Article 7, registration had to be in writing. A distinction was made between Dutch Jews and immigrants, but both groups had to submit their names, forenames, place of birth, date of birth, address, religious congregation, occupation, civil status and number of Jewish grandparents.[13]

> For persons who immigrated to the European part of the Netherlands after 30 January 1933, the last place of residence in the present territory of the Greater German Reich (including the protectorate of Bohemia and Moravia) or in the occupied Polish territory has also to be declared.

The registration duty was observed on a massive scale. By 22 August 1941, when 160,820 registration cards had been received, 140,522 Jews were recorded as full Jews on receipt of their cards, 68,388 full Jewish men and 72,164 full Jewish women. Of these, 22,252 (including 14,652 Germans) were not Dutch. Amsterdam had the largest number of Jews living within its boundaries, namely 79,410.[14]

Because such large numbers of Jewish citizens registered their names, Seyss-Inquart gained a thorough overview of the composition of Dutch Jewry. However, the stream of data, designed to ensure that the planned looting campaign was unlikely to misfire, had not yet come to an end. In 1942 the *Statistiek der Bevolking van joodschen bloede in Nederland* (Statistics of the Population of Jewish Blood in the Netherlands) was published – once again by the Dutch Government Census Office.

That same year, finally, there also appeared the *Statistische gegevens van de joden in Nederland* (Statistical Data on the Jews of the Netherlands). This publication was mainly concerned with Amsterdam and contained a detailed plan of the distribution of Jews in that city. In addition, it gave the distribution of Amsterdam Jewry by sex, age, nationality, denomination and occupation. The number of Jews in the Netherlands at large was also recorded.

In Chapter 1 of this book it was pointed out that the number of Jews who failed to register is not known, although it may be taken that, in the case of full Jews, it was very small: 'Their absence, accordingly, does not detract from the statistical value of our data.' The relevant figures were taken, among other places, from the population registers, from files of the Central Office for Jewish Emigration and from Section IV B 4 of the Befehlshaber der Sicherheitspolizei und des SD.

Directly after Seyss-Inquart took office, on 25 May 1940, a flood of anti-Jewish measures and *Verordnungen* began, all of them designed to render the life of Jewish citizens harder and to exclude them from public life. The first *Verordnung* specifically directed at Jews was VO 80/1940 of 31 July 1940, banning ritual slaughter. It was still a far cry from expropriation, though its anti-Semitic tenor was unmistakable: it made it impossible for orthodox Jews to eat meat.

VO 108/1940 arrived on 20 August 1940, empowering the Reichskommissar to dismiss certain groups of public officials; it was followed on 13 September 1940 by VO 137/1940 concerning the appointment or dismissal of civil servants (no special mention was made of Jews), regardless of the prevailing laws. The result of these two VOs was that all Jewish civil servants were dismissed on 4 November.

At the time, the Dutch authorities did not know which of their officials were Jewish and which were 'Aryan'. The civil servants had to provide that information themselves. The Ministry of Internal Affairs accordingly sent out a circular that was to enter history as the 'Aryan attestation'.

In addition to the Jews' racial origins, the Germans were very interested in their earnings and assets. In 1941, various measures were announced, once again making the life of Jews more difficult. Thus German domestic servants were no longer allowed to work in Jewish households (VO 200/1941), while a growing number of regulations stipulated that Jews could only work or provide services for Jewish clients. On 15 April 1941, Hanns Rauter, the Höhere SS- und Polizeiführer

(Senior SS and Police Commander), published a proclamation in the daily press to the effect that all Jews were to hand in their wireless sets within two weeks. That proclamation was based on Article 1 of VO 26/1941 (11 February 1941), which laid down that wireless sets could be confiscated whenever there was a suspicion that they might be 'misused' for listening to banned transmitters. The Security Police acted on the assumption that Jews as a whole were guilty of illegal listening.

Jews were deprived of their bicycles in two stages. On 22 June 1942, those of them living outside Amsterdam were ordered to hand in their bicycles to the police under VO 138/1941; less than a month later, on 20 July, the measure was extended to Amsterdam Jews. Radios and bicycles admittedly did not amount to vast fortunes, but as part of the body of intimidating decrees, these measures made a considerable impact.

In order to take administrative control of the loot, Seyss-Inquart set up a central loot pool: the Vermögensverwaltungs und Rentenanstalt (the Institute for the Administration of Property and Pensions, or VVRA).

Specialized looting agencies set up by the Germans, such as the Niederländische Grundstücksverwaltung (Netherlands Real Estate Administration), the Wirtschaftsprüfstelle (Economic Inspection Bureau), and the Devisenschutzkommando (Foreign Exchange Protection Commando), together with the Befehlshaber der Sicherheitspolizei und SD (Commander of the Security Police and of the Security Service), who was in charge of confiscated goods, and last but not least the robber bank, Lippmann, Rosenthal & Co., jointly transferred many hundreds of millions of guilders, stolen from Jewish Netherlanders, to the VVRA. The Reichskommissar could make free use of all VVRA funds, inter alia handing some twenty million guilders to the SS for use in Westerbork and Vught camps.

At first, Lippmann, Rosenthal & Co. was completely independent of the VVRA; it was only in the course of 1943 that the robber bank made its first payments to the VVRA, where they were they were credited to the *Sammelkonto* (joint account) of Lippmann, Rosenthal & Co.

The proceeds of the liquidation of the Masonic lodges (approximately one million guilders) also finished up in the coffers of the VVRA, which made further gains by investing the money in equities, consisting of German and Dutch treasury bills and of Dutch government bonds.[15]

Enemy Property

The Deutsche Revisions- und Treuhand AG (German Audit and Trustee Company, the DRT) was set up to administer enemy property. It processed registration forms and advised on the running of enterprises and the appointment of *Verwalter* (administrators), over whom the DRT exercised a supervisory function.

VO 26/1940 of 27 July 1940 laid down that all enemy property had to be registered with the DRT at 22 Alexanderstraat, The Hague, within one week, thereafter to be run by an administrator appointed by Dr Hans Fischböck, the General-Kommissar für Finanz und Wirtschaft.

The DRT was a large accounts office run as a limited company (Aktiengesellschaft, AG) and registered in Germany. The establishment in The Hague was a branch (Zweigniederlassung). It was probably opened in close consultation with the Reichskommissariat. In any case, the DRT was charged with such semi-official tasks as the administration of enemy (and Jewish) property.

The *Verordnung* concerning enemy assets covered all forms of property, that is, movable and immovable goods, pay, shares, rights, claims, and so on, belonging to enemy subjects and to Netherlanders who on 10 May 1940, the day of the German invasion, were to be found in enemy territory, even though they had not given up their Dutch residence.[16]

The names of citizens who had stored furniture and household goods with removal firms or in warehouses had to be reported to the DRT, which then passed the information on to the Sammelverwaltung feindlicher Hausgeräte (Joint Administration of Enemy Household Goods). All in all, 3,000 cases were dealt with. Part of the furniture was rented out by the Heim in Holland (Home in Holland) organization to German officials in the Netherlands. Most of the goods, however, were sold by Dutch auction houses, chiefly by Van Marle & Bignell in The Hague. The proceeds were transferred to the DRT, which then 'credited' the appropriate sums to the original owners. About one-third finished up with the Oberfinanzpräsident (Chief President of Finances) in Mannheim, Germany.[17]

From a report dated 30 May 1944, at a time when the Germans may be supposed to have had a detailed idea of the extent of enemy property in the Netherlands, it appears that *Verwalter* had been appointed by virtue of VO 26/1940 for

- 411 industrial and commercial companies;
- 158 banking and credit institutes;
- sixty-nine insurance companies;
- twenty-seven minority holdings;
- eighty-eight properties of various types.

In August 1941, that is, before the United States entered the war, enterprises with a combined capital of 947,730,000 guilders were registered. The share of enemy property came to a nominal 260,791,000 guilders. The real value was, however, much higher and is put at 400 million guilders. In December 1941, when the United States entered the war, a further 62 million guiders was added, so that the nominal enemy share in Netherlands enterprises came to more than 330 million guilders, while the actual value was put at more than 500 million guilders.

These figures do not include the proportion of enemy property in a number of large concerns such as the N. V. Koninklijke Maatschappij tot Exploitatie van Petroleumbronnen in Nederlandsch-Indië (Shell), the N. V. Philips Gloeilampenfabriek, the Oranje-Nassau Mijnen, the N. V. Nederlandsche Steenkolen Mijnen 'Willem Sophia', and the Maatschappij tot Exploitatie der Steenkolen Mijnen. All these concerns had been placed under administrators for economic reasons and not because of the enemy property decree.

Apart from companies, all types of property, such as real estate, patents and other rights, legacies, works of art, claims on third parties, and the contents of safe deposits could be treated as enemy property. The Abteilung Feindvermögen (Enemy Property Section) of the DRT controlled property to the tune of approximately 1.2 billion guilders.[18]

Real estate belonging to Netherlanders who had fled abroad in May 1940 was also treated as enemy property. However, the Germans sold such property no more than sporadically, probably because they were afraid of similar measures against their own assets in enemy territory. German property on United States and British soil, including the British Commonwealth, was administered by the Enemy Property Custodian.

Jewish property was treated differently from the property of non-Jews: all of it was sold in 1942–3. The proceeds were paid into the DRT account with Liro.[19]

Non-profit-making Societies and Foundations

As we have seen, the liquidation of both Jewish and non-Jewish non-profit-making societies and foundations occurred in two phases under VO 145/1940 and VO 41/1941. The first phase involved registration, the second the actual liquidation. Though both *Verordnungen* were of a general character, inasmuch as they were not specifically anti-Jewish in form, they had a particularly drastic effect on the communal life of Jewish citizens.[20] The closure of synagogues and Jewish cemeteries was plainly a more far-reaching measure than, say, the liquidation of the Apeldoorn Rabbit and Guinea Pig Society or the Rossum Goat Breeders' Association.[21]

On 18 March 1941, H. Böhmcker, the Reichskommissar's Beauftragte for the city of Amsterdam, addressed a letter to the Jewish Council in the capital. That month as many as 120,000 Jewish and non-Jewish organizations had already been placed under administrative control, at least 4,000 of which were eventually dissolved.[22]

Böhmcker thought it desirable that all Jewish organizations (other than religious societies) came under the control of the Jewish Council. Coincidentally, he also asked the Jewish Council for a list of Jewish societies and foundations.

To show that he was in earnest, he dissolved a number of organizations – not all of them Jewish – as early as 20 March. On the evening of that day, Böhmcker told the Jewish Council that though a number of societies had been dissolved, he realized that certain activities had to be continued, for instance aid to needy Jews. If necessary the frozen funds would be released again. The reason why the Jewish Council was being handed responsibility for Jewish organizations was, according to the Beauftragte for the city of Amsterdam, purely practical: it made it easier for him to do his work. That was why he also needed a list of Jewish societies and foundations.

In this way, the Jewish Council was made an accomplice in the German liquidation plans. Had it refused to cooperate, the Jewish organizations would have run the risk of the immediate liquidation and confiscation of their assets. On the other hand, if it did cooperate, then it faced the very real danger of being accused of complicity in the German crimes.

The German aim was to dissolve small and relatively unknown institutions while amalgamating the more prominent ones. In that way, the supervisory work of the German authorities would be rendered considerably easier during the short interval during which it was still needed. Once the time for definite liquidation had come, the yield could be gathered in smoothly and without too many diversions.

The Jewish Council faced a terrible dilemma, and in the circumstances could do very little more than try to delay the inevitable liquidations and the associated confiscation of property for as long as possible. In November 1941, the responsibility of the Jewish Council for non-profit-making foundations and societies was extended from Amsterdam to the Netherlands as a whole.[23]

Seyss-Inquart made optimum use of the Amsterdam Jewish Council, which, as he put it in a confidential letter (*'Vertraulich! Nur zu eigenen Händen'* – 'Confidential! For your attention only') to a number of high German officials:

> [will be] turned into an agency for the transmission of orders by the relevant German bodies in such manner as to make it clear to the Jews that all orders issued by German administrative offices covering Jews in general will be issued through the Jewish Council in Amsterdam, and that any failure to comply will be punished appropriately, as a breach of orders, by the German administration.[24]

All Jewish organizations and institutions would ultimately be liquidated or virtually ransacked. Thus the synagogue in J. D. Meijerplein, Amsterdam, was 'emptied by the truckload by the Einsatzstab Rosenberg'.[25] Only a small number of unsaleable items, including some buildings in the Amsterdam Jewish Quarter, were left undisturbed.[26]

A report by Max Bolle, a senior official of the Jewish Council, listed 981 Jewish societies on 13 May 1941. On 8 May, the Jewish Council had been given orders by

The Looting of Jewish Property

the General-Kommissar zur besonderen Verwendung, Abteilung Vereinswesen (General Commissioner for Special Duties, Societies Section) to examine which societies could be considered for dissolution. Bolle did what he could, but complained that it was impossible to do 'really serious work' because the reply had to be sent by return. In his view, at least two months was needed to do the job properly.

According to Bolle, the list of 981 names submitted to the General-Kommissar was unreliable. For instance, 'the classification of societies . . . was well intentioned but of little use'. In some particulars the compilation was completely wrong. It involved the following categories:

1. Foundations and funds (subdivided inter alia into burial societies, family and pension funds);
2. Youth associations;
3. Palestine support associations and the Zionist Union;
4. Societies for the practice and advancement of Judaism;
5. Welfare societies;
6. Women's societies;
7. Jewish professional associations;
8. Sports associations and
9. Various.

Bolle argued that 'the most glaring mistakes in spelling and classification of names had to be corrected'. In the end, thirty-four names were added, bringing the total to 1,015.[27]

There is no absolute certainty about the total value of the assets stolen from these funds, associations and foundations. The accounts of Müller-Lehning, the Commissioner for Non-Profit-Making Associations and Foundations, were found to be incomplete; he himself committed suicide in May 1945, after the end of the war.

In a post-war attempt to reconstruct the course of events, some 700,000 guilders in cash and about 1.1 million guilders in securities could be retraced through banks. In addition, a large quantity of practically worthless securities was unearthed, including many old Russian and Austrian shares.

At the end of 1945, the looted societies put in claims for stolen cash to the tune of 2.6 million guilders, a sum considerably greater than the 700,000 guilders registered by the banks. In addition, the societies called for the return of a large number of securities and demanded damages for stolen furniture and fittings.

Part of the confiscated fortunes seems to have gone to Liro (237,500 guilders), to Winterhulp (112,000 guilders) and to the Nederlandsche Volksdienst (Dutch People's Service) (1,525,000 guilders). It seems quite clear that the amounts transferred to Liro came from liquidated Jewish societies and foundations. Winterhulp and the Nederlandsche Volksdienst probably drew on the funds of Jewish charitable organizations. By contrast, it is unclear where the funds that the commissariat did not make over to Liro, Winterhulp and Volksdienst eventually ended up.[28] The liquidation of Jewish organizations was ultimately calculated to have yielded more than 10 million guilders.[29]

Aryanization

One of the first *Verordnungen* proving that the Germans were specifically after Jewish property[30] was VO 189/1940 of 22 October 1940, 'concerning the registration of businesses'. All Jewish concerns were instructed to register with the Bureau for Economic Investigation in The Hague before 30 November of that year.

The bureau, which was to become better known as the Wirtschaftsprüfstelle (WPS), was directed by Dr Hans Fischböck. It worked in close collaboration with the Deutsche Revisions- und Treuhand AG (German Audit and Trustee Company) (see above), which had sprung up from the economic division of the pre-war German consulate-general in Amsterdam. Fischböck probably wished to avail himself of the knowledge and expertise the Generalkonsulat had accumulated before the war. For the implementation of the Aryanization measures, four new subsections (Referate) were opened, namely the Planungsreferat (Planning Section), the Treuhandsreferat (Trustee Section), Rechtsreferat (Legal Section, called the Arisierungsreferat, or Aryanization Section, after the summer of 1942), and the Liquidationsreferat (Liquidation Section).

The Planungsreferat took the administrative measures, while the Arisierungs-, Rechts- and Treuhandsreferate ensured that these measures were implemented. The Treuhandsreferat appointed *Treuhänder* (trustees), issued guidelines for them and supervised their activities.

The *Verordnung* of 22 October 1940 was a warning; it heralded the total control of Jewish businesses. The definition of 'business' was an extremely wide one, and everything linked directly or indirectly to it had to be registered. Real estate was not specifically mentioned, but was certainly considered to be due for registration. The assets and liabilities of a business, at home and abroad, had to be entered on special forms issued by the Chamber of Industry and Trade. VO 154/1941 retrospectively covered any real estate that did not fit into any of the listed categories. VO 189/1940, incidentally, also applied to businesses and industries whose board contained Jews on 9 May 1940, that is, before the outbreak of war.

Once the businesses had been registered, the 'legal' basis of their expropriation was specified on 12 May 1941. VO 48/1941 relied on the data obtained thanks to the compulsory registration.

For every change in a company covered by the VO, however trivial, Fischböck's approval had first to be obtained – the so-called 'First Section' of this 'Aryanization order'. The 'Second Section' stated that the Wirtschaftsprüfstelle was entitled to appoint administrators exercising all the rights of the proprietors, and that the business itself had to pay for the costs.

Anyone still in doubt about German intentions was brought down to earth by Article 20, for it could not have been put more plainly: VO 48/1941 would henceforth be referred to as the '*Verordnung* for the removal of Jews from economic life' – the process that would enter history as the *Entjudung* (de-Jewing) or 'Aryanization' of the Dutch economy. Jewish concerns could henceforth be placed under an administrator and then be Aryanized or liquidated by him.

In practice there were two types of administrators, namely *Liquidations-Treuhänder* (liquidation trustees) and *Verwaltungs-Treuhänder* (administrative trustees), who took charge of a business during their term in office. The first were generally referred to as *Treuhänder* for short, the second as *Verwalter* (administrators). The Wirtschaftsprüfstelle appointed a *Treuhänder* if the business – usually a small or medium concern – was due for liquidation, or a *Verwalter* if the business was to be sold or placed under administration. The *Verwalter* was responsible to the WPS, and *not* to the owner.

Treuhänder were generally appointed by Omnia Treuhandgesellschaft G.m.b.H., a firm of German accountants. The main office, usually referred to as Omnia, was located in Prague, where it had been able to gather ample experience in the liquidation of Jewish businesses. The Protectorate of Bohemia and Moravia, occupied by Hitler since 1939, served Omnia well as a laboratory.

In the autumn of 1941, a branch of Omnia was opened in The Hague. That office, responsible for most of the liquidations in the Netherlands, since there were many more small than large businesses, employed a staff of about fifty, of whom two-thirds came from the Netherlands and the rest from Germany. They supervised the liquidations from about ten Sachbearbeiterbüros (offices responsible for special subjects) set up in various Dutch towns.

Prosperous concerns were not liquidated as a rule but handed over to non-Jews. These might be a *Verwalter* or a German or Dutch purchaser, and were frequently NSB members or other pro-German Netherlanders. It often happened that a *Verwalter* bought the business he administered at a price he could only have dreamed of in peacetime. The valuation and the subsequent sale were effected through the Niederländische Aktiengesellschaft für die Abwicklung von Unternehmungen (Netherlands Joint-Stock Company for the Liquidation of Businesses, or NAGU). The price generally bore no relation to the real value. Within the looting structure, quite a few *Verwalter* behaved like robbers on their own account.

The main complaint of the stripped owners was that it was the purchase price, which thus bore no relation to the real value, which was recorded in the account books. After the war they could only claim the recorded and hence verifiable price, and not the real value, which could easily be three times the sum for which the business had been sold and that had been paid into the former owner's bank account, a sum over which, moreover, he had had no control. It was chiefly in this area that the greatest financial blows were struck at Dutch Jewry.

When it came to the larger businesses, by contrast, it proved fairly difficult to find buyers. Slightly smaller concerns were often left under German administrators driven by opportunistic self-interest. There were some administrators who controlled thirty or forty concerns and some who even ran more than a hundred concerns or small companies.

The reason why large businesses were difficult to sell was probably that the sales were easy to trace. This meant running an extra risk: should Hitler lose the war, the businesses would certainly be recovered from the new owners, a fact that was regularly reiterated by the Dutch government-in-exile from London.

There were only a few cases of the Aryanization of large or medium-large concerns. The best known were the department store De Bijenkorf in Amsterdam, and the outfitters Gebroeders Gerzon, N. V. Hirsch & Co, and Maison de Bonneterie. If businesses seemed worth the trouble of being kept in existence, they were sold or placed under an administrator, but they were, in any case, kept going.

The Netherlands Joint-Stock Company for the Liquidation of Businesses in The Hague, specially entrusted with the valuation of confiscated businesses or with finding suitable buyers or administrators, was mainly interested in large concerns. NAGU was a kind of accountants' office, composed of four separate audit bureaus. It also set the selling prices and negotiated with prospective buyers.

Omnia was mainly involved in the liquidation of small, generally not very profitable one-man businesses, which were of little economic interest to the Germans but had provided the main source of revenue for many Jewish families.

Omnia used many of the same liquidation methods as NAGU. The Wirtschaftsprüfstelle, with which the businesses had originally had to register, gave instructions to a Sachbearbeiter (special clerk), who would then open a bank account in the name of the Jewish concern.

The banks involved in the Aryanization process included the Handelsmaatschappij H. Albert de Bary & Co., the Rijnsche Handelsbank, the Bank voor West-Europeeschen Handel and the Bank voor Nederlandsche Arbeid, all of which had close links with German banks.

Outstanding debits and credits were transferred to accounts opened in the name of the Jewish owner. It goes without saying that the account holder had no right to draw on his account.

The funds of the liquidated or sold businesses did not go direct to NAGU or Omnia, so that no direct links can be retraced. Once the expropriation was completed, any possible credit balance was paid into the account of the Jewish owner. In due course, the Wirtschaftsprüfstelle took direct control of the sale of most businesses.

The proceeds of the liquidations and sales eventually ended up in the account of the Vermögensverwaltungs- und Rentenanstalt (VVRA) at the robber bank in Sarphatistraat, Amsterdam. The VVRA was instructed to pay out the former Jewish owners in one hundred quarterly instalments.

In all such cases, the Jewish owner would receive a letter from the Wirtschaftsprüfstelle sanctioning the takeover of the entire share capital, as happened for instance with the sale of the N. V. Spiegel- en lijstenfabriek (mirror and picture-framing works) by S. Hekster to J. Keyzer:

> Permission is granted on condition that the purchase price of 18,000 guilders is paid within fourteen days of receipt of this permit by the vendor S. Hekster into one of the accounts of the Vermögensverwaltungs- und Rentenanstalt, at The Hague.
>
> The Vermögensverwaltungs- und Rentenanstalt in The Hague will remit the sums due to the vendor in 100 equal quarterly instalments, starting immediately and not later than 10 days after payment of the sums into an account of the Vermögensverwaltungs- und Rentenanstalt. Payments to the Vermögensverwaltungs- und Rentenanstalt earn no interest.
>
> No legal claims for payment of money lodged with the Vermögensverwaltungs- und Rentenanstalt are admissible. The same applies to all enforcement orders circumventing this prohibition of transfers and disposals.

In practice, this amounted to a settlement spread over twenty-five years – that is, to a repayment at the rate of 4 per cent per annum. No interest was paid. The low percentage did not really matter, of course, because when the VVRA was founded by Seyss-Inquart in 1941 – with an initial capital of no more than 100 guilders – it had already been decided that all Dutch Jews would be deported. All that the 'settlement' really meant was that an account was opened in the name of every Jew whose business had been taken over.

That, for instance, is what happened in the case of S. Hekster. On 8 June 1942, he was informed by the VVRA that the first instalment of 180 guilders covering the period from 1 June 1942 to 31 August 1942 had been paid into his account with Liro, and that future payments would be effected in the same way, but without any further notice by the VVRA. Hekster then received a notification from Liro that his account had been credited with 180 guilders. This was repeated three times, and then the entries stopped. In any case, neither Hekster nor his fellow victims ever had any control of their Liro accounts.

The staff of the VVRA, which moved soon after its formation from The Hague to 460 Herengracht in Amsterdam, was minimal, with just a few employees besides Bühler, the Geschäftsführer (office manager), the deputy managers Schönthür and

Dahmen, and the bookkeeper Friedrich Fromm, who bore the title of Abteilungsdirektor (divisional director) as a sign of his importance. There was also a typist. In practice, the VVRA seems to have served as a pool of stolen assets, at least until February 1943, when the purchase price for expropriated Jewish businesses went straight to Liro.

When it came to Aryanization, as we have seen, the VVRA was mainly concerned with the bigger enterprises. The purchase price of smaller business and the proceeds from liquidated businesses (which were small by definition) were paid into Liro.[31]

The question of how much money the Aryanization of Jewish concerns brought the Germans is not easy to answer, nor is it possible to state the number of businesses affected by the Aryanization measures. Of the 21,000 or so Jewish businesses, big and small, ranging from a big department store such as De Bijenkorf to humble rag-and-bone dealers, about two thousand were eventually 'de-Jewed'. The rest were liquidated. However, the Wirtschaftsprüfstelle did not manage to close the net completely; in May 1945, there were still a thousand cases on its lists waiting to be processed.

The first thousand cases had been dealt with as early as January 1942, as Seyss-Inquart reported to Berlin: 400 concerns had passed into Dutch hands; 340 had been taken over by Germans, while the remaining 260 had been reserved for *Kriegsteilnehmer* (front-line soldiers).

Half the Jewish concerns registered with the Wirtschaftsprüfstelle had no more than a 'Jewish influence', that is a Jewish director, deputy director or board member. With the consent of the Wirtschaftsprüfstelle, these people could be replaced, albeit for a fee that looked very much like a fine: 1 per cent of the share capital.

In a report by the Befehlshaber der Sicherheitspolizei und des SD, the total yield was put at between 700 million and a billion guilders; in his 'Aryanization report' to Berlin, dated 27 January 1942, Seyss-Inquart came up with a figure of 1.5 billion guilders. This clearly included the amount he hoped to collect in 'fines'.[32]

The VVRA collected approximately 65 million guilders from the sale of Jewish businesses through NAGU.[33] However, it is known that not all the sales were effected by NAGU, and that the liquidation work of Omnia also brought in money (approximately 6.5 million guilders). In addition, many sales were handled direct by the Wirtschaftsprüfstelle, sometimes after substantial tinkering with the accounts.

Another factor impeding reliable estimates was that the NAGU and Omnia archives could not be found after the war. With a great deal of ingenuity, the Dutch authorities were able to come up with a reconstruction of the VVRA accounts. To that end, they produced an entirely new, though of course incomplete, bookkeeping system, by asking banks for duplicates of all the accounts the VVRA had held with them during the war.

The winding up of the VVRA was to take twelve years. But even more accurate figures would not have helped to paint a reliable picture, for, as A. J. van der Leeuw has put it:

> it is perfectly clear that at no point was so much Jewish property stolen than at the time when the liquidation of enterprises – which was so hard to control – took place. Often the owners as well as the liquidators were obviously anxious to keep the visible assets as low as possible. Moreover, the selling price of Aryanized concerns was generally kept low.[34]

The Aryanization of the Jacob Stodel Fine Arts Company

Jacob Stodel's fine arts company in Rokin, Amsterdam, may serve as our model of a business that had to deal with VO 48/1941 and was paid far too low a price for its assets. At the end of October 1941, ten Germans – including two members of the Grüne Polizei – burst into the premises. Owners and staff were questioned at length, each one separately. The Germans were particularly interested in the provenance of works for sale on commission.

The fate of Stodel's company was quickly sealed. The stock was placed under an administrator until further notice, all keys were called in, and the building was sealed, in case staff members decided to try to rescue any paintings.

In December 1941, the owners and staff were summoned to the business premises. There they met the *Verwalter*, Joseph Kalb, appointed by the Reichskommissar in person. Kalb used to work for Lippmann, Rosenthal & Co. in Nieuwe Spiegelstraat, and knew little if anything about the art trade. He explained that the business would henceforth be run under his control. Salomon and Bernhard Stodel, the former proprietors, and their staff were offered employment under him for a weekly salary of 125 guilders; Kalb himself drew twice as much. In the flourishing art market, the former bank clerk acquitted himself very well: at the end of May 1942, the accountants recorded that during the first six months of his work for the company, Kalb made a net profit of 100,000 guilders.

However good that news may have been, it did not really please the new manager, who wanted to buy and continue the business under his own name. For that reason, the value was reduced to a third after a 'corrected' estimate of the stock. All the books and other records were destroyed. As a result, Kalb managed to 'buy' the business for one-third of its value. The Stodels did not see a penny of the purchase price.[35]

It appears that arriving at a reliable estimate of the full scope of the Aryanization measures will have to remain a pious wish. The only certainty is that at the time when most of the measures were taken, in 1941, the Germans had decided to deport all Jewish citizens. What is also clear is that the Germans went out of their way to disguise their real intentions. They took considerable trouble to set up Lippmann, Rosenthal & Co., a bank with a Jewish name but in fact a robbers' den, in which Jewish money and other assets had perforce to be deposited 'for safe-keeping'. The payment of the purchase price to the Jewish owners over a period of twenty-five years was clearly intended to pull the wool over the eyes of the victims. The lessons learned during the Aryanization campaign in Germany, begun as early as 1933, had been taken to heart and extended to other countries.

The Aryanization of the Diamond Industry

Just one branch of business life was to escape dancing to the Aryanization tune for a while, even though 80 per cent of it was in Jewish hands, and that was the diamond industry. Hitler's war machine could not run without it and so it was left alone at first. Germany had a crying need for diamonds: cut diamonds for foreign currency and rough diamonds for industrial purposes. Dutch diamond workers were famous throughout the world and their work so skilled that they could not readily be replaced. Because they were indispensable, they and their families were originally spared from the deportations, which began in July 1942. During the major raids in May and June 1943, however, most members of this group were picked up as well and carried off to Westerbork.

The larger diamond companies escaped direct German intervention in the form of a *Verwalter* until the end of 1944, the underlying hope being that the status quo might help Germany to gain an international diamond-cutting monopoly. At the time, the leading world centres of the diamond-cutting industry were Antwerp and Amsterdam. Once the war was won, Germany, with her diamond works in the Low Countries, would be a worthy match for the South African diamond-mining concerns.

Hermann Göring saw the advantages of this plan, and the result was that no Jewish diamond business was saddled with a *Verwalter*. The industry and its employees were saved, at least for as long as the Germans thought it best to leave them alone.

There was yet another factor persuading the Germans to exercise restraint: the fear that Jewish diamond dealers might spirit a large number of diamonds away. Precious stones, taking up so little space, are easily hidden and easily traded, and hence ideal contraband for anyone trying to flee the country or going into hiding. In other words, there was a good chance that a hasty deportation or attempt to place a business under administrative control might result in serious losses of diamonds to the Germans.

Deferment from deportation to the East until further notice was reserved for those holding a *Sperrstempel* (exemption stamp).[36] Jews handing in diamonds would be issued with such a stamp; in fact, the only reason for issuing these *Sperrstempel* was to win possession of diamonds.

After the raids in May to June 1943, when the Sicherheitspolizei became convinced that significant quantities of diamonds were still being held back, they ordered the (temporary) release from Westerbork of a number of businessmen who had owned a diamond company before their deportation. The acute foreign currency shortage of the Third Reich was the reason for this measure.

The missing diamonds were to be recovered not by confiscation but by sale to the firm of Bozenhardt Bros. Several German diamond-cutting works were instructed to sell the stones abroad for hard currency.

The sham transactions were intended above all to deceive the Allies, for the Germans realized that stolen stones were more difficult to sell than those bought for cash. Large-scale confiscation would have attracted too much attention and was therefore undesirable; it might impede sales in neutral countries and perhaps even prevent them altogether.

The camouflaged robbery succeeded thanks to a number of sham sales and resales and was so complicated and impenetrable that even the Bozenhardts, who purchased the major proportion of the Dutch diamond supply for the German Four-Year Plan, were often unable to fathom the precise ins and outs of the business.

The Bozenhardts purchased the diamonds with the approval of the Rijksbureau voor Diamant (State Diamond Office) and paid the official price, which was essential if the transactions were to have the appearance of legality. Amsterdam diamond merchants were paid 9.4 million guilders in total as part of the so-called Aktion Bozenhardt.

The Jewish diamond merchants sold their stones under duress, and had no option but to agree to the sales of stones they would much sooner have kept, not least because in those hard times diamonds were not only highly desirable merchandise but also fetched far more than the official price. This campaign had the blessing of Göring, to whom the stones were sold in his capacity as leader of the Four-Year Plan. It was not only as the responsible government official but also in his personal capacity that he took an enthusiastic interest in the diamond business.[37]

The Bozenhardt Action had yet another consequence: the so-called 'Hanemann gift'. In September 1943, a number of Jewish diamond merchants assembled a parcel of diamonds and other jewels, and offered them as a 'gift' to Carl Hanemann, the official German representative in the State Diamond Office.

Hanemann had previously exerted himself to have the 'diamond Jews' released from Westerbork, with the clear intention of using them as part of the Bozenhardt Action. As a token of their gratitude for his intervention, he now demanded part of the assumed 'black' supply of diamonds held by Jewish diamond companies. Each of them was expected to hand in stones to the value of approximately 30,000 guilders, more or less the going 'tariff' for a *Sperrstempel*. Thus twenty firms contributed a total of about 600,000 guilders to Hanemann's 'gift'.

During the raid of 29 September 1943, that is, a few days after handing over the present, practically all the 'diamond Jews' were rearrested and carried off to Westerbork for the second time. This time, they did not return home. Hanemann handed his gift over to the Four-Year Plan authorities in Berlin.[38]

Besides *Sperrstempel*, employers and workers in the diamond industry had yet another means of avoiding deportation for a time. Employers taken off the transport registers were entered on List I, and employees on List II. Family members of both categories had a chance of being entered on List III, which, like the *Sperrstempel*, promised exemption 'until further notice'. To be eligible for inclusion in List III, these family members had, however, to hand in 50 carats of industrial diamonds (mainly 'bort' or inferior diamonds); at a later stage a further 50 carats was required. As a result, the black-market price of 'bort' soared to 3,000 guilders a carat as against the pre-war price of three guilders. A place on List III eventually cost 15,000 guilders instead of the original 150. List III was opened in the summer of 1942. Roughly six months later, the Germans believed they had collected all the loot there was. 'Until further notice' thus turned out to be about December 1942. Approximately two hundred 'diamond Jews' were packed off to Westerbork Transit Camp, ready for their final deportation.

The Amsterdamsche Bank was designated as the diamond collection centre; the ultimate destination was the Reichsstelle für technische Erzeugnisse (Reich Office for Technical Products) in Berlin. It paid the Amsterdamsche Bank a fair price, but the Second Liro *Verordnung* prevented the bank from paying the money over to the Jewish suppliers. Nor did the bank transfer the money to Liro in Sarphatistraat, Amsterdam, in which case the rightful owners could have been recompensed after the war – at least if they or their heirs had survived. [39]

Agricultural Property

On 27 May 1941, a further attack on Jewish property came in the form of VO 102/1941. This time it was aimed at land held by Jews or Jewish businesses involved in the agricultural and fishery sectors. All such land had to be transferred to non-Jews by notarial deed before 1 September 1941. The sales contracts had to be approved by a still-to-be-set-up 'Approbation Bureau' of the Ministry of Agriculture and Fisheries.

Agricultural property had to be registered with so-called *Pachtbüros*, later called *Grondkamers* (provincial authorities responsible for leasehold contracts) and responsible to the Ministry of Agriculture and Fisheries. These bureaus supervised the sale of land to non-Jewish Dutch farmers. In the event, only a few Jews were discovered in the agricultural sector – of the entire Dutch agricultural holdings less than 1 per cent (0.9 per cent, that is, 9,000 hectares) was in Jewish hands.

The *Verordnung* mainly affected Jewish landowners in Groningen province, although in practice little came of the whole campaign because it proved difficult to find buyers. All the proceeds of the sales, amounting to 17 million guilders, went into the coffers of the VVRA.[40] The value and size of Jewish-owned building sites, with or without buildings on them, by contrast, was much greater. Small wonder then that, just over two months later, the Germans cast their greedy eyes over non-agricultural property.

Non-agricultural Property

The Niederländische Grundstücksverwaltung (Netherlands Estate Administration, the NGV), at 45 Juliana van Stolberglaan in The Hague, was charged with the liquidation of all Jewish real estate and mortgages. That was laid down by Seyss-Inquart on 11 August 1941 in VO 154/1941 'concerning Jewish real estate'. Little time was allowed for registration, because the relevant forms – obtainable from the Chambers of Trade – had to be handed in before 15 September 1941. The proceeds went to the VVRA.[41]

VO 154/1941 covered not only parcels of land and the buildings on them but also the income from them in the form of rent, building rights (the right *in rem* to build on the land of others), hereditary tenure, mortgages and other property rights.

In practice, the *Verordnung* mainly affected private property: houses, building sites, claims on real estate covered by mortgages, and other property rights. All these assets and rights had to be registered with the Netherlands Estate Administration. In total, some 20,000 parcels of land and 5,600 mortgages with an estimated value of 150 million guilders and 22 million guilders respectively were registered.[42]

Control of confiscated properties was again vested in a *Verwalter*. He collected rents, paid off mortgages and insurance premiums and was responsible for the (inevitable) ultimate sale. Originally all these tasks were supervised by the NGV, but soon afterwards it handed its work over to the Nobiscum administrative office and the Algemeen Nederlands Beheer van Onroerende Goederen (General Netherlands Administration of Real Estate, the ANBO) which had numerous branch offices in all parts of the country. Both organizations were associated with the NSB and each appointed assistant administrators. Thus the firm of P. Everout was appointed for Amsterdam and surroundings where most Jewish real estate was concentrated. A fee of 5 per cent was charged for the administration of expropriated estates, half of which went to the assistant administrators.

In 1943, the administrators collected over 1.4 million guilders in rent, and in the first six months of 1944, by which time many parcels of land had been sold, another 80,000 guilders. The rentals and proceeds of sales were made over to Lippmann, Rosenthal & Co. in Sarphatistraat, Amsterdam, after having been checked by the VVRA.

Like Aryanized businesses, the owners were ostensibly entitled to collect their money in one hundred quarterly instalments (that is, within twenty-five years), and once again this was a farce because the Germans had never had the slightest intention of handing the money over to the expropriated owners.[43]

Quite apart from the fact that the Jews had no control over the proceeds of the sales, these were also much too low. From the minutes of the ANBO it appears that the figures were juggled drastically, and that houses were frequently sold far below their market value. Thus a house with an estimated value of 5,000 guilders changed owners for a mere 1,600 guilders. Moreover, an ANBO meeting concluded that

> a very large proportion of Jewish houses are falling into the hands of buyers who work hand in glove with black marketeers, the percentage of houses that actually pass into the hands of private individuals being relatively far too low. Ultimately the houses do end up with private individuals, but not at prices we could justify.

The war prospects also seemed to have an influence on the sale of houses. After the fall of Stalingrad, in the winter of 1942 – often described as the beginning of the end of the Third Reich – the clear stagnation in the sale of Jewish property reflected fears of post-war restitution claims.[44]

The new owners paid a commission of 2 per cent for their acquisitions, half of which went to the estate agent and the other half to the NGV. The commission in no way reflected the actual profit accruing to the new owner – which came to nearly 100 per cent after deduction of the costs incurred by the new occupier – because the houses had generally been sold to a front man at far below their real value, and then sold on for a more realistic price.

Remarkably enough, all the sales contracts explicitly excluded an indemnity clause (that is, indemnity from possible claims by third parties).[45] Just as remarkably this form of defeatism was tolerated or at least ignored.

For what else could that exclusion signify than that the NGV was afraid of Jewish claims for restitution from the NGV? That danger only threatened if Germany lost the war. Now the jurist Professor M.H. Bregstein, who was particularly active for the Dutch government in restitution matters after the war, has pointed out that NSB-men, black marketeers, and 'other unpatriotic elements' were quite prepared to wager on a final German victory. Faith in a future under Germany was evidently great.

In the provinces, things were quite different; here 'property racketeers' were able to talk many *bona fide* but ignorant members of the public into investing their money in confiscated houses. Often they concealed or denied the fact that these houses were Jewish property. In practice, the more frequently a house changed owners, the easier it was to disguise its Jewish origins.[46]

One problem for many prospective buyers was that they could only clinch the sale after taking out a mortgage. Dutch mortgage banks, however, were generally – and for good reasons – reluctant to issue mortgages on Jewish property. As a result, the NGV was forced temporarily to issue mortgages itself, for the sake of speeding the transfers.

The mortgage banks were put under increasing pressure and even admonished officially to co-operate, but to little avail. To tighten the screws, the Germans appointed administrators over several mortgage banks that had had Jewish directors or board members in May 1940. The fact that these board members had had to resign much earlier in the wake of the Aryanization measures seemed to be irrelevant. The Germans, moreover, insinuated that a non-cooperative attitude might well lead to arrests. All these methods were expressly designed to extort mortgages on expropriated Jewish property.

In part, the Germans were successful, but the banks continued to be reluctant agents for them, and decided to use new tactics. Mortgage requests would no longer be turned down out of hand, but investigated with exceptional care, the aim being to discover grounds for turning applications down on technical or legal grounds. In order to put an end to the ensuing stalemate, the Germans instructed two NSB members, D. H. de Vries and H. C. van Maasdijk, to set up the Landelijke Hypotheekbank (Rural Mortgage Bank).

The Landelijke Hypotheekbank was also used to put a stop to Jewish mortgage claims on 'Aryans'. VO 37/1943 of 19 April 1943, 'concerning the termination of monetary demands secured by mortgages by Jewish natural or juridical persons or associations of persons', laid it down that such mortgages could be terminated within three months. In practice, this VO only applied to loans to non-Jews, since all Jewish property had passed into German hands under VO 37/1943. The Germans had issued that *Verordnung* because insurance companies and banks refused in many cases to hand over to Liro all funds belonging to Jews. They cited legal objections as their justification.

In these cases, too, the mortgage banks were not very anxious to take the mortgages over, because the NGV would claim that – following the transfer of the debt – it was acting as the representative of the Jewish creditors. The legality of this construction was rightly considered to be dubious by the mortgage banks.[47] VO 37/1943, intended chiefly to speed up the attempts by financial institutions to wind up Jewish mortgages, failed to have the intended effect, and threatening letters by the Reich Commissioner's Office were needed to make them act.[48]

VO 89/1943 of 25 September 1943, 'concerning the termination of monetary demands not covered by mortgages', was a supplement of VO 37/1943 (which concerned claims covered by mortgages). Like VO 37/1943, it revoked the contractually agreed terms, opening the way for Liro to turn these demands into cash.

It is difficult to determine whether the uncooperative attitude of the mortgage banks was based on principle or on commercial considerations. This applies no less to the release of capital for expropriated houses – to which they were fiercely opposed – than to the transfer of debts to third parties. In either case, a German defeat would have caused them great difficulties.

In the countryside, the tendency to cooperate with the German measures seems to have been, if anything, even less enthusiastic than, for instance, in Amsterdam. Many Jews lived in the capital and it was not always easy to establish whether a parcel of land or a house had originally belonged to one of them. In the countryside, where there were relatively few Jews, these facts were more widely known.

–6–

The Robber Bank in Sarphatistraat, Amsterdam: Lippmann, Rosenthal & Co. (Liro)

Introduction

Lippmann, Rosenthal & Co., the 'robber bank', has already been mentioned briefly several times; it was not a bank in the normal sense of the word, but was given the title in order to deceive. In practice, Liro was far more of a storage depot and sales office for stolen Jewish property than a financial institution. It was an executive agency under the direct supervision of the Reichskommissar; its most important task was the realization (*Verwertung*) of the Jewish assets it collected. Liro did not engage in typical banking activities, although at first it issued regular statements to its clients, listing all deposits and withdrawals from the accounts they had been forced to open.

There were two establishments in Amsterdam by the name of Lippmann, Rosenthal & Co. To distinguish between them, they were referred to respectively as Nieuwe Spiegelstraat and Sarphatistraat, the Amsterdam streets in which they were located. Oddly enough, the name Sarphatistraat was in use for the duration of the war, although the letterhead bore the address of 'Muiderschans'. Sarphatistraat itself had been named after the Jewish physician Samuel Sarphati (1813–66) and in common with all other streets named after Jews, was renamed in 1942. Everything Jewish or that recalled a Jewish connection had to be exorcized from public life.

The name of the new 'bank' was chosen deliberately. A Jewish bank by the name of Lippmann, Rosenthal & Co. had been trading at 6–8 Nieuwe Spiegelstraat in Amsterdam before the war. It had an excellent reputation and seemed well equipped to calm, or better still prevent, Jewish fears and the anticipated panic over registrations and transfers as much as possible. Another reason for using the name was to strengthen confidence abroad. There was little doubt that rich Jews had moved their assets to foreign banks, and Seyss-Inquart had plans to lay his hands on those assets as well. The name of Lippmann, Rosenthal & Co. not only stood for reliability and integrity but inspired trust, and the Germans made good use of these qualities when they set up the fictitious branch in Sarphatistraat. Apart from the name, the two banks had nothing in common, and were administered quite separately.

Needless to say, the genuine bank of Lippmann, Rosenthal & Co. in Nieuwe Spiegelstraat had been placed under German control as part of the 'Aryanization' process. Edgar Fuld and Robert May, the two Jewish proprietors, were forced in May 1941 to hand over control to Alfred Flesche, who in addition to being a director of the Rhodius-Koenigs Handelsmaatschappij and president of the German Chamber of Commerce for the Netherlands now also became 'commissarial administrator' of the famous bank in Nieuwe Spiegelstraat.[1] Flesche had been with Lippmann, Rosenthal & Co as a *Verwalter* since 8 July 1940 under the enemy property decree of 24 June 1940, following the escape to England of Ellen von Marx-May.[2]

Ellen was the heir of Paul May and his wife Rosa Fuld, both of whom had committed suicide on 15 May 1940 (Paul May and his brother Robert had been board members of Lippmann, Rosenthal & Co., Nieuwe Spiegelstraat). Ellen von Marx-May had fled to England with her family one day earlier, that is on 14 May. Paul May's estate, or at least Ellen von Marx-May's share, was treated as 'enemy property' because she had fled the Netherlands. It was on those grounds that the bank had been saddled with an administrator.

Liro was the first large Jewish concern to be placed under an administrator, albeit only in part. Alfred Flesche had a good name as an independent banker and, as he later testified, tried to show his good intentions by running the company entrusted to him to the best of his ability.

The two Jewish partners, Fuld and May, continued to work in the bank until close to the end of the war, which both of them survived.[3] To a large extent, that was undoubtedly due to Flesche's efforts. But there was yet another reason: the Devisenschutzkommando (Foreign Exchange Protection Commando, or DSK) needed the two partners 'urgently' for a major currency transaction with Portugal involving between 70 and 80 million escudos. The DSK made it known that the continued freedom of the two partners depended on the completion of this escudo transaction.[4]

Liro Saphatistraat was opened on 8 August 1941 by virtue of VO 148/1941 'concerning the handling of Jewish capital assets'. This was the first *Verordnung* affecting the private property of Jews, and was to become known as the First Liro *Verordnung*.[5] Jews, having first been driven out of the business world, social life and the civil service, now found their private property under attack as well.

The removal of Jews from public life was invariably accompanied by a string of euphemisms and misrepresentations, all intended to hide the naked truth. Especially in 1941 and 1942, the years in which the two Liro *Verordnungen* were promulgated, the Germans made a constant effort to mislead Jews by hinting that all these measures were no more than temporary expedients. This ploy was part of a policy that continued to the bitter end: even the gas chambers in the extermination camps were presented as showers.[6]

When the Jews were forced to register their private possessions and liquid assets with Liro, few of them could have known that they would soon be destitute. They had indeed lost the right to dispose of their possessions, but many of them must have thought, or at least must have hoped, that it was a temporary measure. Even the fact that they were allowed to draw money for living expenses and their 'credit balance' was consequently reduced contributed to this misconception, the more so as every request to withdraw money was judged individually by the bank's 'Inspectorate' division, which enjoyed complete freedom of action.

Nor was that the only ruse to deceive the victims. Receipts were issued for all goods handed in; statements were issued regularly, as by a normal bank; interest was added and fees were charged. Customers were even sent a form setting out 'conditions for dealing with our clients', with a request to sign and return it. Originally, moreover, clients could still give instructions for buying and selling shares through Liro.

The pseudo-bank even tried to maximize its 'profits' like any normal bank. 'One might easily have gained the impression,' wrote the post-war administrators/liquidators of Liro in their final report, 'that the Liro administration had had no knowledge of the German intention to confiscate all Jewish assets.'[7] It is no longer possible to decide if that was indeed the case. However, Liro's clients probably did not suspect that their deportation had been decided on even before VO 148/1941 was officially issued. Yet as early as May 1941, Seyss-Inquart and his associates knew that the complete removal of Jews from Dutch society was a foregone conclusion.[8]

Despite the fact that the top German echelons knew all about these plans, Liro did not seem fully prepared for its task, since on 8 August 1941, when the First Liro *Verordnung* was issued, the inflow of parcels of shares and bank notes was so great that the staff proved quite unable to cope. In May 1942, when the Second Liro *Verordnung* came out, Liro had still not finished dealing with the enormous volume of paper unleashed by the First Decree, so that many parcels of shares had to be left unopened while awaiting further attention.[9]

The Second Liro *Verordnung* was to cause an even greater inflow of parcels than the first. The incoming material was numbered sequentially, which helps us to reconstruct the course of the surrender process fairly accurately.

Up to 23 May 1942, six hundred consignments arrived in response to the First Liro *Verordnung*. From 24 May 1942 to 31 December 1942 the inflow was largely made up of parcels containing material sent in on the basis of VO 58/1942 (the Second Liro *Verordnung*), 16,097 consignments in all. The yield from 1 January to 30 September 1943 – the peak had been passed by then – was 6,050 consignments, nearly 10,000 consignments less. The number of items per parcel was estimated at twenty-five.

By 30 September an estimated 586,675 items had passed through the hands of Liro employees. Often, a single number would cover an enormous quantity of items: thus No. 16723 contained no fewer than 1,103 items and parcel No. 1857 contained 1,414. The figures could be even higher than that, as for instance in the 'collective parcel' No. 7416, which contained 8,872 items, although the names of the senders were not recorded in the rush.

The Second Liro *Verordnung* yielded a total of 12,701 parcels.[10] At one point, Liro was left with an enormous backlog, because during the M-Aktion (the theft of *Möbel*, furniture, by the ERR), part of the loot was handed in to Liro, even though it was not covered by the Second Liro *Verordnung*.

From the middle of 1942 to the summer of 1943 the flow of items into Liro was so huge that the need for additional storage space became urgent. To that end the buildings of the Handwerkersvriendenkring (Artisans' Friendly Circle, now the Kriterion Cinema, in Roeterstraat) and of the Diamond Bourse in Weesperplein were taken over.[11] This colossal inflow involved items of the most varied kinds, very often including some virtually worthless pieces. The building in Roeterstraat had been rented, with an eye to the Second Liro *Verordnung*, as early as 1 May, for a period of one year at a rental of 6,500 guilders. When storage space still appeared to be inadequate, two floors in the Diamond Bourse were hired from 1 February 1943 to 31 October 1943, notice to quit one floor being given on 31 October 1943. The annual rental for both floors was 14,000 guilders.[12]

It had not been intended, but ordinary household goods (*reiner Hausrat*) were handed in as well, something against which Liro protested repeatedly:

> Should the Einsatzstab Rosenberg have no use for certain household effects, they ought to be put at the disposal of the N.S.V. [Nationalsozialistische Volkswohlfahrt, the National-Socialist People's Welfare, which was part of Winterhulp. G.A.], but in any case not delivered to our goods division.

Articles of artistic value 'due' to be surrendered to Liro under the Second Liro *Verordnung*, such as antique furniture, were naturally accepted by the robber bank, just like money or equities found in the houses of deported Jews.[13] All these effects were covered by the two Liro *Verordnungen* and Liro was therefore 'entitled' to them.

On Tuesday 15 June 1943 instructions were issued that in future none but articles covered by the Second Liro *Verordnung* – that is, collections of all kinds, works of art, gold, silver, platinum, pearls, precious stones, and so forth – would be taken in. The rest would have to be rejected. From the instructions it appears that the Zentralstelle für jüdische Auswanderung (Central Office for Jewish Emigration), which played a central role in the looting of household effects, had been notified of this decision. The Zentralstelle along with the ERR were told to find storage depots of their own. Goods brought in from Westerbork transit camp and not covered by Article 10 had also to be taken to these depots. However, Liro, and this was emphasized, would continue to take in 'cash, shares and other securities'.[14]

All Jews arriving in Westerbork were searched by Liro officials for what cash and objects of value they had been able to secrete. As a result, many of their possessions finished up in Sarphatistraat after all.[15] Liro-Westerbork, which from July 1942 to the middle of October 1943 employed a staff of six to eight and later of four, was able to extract 825,000 guilders in cash in this antechamber of death. At first, amounts of less than 250 guilders were ignored, but from October to November 1942 practically anything was seized. Sometimes the victims were left with ten guilders, but that was up to the discretion of the Liro member on duty. The money was paid into the Liro account of the Amsterdamsche Bank in Assen and later transferred to Amsterdam. Upon any eventual release from Westerbork, for instance of Jewish partners of mixed marriages, the confiscated possessions were returned.[16]

While Liro was quite unable to cope physically and administratively with the flood of goods pouring in, the 'bank' nevertheless complained that many valuable items were being withheld, in particular such 'interior fittings' as antique furniture, paintings and objets d'art in houses and apartments confiscated on behalf of the German army. According to Liro, these fittings belonged to the bank on the basis of the Second Liro *Verordnung*.[17]

Liro also had an eye for detail. Thus an internal note was issued on 9 January 1942 about correspondence with clients, proscribing the use of all polite forms of address such as 'Sir' or 'Madam'. Plain 'Mr', 'Mrs' or 'Miss' had to suffice. Formal salutations and signings-off in a letter were to be omitted. It was stressed that these instructions applied exclusively to correspondence with Jewish persons.[18]

The Establishment of Liro Sarphatistraat

On 22 July 1941, Flesche was instructed to 'make organizational preparations for the seizure of Jewish capital assets'. A building belonging to the Amsterdamsche Bank at 47–55 Sarphatistraat was rented as a storage depot for the booty. The cellars of the premises held two large vaults, one of which contained safe-deposit boxes. The Germans agreed to pay a rental of 35,000 guilders. In addition they agreed to pay the removal expenses of the Amsterdamsche Bank, which came to 8,711.21 guilders. They also paid 69,355.88 guilders for the inventory as well as 8,743.20 guilders for various small structural alterations.[19] All in all, these initial expenses and the capital outlay were a mere trifle compared with the hundreds of millions in the form of money, credits, claims, shares and, at a later stage, objets d'art, diamonds and precious metals that poured into 47–55 Sarphatistraat.

There was just one small stumbling block: finding a new home for the Amsterdamsche Bank's safe-deposits boxes. However, as the Amsterdamsche Bank itself managed to rent a building within a few days and moved into it that same weekend, the pseudo-branch of Liro was able to take over the new premises as early as Monday, 28 July 1941. It took less than two weeks to refit the building; on 8 August 1941, when the first Liro *Verordnung* came into force, the great robbery could begin.[20]

As early as 7 July 1941, Flesche had been informed by confidential letter of the German plans to open deposit and current accounts in the Bankhaus Lippmann, Rosenthal & Co. in Amsterdam. These accounts were euphemistically called *Sicherungskonten* (security accounts) and *Sicherungsdepots* (security deposits). What was to be secured and for what purpose was specified in the strictly confidential letter to Flesche:

a) for paying and securing taxes, fees, fines and dues to sick funds and notaries;
b) for paying contributions, levies and other dues to the Jewish religious community.'

Mention was also made of medical costs, veterinary fees and burial charges. Finally, it was specified that the 'security precautions' would also guarantee payments connected with emigration, such as travel and transport costs.[21]

Once again, the true state of affairs was being camouflaged; the real German intentions could not possibly be inferred from the text. Admittedly, the measures were patently anti-Semitic, but that did not seem particularly worthy of notice among the mass of anti-Jewish *Verordnungen* promulgated by the Third Reich. People may – and will – have wondered why this measure applied exclusively to the Jewish population, but few could have suspected that it was one of the first major steps towards the total confiscation of Jewish property.

The Liro Board of Directors

It was the intention of Fischböck, the man who had thought up the whole Liro idea, that the robber's den appear like a normal bank to the outside world. That meant a normal board of directors. It seemed obvious that Alfred Flesche, the *Verwalter* of Lippmann, Rosenthal & Co. in Nieuwe Spiegelstraat, would be appointed the new head. And so he was, formally, but in practice Dr Walter von Karger and his successor Otto Witscher were in charge of the business, though they did little more than carry out the instructions of the Reichskommissar.

The Robber Bank in Sarphatistraat

Alfred Flesche, the prospective managing director, had lived in the Netherlands since 1926. He was a member of the NSDAP, but was not a fanatical anti-Semite and as head of Liro he never exceeded his formal duties. That emerged during interrogation after the war, not only from declarations by Flesche himself (who naturally had every interest in putting his own role in the best possible light), but also from declarations by Bühler, the German Beauftragte in the Nederlandsche Bank, by Generaldirektor von Karger, and the divisional heads R. von Blaschke and K.V. K. Mulisch, not forgetting Edgar Fuld and Robert May, the two partners in Lippmann, Rosenthal & Co., Nieuwe Spiegelstraat.

Flesche himself wanted nothing to do personally with 'Sarphatistraat', although he never said so expressly to his superiors. He obviously neither could nor would assume responsibility for the robber bank. According to him, and also according to Bühler, Sarphatistraat and Nieuwe Spiegelstraat were to be kept strictly separate. That met with resistance from Fischböck, who wanted to present Liro as an undivided, normal bank.

Flesche also had reservations about concentrating all Jewish assets in one central institution. When the subject was mooted for the first time, he could not yet have known that all registered assets were to be confiscated. Flesche was afraid that the company might go bankrupt, and that was something he was anxious to prevent. He avoided all official meetings and discussions about developments at Sarphatistraat.[22]

Orders and instructions from the Reichskommissariat were always sent direct to von Karger and, after his dismissal, to Otto Witscher, but never to Alfred Flesche. None of this of course altered the fact that Flesche was and remained legally responsible for what happened at Sarphatistraat.

From Flesche's dossier it emerges repeatedly that he made consistent efforts to avoid involvement with Liro Sarphatistraaat, but that Hans Fischböck tried just as often to put a spoke in his wheel. Flesche had it recorded annually that he received no financial remuneration for his compulsory administratorship. Moreover, an agreement between Flesche and Witscher specified that from 15 August 1943 Witscher was in charge of the fiduciary administration of Liro Sarphatistraat, whereas Flesche's responsibility was confined to Liro in Nieuwe Spiegelstraat: 'Herr A. Flesche accordingly bears no responsibility, from the above-mentioned day, for the business and administration of the firm of Lippmann, Rosenthal & Co., Sarphatistraat, Amsterdam.'[23]

Flesche stood out from the many who left no stone unturned to derive personal profit from the situation. True, he never refused to follow orders out of hand, probably because he lacked the courage to do so, but he was never one of the unthinking 'orders are orders' brigade either. 'One rarely senses so strong a feeling of guilt about Nazi collaboration as one does in his correspondence,' A. J. van der Leeuw of the Netherlands State Institute for War Documentation was to write later.[24]

Von Karger and Witscher

The Generaldirektor of Liro, Dr Walter von Karger, was a banker by profession, but leadership was not his strongest point, and anyway he preferred black-market activities. In May 1943, he was dismissed by Alfred Flesche, but he had actually been suspended as early as March and replaced by deputy director Otto Witscher. The ostensible reason for von Karger's dismissal was a report by the trustees criticizing his business conduct. According to von Karger, however, the real reason for his dismissal was that Flesche wanted to make sure that he had someone he could trust in Sarphatistraat, and that person was Witscher.

The reorganization involved several phases. First a control section was set up under Witscher's leadership for the express purpose of keeping an eye on developments in Sarphatistraat. Even von Karger had to submit all his incoming and outgoing correspondence to Witscher, as a result of which he, the Generaldirektor, felt that he had been placed under a subordinate and lost 'all interest' in the bank.

After a while, Witscher was appointed deputy to Flesche, who continued to be the formal head of Liro Sarphatistraat. According to von Karger, Witscher had his eye on his superior's job and managed to turn various German officials against von Karger.

After a serious reprimand from Flesche, von Karger tendered his resignation and stopped working for Liro. Back in Berlin, he was arrested by the Security Service on suspicion of theft, together with Liro's 'art adviser', Baron von Stechow.[25]

Witscher was no more of a dynamic businessman than von Karger. If Witscher had had his way, the entire Liro records would have been burned to wipe out all traces of the looting. As the Allies approached Amsterdam, so Witscher's nervousness grew. From many of the interrogations of his closest colleagues it appears that, when the German defeat seemed close, his nerves gave way. The rest of the Liro top brass opposed the destruction of the records 'even if that means personal difficulties'. No doubt they were afraid that the burning of the archives would be held against them as an additional offence.

On 4 September 1944, one day before *Dolle Dinsdag*, when the people of the Netherlands thought wrongly that their liberation was imminent, Witscher started to burn the documents in his own archive. The Treuhänder Archiv (fiduciary archive) with the entire secret correspondence between him and his superiors went up in flames. This work took him two days. Two of his closest collaborators, Mulisch and von Blaschke, declared that on that hectic Tuesday Witscher could barely keep control of himself during a board meeting and ordered

> everyone present to burn all the documents of his particular section. He himself expressed the intention of leaving for Germany at the first opportunity. We did not prevent this departure; on the contrary, we did all we could to get rid of him as soon as possible, not

least in order to prevent the wholesale incineration he had ordered. After Witscher had left the office on 5 September 1944 at about noon, preparing to flee the country, we immediately . . . reconvened and decided unanimously not to burn anything, and to lock up all important papers in the safe as usual.[26]

The Liro Staff

The size of the Liro staff is one way of forming some idea of the scale of the looting activities. While Liro could still make do with a staff of 268 (fifty-three women and 215 men) at the time of the First Liro *Verordnung*, 160 of them working in the banking division, the number was nearly doubled in 1942 (125 women and 385 men), to drop back again to 299 (fifty-six women and 243 men) in 1943.

Throughout this period, the banking section remained the largest division. From the scant material on the running costs of the bank it would appear that, apart from rentals, these costs were mainly made up of salaries. Thus, in 1942 when looting went into top gear in the wake of the Second Liro *Verordnung*, the wage bill came to 1,053,187.44 guilders. Liro's contribution to Winterhulp was 4,479.94 guilders.

The so-called *Kolonnen* (columns) working for the Zentralstelle für jüdische Auswanderung, which we shall be discussing at some length below, were paid from April 1942 by Liro on the orders of the Beauftragte für die Stadt Amsterdam (commissioner for the city of Amsterdam), although these columns did not work directly for Liro. They had roughly the same staff fluctuations as the robber bank: after quickly growing to 350, the number fell to just over thirty in the course of 1943.[27]

The employment contract of the column leader, W. C. H. Henneicke, has come down to us. It appears from it that Henneicke, 'acting on the orders of the Beauftragte for the city of Amsterdam' was paid a monthly salary of 270 guilders 'for certain temporary services'.[28]

The original core of the Sarphatistraat staff came from the 'genuine' Lippmann, Rosenthal bank in Nieuwe Spiegelstraat. Towards the end of 1941, the entire staff was summoned and informed by Director Fuld that some of them might be transferred to the new Liro branch in Sarphatistraat. Fuld was unable to give precise details, because he did not know them himself. All that was certain was that banking and trustee matters would be handled in Sarphatistraat.

At the end of the meeting, the staff were ushered into Fuld's office in groups, where they were told whether or not they would be transferred to the new branch. They were given one day to think about it, but Fuld advised them to agree to the transfer, because Nieuwe Spiegelstraat had already been placed under German administration so that its continued existence was uncertain. Those choosing to transfer to Sarphatistraat would at least be sure of continued employment. On

1 August 1941, some twenty-five employees made the move from Nieuwe Spiegelstraat to Sarphatistraat. Seven days later, on 8 August, the First Liro *Verordnung* came into force.

The Structure of Liro

The organization and not least the size of Liro underwent considerable changes during the four years of its existence, due to its varying activities and the progress of the *Auswanderung* (emigration), as the deportations to the East were euphemistically called.[29] Towards the end of 1941, roughly four months after the First Liro *Verordnung* came into force, Liro consisted of four main divisions:

- The Banking Division (*Bankabteilung*);
- the Inspectorate (*Prüfungsabteilung*);
- the Credit Division (*Kreditabteilung*);
- the General Division (*Allgemeine Abteilung*).

J. P. Koffieberg, who had joined the Liro Credit Division towards the end of September 1941, declared during his post-war interrogation that he never understood the purpose of his division. The Credit Division was in fact dissolved after a few months.[30]

One year later, towards the end of December 1942, the organizational structure was altered to:

- The Banking Division;
- the Inspectorate;
- the Third Division.

The Banking Division was divided into twelve subdivisions, which dealt with the various assets surrendered in the wake of the First Liro *Verordnung*. Alfred Flesche was the nominal Treuhänderdirektor (fiduciary director), but left the running entirely to Generaldirektor Dr Walter von Karger.

The Inspectorate under Otto Witscher dealt with the problems arising from the implementation of the First (and later also of the Second) Liro *Verordnung*. This section dealt with Jewish requests for money to cover living expenses and, if there was reason to do so, conducted supplementary investigations into undeclared assets.

The Third Division was mainly concerned with gold, silver, objets d'art, Jewish claims against non-Jews and insurance policies handed in under VO 58/1942. The Third Division, too, had several subdivisions: 'Emigration' (which was suspended soon after its creation), 'Claims and policies', 'Merchandise' and 'Subsidiary companies'.

Koffieberg, who after the closure of the Credit Division was transferred to 'Emigration', was unable to stay there for long; that division, too, was quickly dissolved and absorbed into the Merchandise Division. At 'Emigration' (a strange division for a bank) Jews who had been given permission to emigrate had to hand in all their possessions. The Zentralstelle für jüdische Auswanderung, which fell under the Sicherheitspolizei in Amsterdam, passed these possessions on to Liro. K. V. K. Mulisch was in charge of the Third Division, and at the same time head of the General Division, which was in charge of staff and internal affairs. Since the end of 1941, Liro had thus been handling valuable objects extracted from Jews through the so-called Auswanderer Durchschleusungsverfahren (Emigrants' Processing Procedure), that is, long before the promulgation of VO 58/1942.

From a brief survey of activities in 1942 and part of 1943, it appears that the Emigration sector sold merchandise to the tune of 166,450 guilders. By 30 September 1943 these sales had dropped to 69,639 guilders. It can no longer be determined to what extent the Jews concerned were actually allowed to emigrate, but the number of emigrants was in any case very small. From April 1942, Liro also received goods seized by the Hausraterfassungsaktion (household goods collection campaign). Even before the Second Liro *Verordnung* was published, some six hundred consignments had been handed in.[31]

In October 1943, the structure of Liro was again modified: the number of divisions was increased to seven, indicated by Roman figures. Seyss-Inquart's wish that all Liro activities be concluded by 1 April 1943 had by then proved impracticable.[32]

Division I, the Banking Division proper, had been retained and continued to be responsible for ongoing banking transactions, general accounts and monthly balance sheets. This section was headed by R. von Blaschke, a naturalized German.

Division II was new and was mainly concerned with securities. It also ran the personnel section, the internal affairs section and the general business section. It was headed by Mulisch.

Division III specialized in the liquidation of Jewish claims against non-Jews and the redemption of insurance policies. It was headed by J. T. van Rossum.

Division IV took over part of the work of the former Inspectorate, which had been rendered redundant by the introduction of the *Sammelkonto* (collective account). It also dealt with the return of wrongly confiscated property. It is not clear who ran it.

Division V dealt with legacies and was headed by W. H. Woortman, Liro's chief clerk.

Division VI dealt with bequests to non-Jewish children from mixed marriages.

Division VII, the Merchandise Division, administered the remaining gold, silver, objets d'art, jewels and household utensils. Like Division II, it was run by Mulisch.

Fire and Theft Insurance

Normal businesses insure against fire, flood, burglary, theft and various other commercial risks. Nothing indicates that the board of the 'robber bank' felt and behaved differently from an ordinary banking institution. The board made sure that the relevant insurance policies were actually taken out, and reviewed the situation from time to time to ascertain if changes were needed to meet the constantly changing conditions.

On Thursday 4 March 1943, for instance, the board examined the various insurance policies and discussed the current state of affairs. The fire and theft insurance for the contents of the three Liro vaults with a joint insurance value of five million guilders was to be doubled to ten million. The board also wondered if the fire and theft insurance on the paintings in the storerooms in Sarphatistraat and in the Diamond Exchange did not need to be increased from one million guilders and ordered the estimated value to be reassessed. The insurance for war damage to the paintings in the two buildings had been put at two million. The transport insurance for money, securities, and precious metals inside the Netherlands and during transport to and from Germany, Belgium and France came to 500,000 guilders. Furniture and carpets in the Roeterstraat depot had been insured for 200,000 guilders against fire and theft, quite apart from jewellery and other trinkets.

All in all, the board was not satisfied with the insurance situation, particularly because certain items were not covered, namely:

a) fire and burglary for silver
b) idem, furniture, carpets, etc. outside Roeterstraat
c) damage to silver
d) ditto for furniture, etc. outside Roeterstraat
e) transport insurance for more than 8 daily deliveries of securities in Amsterdam by bank messenger
f) fraud insurance.

At the meeting it was also pointed out that the office equipment in Sarphatistraat, which had cost 250,000 guilders, was only insured for half that amount. Here too, the board demanded that the necessary steps be taken to remedy the situation.[33]

Insurance continued to be a cause of constant concern for the Liro board.

The Robber Bank in Sarphatistraat

In view of the great importance I [Witscher] attach to this matter, I would kindly request you to let me have your thoughts on our current insurance situation at least once a month, submitting possible suggestions for changes or increases in cover to me in writing.[34]

If we did not know better, we might really think that we are describing a normal bank and not a 'robbers' den' taking out insurance for stolen goods.

Internal Fraud and Theft

One problem for which no cure (or insurance) seemed available was theft by insiders. The Liro board was fully aware of this problem. Flesche worried about the many opportunities offered to thieves and wondered, on the basis of four carefully constructed 'theoretical models', how and by whom such 'irregularities' could be detected. Flesche examined the following models:

- The cashier conspires with a staff member who hands the incoming money over to him. The cashier does not record the amount, and the money, as well as the receipt for it, is misappropriated. The cashier and the employee pocket the money between them.
- When a parcel of shares without a list of contents arrives, the shares are easily misappropriated.
- Two Liro employees, both of them entitled to sign documents, draw a cheque on the *Sammelkonto*. They send the cheque to the address of an acquaintance where they collect it and cash it themselves.
- The same trick, but with a variation. A sum of money is released to the *Sammelkonto*. The cheque is again sent to an accommodation address, where the fraudulent official collects it and then cashes it.

According to Flesche these examples could be multiplied and endlessly varied. Embezzlement was possible both before and also after the registration of goods. The answer to the question: 'Who notices it, when and how?' was 'No one and never,' according to Flesche. Normally, the clients would have complained, but at Liro things were not normal. The clients had gone 'away' – in other words, had been deported. The impossibility of carrying out adequate checks was therefore not so much due to the nature of the *Sammelkonto*, as to the fact that the clients never raised the alarm.[35]

The opening and emptying of safe-deposit boxes, too, seemed to give cause for concern. One memo complained that this type of work was increasingly being done by one employee instead of two, which greatly increased the chances of fraud. The Liro board was afraid that valuable items would vanish before they were registered with the bank.[36]

In view of all these complaints, it would seem that embezzlement must have assumed considerable proportions, but the exact situation is hard to reconstruct. One result was that the embezzled objects or sums of money could not be retraced during the post-war restitution attempts.

J. P. C. Rosier, head of the Merchandise Division, was arrested for theft and interned in Amersfoort concentration camp. He did not survive his imprisonment. Rosier was caught because when he was taken on by Liro in 1942 he was almost destitute, but only one year later he was the proud owner of three yachts and his own house.[37]

Rosier managed his embezzling activities in close collaboration with Thilo Carl, Baron von Stechow-Kotzen, the official Liro sales expert on paintings and art. The pair sold jewellery and paintings to Herman Olij, also known as Dr Bosch.[38] Von Stechow apparently not only sold goods clandestinely to Olij, but also decorated his home in Berlin with objets d'art he had embezzled in Sarphatistraat. During a search of his house, the police took possession of numerous *Wertsachen* (valuables). The list mentions tables, chandeliers, clocks and chairs, but above all thirty-two (mainly Persian) carpets and thirty-six paintings.[39]

Baron von Stechow was in charge of the sale of objets d'art to German dealers after valuation, a job originally done by Rosier. The baron charged his clients an extra 10 per cent commission, which he put into his own pocket.

The affair came to light when a dealer in Lübeck refused to pay the extra commission. When he received a visit from a tax officer soon afterwards, on suspicion that he had failed to pay import duty on carpets from the Netherlands, the Lübeck dealer suspected that von Stechow had done him a bad turn and informed the authorities.

Since the suspicion then arose that other dealers, too, might have had imported carpets clandestinely from Liro, it was decided to launch a closer investigation. The Sicherheitsdienst in Amsterdam was informed, and von Stechow was arrested.

Koffieberg, through whose hands all the merchandise passed and who was therefore thought capable of identifying the stolen objects, was given instructions to join an SD-man in a search of the baron's home in Berlin. During the first visit, Koffieberg identified a number of objects of Liro provenance. But when he returned next morning to Bismarckstrasse to continue his search, the whole street had gone up in flames. Von Stechow's home seemed to have been razed to the ground during a British air raid.

It thus proved impossible to gather enough evidence to indict the baron, but the investigation continued all the same. It then emerged that von Stechow had pocketed 90,000 guilders in commission from the Berlin trader Reinheldt alone.[40]

But even 'investigator' Koffieberg was one of the Liro employees to enrich themselves 'in a most improper manner' from the stream of goods pouring in. He had in fact misappropriated so many items that his home was nearly filled to capacity and he was forced to rent a storeroom. Paintings, bookcases, encyclopaedias, decorative Chinese plates, mantel clocks, antique furniture, tapestries, dressers, camphor-wood chests and scores of other objects – he was interested in everything.

At the beginning he had bought the goods from Liro officially. All the staff had been offered an opportunity to do that, although that fact had never been made public. Later he also bought goods from the German buyers. He would hand them the estimated value plus a small premium, but even so the goods went to him at giveaway prices.

It is not known to what precise extent Koffieberg acquired goods illegally, though it is certain that he could not possibly have paid for the many new acquisitions out of his salary. Moreover, his attempt to destroy documents that would have shown which articles had been bought legally by staff members, suggests that he had something to conceal.[41]

The *Sammelkonto*

If the Liro board had indeed had no inkling originally of the intention to 'confiscate Jewish property in its entirety',[42] as the Liro liquidators put it in their final report, then the situation must have changed on 21 November 1942.

That day the board received a letter from Dr Hans Fischböck, the General-Kommissar für Finanz und Wirtschaft, instructing them to close all the accounts of so-called 'full Jews' and to transfer the balances on 31 December 1942 to a collective account – a *Sammelkonto* as it was called in German. All moneys received after New Year's Day 1943 had to be credited to the *Sammelkonto*. As a result, the individual credit balances of Jews could no longer be determined and had, to all intents and purposes, been liquidated. The disentanglement of the *Sammelkonto* was to take many years and a great deal of manpower after the war.

The accounts of Jews from 'mixed marriages', of *Feindjuden* (Jews from countries with which Germany was at war) and of Jews of foreign nationality continued to be kept separately for a while. As we shall see, mixed marriages faced the Liro machine with considerable problems, while interference with the property of non-Dutch Jews threatened to provoke counter-measures against German residents in the countries concerned.[43]

The introduction of the *Sammelkonto* led to the closure of some 26,000 private accounts between 31 December 1942 and the end of March 1943. Some 5,000 accounts remained, mainly those of Jews from mixed marriages, *Feindjuden* and Jews of foreign nationality. The rest consisted of business accounts, frozen accounts, and accounts to which 'Aryan' heirs had laid claim.[44]

On 15 December 1943 it was finally admitted that, after the creation of the *Sammelkonto*, official sequestrations were no longer needed, inasmuch as credits to the *Sammelkonto* were in practice tantamount to confiscation. An exception was still being made for *Feindjuden*, for Jews exempted from wearing yellow stars, and for partners in mixed marriages.

The whole subject was raised at a discussion between Otto Witscher and Guth, the head of the Devisenschutzkommando (DSK). The DSK confiscated goods following punishable offences, one of which was ignoring the instructions to surrender goods and money. The monetary value of all goods confiscated by the DSK was credited to the *Sammelkonto*, while the possessions of Jews who still had a bank account were handed over to the Deutsche Revisions- und Treuhand AG. Property confiscated from Jews exempted from wearing the yellow star and from mixed marriages was handed over to the SD.[45]

Like the DSK, the SD also confiscated property that had 'wrongfully' been kept back. In most cases, these items were no longer handed in to Liro, but to the Asservatenstelle IV B 4 (the depot for confiscated exhibits) of the Commander of the Security Police (BdS) in The Hague.

Payments to Jews from Liro Funds

Fischböck also gave orders to stop all maintenance payments. As a result the Inspectorate Division was wound up for lack of work. Its duties were taken over by the Jewish Council, which obtained the necessary means from Liro funds allocated to the Council by Fischböck.[46]

In 1942, the Inspectorate received maintenance applications to the tune of 7,377,708.68 guilders, but released no more than 5,734,014.78 guilders. The applications for 'other purposes' such as tax demands, mortgage repayments and sundry debts came to 21,531,482.01 guilders, of which 16,689,677.17 guilders were granted, representing an approval rate of 67.5 per cent (total requests 28,909,550.69 guilders; remittances 19,502,361.05 guilders).

The Jewish Council received a total sum of 1,610,523. 26 guilders. In 1942, the greatest number of applications was received in October, for reasons that are unclear. The inspection costs involved were listed as 406,901.55 guilders.[47]

The transfer of duties from the Inspectorate to the Jewish Council took place on 1 January 1943. The *Joodsche Weekblad* of 18 December 1942 carried the following announcement:

> Since the firm of Lippmann, Rosenthal & Co., Sarphatistraat, will cease to make payments to Jews from 1 January next, and since, as from that date, such benefits will be paid by the Jewish Council, it is essential that everybody who has been drawing, or

The Robber Bank in Sarphatistraat

has applied for, benefits in accordance with *Verordnung* 58/1942 in November and December 1942 from the above-mentioned firm, resubmit these applications forthwith to the Jewish Council.

You are requested to remit these applications with the necessary details accompanied by such proof as debit notes, etc., to the offices of the specially constituted 'Committee for Financial Matters' at 10 Vening Meinezkade, Amsterdam-C . . . Requests for the payment of taxes must not be submitted to us.[48]

The settlement of Jewish debts was also proscribed. Liro was 'neither obliged nor authorized to settle Jewish liabilities', the bank informed the electricity company, which had been trying to get Liro to pay a bill. The tax authorities could no longer be paid through Liro either. All the remaining shares and assets of Jews had to be sold as soon as possible. The proceeds were added to the *Sammelkonto*.[49]

Towards the end of 1943, the Jewish Council asked J. M. Goudsmit, an Amsterdam barrister, to join several other respected persons to take charge of the maintenance of needy Jews, from whom the social service department of the municipality had been ordered to withdraw support as from 1 January 1944. The original intention was to pay every Jewish family in need of support, regardless of its size, 10 guilders a week through Liro.

Objections were raised to this proposal, for reasons that are no longer clear, but the result was the foundation of the Jüdische Unterstützungsstelle (Jewish Benefit Agency), with Goudsmit as director. It was run on much the same lines as the Amsterdam social services department. It employed inspectors and a doctor. Every week, the agency drew up lists of money to be paid to indigent Jews and handed them in to Liro. From January 1944 to March 1945, a total of 300,000 guilders was paid out.[50]

Liro's Administrative Problems

Every new measure designed to rob Jews of their possessions involved a flood of special regulations and exceptions, which interfered with the smooth running of the Liro administration.

One acute problem for the robber bank was to decide what to do about the share of the property of Jewish partners in mixed marriages, with or without children. Seyss-Inquart had laid down that the Jewish share of the property of childless mixed marriages must not be handed over to the Jewish partner, but that non-Jewish children from mixed marriages did have a claim to that share, at least if they were not stepchildren, or adopted or fostered. This apparently clear directive produced a flood of questions to Liro by a host of desperate people:

General Questions

A. Should assets be released at the request of those entitled to them or of their authorized representatives, or should they be released on our own authority? A public announcement of the decision is in any case urgently needed.
B. Does the measure apply exclusively to assets deposited with us or also to assets not administered by us, such as land, houses, household utensils, claims, life insurance policies, etc.? If so, how is the measure to be implemented (realization of these assets)?
C. Does the measure also apply to estates?
D. Should the measure also be applied 'logically' to the assets of divorced marriage partners, widowers and widows, inasmuch as they have half-Aryan children?

True, the Reichskommissar had decreed that the Jewish share must not pass to the partner, but did this also apply, the Liro administration wondered, to people married in community of property and to childless couples? For according to the Liro board, what generally happened was that the 'wife is Aryan, and hence is legally entitled to half the property'.

Couples with children caused a different set of problems, because: 'Who is entitled to dispose of or receive property belonging to minors?'

And did assets have to be turned over to children resident in non-hostile foreign countries? These two questions were no more than the beginning of a series of eight, which make it clear that Liro Sarphatistraat was not willing to leave anything to chance:

3. If some of the children live in hostile foreign countries, should the rest of the surrendered assets be divided among the children left behind, or should the number of children living in hostile countries be taken into account during the division? (In the latter case, the share due to the children living in hostile countries would naturally remain with us.)
4. How is the number of children to be determined in every individual case, seeing that care must be taken to ensure that the parent's information on the subject is correct? Children might well remain undisclosed for some reason, for instance in order, if possible, to keep the assets together pending an agreed legitimate distribution at a later stage. In view of the ongoing transportation of Jews, the determination of the number of children is no simple matter.
5. Should provisions be made to prevent parents from disposing of assets transferred to their (especially minor) children?
6. Does the Jewish marriage partner remain subject to the exemption limit laid down in Section 9 of VO 58/42) [i.e., the Second Liro *Verordnung*], so that he or she has to keep remitting contributions of more than 250 guilders, which have then to be handed over to the children?
7. Does the Jewish marriage partner have the right to apply for maintenance and support to the Jewish Council, if he or she has no income, or must he or she rely for support on

his or her children, having transferred his or her assets to them, the children being obliged to provide such support by law?

8. If the decision of the Herr Reichskommissar also applies to estates of which an Aryan parent and half-Jewish children are the beneficiaries, shall the Aryan parent, too, be excluded from the distribution of the assets, all of which shall go to the children?

(This question is particularly important in the case of estates from couples living in community of property, in which the surviving marriage partner is entitled to half of the estate and a child's portion.)

In a few concluding comments, Liro pointed out that in the case of mixed marriages, the Aryan marriage partner living in community of property did not have the duty to surrender his possessions. That meant that the (Jewish) wife became his heir by law.

The robber bank wondered if measures should be taken straightaway to ensure that the estate went, not to the wife but to the half-Aryan children. Finally Liro noted the absence of regulations granting half-Aryans the usufruct of Jewish assets. 'Should such assets be handed over to the beneficiaries with binding limitations or in what form can the usufruct be safeguarded for the future?'[51]

It would be impracticable but also unnecessary to enter in detail into all exceptional cases and special regulations that arose in practice. An example will serve to convey an idea of the confusing and complex Liro world.

The First Liro *Verordnung* banned Jews from having bank and giro accounts in banks other than Liro Sarphatistraat. A maximum amount of 1,000 guilders a month could be freely withdrawn. But doctors, lawyers or accountants had frequently to make payments in connection with their work, not least to non-Jews. They were granted permission to open a separate account with Liro, 'on the understanding that they are obliged to credit any amounts that, after deduction of their professional costs, exceed the permitted monthly maximum of 1,000 guilders, to their current account with us.'

Lawyers and accountants could also obtain permission to open accounts for third parties whose funds they administered, provided that 'the clauses of the above-named *Verordnung* do not apply to these third parties, inasmuch as, if they do, Article 1 . . . of this *Verordnung* comes into effect.'[52]

–7–

The First Liro Decree in Practice

Introduction

VO 148/1941 'concerning the handling of Jewish financial assets' of August 1941 (the First Liro Decree) laid down that 'Jews liable to surrender their assets' were to transfer all their ready money to an account at Liro Sarphatistraat that had been specially opened for the purpose.

If we are to believe the post-war testimony of some leading Liro officials, all employees, including the managerial staff, were deliberately misled:

> This *Verordnung* – or so at least it was put to us at the time and indeed as it was first applied in practice – was simply meant to concentrate Jewish monetary and share transactions, etc., at the Bank, and moreover in such a manner that the customers would, in principle, not be treated any differently than they would be in other banks, the Bank providing its clients with normal banking services, such as the buying and selling of shares, the granting of loans, the extension of credit facilities and the payment of dividends and interest into current and fixed-term deposit accounts.
>
> The sole difference from other banks would be that clients would have to declare the purpose of their cash withdrawals and/or payment orders. They were entitled to draw living expenses of up to 1,000 guilders per month, and in addition were entitled to make payments for other more particular purposes, such as doctor's, dentist's or hospital fees, repairs of all kinds, insurance premiums, school fees, assistance to family members, removals, dowries, etc.

Soon afterwards, the staff was overwhelmed with a flood of work: 'The surrender or transfer of the shares and cash of Jewish clients was mostly effected by local banks in all parts of the Netherlands and produced such pressure at the office that a backlog of several months was quickly created.'[1]

Foreign currency and cheques were treated like cash. In addition to money and cheques, securities deposited with banks, saving banks, postal banks and other financial and credit institutions had all to be transferred to Liro.

Every client was allowed to keep 1,000 guilders and to dispose of it at his discretion. The thousand guilders were considered to be the 'free maximum'. Also exempted from compulsory surrender were Jews whose net assets did not exceed

10,000 guilders and whose taxable income in the previous year (1940–1) had not been more than 3,000 guilders.

These sums could not be set off against each other. Thus if someone had assets amounting to 11,000 guilders and an income of 2,500 guilders, he was nevertheless subject to the *Verordnung*, just like persons whose net assets did not amount to 10,000 guilders but whose earnings came to 3,500 guilders.

In themselves, the various provisions seemed fairly clear. However the taxable income was not invariably the same as that stated on the tax demand for 1940–1, because the following items had to be added:

a. deductions from the gross income for losses during previous years;
b. amounts deducted from the gross income due to personal obligations, such as interest on debts not directly linked to parts of the income; premiums on life insurance policies; maintenance allowances.[2]

In other words, if a person had an income of 1,000 guilders, arrived at after deduction of, say, 1,500 guilders for losses and 1,000 guilders for maintenance, his income was put at 3,500 guilders. Hence he had exceeded the limit of 3,000 guilders per year in taxable income, and so fell under VO 148/1941.

The Surrender of Assets

The transfer of money and goods to Liro did not always go smoothly. Banks were obliged to send their clients a form on which the clients had to declare whether or not they were Jews, but not all the forms were filled in and returned. The director of the National Giro Bank repeatedly informed Liro that some account holders refused to supply the required information. What was to be done in such cases?

Liro's reply was that all such accounts must be treated as Jewish accounts and hence transferred to Sarphatistraat. Only if the non-Jewish identity of the account holder was absolutely certain could an exception be made. The reply stated expressly that this guideline also applied to funds in other banks and financial institutions.[3] Dutch notaries were informed by Liro in writing that all cash, credits and securities bequeathed under Jewish wills proved after 8 August 1941 had to be surrendered.[4]

Not all institutions seemed prepared to sanction the transfer or registration of Jewish property without demur. In March 1943 – by which time the Second Liro Decree was in force – the Bedrijfsgroep Handelsbanken (Commercial Banking Confederation) and the Bedrijfsgroep Effectenhandel (Securities Trading Confederation) sent out a circular at the prompting of Liro to the Hoofdgroep Banken (Main Banking Confederation) complaining that all Jewish assets had not yet been

The First Liro Decree in Practice

registered with Liro Sarphatistraat. The circular emphasized that breach or circumvention of the Liro Decrees, even if due to 'negligence', would be severely punished. Hence it was in the institutions' own best interest to implement the two Decrees with due care and attention.[5]

All Jews liable to surrender their property were thus forced to open accounts with Liro, but had no control over these accounts. True, they could, albeit with a mountain of paperwork, put in an application for control over part of their property, but generally the amounts they received were far below what was requested. Liro charged a 'commission' of 1 per cent for every transaction of less than a thousand guilders, and of 1½ per cent for larger amounts. Moreover, the 'bank' charged the commission not on the amount released but on the amount applied for.

In view of the maximum withdrawals allowed, these measures were obviously confined to the more prosperous clients. The impecunious masses could only dream of such sums.

During the first six weeks, Liro received the following sums and credits from various banks:

In the week from 11–16 August 1941	Hfl. 398,681.32
In the week from 18–23 August 1941	Hfl. 1,991,397.82
In the week from 25–30 August 1941	Hfl. 3,743,363.60
In the week from 1–6 September 1941	Hfl. 3,438,783.46
In the week from 8–13 September 1941	Hfl. 1,616,871.58
In the week from 15–20 September 1941	Hfl. 1,618,604.61
In the week from 22–30 September 1941	Hfl. 2,352,958.17

Within seven weeks, Seyss-Inquart thus gained control of more than 15 million guilders in cash and credits from private Jewish sources, quite apart from shares and bonds. On 30 September 1941, the number of compulsorily opened Liro accounts stood at 3,963.[6]

In practice, Jews had as good as lost all say over their Liro accounts, although in theory they continued to have some control over them. By the Second Liro Decree, that control was even more drastically cut, but even before then, in March 1942, the Reichskommissariat issued a notice abolishing the exempt limit of 10,000 guilders. Banks were sent instructions to transfer all Jewish credit balances and securities to Liro Sarphatistraat. Giro accounts had to be closed.[7]

All in all, Dutch Jews transferred between 325 and 455 million guilders in cash, cheques, bank and Giro deposits to the robber bank. Some of the shares were not actually surrendered to Liro but merely registered with them, the share certificates remaining in the banks in which they had been deposited originally.[8]

The Price of the Surrendered Shares

It is impossible to determine the precise value of the stolen securities. To begin with the prices fluctuated from day to day, just as in peacetime, and secondly the surrender to Liro did not occur on a particular date but took more than a full year to accomplish. Even after that year, shares were still being surrendered to Liro, be it on a modest scale.

As an example of major share fluctuations we might look at Koninklijke Olie (Shell Oil), the prices of which fluctuated in 1941 between 201 and 350 points and in 1942 between 177 and 402 points. Expressed in guilders, a share in Koninklijke Olie was quoted at 1,770 guilders (the 1942 low), and at 4,020 guilders during the high that same year. The value was obviously dependent on the surrender of shares to Liro on a particular day. A significantly large number of shares was handed over during the first months of 1942, at a time when East India shares plummeted due to the war in that part of the world. An analysis of the prices of Koninklijke Olie (KO) and Amsterdam Rubber (AR) shows clearly to what large extent prices were influenced by the course of the war (see Table 7.1).

What was true of East Indian securities was also true of shares in trading companies, industries, banks, shippers and not least American shares. To determine the value of securities handed in by Jews, one would have to determine what particular shares each individual handed in at the price they fetched on the day of their surrender. In practice, that is an impossible task. However, a rough estimate of the value of the shares during the surrender period at the beginning of 1942 put the figure at between 250 and 300 million guilders. In the middle of 1942 the total was estimated at 5,000 million guilders.[9] It seems reasonable to put the value of the surrendered securities at between 300 million and 400 million guilders. All in all, some 500,000 shares[10] were surrendered by 12,815 persons.[11] The number of Jews forced to hand in their assets and the number of surrendered items do not, of course, tell us anything about the value of the items, but they do convey a picture of the magnitude of the looting.

Table 7.1 Prices of Koninklijke Olie (KO) and Amsterdam Rubber (AR)

	Maximum price, 1941	6/12/41	30/12/41	17/2/42	5/3/42
KO	340	327.5	215.5	187	108
AR	350	343.5	241.5	250.5	189

The First Liro Decree in Practice

The Administrative Handling of the Shares

In addition to private persons, banks, lawyers and accountants were also obliged to hand the securities of their Jewish clients over to Liro. This could be done over the counter in Sarphatistraat, where numbered vouchers were issued by way of receipts. The number was also recorded on every parcel of shares and marked with an L (*loket*, or counter) to show that the parcel had been handed in over the Liro counter. Parcels of shares that arrived by post were stamped with a P, indicating that they came by post from the provinces. Originally, a chit listing the contents of parcels was issued soon after the surrender of the shares upon production of the numbered voucher. People sending securities from the provinces had the receipt posted to them. However, after only a few weeks, the work began to falter. The flow of securities became so overwhelming that the board decided to stop issuing receipts. These would thenceforth be issued exclusively to banks, and then only after repeated requests. At first, a detailed list in triplicate had to accompany every parcel of shares. This measure was intended to simplify the confirmation of the receipt of securities. However, checking the certificates against the accompanying list took up so much time that the work ground to a halt within a few weeks: parcels, which had arrived at the rate of a few hundred a day at first, now poured in at the rate of more than a thousand a day. Another factor contributing to the growing chaos was the lack of trained staff.[12]

On 30 September 1941, more than a month after VO 148/41 was issued, the value of the pilfered shares was put at over 20 million guilders; one month later, on 31 October 1941, the figure had risen to close on 38 million guilders.[13]

Chaos was complete when all securities (those processed and those not yet processed) were transferred to two banks in Berlin. Shares went to Merck, Finck & Co.; bonds, premium loans, and so on to Delbrück, Schickler & Co.

The reason for the sudden transfer was probably the fear of an imminent invasion of the European continent from England – the direct impetus is said to have been the British raid on Dieppe.[14] The transfer of equities to Berlin made it necessary to open a Liro section in the two banks to which they were sent so as to catch up with the administrative work. The Liro sections in Berlin were manned exclusively by NSB staff from Sarphatistraat. As far as possible, all the securities were listed by type. The result, although still inadequate, was intended to form the basis of a new system meant to replace the one that was hopelessly bogged down in Amsterdam. On the basis of the lists compiled in Berlin, a new administration was set up in Amsterdam for dealing with the funds deposited in the two Berlin banks. What few securities had been left behind in Amsterdam were also registered on lists based on the Berlin model.

After the end of 1943, when the Allied air raids on Berlin grew more intense, most of the securities were gradually brought back to Amsterdam, where the

Sammelkonto had been introduced on 1 January. At the beginning of 1944, the Liro depots in the German capital were wound up.

The chaos caused by the processing of securities had a demonstrably negative effect on the value of the equities surrendered to Liro, so much so that the lawful owners were repaid far less than their due after the war. In particular, poor bookkeeping was responsible for the failure to collect thousands and even millions of guilders' worth of interest accruing from the securities. Even the redemption of dividend coupons proved almost impossible in these circumstances.[15]

Liro Sarphatistraat as Accredited Stockbroker

The separation of Liro into two distinct 'branches' appeared to be a great advantage when it came to the sale of equities: Lippmann, Rosenthal & Co., Nieuwe Spiegelstraat, was a member of the Vereeniging voor de Effectenhandel (VvdE, or Stock Exchange Union), and so enabled its sham daughter to gain entry into the Stock Exchange in Damrak, Amsterdam. By that ploy, the Germans were skilfully able to disguise the sale of stolen equities through the Stock Exchange.[16] The board of the VvdE used the argument that Liro was a normal stockbroker to justify the sale of securities deposited with Liro.

> In the register of companies . . . the Sarpahatistraat office appeared as part of Lippmann, Rosenthal & Co. with headquarters in Nieuwe Spiegelstraat. Only after the Liberation was Lippmann II declared to be an independent juridical body by the Beheersinstituut [the Netherlands state administration of confiscated goods], thus stressing the fact that Lippmann II had not been an independent body during the occupation.[17]

This was a purely formal definition; in practice Liro Sarphatistraat had always been independent of the head office in Nieuwe Spiegelstraat.

At first Dr Hans Fischböck, the General-Kommissar for Finance and Economic Affairs, had planned to have the securities sold in Berlin by German banks, but Anton Bühler, the German Beauftragte in the Netherlands Bank, was opposed to the idea; in his view it was fairer to keep the proceeds in the Netherlands. Bühler's rather equivocal attitude has been mentioned before. Seyss-Inquart did not really care one way or another and so raised few objections to Bühler's argument. To the Reichskommissar it did not really matter because the proceeds would in any case end up in the coffers of the VVRA, a body firmly under his control.[18]

Bühler discussed the sale of the securities on the Amsterdam Stock Exchange with Carel F. Overhoff, chairman of the VvdE. He argued that the sale through the Amsterdam Exchange was the only way of keeping securities of Jewish provenance in the Netherlands. Otherwise the securities would all be sold across the border, in Berlin. Overhoff thereupon consulted, amongst others, the board of the

VvdE and L. J. A. Trip, the former president of the Netherlands Bank. As a result, the VvdE decided that Liro Sarphatistraat must not be denied access to the Stock Exchange, the less so as the old and reputable bank of Lippmann, Rosenthal & Co., Nieuwe Spiegelstraat, was a normal and respected member of the Exchange.[19]

To provide a legal basis for this interpretation, the VvdE sought the advice of the lawyer M. van Regteren Altena, who allegedly concurred that Liro must be admitted to the Stock Exchange.[20] That at least was how the chairman, C. F. Overhoff, put it after the war, claiming that the board of the VvdE had had no way of preventing the sale of the stolen Liro securities on the Amsterdam Stock Exchange.

Where Overhoff obtained this particular explanation is not clear; it was certainly not based on the opinion of Van Regteren Altema, who had declared the precise opposite when giving his opinion. Referring to the expulsion of Jews from the Stock Exchange as from 1 November 1941, he argued that Jewish stockbrokers had lost their trading rights precisely *because* they had been barred from the floor. The partners in the old Liro Bank in Nieuwe Spiegelstraat, Robert May, Edgar Fuld and H. P. Rahusen, had been members in their own right, that is, not in the name of the bank, so that their membership could not pass to A. Flesche, the *Verwalter*. In other words, the partners had been members of the Stock Exchange, and *not* the firm of Lippmann, Rosenthal & Co. The jurist's conclusion was that Liro Sarphatistraat had no right to be in the Stock Exchange, but for one reason or another that opinion was not welcome to the board of the VvdE. In any case, the board argued that the Jewish brokers, and hence also the Liro partners, had lost no more than *part* of their power to act. True, they had been expelled from the floor of the Stock Exchange, but they continued to be members. According to the statutes of the VvdE, only bankruptcy or receivership entailed a total loss of trading rights, and neither was involved here.[21]

Liro Securities and Normal Stock Exchange Transactions

The VvdE also came up against the question of whether or not the surrender and sale of securities from Jewish sources could be reconciled with the WOL convention. There was clearly a feeling that everything was not as it should be. On this matter, too, the VvdE took legal advice, but

> all authorities on the subject during the years of the occupation, could see – possibly after consulting with one another – no conflict between the German orders to surrender and sell Jewish shares and the War on Land Convention. In view of the ruling by the Hoge Raad [the Supreme Court of the Netherlands] of 12 January 1942, it may be taken that that no legal objection could be made to the trading in so-called Jewish equities. Far from considering the latter 'stolen' or 'embezzled', the securities trading division of the VvdE maintained that they could be traded in the normal way.

The board of the VvdE never raised any objections in public to the trade in equities from Liro, so that its members, whose interest the VvdE was thought to defend, could assume that they 'could safely trade in the above-mentioned securities'. So, at least went the argument of stockjobbers trading in Liro securities. Had this not been the case, the VvdE would surely have 'warned its members not to trade in them'.[22]

Overhoff's interpretation of the Supreme Court ruling was remarkable. He gave its contents a twist to shore up his own view, precisely as he had done with the opinion of Van Regteren Altena. In fact, the Supreme Court had argued that though the legality of the German *Verordnungen* could not be denied in Dutch law, Dutch judges could neither pronounce on the inner merits or the fitness of a law nor judge it in terms of 'a treaty such as that of which the War on Land Convention of 1907 is a part, or in terms of such decrees as the *Führererlass* of 18 May 1940 on government authority in the Netherlands . . .'.[23]

The Supreme Court approval of the right to trade in Jewish equities, which Overhoff read into the opinion, was thus never given. The Supreme Court merely recognized the right of the occupying power to pass laws, but could not and would not judge the probity of these laws because that was not its proper task. For the rest, Article 46 of the WOL convention, on which Overhoff based his defence, states explicitly that private property cannot be confiscated, which is precisely what had happened to the Jewish securities.

The board of the VvdE, as represented by Overhoff, thus based its case on the legality of his decision to allow trading in Liro equities. The VvdE ignored the explicit warnings by the London government in exile against trading in stolen property. Conspicuously absent, too, is any reference to Article A 6 of the London emergency decree, which proscribed all dealings with the enemy without prior consent. The repeated admonitions over Radio Oranje (including the broadcast of 3 June 1942 mentioned earlier), warning, inter alia, against the purchase of stolen Jewish securities, were not mentioned either. That Liro Sarphatisaat was a German, and in that sense an enemy, creation, was something everybody must have known. And finally, Anton Bühler, despite the flexibility he displayed, was nevertheless a representative of the occupying power, and personally negotiated the sale of Liro stock with Overhoff.

A frequent excuse for trading in confiscated Jewish stock was that the securities were at least kept in the Netherlands, so that they could be more easily restored to their legitimate owners after the war. The broadcast of 3 June 1942 warned explicitly against this argument as well: 'The occupier is cunning. He has NSB members say: "Dutchmen, feel free to buy Jewish property, since by so doing you stop it from falling into German hands."'[24]

Five years after the war, on 20 July 1950, during a discussion by the board of the VvdE about 'several matters concerning the trade in securities during the occupation', the question of whether or not the trade in stolen Jewish securities must be considered in conflict with the War on Land Convention was raised once again. The answer was an unequivocal 'no'.[25]

Does that mean that leading members of the VvdE never raised objections to the sale of confiscated securities coming from Liro or from 'similar institutions' through the Amsterdam Stock Exchange? According to a 'strictly confidential' circular to members of the VvdE that matter was never discussed.[26]

It looks very much as if many members of the VvdE shared the view of the board that securities from Liro could be traded normally. The crucial question was whether the stock had been obtained in 'regular Stock Exchange transactions'. In other words, had the buyers of Liro securities acquired them in good faith? According to the VvdE they had done just that. Liro was a normal member of the Stock Exchange, and trading with a fellow Stock Exchange member could not be refused in accordance with the rules.

It is an open question whether the reason why Overhoff, the chairman of the VvdE, succumbed to the blandishments of the occupying power may be linked to his embezzlements in the stockbroking firm of Kerkhoven & Co. in Herengracht, Amsterdam, where he had worked since 1913. In 1918 he became a partner and, when the company went bankrupt in 1948, it emerged that Overhoff had embezzled the funds of clients. He was sent to prison and forced in October 1948 to resign as chairman of the VvdE. For at least ten years, Overhoff had made unauthorized and practically untrammelled use of the money his clients had entrusted to his stockbroking firm. As a result, a deficit of about three quarters of a million guilders had been accumulated.

It is unlikely that the Germans were aware of Overhoff's professional misconduct and used that knowledge to put him under pressure. But unintentionally the pressure exerted by the occupying power might well have had the same effect: his position as chairman of the VvdE provided, thanks to the status it reflected, a measure of protection against the exposure of his malpractices. But if he had been dismissed from the VvdE and had become wholly dependent on Kerkhoven & Co., which was teetering on the brink, then bankruptcy was a very real threat. After the war, a judicial committee looked into the question of why Overhoff had succumbed to the pressure of the occupying power and came to the following conclusion:

> The collapse of Kerkhoven & Co. has unfortunately clarified much that seemed puzzling at first. The Committee cannot avoid the conclusion that, had Overhoff refused to accommodate them, the Germans would have forced him to resign as chairman and perhaps to liquidate his company. That would have brought to light certain facts that might have proved fatal to him and to his company. But how would the Stock Exchange as such, which was known as a centre of anti-German propaganda, have appeared in the eyes of the Germans and the NSB, if their chairman had been unmasked as a bankrupt with a sizeable deficit?[27]

In order to sell the confiscated securities, the VvdE, through its chairman, sheltered behind the Stock Exchange regulations. This does not mean that all stockbrokers dealt in Liro securities, but what is certain is that the board of the VvdE did little if anything to oppose the German plans to realize Jewish assets through the Amsterdam Stock Exchange. In any case, the board of the VvdE agreed with Bühler's plan to sell the securities in Amsterdam rather than in Berlin. There is no doubt that the VvdE was fully aware of the coercive nature of the surrender of the securities, which is also reflected in the legal advice they took in connection with possible breaches of the War on Land Convention. Quite clearly, the VvdE was anxious to work under a legal cover.

To a certain extent, Overhoff was right when he said of Liro's clientele: 'They opened accounts, sanctioned the cashing of coupons and dividends and the repayment of debts, and allowed exchanges and reinvestments.'[28] However, that 'freedom' did not last very long and did not amount to very much. The proceeds of the sales could only be converted into Dutch government bonds, industrial bonds and mortgage bonds; the purchase of other securities was forbidden, while the purchase of bonds was soon restricted to the acquisition of Dutch government bonds. These limited 'freedoms' were small consolation indeed for the forced sale of securities.[29]

We may take it that the chairman of the Stock Exchange knew about these developments, and that he was aware of the true plans of the occupying power for dealing with the confiscated securities. Compulsory Aryanization was in full swing at the time and that drama could hardly have escaped any stockbroker.

Overhoff's further arguments smack of an apology, and are of a naiveté one would have thought impossible in the chairman of the VvdE. It looks very much as if he was not so much incompetent as trying to defend the indefensible:

> In the course of time, obviously because the enemy believed that Jewish property in the Netherlands was the property of the Great German Reich, this approach *seems* to have been abandoned gradually, shares in large quantities being sold en masse on behalf of the companies concerned without further ado.[30]

There is no doubt that, in the given circumstances, the VvdE had few formal means of keeping Liro Sarphatistraat off the Stock Exchange floor, just as there is no doubt that it made no attempt to do so. Members were at least given no official warnings.

According to the VvdE, shares offered by Liro were traded in keeping with 'regular Stock Exchange practice', that is, 'in good faith'. There was therefore nothing wrong with such transactions. The VvdE continued to defend this viewpoint doggedly, until the judge brusquely put an end to this fiction in May 1952 during a rehabilitation trial. We shall return to this subject in more detail when we examine the post-war rehabilitation process.

Even after the war, Overhoff, for his part, stuck obstinately to his version of the events, namely that Liro shares were traded in keeping with normal Stock Exchange practice and in good faith.[31]

Sales through the Stock Exchange

In January 1941, Liro started to sell securities on the Stock Exchange floor, Seyss-Inquart having issued instructions to that effect on 17 November 1941. Some 100,000 buyers are estimated to have bought securities offered by Liro for between 110 and 145 million guilders.[32] All in all it is estimated that Jewish securities worth 250 million guilders were sold. That means that another 100 million guilders' or so worth of stolen equities changed hands outside the Stock Exchange.[33] In the beginning the shares were still accompanied by a pro forma declaration that the (Jewish) owner had freely agreed to the sale, but this was soon dropped.[34] The change in attitude was also reflected in the statements Liro sent to its account holders. While originally the statement specified that the shares had been sold 'on your instructions', this was changed at the beginning of March 1942 (that is, a few months after Liro had begun to make serious efforts to realize Jewish securities), when the words 'on your instructions' on the statements to the account holders were crossed out and replaced with 'sold on your behalf in the Stock Exchange'.[35] Liro clients were forbidden to purchase securities, which was the sole prerogative of Liro itself.[36]

The VvdE did admittedly ask Bühler formally to specify on the basis of what ruling Jewish equities could be sold without instructions from their owner. The answer was short: *suprema lex*. But Bühler himself was not satisfied with that. He asked Seyss-Inquart on what legal grounds the liquidation of Jewish assets deposited with Liro was based. The answer was vague: the liquidation was part of normal administrative activity. In addition, Seyss-Inquart based himself on the declaration by Reichsminister L. von Schwerin Krosigk to the effect that all Jewish assets were the property of the Third Reich.[37]

The sale Seyss-Inquart ordered in November 1941 started slowly; it took an extra prod from Fischböck before Liro began offering the shares on the Stock Exchange floor in the middle of February. It quickly became clear that this was an unpropitious moment, because the Japanese invasion of the Dutch East Indies had led to a stock-market slump.[38] The enforced sale of Liro securities in what was already a depressed Stock Exchange climate drove the market down even further. At the beginning of March it began to look as if Liro's ill-considered action had caused the situation to get completely out of hand. For a number of days, the robber bank offloaded large numbers of shares on the Exchange and tried to get rid of them at any price. Liro's rash policy ushered in what has become known as the 'dumping days'. Friday, 6 March 1942 turned out to be the chief 'dumping day' with scenes reminiscent of the Wild West.[39]

The daily press covered these events at great length. Thus *De Telegraaf* reported that on the Friday in question 'excited and unprecedented conditions' had occurred at 3.00 p.m. during the sale of Koninklijke Olies shares. The paper continued:

> The situation grew so out of hand that two large corners were formed in which quite distinct prices were being quoted. In one corner, which literally overran the Philips corner, the price of the above-mentioned special and one-sided offer remained at 184–185, but in the other corner 186 was readily being paid. As the closing gong was about to be struck, the excitement came to a head. Olies shares dominated the entire exchange and trading was disrupted . . . Naturally the Olies transactions caused heated discussions and long after the end of business, all talk was of the way the leading stocks had been traded that day.

The *Amsterdamsch Effectenblad* spoke of large blocks of shares being offered by a 'certain party'. But however large the offer, it vanished, so to speak, into a bottomless pit, in particular the sales of Koninklijke Olie, Amsterdam Rubber, H.V.A. and Unilever shares. The paper mentioned 'the' vendor and 'the big vendor' without referring to Liro by name.

J. H. Wijnand, the financial editor of *De Telegraaf*, testified after the war that Jewish shares were not so much sold as dumped at the Stock Exchange, and that he noticed that it was chiefly NSB members who had the shares bought by front men.[40] It was no secret either that Liro was behind the sales, since it was M. G. Hali, Liro's stockbroker, who was offering the shares in large quantities. In Stock Exchange circles, Friday, 6 March, 'dumping day', became generally referred to as 'Hali-day'.[41]

According to Otto Rebholz, the vendors of Liro shares had a disruptive effect on Stock Exchange transactions in early spring, because they acted quite unprofessionally. Overhoff shared this opinion, and discussed the matter with Bühler. He also asked for and obtained the support of Rebholz: 'In particular, the sale of leading Dutch securities such as Kon.Olie and H.V.A. depressed prices throughout the exchange by about $1/3$. There were exceptionally large losses all along the line.'

The approach to Bühler proved successful almost immediately: on Fischböck's orders a stop was put to the sale of Liro shares until further notice. At the same time an investigation was launched, as a result of which Bühler was put in charge of the sale of Jewish securities. Bühler for his part appealed to Rebholz to guide the sale of Liro securities into the right channels. Because of the 'public importance' of the matter, Rebholz felt that he could not refuse[42] – a declaration we must take with a pinch of salt. After the war, he declared repeatedly that he felt obliged to lend his cooperation, because that was the only way of keeping the Jewish securities in the

The First Liro Decree in Practice

Netherlands. The same argument, incidentally, was also used by Overhoff (and many others) and is not, in fact, lacking in a certain logic. It proved very much easier to trace securities that had been kept within the Dutch borders than any that might have been scattered all over Europe (or even all over the world). However, the alacrity with which members of the Amsterdam Stock Exchange acquired Liro shares suggests that their motive was profit rather than the wish to have the shares handed back to their rightful owners.

Although 1942 was a turbulent year for the exchange, the following year was calm, at least after 2 March 1943. That day, Rost van Tonningen's intervention led to the end of 'free trade' in the Amsterdam Stock Exchange, where a price freeze was introduced. The cause was the unchecked rise in the price of shares, which had become a constant source of anxiety as early as 1942. Thanks to the increase in liquid assets, the dwindling of supplies due to the continuing war, and the unstoppable black market, the demand for shares had begun to exceed the supply.

The black market proved a scourge for the Stock Exchange. Thus the black-market price for Koninklijke Olie was 1,200 for a time, as against the official price of 361, with the result that the much-sought after Koninklijke shares (and other popular equities as well) became increasingly hard to acquire. On 3 March, Overhoff was given instructions to make sure that share prices did not exceed those quoted on 2 March 1943 until further notice. However, that instruction could not prevent the demand from remaining high, or the supply of most shares at the frozen price remaining limited.[43]

Even so, some shares were sold *below* the frozen price, namely shares offered by Liro. Rebholz had divided his price lists into two columns: frozen price and selling price. With the help of these lists he was able to show potential clients 'that the equities on offer were not so-called Aryan shares, which in most cases were unobtainable at the frozen price, but Jewish shares.'

When the sales price was *below* the frozen price, the shares in question were generally Jewish securities.[44] Jewish shares were cheaper because of the risk that they might have to be returned to their original owners, should Hitler lose the war.

Between December 1942 and the end of 1944, Rebholz sold leading Dutch shares to the tune of about 14 million guilders. According to him, large blocks of shares of Liro origin were offered at attractive prices up to May 1942, and most stockbroking firms, looking for bargains, jumped at the opportunity.[45]

American Shares

When the Amsterdam Stock Exchange began to trade in American shares, there was one major drawback, namely that these shares were nominative shares – that is, they bore the name of the registered owner, and not bearer shares, like most

Dutch issues. That meant that every sale involved a name transfer in the United States. This was clearly impracticable, and in order to resolve the problem administrative offices for American securities were opened in Amsterdam. They issued bearer-share certificates, so that the securities could easily be traded in the Stock Exchange. The administrative offices bought original shares in the United States in their own name and issued certificates that could be traded on the Stock Exchange as normal bearer shares.

The certificates had to be accompanied by a 'chain declaration' to the effect that the shares had been owned continuously by Dutch citizens since May 1940. This measure was intended to overcome resistance abroad to the purchase of what might be confiscated shares, and it must be seen as an attempt to calm the conscience of buyers. After all, if they had been in Dutch ownership since the specified date, these shares could not have been stolen by the Germans. According to the Allied Declaration of 5 January 1943, no goods from the occupied territories could be traded without a *bona fide* declaration, unless the purchasers were prepared to run the risk of having the goods restored to the legitimate owner after the war. Jews were forced to sign a chain declaration, but once the deportations to the East had started, such declarations proved increasingly difficult to obtain, and Liro then solved the problem by issuing declarations of its own.[46]

The Allied Declaration did indeed seem to succeed in raising fears because the zest in neutral countries for buying shares from German-occupied territories declined as the Allied chances of victory grew.[47]

The sale of certificates accompanying American shares (called *Amerikaantjes* or 'Little Americans') constitutes a separate chapter in the history of share trading. They could not be sold abroad – which they certainly would have been in view of the German shortage of foreign currency – because the debtors were Dutch institutions. The prices of 'Little Americans' rose throughout the occupation, mainly reflecting the decline of the guilder against the US dollar. The 'Little Americans' owed their popularity to their possible conversion after the war into American stock, which naturally meant a considerable profit. Trading in 'Little Americans' was admittedly allowed during most of the occupation, but only, because of their special (foreign) nature, exclusively under licence from the foreign currency institute, which considered them to be foreign shares. Licences were usually issued separately for each transaction, but Liro and Otto Rebholz were alone in having a general licence issued to them.

At first, for the five months from June to 12 November, the sale of certificates was the prerogative of a consortium consisting of Rebholz's Bankierskantoor, Kol & Co., Van Essen and the Bank voor West Europeeschen Handel (BWEH). Each member of this 'Konto Quarto'[48] was responsible for a quarter of the funds, listed in alphabetical order. According to Otto Rebholz, the chairman of the consortium, the sale quickly degenerated into fierce competition. In addition, he suspected that many shares ended up on the black market. Bühler, too, observed that competition had led to a serious fall in prices.

Apparently Rebholz then felt obliged to put an end to this practice. With Bühler's consent, his own firm assumed the sole selling rights. The Konto Quarto had jointly sold *Amerikaantjes* to the tune of about 1,500,000 guilders. During the next period, from December 1942 to the end of 1944, Rebholz alone sold stock worth 20,500,000 million guilders.[49] Rebholz and Liro, as we have seen above, enjoyed a special position in the sale of *Amerikaantjes* because they held the rarely granted general licence (the 'A-licence'), which meant that they did not have to apply to the foreign currency institute for every new transaction. Article 9 of the Foreign Currency Decree passed in 1941 laid down that the purchaser must obtain the foreign currency licence number of the vendor *before* delivery. Thanks to a whispering campaign, the licence numbers issued to Liro and Rebholz were soon known all over the Stock Exchange.

Some dealers showed considerable restraint when it came to the purchase of *Amerikaantjes*, despite the great demand. But quite apart from the fact that licence numbers issued to Liro and Otto Rebholz were common knowledge in the Exchange, there was yet another way of discovering whether the stock came from a contaminated source: individual stockbrokers could sell only limited amounts of *Amerikaantjes*, while those stemming from Rebholz and Liro were being offered in large quantities. Small parcels thus came as a rule from a non-suspect source, big ones from a German robber agency.[50] Because a general licence was so seldom issued, it could not have been too difficult to spot the licence holders.[51]

G. M. Muller, a jurist in the Foreign Currency Institute, was to testify after the war that 'reliable officials of the Foreign Currency Institute regularly informed the Stock Exchange by means of a whispering campaign of the numbers of these extorted foreign-currency licences, something widely known at the time in the Exchange.'[52]

Rebholz denied the existence of a whispering campaign, adding that, had it existed, then many firms, 'including that of the former chairman, many board members [of the VvdE] and leading banks . . . never heard anything about it, or paid any attention to it.'[53]

Anyone looking at the list of members of the VvdE who bought *Amerikaantjes* from Rebholz's banking institute, can do little but confirm that many firms were either deaf to the whispering campaign or else pretended to be. The list contains 136 of the 375 or so members of the Amsterdam Stock Exchange and twenty-nine 'external members' with registered offices outside the city.[54] These figures, taken from the administration of Rebholz's Bankierskantoor, do not include the name of firms that bought *Amerikaantjes* through jobbers; it is impossible to tell by how much the number of names was increased as a result. Kerkhoven & Co., Overhoff's firm, appears on the list as well, as do the names of such then renowned banking houses as the Amsterdamsche Bank N. V. ('and various branches'), the Incasso Bank N. V., the N. V. Nederlandsche Middenstandsbank, the Rotterdamsche Bank N. V., the N. V. Nederlandsche Handel-Maatschappij ('and various branches') and the Twentsche Bank N. V. Most of them are still in existence, although they have been merged into larger conglomerates over the years.[55]

If we compare this list with a list of 'black members', that is, members expelled after the war because of membership of the NSB, we find that no more than two of these NSB members bought securities from Rebholz. In addition, three NSB members are mentioned who were originally suspected of Nazi sympathies – and who did buy tainted *Amerikaantjes* from Rebholz – but who were not expelled in the end.[56] Not only the licence numbers, but also the price lists published by Rebholz showed clearly that the *Amerikaantjes* on offer were 'tainted' because the prices were well below the frozen level.

Rebholz's Discount

Rebholz tried to overcome the initial reluctance of brokers to the purchase of *Amerikaantjes* by offering them a discount. He did his best to offset the greater risk attaching to *Amerikaantjes* – it was difficult after the war to plead ignorance about their origin – with the promise of greater profits. This bait was intended to win over potential buyers, and it succeeded. Not even Overhoff, the chairman of the Stock Exchange board, proved immune to this temptation, any more than the 135 Stock Exchange members who bought *Amerikaantjes*.[57]

As late as 11 May 1943, Overhoff protested in an internal circular against these 'investment commissions' and demanded that a stop be put to them. 'It was my intention to end to the sale of Jewish shares with this circular,' he declared during interrogation after the war. In the circular he had not, of course, been able to say such a thing frankly, but the import was clear to all members of the Stock Exchange. After consultation with L. Proos Hoogendijk and J. C. van Essen, the two vice-chairmen of the VvdE, Overhoff declared:

> I consider this practice undesirable and unnecessary when no special services are involved, but class it as debatable and questionable when – as in the case in point – such rewards are paid at a level that bears no relationship to the service rendered . . . I consider the granting and enjoyment of such extra rewards for a simple transaction to be in general conflict with what is fitting for a respectable businessman and most certainly not in keeping with the views and customs members of our Society uphold and must be expected to uphold.

That the brave stand of the chairman changed very quickly may be gathered from his circular of 27 May 1943, in which he wrote that he had come to approve of the commissions, provided they were 'normal' and 'modest'.[58] Following the circular of 11 May, Overhoff had a discussion with Rebholz and the latter explained to him that he considered the sale of *Amerikaantjes* in the Stock Exchange in the interests of the Netherlands. Foreign shares in Dutch possession were under threat with the increasing interest in them shown by the Germans, Reichsmarks proving to be of little use to them, even in France or Belgium. In the circumstances, Rebholz thought it important to keep the *Amerikaantjes* in the Netherlands. The proceeds went to Seyss-Inquart, it was true, but that was of secondary importance right then. The shares could still, at any rate, be traced back to their original owners. The banker estimated the number of American shares at 100,000, with a total value of 35 to 40 million guilders.[59] *Amerikaantjes* constituted a highly desirable prey for foreign-currency starved Germany and would not have been difficult to sell in South America or in neutral European markets, be it at cut prices. In addition there was a flourishing black market. Because of their dubious origin, the shares would have to be sold at far below the market price. The same considerations held for the Dutch international securities Liro sold on the Stock Exchange.[60]

However the real reason for Overhoff's about-turn was not his discussion with Otto Rebholz but a reprimand from Bühler, as a result of which he found it imperative to 'tone down the first circular.'[61] 'Toning down' was an obvious euphemism; Overhoff not only revoked his circular but even profited from the change, pocketing a commission of 637.50 guilders from Rebholz between 1 December 1943 and 1 March 1944. That it was quite possible to issue warnings on the Stock Exchange floor may be gathered from Overhoff's defence: he had warned his clients that the shares were of Jewish origin, but when a client 'gave express orders for such purchases' he did nothing to stop him. When Overhoff was confronted with the list of VvdE members who had taken a commission, he admitted that these members came from ordinary Amsterdam stockbroking firms with few exceptions, not from so-called NSB offices. But 'perhaps' these orders too had been 'executed at the express wish of clients'.[62] The commission over which the members caved in came to an average of about 1 per cent.[63] According to Rebholz, clients who had demanded shares of non-Jewish origin were in many cases swindled by being fobbed off with shares at inflated prices, when in fact they came from Liro.[64]

How Much did Members of the Stock Exchange Know?

It is unclear how stockbrokers could tell that they were buying tainted shares. They could not, of course, tell from the shares themselves whether they came from Liro or from *bona fide* sources. After all, people bought shares in a company and not specially marked certificates issued by a particular trader.

At the time, jobbers (*hoeklieden*, or cornermen) played an important role in the Amsterdam Stock Exchange. The trade in the shares of each officially quoted company was confined to a particular position, the so-called *hoek* (corner) of the floor, allocated by the Stock Exchange board. Members specializing in a particular stock assembled in their particular corner and took orders from fellow members, that is, jobbers trading in that particular stock. Leading shares were traded in an 'open corner', less marketable stocks in a 'closed corner'. When the exchange was open, jobbers congregated in their particular 'corner' and helped to set the official price of the stock. Stockbrokers placed their clients' orders with these jobbers, who acted predominantly on the instructions of fellow Stock Exchange members, although some also traded on their own account, mainly in order to maintain regular price levels. The jobber's commission was fixed by the exchange rules. Jobbers held the key to the question of whether or not exchange members knew (or could have known) if tainted shares were being traded.

They had to be careful what they bought; if they went straight to Liro, the chances were that they were dealing in tainted securities. Jobbers could tell from their commission statements who was offering which shares.

When a broker bought a Liro-supplied share through a jobber, there were two possibilities: either the jobber wrote 'Liro' on the sale note or he failed to do so. In the second case, the Liro shares were sold in the name of the jobber, who was considered to be the vendor. In all cases, however, the jobber knew the names of both vendor and buyer from his commission statements. The VvdE always argued that, in terms of the Stock Exchange rules, jobbers had no right to refuse to deal with Liro, a fellow Stock Exchange member. Precisely because Liro was a member of the Exchange, shares bought from the robber bank had been obtained 'by normal Stock Exchange practice'. According to the VvdE, a jobber was therefore prohibited by the exchange rules to refuse buying shares from Liro, a fellow Stock Exchange member.[65] That applied to open as well as to closed corners.

However, there was nothing to stop members from informing buyers that the shares on offer had come from Liro. In addition, buyers could ask for guarantees, and stipulate that they did not want to be sold securities of Jewish origin. Overhoff has confirmed that while it was possible to make such conditions, doing so was pointless 'because the market was awash with shares of Jewish origin and buyers had to wait an inordinately long time for "good shares".'[66] According to the chairman of the VvdE, it was possible even after May 1942 – when shares sold like hot cakes – to stipulate that shares of Jewish origin were not wanted.[67]

A dealer who did direct business with Liro must have known that he was skating on thin ice and that he was, in all probability, buying stolen securities.[68] Traders who bought confiscated *Amerikaantjes* had two (and after May 1943, even three) ways of telling whether they were dealing in shares of Jewish origin:

- from the three foreign-currency licence numbers;
- because the shares were being offered well below the frozen prices, which in practice almost invariably meant that Jewish securities were involved, and

- because an extra commission was being offered to render the purchases more attractive.

In sum, it can be asserted that members of the VvdE had every opportunity of avoiding the purchase of stolen Jewish securities. Those members who nevertheless bought tainted shares, did so in the full knowledge of what they were doing, or because they could not resist the appeal of specially reduced prices or of Rebholz's commission. Of course, a combination of these factors was often at work. Of the 375 or so members of the VvdE, nearly 140 bowed to Mammon in the years 1942–4.

Moral, Legal and Economic Considerations

It was pointed out earlier that the justification of the purchase of confiscated Jewish securities was based on the argument that, as a result, the shares remained in the Netherlands, so that the post-war restitution of property rights was rendered that much easier. That was Rebholz's argument no less than Overhoff's, and was pleaded by practically everybody who had anything to do with buying or selling these securities.

A. J. van der Leeuw, a member of the Institute for War Documentation of many years' standing, has shown how specious that argument really is. He does not go into the restrictions (prohibitions) issued by the Dutch government-in-exile or the Allied Declaration of 1943, but examines the sale of stolen Jewish securities from a practical point of view. He argues that anyone viewing the subject from a purely moral angle does not need a lot of time to make up his mind. It is reasonable to suppose that, in nearly every case, the buyers acted in full knowledge of the fact that they were buying property stolen from Jews. They were simply receivers of stolen goods, as several leading lawyers have stressed.

While the charge of receiving stolen goods cannot be swept under the carpet, it is also possible to view the subject in the light of its economic merits. In the case of *Amerikaantjes* and international Dutch funds such as Shell and Philips, in particular, it is true that sales outside the Dutch borders would have made it much more difficult, if not impossible, to trace them back to their legitimate owners. The proceeds might have ended up in the coffers of Seyss-Inquart – which seems unlikely – but would in any case have been much smaller because securities of a dubious type had invariably to be sold well below the normal price. The foreign currency acquired in that way would probably have been used for the purchase of strategic material on the world market where Reichsmarks were not welcome.

There seems therefore to be a fundamental conflict between the moral and the economic assessment of these sales.[69] It is an open question whether those buyers who claimed to have acted for patriotic motives had not in fact been motivated by avarice. Inasmuch as Rebholz's commissions tempted many a buyer, it seems unfortunately true to say that the second was the more likely explanation.

Sales outside the Stock Exchange

Not all the securities surrendered to Liro were sold in the Amsterdam Stock Exchange. As part of *Kapitalverflechtung* (see Chapter 1) a number of shares changed hands without the intervention of the Stock Exchange. According to Hali, Liro's Stock Exchange clerk whose name is inseparably associated with the 'dumping days', marketable as well as unmarketable securities were sold underhand without the intervention of Liro's Stock Exchange section.[70] Part of these securities undoubtedly slipped out under the aegis of *Kapitalverflechtung*.

In addition there were auctions involving both officially quoted shares and shares that were not included in the daily list of quotations, the so-called unlisted stock. The most important unlisted shares were published in periodic price bulletins, on the basis of which prices were set. These bulletins were issued by such specialists as Brand's Effektenkantoor and the Commissiebank voor Incourante Fondsen. Both were members of the VvdE and ran share auctions. In addition, shares were also sold privately.[71]

As in the Stock Exchange, here too buyers had the means of stipulating that they did not wish to buy securities of Jewish provenance. Brand's Effektenkantoor actually asked Liro if they were obliged to declare that certain shares came from Jewish sources. Liro replied that the answer was an emphatic 'no', seeing that there was no regulation demanding that type of declaration. Brand was then forbidden to refer to the origins of the securities. Liro's letter said nothing about clients who enquired explicitly about the origins of the securities.[72]

Overhoff, who was asked by VvdE member Brand if a distinction must be made between the sale of officially listed and other Liro equities, replied that there was 'no difference between them'. It has already been pointed out that Overhoff had no objection to the sale of listed shares of Liro provenance traded as part of 'normal Stock Exchange practice'. It now appeared that he had no more problems with the sale of non-listed securities sold outside the Stock Exchange.[73]

A solution was also found for shares issued not 'to bearer' but to named holders (and hence more easily identified). J. H. L. Aufenacker, a Liro staff member, was handed forms for signature by which nominative shares were made over to his name. Aufenacker is said to have objected, but in the end he concurred because the proceeds were credited to the client's account. These name-transfer forms had the following wording:

> The undersigned, A.C.P., represented by the firm of Lippmann, Rosenthal & Co., Sarphatistraat, administrators of Jewish assets by virtue of VO 58/1942, and residing at

47–55 Muiderschans, Amsterdam, hereby requests the board of the NV Maatschappij tot Exploitatie van het Nederlandsch Sportpark in Amsterdam to transfer share no. 222 D valued f. 250.00 to J. H. L. Aufenacker, 60a Leidschegracht, who declares that by signing this form he agrees to adhere to the Statutes of the above-mentioned company. Amsterdam, 21 September 1943. Lippmann, Rosenthal & Co. Sarphatistraat.

Aufenacker then asked the company concerned to transfer the share to a third person, say, to Jansen. In quite a few cases, nominative shares also found their way to buyers without changes of name. In that case the price was usually so low that the new buyer swallowed his objections. The Incasso Bank, too, seemed to have few problems with the acceptance of nominative shares, even if they had been issued to a person with an obviously Jewish name (for instance Polak) and had been transferred by Liro to another name.[74]

Not all Jewish securities were surrendered to Liro. A small proportion of Jewish-owned securities was confiscated by the Sicherheitsdienst or the Devisenschutzkommando. The sums involved were relatively small: 3.5 million guilders in all. Not all these cases, incidentally, were Jewish, for shares in the hands of black marketeers were also confiscated. Here, too, Rebholz acted as sales agent.[75]

From the spring of 1943, foreign securities from Jewish sources deposited with Liro were sold abroad, mainly in Switzerland, France and Portugal, largely for the benefit of the Four-Year Plan. The cash equivalent of the securities sold was credited to the account of the Liro 'clients' concerned. Sales to Switzerland and then on to Portugal were begun in March 1943. The shares sold consisted largely of Portuguese, South American and Egyptian government bonds, mainly issued in pounds sterling. Shares to the value of 740,000 Swiss francs were sold to Switzerland and to Portugal for approximately 10,400 escudos.[76] There was no interest in British securities; the risk was probably considered too great. Buyers grew increasingly cautious, not least in the wake of Allied warnings against dealings in stolen property in the occupied territories. For that reason, a new market was sought and eventually found in Paris.

Sales to France were considerable and ran to about 20 million guilders. American dollar bonds and other securities issued in dollars were readily offloaded. In Paris there was an extensive black market in which the Germans, too, were actively involved. Here Spanish pesetas could be bought with French francs. With the pesetas the Four-Year Plan paid for Spanish tungsten, an essential raw material for the munitions industry. In August 1944 Rebholz used his own car to fetch the remaining 180 million francs (the proceeds of shares already sold) to Amsterdam. According to Rebholz's testimony, he dealt with just one intermediary in France, a man by the name of Robineau. The Nederlandsche Bank refused to change francs and the Reichsbank in Berlin, where they were sent next, seemed equally reluctant to do so. The francs were therefore deposited in a bank and after the war probably confiscated by Soviet agents. Rebholz conducted the transactions on Bühler's instructions.[77] In 1944, the Continentale Bank sold Belgian securities in Belgium on behalf of Liro to the tune of approximately 2.1 million guilders.[78]

On 5 September 1944 (*Dolle Dinsdag*), Seyss-Inquart panicked and had Liro's remaining parcels of foreign securities sent to Berlin. The panic was caused by the rapid Allied drive through Belgium towards the Netherlands. Breda had fallen at the beginning of September – at least according to a rumour that spread through the country like wildfire – and Seyss-Inquart thought it best to save as many securities as possible. Bühler was given orders to transfer the most important parcels of foreign-currency shares (mainly British War Loans, Funding Bonds and Argentinean pesos) to the VVRA, which in its turn was expected to transfer them to the Reichskreditgesellschaft in Berlin. Ten days after Mad Tuesday, Rebholz was instructed by Bühler to separate the most important foreign securities from the remaining Liro holdings and to transfer them to the VVRA. That parcel was henceforth known as the '*Dolle Dinsdag* parcel'. Von Blaschke has put its value at 12 to 15 million guilders. By way of Almelo, where the German agencies evacuated from the western Netherlands had taken temporary refuge, the parcel disappeared into the vaults of the Reichskreditgesellschaft in Berlin. After the fall of the German capital the parcel vanished without a trace. A part was probably burned; the rest must have found its way to various foreign countries.

Securities worth several million guilders were handed over to several, often influential, German agencies, for instance the RSHA, no doubt because Seyss-Inquart thought doing so might enhance his reputation.[79]

It is not easy to establish what securities slipped across the border through the black market or by other complicated transactions. According to a declaration by Rebholz, large blocks of Dutch stock (such as Koninklijke Olie) changed hands abroad at very low prices. The Otto Wolff concern in Cologne played a leading role in this process. The securities were sold in Switzerland for one-third or a quarter of their value. The Otto Wolff concern, which was closely linked to the Four-Year Plan, needed the foreign currency to buy raw materials not obtainable for Reichsmarks. The concern tried to keep its activities secret, and therefore conducted its security transactions through Knauth, Nachod & Kühne of Leipzig. The secrecy simplified purchases on the world market, because the vendors found it hard or impossible to tell where the foreign currency came from.

Towards the end of 1941 Otto Wolff received instructions from the Four-Year Plan administrators to make large-scale purchases of foreign and international securities on the Dutch market and was granted sweeping powers to do so.[80] It is not clear to what extent Jewish securities were involved.

During the occupation, Liro also transferred securities to the VVRA and the DRT.[81] No proper books were kept about these transactions, especially with the VVRA, no doubt for reasons of obfuscation.

After the Liberation, it appeared that not all the securities lodged with Liro had been sold. The remainder were kept in the safe deposits vaults in Sarphatistraat, on deposit with Amsterdam or German banks, or with other German agencies to which they had been surrendered on the orders of the Wirtschaftsprüfstelle. The securities lodged with German banks (mainly in 1944) proved to have disappeared without a trace after the Liberation. However, of the approximately half a million shares handed in, no more than a few score disappeared 'without apparent cause'. Misappropriation by Liro employees was the likely explanation. In this context, 'without apparent cause' means that though the receipt of the securities had been recorded, their ultimate destination was a mystery. The destination of the securities sent to Germany in 1944 is easier to determine – they were delivered to designated banks in Berlin.[82]

From an internal search of stolen securities held by Liro, it appears that the number of 'stolen' or 'missing' shares was relatively small; in December 1942, there were twenty-four shares in all and the names of the thieves and the methods they used are known.[83]

Securities and Banks

We have already seen that a number of banks were unable to resist the temptation of an extra commission of 1 per cent *ad valorem*. After the war, when Rebholz was called to account for his actions, he pointed out several times that he was not the only banker to have dealt in Jewish securities. This German, who became a naturalized Dutchman (and was 'de-naturalized' again in 1943), had no wish to play the role of scapegoat, as he saw it, and together with his lawyer, J. H. de Pont, he launched a counter-offensive. In essence, their argument was that 250 million guilders of Jewish securities had been sold, and that Rebholz's share had been no more than 30 million.[84] Now that was no more than a fraction of the total and so raised an explosive issue: if Rebholz could be held responsible for no more than some 30 million guilders, the rest of the 250 millions' worth of Jewish securities must have been traded by others. A. A. L. F. van Dullemen, the Attorney-General of the Amsterdam Court of Justice, seemed ready to accept that argument. One day after De Pont drew his attention to the figures, Van Dullemen sent a ('secret and personal') letter to A. A. M. Struycken, the Minister of Justice. From this, it emerges that Van Dullemen had come to entertain grave doubts about the 'expediency' of proceeding with the case. His opinion was shared by G. R. Nubé, the Public Prosecutor, who went so far as to argue that taking the matter any further was 'entirely inexpedient'. Nubé had come to this conclusion because the 'case for the defence was more substantial and well-founded than that of the prosecution'. In addition, it was impossible to find new financial experts to review the case, not only because there was no time for so complicated and comprehensive an investigation, but also because

> like Rebholz, they prefer not to unmask their 'connections' in the financial world, who equally live in glass houses, and because the entire case would turn into a contest between prosecution and defence experts, from which in the end not even the judge will be unable to arrive at a verdict of guilty.

The opinion of the public prosecutor, Van Dullemen wrote to the minister, was shared by the auditor and the examining magistrate familiar with the Rebholz case. Moreover:

> The main argument *against* proceeding with the case is, however, that other, 100 per cent Dutch financiers in our city did precisely the same thing as Rebholz, trading in at least ten times the number of Jewish securities. To bring up the names of so many very well-known bankers today – after so many years have passed – and possibly or even most probably to obtain an *acquittal* is *most inadvisable*.

Rebholz and his lawyer, De Pont, had in fact conceived the plan of putting a number of prominent personalities, some from Amsterdam's leading financial circles, into the witness box:

> 1) Professor de Jongh and *Mr.* van Taalingen, directors of the Nederlandse Bank, which is or was implicated in this affair to the amount of several (30) million guilders; 2) Mr. Carel Overhoff . . .; 3) Messrs. de Graaff and Schrikker of the present Board of the Stock Exchange; 4) the *Germans* Dr. Bühler, Dahmen, Fahrenholz and Egner; 5) one or more directors of the Nederlandse Handelsmaatschappij, which is also said to have sold securities to France; 6) several other leading figures from the banking world, including our present highly respected Mayor, *Mr.* d'Ailly, then a director of the Amsterdam Kasvereniging; etc., etc.[85]

Two financial experts, H. ter Meulen and G. Vleming, who had conducted the preliminary examination of Rebholz on behalf of the chief counsel to the Amsterdam Special Court, also proved far from enthusiastic about starting legal proceedings, and voiced their fears about the 'repercussions' that might result from a public airing of the Rebholz affair:

> In the first place, sight should not be lost of the fact that in many of the transactions for which he is now being blamed, he enjoyed the support of Dutch financial institutions.
>
> Moreover, several important institutions asked to be allowed to participate in several of these transactions, even offering him credits for that purpose.
>
> At the end of the transactions, one of these institutions expressed its cordial thanks to Rebholz for his collaboration.

The First Liro Decree in Practice

> We would further point out that while Rebholz sold French bonds to the value of approximately two million guilders to Degobank, several large banking institutions did likewise and, moreover, for many times that amount, namely for about twenty-two million guilders. There is little doubt that Rebholz's defence will not fail to draw attention to this fact.
>
> In addition, the undersigned believe that the public airing of the Rebholz affair will reveal that a large number of members of the VvdE bought discounted American shares from Rebholz.[86]

After the war, Liro's 'confidential banker' was in a position to expose the actions of many financial institutions, bankers and stockbrokers who had taken to trading in Jewish securities, and he was fully determined to do so by summoning them as witnesses should he be taken to court. Rebholz refused to shoulder the collective guilt of the financial world. The role of scapegoat, as we have said, did not appeal to him. The trial threatened to end in a major scandal.

True, not all the witnesses he proposed to call were guilty of collaboration or of receiving stolen securities, but under oath they could nevertheless have been forced to give evidence against former colleagues, whose slate was not quite so clean. And the list of names of proposed witnesses was far longer than Van Dullemen had given in his letter to Struycken.[87] In short, a trial was not an attractive option for anyone concerned, and would, moreover, not have been 'in the general Dutch interest'. Rebholz, for his part, would not have minded the public exposure, because he believed it would help his 'legitimate defence'.[88]

To the probable relief of all those concerned, his case was never brought to trial. In April 1954, Rebholz received a five-year prison sentence *in absentia*, three of which he had already served on remand. The former banker learned of his sentence in Liechtenstein, his new domicile.

Dutch financial institutions were alleged by Van Dullemen, as we have seen, to have jointly traded some ten times as many Jewish securities as Otto Rebholz. The avarice of the banks, as described in their letter by the financial experts Ter Meulen and Vleming, was blatant. What is the explanation for this?

At a meeting on 19 August 1941, about one week after the promulgation of the First Liro Decree, the Amsterdam Bankers' Association and the VvdE voiced their concern about the concentration of Jewish assets in Liro. According to the bankers' calculations this meant a drop of 4 to 5 per cent in their turnover. As compensation, the banks asked Bühler to allow them to participate in the sale of these securities. The Handelstrust West, a branch of the Dresdner Bank, was also present at the meeting because that company too plainly hoped for a share of the action. After the war, the VvdE claimed that they had attended the meeting in the belief that Liro was holding 'compulsory deposits', and that they had merely tried to ensure that the Jewish clients were allowed to decide which banks they wanted to handle their shares. The reason put forward for the meeting – the anticipated drop in turnover – had been meant to deceive Bühler, since the real motive had been the endeavour to keep the matter 'in house'.[89]

Stock Exchange practice casts doubt on this claim. The attempt by a large number of banks and stockbrokers to chase after profits has been mentioned earlier, as has the fact that those clients who did not want to be fobbed off with Jewish securities were able to say so quite freely. On the other hand, it seemed equally possible to *order* securities of Jewish origin from a number of banks. Such orders could be placed with numerous stockbrokers and banks, including, for instance, the Amsterdamsche Bank and the Rotterdamsche Bank. The price was about 10 per cent below the usual quotation. The Amsterdamsche Bank had also, certainly compared to other large banks, purchased a large number of government bonds from Liro.[90]

Sometimes things went wrong and buyers who had explicitly asked for 'Jewish' securities were supplied with the 'wrong' stock, that is, 'non-Jewish' shares. That happened to the Rotterdamsche Bank on 18 October 1943, when the Heerlen branch ordered two $^2/_{10}$ Shell-Union Oil certificates. One client had specified 'non-Jewish' sources; the other had specified 'Jewish' sources with equal emphasis. The price of the Jewish share was 38¼, that of the non-Jewish share 42. The mistake came to light when the 'good' shares finished up with the 'wrong' client through an administrative error.[91] 'Numerous clients' were prepared to run the risk that the securities they bought had come from Liro. Clients who insisted on 'good' securities were often placed on waiting lists.[92]

The Twentsche Bank took advantage of the occupation in a different way, by buying large quantities of their own shares and share certificates direct from Liro. All in all, Liro supplied the Twentsche Bank with original shares with a nominal value of 368,000 guilders and with Twentsche Bank share certificates with a nominal value of 538,100 guilders. As a wholesale purchaser of its own shares, the bank also used the services of two intermediaries, the jobbers J. F. Grossouw and H. B. Willemsen. Other, more modest, buyers of these shares were the Incasso Bank, the Nederlandsche Handel-Maatschappij, the Amsterdamsche Bank and the Rotterdamsche Bank.[93]

In the context of *Kapitalverflechtung,* the Handelstrust West purchased securities direct from Liro, that is, by-passing the Stock Exchange. In most cases, this was done on the orders of German industrial concerns. From 1942 to 1943 the Handelstrust West bought securities with a nominal value of four million guilders.[94]

From the middle of 1943, the Handelstrust West was also a member of the VvdE, but this branch of the Dresdner Bank appeared rarely, if ever, on the Stock Exchange floor 'out of consideration for the other banks and for the stockbrokers'. Instead of dealing directly at the Exchange, they made use of the stockbrokers and banks whose feelings they were so anxious to spare. What is clear is that the Handelstrust West wished to do business discreetly, and that all the big banks in Amsterdam, such as the Incasso Bank, the Twentsche Bank, the Rotterdamsche Bank, the Nederlandsche Handel-Maatschappij, and many stockbrokers respected and honoured this attitude by not withholding their services as intermediaries. The largest proportion of the purchased securities administered by the Handelstrust West was lodged with the Kasvereeniging. How many Liro securities were involved cannot be determined; in any case it was all a forbidden form of trading with the enemy. By their actions, the banks no doubt contributed to *Kapitalverflechtung*, which incidentally proved a failure.[95]

The banks were thus used by the Handelstrust West as intermediaries, but they also made use of front men to buy securities on the Stock Exchange. Such jobbers as Grossouw and Willemsen, who worked for the Twentsche Bank, were, in fact, covers. In 1942, the broker G. P. J. Monker bought Netherlands bonds to the value of nearly 1.9 million guilders from Liro for the Amsterdamsche Bank.[96] Rebholz referred to the use of front men on several occasions, and Wijnand, the financial editor of *De Telegraaf*, mentioned them in his article about the great 'dumping day'.

However, it should not be forgotten that Rebholz had good reason to blacken his business partners: it would minimize his own role. On the other hand, it has to be said that Rebholz, not least thanks to his position of confidential banker, was well aware of what was happening at Liro and at the Stock Exchange. Rebholz was without any doubt an important source of information, and, in most cases, proved to be reasonably reliable.

To recapitulate, it may be asserted that the major proportion of the Jewish shares, both surrendered and sold, remained in the Netherlands. On the Amsterdam Stock Exchange, Liro securities to the value of some 145 million guilders were traded, but Jewish securities were also sold at auctions, through banks or directly through Liro. A very small proportion crossed the border (especially to Germany, France, Switzerland, Belgium and Portugal). Another portion disappeared on the black market, abroad as well as in the Netherlands.

The unsold portion was discovered after the war in Liro, the VVRA and the vaults of various banks in Amsterdam, which had not yet surrendered them. The nominal value of these (mostly unlisted securities) came to about 128 million guilders. In addition, some 26,000 shares without a nominal value and some 35,000 United States share certificates were recovered.[97] Because of all these factors, the return of the securities to their rightful owners after the war was to prove an exceptionally complicated and long-drawn-out process.

–8–

The Second Liro Decree in Practice

The Second Liro Decree, VO 58/1942, 'concerning the treatment of Jewish assets', was the second and definitive attack on private Jewish property. It was issued on 21 May 1942. After the Jewish businesses, foundations, associations and some of the private Jewish cash and shares called in by the First Liro Decree, it was now the turn of the rest of private Jewish property. 'Claims on third parties of every kind', including annuities and life insurance policies, had to be registered with Liro 'no later than 30 June 1942'.

According to a special notice, claims could be of many types:

> outstanding loans; debt-register claims; rentals, leases, mortgage interest, etc.; fixed salary claims, wages, retirement pensions, annuities, life insurance payments, etc. Professional fees of self-employed persons (doctors, lawyers, etc.); claims on individuals or institutions abroad. Bank balances are of course also included.[1]

Creditors and debtors alike were obliged to submit all claims in writing, together with all the relevant information.

In practice the decree meant that Liro was about to become a new creditor and that all claims would flow into its coffers. This was not yet so on the day that the decree was issued in May 1942 – all that was required then was registration. However, it was widely known where registration would lead.

In addition to claims, rights constituting part of the assets of all persons 'subject to registration' and not normally treated as claims had to be registered, including:

a) rights to assets in other countries . . .;
b) rights to rented safe deposits;
c) life insurance policies and outstanding annuities; fire and theft insurance policies; jewellery insurance policies, etc.;
d) usufructuary rights.[2]

Finally, it was laid down that that all patent rights, authors' rights, trademarks, concessionary rights, share entitlements and hereditary rights had to be registered with Liro.

The exemption from registration duty of assets worth less than 10,000 guilders and of incomes of less than 300 guilders was revoked. Henceforth all credit balances, cash, cheques, shares and deposits that had escaped from registration duty in August 1941, had to be 'paid into, deposited with or transferred to Liro', and, what was more, before 30 June 1942. The exempted maximum allowance of 1,000 guilders a month in cheques or cash per person was cut to 250 guilders per family.

According to Article 10, Jews were obliged to hand over to Liro 'collections of all kinds, works of art, gold, platinum and silver objects, together with polished and unpolished precious and semiprecious stones and pearls'. 'Mixed marriages' were covered by special regulations.[3]

Article 10 covered almost all valuables other than money, claims, rights or securities. 'Collections,' one notice explained, 'naturally' comprised:

> postage stamps, books, coins and porcelain. Works of art include, among other things, paintings, sculptures, etc. These objects are to be handed in, even if they are *economically* indispensable to the person obliged to surrender them. If any such objects have been assigned to a third party as security for a debt, then that person is obliged to surrender them, in accordance with Article 14.[4]

Some exceptions were specified: one's own wedding ring (including that of a deceased spouse) and silver watches for personal use. The exemption also applied to used table silver, though with certain limitations. Every family member was entitled to one 'knife, fork, soup spoon and dessert spoon', but teaspoons were not mentioned and had therefore to be surrendered. This cutlery list was expressly 'restricted'. To leave no doubt as to its restrictive nature, an explanatory note in the Second Liro Decree underlined the fact that 'teaspoons, for instance, *cannot* therefore be retained.'[5]

There was yet another exception, and in retrospect it was a gruesome one: 'dental fillings made of precious metal and in personal use' could also be kept back. One wonders why this stipulation was thought to deserve separate mention. As we know now, even this concession was only a postponement of the surrender of the objects concerned, not its cancellation. However, on 2 November 1942 it was decreed that dentists who used precious metals for fillings would no longer have their expenses paid.[6]

The Germans seized the remaining cutlery after the deportations, which started in the summer of 1942. The other 'exempted' possessions – including the dental fillings – did not escape their rapacity either. After their death, the clothing of murdered Jews was searched for valuables. Gold, silver and coins were found sewn into coats or hidden elsewhere – small items of great value, relatively easy to transport and to secrete. After the gassings, special teams pulled the gold teeth and fillings out of the mouths of the dead. 'Dead man's gold' (*Totengold*) became a ghoulish catchphrase. What share Dutch Jewry contributed to it will never be known.

The Second Liro Decree in Practice

The SS collected some seventy-six loads of gold, silver, and so on to the value of 36 million Reichsmarks from the concentration camps (and occupied territories). The loot was made up as follows:

- foreign banknotes, RM 21.88 million;
- gold and silver coins and gold bullion, RM 10.67 million;
- jewellery containing precious stones and precious metal, RM 1.7 million;
- dental fillings and second-grade jewellery, RM 1.65 million;
- shares and postage stamps, RM 0.27 million.

The transport of these valuables was organized by Bruno Melmer. He worked as a plain-clothes SS-officer, so that the SS could not be linked directly to the transports. The trucks were also escorted by SS-men in civilian dress.

The consignments went to the precious metals division of the Reichsbank and were credited to Melmer's account. Melmer's name was used on all bookkeeping entries and reports.

The SS loot was sold through the Reichsbank (money and shares); the Prussian Mint ('damaged' gold, including gold fillings, gold and silver watches and gold and silver jewellery), and the Municipal Pawnshop in Berlin (the rest of the jewellery). All the proceeds went to the account of Max Heiliger, a fictitious name used by the German ministry of finance. The first load of dental gold (*Totengold*) arrived in November 1942. All the negotiations between the SS and the Reichsbank were conducted verbally, so that the strictest secrecy could be maintained.[7]

Lippmann-Rosenthal were granted the right to dispose of the collected objects, cash, securities, rights and claims, but remained responsible to the General-Kommissar für Finanz und Wirtschaft, while the General-Kommisar für das Sicherheitswesen bore ultimate responsibility for the incoming vessels and vehicles, including motor cars.

The many admonitions by the German authorities suggest that they considered the collaboration of the Dutch banks and stockbroking world inadequate and, in any case, too tardy.

On 27 May 1942 the robber bank pointed out that the safes and deposit boxes rented by Jews also fell under the Second Liro Decree. Three months later, in August, the matter was mentioned again with some emphasis: private individuals were reminded to register their possessions with Sarphatistraat, businesses with the Wirtschaftsprüfstelle in The Hague.

In a letter dated 10 July, Bühler also pointed out that the implementation of the two Liro decrees had been too 'dilatory'. He therefore felt it necessary to issue a 'severe reprimand' to banks and stockbroking concerns, which had 'repeatedly neglected their duty to surrender [Jewish assets]'.

On 13 March 1943, Bühler wrote again to the banks, telling them that Liro had complained about a 'striking number of cases in which financial institutions had failed to observe the regulations governing the surrender of Jewish assets'. The Beauftragte in the Nederlandsche Bank urged 'painstaking observance' and mentioned the severe penalties that could be imposed for 'neglect and evasion'.

More than eighteen months later, the matter had not yet been resolved satisfactorily, because in June and August 1944 Liro once more urged implementation of the decrees. The Incasso Bank let it be known that a new examination of the accounts and deposits concerned would be extremely time-consuming, not least because 'in most cases contact would have to be made with the account holders'. The bank furthermore complained about the lack of staff caused by 'labour service and holidays'. Liro clearly took the point; they replied that they were obviously expected to wait 'some considerable time' for the result of that examination but that they had no intention of doing so. The robber bank demanded a complete list of Jewish account holders and depositors in the Incasso Bank within three weeks.[8]

Bühler's admonitions seem to indicate that some banking and stockbroking concerns at least proved rather uncooperative in their dealings with the occupying power. On the other hand, it is also possible that Bühler's letters were part of a deliberate policy to keep up pressure on banks to surrender the assets of their Jewish clients.

The Second Liro Decree was the final blow to private Jewish property. It hit the entire Jewish population. The First Liro Decree had, by virtue of the exemptions it contained, been aimed primarily at the prosperous section of the Jewish population and had been no more than the first phase of what turned out to be robbery unconfined.

Claims

Claims were of various kinds: by Jews against non-Jews, by non-Jews against Jews, by Jews against Jews at home and by Jews against Jews – as well as non-Jews – living abroad. There was, as we have seen, very little that escaped the attention of the German robber agencies.

The collection of the claims was the responsibility of the Third Division. The procedure was by and large the same as that used by the police. The Third Division was helped by the fact that the Decree had laid down that both creditors and debtors had to register all claims with Liro.

Once the robber bank knew that a Jew had a claim against a non-Jew, the debtor was sent a form informing him that the debt had been passed on to Liro and had to be settled with them. If the debtor was in default, he received a letter from Liro informing him that if he persisted with his recalcitrant attitude, the relevant

German agencies would be informed. That threat was little more than a form of paper intimidation. According to a statement by the Reichskommissar for Finance and Economic Affairs, it had become 'irrefutably clear' that he 'could never consider the collection of claims by legal means, obviously because he realized that he had no case in civil law'.[9]

The control of Jewish safe deposits in various banks had also been taken over by Liro. After inspection, they were all emptied.[10]

Claims by Aryans against Jews

Naturally there were not merely claims by Jews against non-Jews, but also 'claims by Aryans against evacuated or missing Jews', certainly at a time when 'so many Jews are disappearing from the country', as Liro's inspectorate put it quite bluntly in a note dated 24 August 1942. The systematic deportations of Jews from Westerbork transit camp to the extermination camps had begun on 15 July 1942, and it is not surprising that Jews who had been dragged from their houses and deported should not have bothered to pay their rent.

The Liro inspectorate did that for them in part. According to the guidelines, outstanding rentals could only be paid for the month of 'a Jew's evacuation' until the 'clearance of his home'. In the case of weekly rentals, only the rental for the week before the 'evacuation until the clearance of the home' could be paid from the Liro account of the 'evacuee' – as the inspectorate kept referring to the deported Jew in question.

The inspectorate did not refund other claims arising from leases taken out by Jews after 9 May 1940, while similar debts involving leases signed before 10 May were open to negotiation.

The settlement of other debts by deported Jews could also be applied for, but the creditors could not count on being paid. For even if they could prove their claims to the full, it would still 'be very doubtful if we would pay them, since anyone giving credit to a Jew under the present circumstances must realize that he is running a grave risk.' If there were any payments, they were debited to the Liro account.[11]

Claims Abroad

Jews who had outstanding claims abroad (shares, credit balances) were obliged to register them in accordance with the Second Liro Decree. Shortly afterwards they received blank transfer forms, which they had to sign. With these forms (by which Jews transferred their rights and claims against third parties living abroad) the Germans hoped to pocket the proceeds as smoothly as possible.[12]

For the administrative handling of these foreign claims, the firm of N. V. Phöbus, Maatschappij tot het voeren van Adminstratie's, Beheer en Financieele Zaken (Company for Administration, Management and Financial Affairs) was founded. Its declared aim was:

> the administration of financial and commercial transactions, together with the management of the shares and bonds of third parties in Dutch and foreign companies and banks, as well as the financing of, and participation in, enterprises with similar objectives, and also the management or joint management of these companies, both in the broadest sense of the term.[13]

In practice, Phöbus did little more than administer the 'non-recoverable' assets of Jewish citizens. According to a balance sheet on 30 September 1943, it controlled assets worth close on 20.7 million guilders. The largest proportion was lodged in the United States. The credit balances there came to a good fifteen million guilders, while outstanding claims against individuals amounted to over two million guilders. For Great Britain, the amounts were respectively over 1.3 million and 200,000 guilders. The amounts in Switzerland may rightly be called modest: just over 7,000 guilders at banks and 44,000 in claims against individuals.[14] These figures seem to bear out the findings given in Chapter 5, namely that the United States rather than Switzerland was considered a safe haven for Jewish capital. It is of course an open question to what extent the registration of foreign capital with Liro may be considered reliable evidence.

Phöbus was a fiasco, inasmuch as the company rarely, if ever, managed to gain control of the claims ceded to it. The major proportion of the booty was in the United States and, thanks to President Roosevelt's Executive Order 8389, untouchable by definition, but London, too, froze the funds and credit balances of foreigners in British territories for the duration of the war. The amounts kept in other countries were too small to be of great interest and in any case the countries concerned refused their co-operation in the transfer of assets to Phöbus.[15]

Insurance Policies

By virtue of the Second Liro Decree, insurance policies had to be registered and more than a year later wound up on the basis of VO 54/1943 of 11 June 1942, 'concerning the termination of insurance contracts with Jews'. This measure covered all life, capital, interest or pension insurances, and obliged the insurers to compute the cash value of the policies and to hand that sum over to Liro by 30 June 1943.

Insurance companies had a duty to transfer the money, even if the policy could not be found or if the possible request for 'proof of survival or state of health' could

The Second Liro Decree in Practice

not be met. The last stipulation cut off the escape route of insurance companies unwilling to help in the liquidation process.

The policies were registered both in the name of the insurer and also that of the insured. This process was extremely time-consuming, not only because Liro lacked the trained staff, but also because, for the time being, the different conditions governing different policies had still to be taken into consideration. Thus a large number of policies could not be liquidated because of special conditions written into the insurance contract.

It was no doubt for that reason that VO 54/1943 'concerning the termination of insurance agreements with Jews' was promulgated on 11 June 1943. The occupying power was probably reluctant to have a legal confrontation with recalcitrant insurance companies, because it had no legal leg to stand on. In such cases, only a special *Verordnung* could remedy the situation, not least because Liro was reluctant to take the matter before a judge, which would have caused a public outcry. VO 54/1943, promulgated to obviate this embarrassment, forced life insurance policies to compute the surrender value of life, capital, and pension insurance policies, regardless of the conditions under which they were entered into, and make that sum over to Liro, where the amount was credited to the account of the customer concerned. The deadline was 30 June 1943. According to J. T. van Rossum, the deputy manager responsible for the Liro administration of insurance policies, the registration was not subject to proper controls – there were clear differences between the declarations made by the policyholders and those given by the insurance companies:

> It happened that Jews handed in policies not found in the submissions of the insurance company; on the other hand policies that Jews failed to hand in were mentioned in the company submissions.

In such cases those concerned were charged. If the fault was the insured's then he had to hand in the policy without further delay, unless, of course, he had meanwhile been deported. If the mistake turned out to be the company's, they were notified of the fact. In practically every case, the policies concerned were then handed in with a statement that the omission had been an administrative mistake. According to Van Rossum it was a remarkable fact that some insurance companies 'paid the biggest policies off first' because they found it advantageous to buy these policies back. Altogether 22,368 policies were handed in at Sarphatistraat with a total value of about 25 million guilders.[16]

Much as the banking and Stock Exchange sectors had, under pressure from Liro, drawn the attention of their members to the liability of Jewish customers to register their assets, so the Bedrijfsgroep Levensverzekering (Life Insurance Group), too, issued similar guidelines at the behest of the Verzerkeringskamer (Chamber of Insurance Underwriters).

The insurance companies were informed by the Group in a circular dated 12 June 1942 that they were expected to send all their customers a form on which the customers had to declare whether or not they were Jewish. In a subsequent circular dated 24 June 1942, the Group issued further instructions. The insurance companies had little choice but to do as they were asked, not least because the Germans kept a sharp eye on them.

The Amsterdamsche Maatschappij van Levensverzekeringen (Amstleven, or Amsterdam Life Insurance Company), too, issued these registration forms. When a number of them had not been returned, Amstleven decided to find out from the registers of births, deaths and marriages whether customers who had not returned their forms must or must not be treated as Jews. Amstleven did this in the first place because all clients not returning their cards were considered to be Jews, in which case non-Jewish policyholders, too, would have been disadvantaged.

However, Amstleven had no need to refer to the registers of birth, deaths and marriages because Liro supplied them with lists of the names of their Jewish clients. The dispatch of these lists took from August 1942 to February 1943. Sarpahatistraat was thus well briefed, probably thanks to the information Jews themselves had supplied in accordance with the Decree.

The *Joodsche Weekblad* of 10 July 1942, moreover, drew its readers' attention, at the behest of Liro, to the fact that annuity and life-insurance policies must be surrendered not later than 24 July. Jews responded on a massive scale, and Liro took full advantage of that. In addition the robber bank obviously kept abreast of the situation with the help of other sources (such as the register of births, marriages and deaths or the 'List of family names of persons of Jewish blood' published on 1 July 1942).

After the promulgation of VO 54/1943, which laid down that all Jewish policies had to be wound up by 30 June, Liro knocked at the door of Amstleven once more, this time with the news that the company would have to buy back all Jewish policies and remit the proceeds to Sarphatistraat. D. Streefkerk, the departmental head of Amstleven, protested against this measure, but he nevertheless felt sure that

> if we ignore the decree, there is the probability bordering on certainty that an administrator will be appointed. Other companies have had difficulties and many have been placed under control . . . Lippmann, Rosenthal & Co. kept hounding us and urging us to pay up.

In the end, Liro had Amstleven buy 84 per cent of the Jewish policies. In most cases, Liro seemed to know all about unsurrendered policies. According to Steefkerk, the company was therefore quite unable to tell which policies were known and which were not. Liro also seemed to know which policies had been terminated by methods other than repurchase, because these policies too were recorded on the lists sent to Amstleven. 'After redemption, they were surrendered to us for non-payment.'[17]

It may be assumed that what happened at Amstleven did not differ significantly from what happened at other insurance companies. The repurchase percentage (84 per cent in the case of Amstleven) may, of course, have varied slightly. Thus the Hollandsche Sociëteit van Levensverzekeringen N.V. surrendered 80 per cent (811 policies) of the 1,005 Jewish policies registered with them.[18]

It is not known to what extent insurance companies, working hand-in-glove with their Jewish clients, tried to devise camouflage procedures to protect Jewish assets. As far as can be ascertained, no mention of the matter was made during the post-war trials.

Jewish life insurance was not an attractive option for insurance companies after May 1940. In view of the spate of anti-Jewish measures, insuring Jews was a risky business. Beyond that, Jews were prevented from taking out life policies at a very early stage, because the First Liro Decree in August 1941 had robbed them of control of their own resources, while from 21 May 1942 all Jewish insurance policies had to be registered. By then, it was not hard to foresee that they would be confiscated.

Even so, some new policies were sold to Jews. The Hollandsche Sociëteit van Levensverzekeringen N. V., for instance, advised prospective Jewish clients not to take out just one redeemable policy for a certain amount but several policies at once. In that way 'such policies – redeemable in combination but not separately – would be kept out of the grasp of the occupying power'.

Although the company declared that in normal times they would have no problem in agreeing to the simultaneous redemption of insurance policies taken out in combination, they turned down Liro applications to that effect. The report does not say so, but it seems obvious that VO 54/143 (which as we have seen laid it down that *all* Jewish policies must be terminated) put an end to this situation as well.[19] In any case, a number of insurers tried to delay the redemption of policies for as long as possible, but to prevent it altogether must have proved impossible in the long run.

–9–

The Looting of Cultural Property from Jews

Introduction

Gold, silver, jewellery, trinkets and watches incorporating precious metals or precious stones, paintings and other works of art, in short, everything that could be fitted under the heading of cultural property in the broadest sense of the term, often had not only economic but also great emotional value for the owner. The market value of articles handed in to Liro was in many cases – exceptions apart – not very great, but to the owners these very articles mattered greatly because many memories were often attached to them. Possibly they lent an extra dimension to their family history; perhaps they were treasured for their beauty or for some other quality. All of them had one thing in common: they were absolutely unique and hence irreplaceable.

Jews were not spared the theft of even these articles. In most cases they went without a trace to some unknown destination – after the war almost anything of even the slightest material value handed over to Liro seemed to have vanished. With the scant evidence available, these items proved almost impossible to find. Nazi bosses, museums, German art dealers and private individuals both in the Netherlands and also in Germany made up the motley clientele of Liro and other robber-institutions. Seyss-Inquart took a personal interest in the objets d'art amassed at Liro following the Second Liro Decree. The Reichskommissar kept a close watch to make sure that no items of artistic merit were sold before Hitler's and Göring's agents had had their pick of them.

Hanns Rauter, the Höhere SS- und Polizeiführer, also belonged to Liro's clientele. He is said to have 'bought' art there to the tune of 136,000 guilders. According to T. J. Hoogland, a Liro employee, Rauter was 'so well off that he paid the bill twice. Unfortunately half the amount was refunded to him.' On 26 March 1943, this police chief bought an eighteenth-century painting of the Dutch School, *Woman Seated*, for 450 guilders. Other leading German Nazis, too, helped themselves regularly at Liro. Paintings were sold at scandalously low prices. It was common for valuable items from the Liro storerooms to be 'lent' to top German officials.[1] However, the cream of the Liro collection was not sold on the open market but went straight to Hitler and other top Nazis.

Kajetan Mühlmann was one of Liro's clients as well. While foraging on behalf of the Nazi chiefs he bought nothing but masterpieces, although he did not spurn canvases of lesser quality. Thus he bought some seventy-five works from Liro, after the canvases earmarked for Linz had already been removed. Dr Erhard Göpel, for his part, picked up about a dozen objets d'art from the Liro storerooms for the 'special Linz mission'.[2]

That Mühlmann, who laid his hands on thousands of works of art, did not always insist on top quality is borne out by the fact that he also bought canvases by unknown masters. Sometimes the description of these works was confined to the phrase 'from the school of'. The schools concerned might be the Dutch, Flemish or French and come, moreover, from different centuries. The prices of these pieces generally ran to no more than a few hundred guilders, with both higher (4,000 guilders) and lower (5 guilders) exceptions. They nevertheless included such well-known painters as E.van de Velde, Van Ostade and Nicolaas Maes.

A relatively small part of the Liro loot was sold at auctions by the Amsterdam firm of Mak van Waay, with other shares sold by Matthias Lempertz of Cologne, who profited considerably from the flourishing Dutch market, as well as by Curt Reinheldt of Berlin. The two German concerns also dealt in carpets and other objets d'art. Another client was the Munich Galerie für alte Kunst, which in December 1942 paid a bill for 289.80 guilders, of which 193.25 guilders was for paintings and the rest for furniture and bronze objets d'art.[3]

It is estimated that between 3,500 and 3,600 paintings were handed over to Liro, the prices ranging from 25 cents to several thousand guilders.[4]

The Liro Sale of Cultural Property

Liro sold cultural property almost directly after taking it in. The sale of gold, silver and jewellery netted 303,000 guilders in 1942, and furniture, paintings and antiques fetched 491,230 guilders. The Second Liro Decree came into force in May 1942 and thus covered items handed in during the second half of 1942. During the first nine months of 1943, the sale of precious stones and precious metals grew apace, as did the sale of furniture, paintings and antiques. The proceeds came to 3,042,650 and 1,432,116 guilders respectively. With that, the sale of Jewish property in these two sectors was almost complete; what little was left over went on loan to various museums or to houses confiscated by the Wehrmacht.[5]

Here and there archival documents reveal that even before the Second Liro Decree was promulgated in May 1942, Liro had put many valuable items up for sale, although the First Liro Decree only covered money, credits and securities. The fact that the robber bank nevertheless disposed of valuable objects from about the end of May 1941 was not the result of some *Verordnung* but of the 'proprietary processing' of Jewish persons wishing to emigrate. Only a small number of cases were involved.[6]

The valuation of Jewish cultural property was a convoluted process. The value of objets d'art and precious stones was assessed not only by von Stechow but also by G. Schilling and Martin Wolf. Wolf and Schilling were German jewellers and buyers; they therefore valued the works they themselves wished to buy.

In addition, Liro also had its loot valued by N. C. A. J. Groenendijk and S. J. Mak van Waay, two Dutchmen.[7] The broker and auctioneer Groenendijk, unlike Mak van Waay, was a member of the NSB. He not only served as an appraiser for Liro but also for the Devisenschutzkommando and for Omnia. In 1943, the proprietor of the auction house De Vijzel collected close on 10,000 guilders for valuations from Liro. In 1942, the figure was 27,094.77 guilders and in 1944, 2,722.01 guilders. The agreed commission charged varied between 1 and 1.5 per cent.[8]

Valuations at the Mak van Waay auction house were held from 23 February 1942 to 23 June 1944 and covered paintings, silver, gold, gold and silver coins, furniture, porcelain and carpets. A total of 13,861.36 guilders was charged in commission. Since the agreed commission was 1 per cent of the assessed value, the value of the goods in question must have been 1,386,136 guilders. H. Nienhuis, who took the auction house over on 1 July 1944, made four further valuations, but the total value was by then no more than 9,356 guilders. S. J. Mak von Waay could not be questioned about his valuation method after the war – he died of a heart attack on Liberation Day (5 May 1945). According to a witness, he did his work 'to the best of his knowledge and conscience' with the aim of obtaining a decent price for Liro's 'clients', knowing that the proceeds would be credited to their Liro accounts.

On the basis of invoices discovered at Liro, it is possible to put the following figures on the cultural property handed in to Liro in accordance with the Second Liro Decree:

Jewellery	2,295,011.80 guilders
Gold	451,176.26
Silver	799,752.74
Carpets	252,642.10
Precious stones	65,723.39
Paintings	684,034.24
Porcelain and earthenware	185,629.92
Postage stamps	190,514.71
Furniture	74,228.43

Ironwork	29,749.75
Asian works of art	43,080.25
Wearing apparel	36,336.15
Various	56,193.38
Total (guilders)	5,163,963.12

The approximate number of articles handed in to Liro is known, although there is naturally no way of knowing to what extent thefts by staff members distorted the figures. All that is certain is that the figures were almost always too low and can provide no more than a vague indication of the real value of the objects handed in.

Jewellery, including ornaments containing polished and unpolished diamonds, pearls, and so on, found their way to the buyers listed in Table 9.1.

Precious stones not worked into jewellery (loose brilliants, uncut diamonds, emeralds, and the like) went to a different destination. They were bought by the Fachuntergruppe der Edelsteinen und Diamantindustrie (Industrial Sub-division for Precious Stones and the Diamond Industry) and paid for on the basis of valuations by employees of that group. The valuation methods varied, but it is certain that the buyers were never overcharged. As we have seen, Schilling and Wolf valued on their own behalf and we may safely take it that they did not do themselves down. Sometimes the pre-war value (May 1940) was paid; in other cases, the value obtaining during the year of the sale. The invoices issued to Goldfalken, Wolf, Schilling and Seidel were at precisely 50 per cent of the assessed value, while Busse & Co, which mainly bought watches, had to hand over 70 per cent of the assessed value. The assessed value of the Four-Year Plan acquisitions was equal to the purchase price, but that was because it conducted its own valuations. General-Kommissar Fritz Schmidt, Seyss-Inquart's political adviser, paid the 'May 1940' price for jewellery, but for other items he often paid no more than a tenth of the

Table 9.1 Prices and values of jewellery items

buyer	purchase price	estimated value
Goldfalken	705,204.40	1,410,408.80
E. Busse & Co.	20,930.00	29,900.00
General-Kommissar Schmidt	999,931.00	999,931.00
Four-Year Plan	166,538.15	166,538.15
Martin Wolf	138,152.25	276,304.50
O. Reichert & Co.	25,000.00	25,000.00
G. Schilling	179,511.00	359,022.00
K. Reinheldt	18,431.50	18.431.50
Otto Seidel	41,268.50	82,537.00
Total (guilders)	2,295,011.80	3,368,117.45

assessed value. Purchases for Goldfalken and Busse were mainly made by von Rautenberg, who had good relations with the Wirtschaftsprüfstelle in The Hague.

Gold was chiefly sold, as early as 1942, for the benefit of the Weihnachtsaktion (Christmas campaign). Liro charged standard prices that bore no relation to the actual price of gold. The Deutsche Gold-und Silberscheideanstalt (Degussa, the German Gold and Silver Refinery) was one of the largest customers, but Liro also sold gold to Busse & Co.

Silver was mainly sold as bullion (which is cheaper to buy), so that the proceeds came to no more than 83,654.95 guilders. The cost of melting the silver down (approximately 6,200 guilders) was borne by Liro, and thus ultimately by the 'client'. Antique or artistic silver objects, too, only fetched a fraction of their normal price. Busse and Degussa were among the biggest buyers of silver.

Carpets were mainly bought by Reinheldt and by Lempertz (Cologne). These companies were also by far the most important buyers of paintings, porcelain, antique furniture, Asian objets d'art, wearing apparel and 'various' items. Of the total proceeds from paintings (694,034.24 guilders), these two firms accounted for 522,552.54 guilders.[9]

It must, of course, be remembered that German agencies such as the Dienststelle Mühlmann and buyers such as Posse and Hofer always had first choice, paying little or sometimes nothing at all. They cornered the best works and precious gold and silver objects for Göring and for German museums, including the Führermuseum in Linz. Because the Reich was acutely short of foreign currency, jewellery went mainly to the Four-Year Plan. After January 1943, Schmidt was given first choice of items for *Reichszwecke* (Reich objectives).[10]

In the case of art, silver and ornaments, the figures mentioned convey an incomplete picture of the activities of the looting sector for yet another reason. From the autumn of 1942, the ERR seized increasing quantities of goods and a fierce competition between the ERR and Liro ensued. The ERR based its predatory acts on the *Führererlass* and paid little heed to the Second Liro Decree.[11] It is quite certain that far more cultural property was stolen from Jews than appears from the surviving Liro records.

On the orders of the Reichskommissariat, some eighty paintings were sold to Himmler. The auction house of Mak van Waay was commissioned to value them, but because Himmler was personally involved, von Karger, the Liro chief, was afraid of falling foul of the Reichsführer and so the art historian Dr Eduard Plietzsch of the Dienststelle Mühlmann was asked to check the Mak van Waay valuations. In most cases, the two sets of figures were practically identical: an average price of almost 1,000 guilders per painting. The works were not intended for Himmler's private collection – for that their value was too low – but as presents to officers.[12]

Hanns Rauter, too, whom we have already met as one of Liro's 'clients', did not always buy goods for himself, but also depleted the Liro storerooms for other reasons. All in all, he seized his chance some 140 times. Apart from purchases for his private use, he bought seventy-eight paintings, forty carpets and seventeen objets d'art from Liro, all destined as prizes for Waffen-SS shooting competitions in Berlin.[13]

Valuable pieces of jewellery in which the Four-Year Plan administration was interested were transferred to the planning offices after payment of a levy to Liro. The rest went to the highest German bidders in the jewellery trade, unless the Reichswirtschaftsministerium (Reich Ministry of Economics) raised objections.

Gold, silver and jewellery largely finished up with German dealers, the two most important of which were the Goldfalken-Juwelengesellschaft GmbH and E. Busse AG in Berlin. Diamonds and second-grade silver and gold objects were in many cases handed over to the Weihnachtsaktion, to which end contact was made with Dr Heinemann or some charity indicated by him.[14] As part of the Weihnachtsaktion some 300,000 guilders worth of jewels were bought from Liro.[15]

Gold and silver articles of no artistic or antique quality were melted down by Degussa in Frankfurt and sent on to the Reichsstelle für Edelmetalle (Reich Office for Precious Metals), but not before Heinemann had been informed and they had been rejected by the Weihnachtsaktion. Like the Four-Year Plan, the Weihnachtsaktion paid a levy based on what the German wholesale trade would have paid to the tax authorities in similar cases.

If gold and silver objects were of artistic value, they were first offered to Kajetan Mühlmann or Hans Posse.[16] Posse advised how best to share out the stolen articles from Jewish sources among German museums, though of course the Führermuseum in Linz always had first refusal.[17] When it came to paintings, tapestries and carpets, Posse, Hofer and Mühlmann also had first choice; next it was Himmler's turn, followed by the German art trade and the Weihnachtsaktion.

The last of the privileged few to have his pick was SS-Sturmbannführer Albert Schmidt-Stähler. He was head of the Hauptarbeitsgruppe Niederland (Main Working Group, Netherlands), a division of the EER, and believed that when it came to art collections Dutch Jews could not hold a candle to their French coreligionists. For that reason he concentrated his efforts on archives, libraries and Masonic lodges rather than on paintings.

In the pecking order the EER thus came after the Dienststelle Mühlmann, which was able to lay its hands on all collections of any importance. 'Degenerate art', despised by the Nazis, was nevertheless important when it came to earning foreign currency and was accordingly earmarked for foreign buyers. Switzerland was the most important market. Portraits of Jews in general and of Jewish writers in particular could not be sold in Amsterdam (probably meaning the Netherlands) under any circumstances, and could only be handled by specially appointed agencies.

The main buyers of confiscated postage stamps and coins were the Reichspost and the Reichsbank. The stamps were sold at auctions run by H. Köhler in Berlin or offered to the Reichsstelle für Papier (Reich Paper Office) for sale abroad. Household goods continued to go mainly to Schmidt-Stähler. He did not have to pay for them but did have to hand over a tax, which was credited to the *Sonderkonto* (special account). In that way, it was possible to keep tabs on what passed through Schmidt-Stähler's hands on its way to the occupied territories in the East, his most important market. Liro was anxious to get rid of these household goods, which were of small value but occupied a great deal of space. What could not be disposed of to Schmidt-Stähler went as quickly as possible to the Weihnachtsaktion.[18]

From the summer of 1943, a mass of household articles (furniture, glassware, and so on) found its way to areas of Germany that had been hit badly by the Allied air raids.[19] Lübeck in particular profited from this source, thanks to Dr H. Böhmker, who was not only the Beauftragte for the city of Amsterdam but also a Lübeck senator. Finally, a very small number of private persons was allowed to 'shop' at Liro, including employees, but their overall share in the transactions was negligible.[20]

In January 1943, just when Liro had begun to turn the stolen loot into cash, General-Kommissar Schmidt instructed the robber bank to put an immediate stop to the sale of diamonds. He himself must be given first refusal to these. The notification was shrouded in great secrecy, so much so that not even the Liro bosses knew the reasons why. All they did know was that 'Reich objectives' were involved and that the Führer himself had issued the order. From March to May 1943, Schmidt bought jewellery and precious stones with a total value of 1,071,205 guilders.

After the war it emerged that the diamonds were worked into caskets for the highest German decorations (above all the *Ritterkreuz des Eisernen Kreuzes mit dem Eichenlaub mit Schwertern und Brillianten* – the Knight's Cross of the Iron Cross with Oak Leaves with Swords and Diamonds). At the Führer's behest, these caskets had to have a 'unique character' and this was obtained with gold and diamonds. A proportion of the diamonds came from the Devisenschutzkommando but reached Munich, where the caskets were made, via Liro.[21] To Liro the law of supply and demand was as irrelevant as it was to Schmidt, who paid the price prevailing on 9 May 1940, although prices had shot up since as the result of the war.[22]

Liro began the clearance sale of stolen Jewish property in January 1943, and within a year most of the property was gone. By late 1943, Mühlmann, accompanied by Dr Eduard Plietzsch, complained during a visit to Baron von Stechow that few goods worth having had been left in Sarphatistraat.

Von Stechow explained that there were several reasons for this. In the first place, Liro had never been meant to serve as a permanent store for confiscated works of art but was expected to turn them into cash, and in that respect the bank had been highly successful. The supply had begun to dry up because not everything that ought to have gone to Liro ended up there. The SD, for instance, had confiscated the property of Jews against whom criminal charges had been laid. The confiscated property was considerable but no one knew where it had gone. In any case, it had not ended up with Liro.

Things were different with the Devisenschutzkommando, which, once it had won a case against Jewish suspects, did hand their property over to Liro. According to the nobleman-turned-art-thief, the DSK was the only agency that adhered strictly to the various *Verordnungen*.

The actions of the DSK were in stark contrast to those of Schmidt-Stähler. According to von Stechow, the chief of the ERR-Hauptarbeitsgruppe Niederlande had been quite wrong to invoke the *Führererlass* as the basis of his actions – Schmidt-Stähler had completely 'misinterpreted' the Führer's orders.

Works of art seized by the ERR or by agencies collaborating with it during house clearances had to be handed over to Liro, but von Stechow had not seen any such works coming in for several months. Moreover, not only the ERR, but Wehrmacht billets, too, kept many works of art out of Liro's hands.[23]

The *Führererlass* of 1 March 1942 was indeed at odds with the Second Liro Decree. The *Erlass* allowed Alfred Rosenberg and his Einsatzstab to search libraries, archives and 'philosophical and cultural institutions of every kind' belonging to Jews and Freemasons for valuable items and to confiscate them. The same applied to other cultural properties of Jews.

In response to von Stechow's complaint, Mühlmann decided to suggest to the Reichskommissar that a Liro representative be present at every house clearance and to have Wehrmacht billets (inasmuch as these had been the homes of deported Jews) inspected by Liro officials to make sure that works of art were not wrongfully being withheld.[24]

With the exception of *Ramschware* (shoddy goods not covered by Article 10 of the Second Liro Decree), the major portion of the surrendered cultural property went to Germany. The index cards in the archives of the Nederlandse Beheersinstituut (the Netherlands Control Institute, or the NBI) held in the General State Archives in The Hague help us to determine which Dienststelle, customer or firm acquired which articles. Almost all their names are therefore known. In only about 1 per cent of the cases do the index cards fail to tell us who had bought a particular item or where it had come from, slips that must probably be blamed on administrative errors. Part of the missing 1 per cent was probably stolen by Liro employees, a number of whom, as we said earlier, were corrupt.[25] In any case, the names of most buyers were known, but it is impossible to tell where the ornaments, objets d'art, precious stones and precious metals they bought ended up.

Of the works of art and the diamonds, only a small proportion could be retraced after the war. Their original destination could admittedly be established, thanks to the surviving lists of the German agencies and businesses that had handled the loot, but the trail from them to the new owners quickly ran cold, especially in the case of smaller or less valuable items. Moreover, the chaotic conditions at the end of the war, in the wake of bombings, military operations and the resulting disruption of German life, did not make the search easier. True, Dutch investigation teams in defeated Germany were in possession of lists of jewellery, watches and other items handed in to Liro, but in the prevailing bedlam a description such as '1 gold gentlemen's wrist watch' with no more than the owner's name and the household-goods confiscation number were very little to go by.[26] Even in calmer times, such summary descriptions would have been next to useless.

Many years later, the original owners were able, by virtue of the post-war *Wiedergutmachung* (reparation) legislation of the German Federal Republic, to claim financial compensation. It is also thanks to *Wiedergutmachung* legislation that we know roughly where the stolen valuables ended up, for it was one of the conditions of receiving compensation from Bonn that the final destination of the goods in question must have been the Federal Republic or West or East Berlin. On the basis of the *Bundesrückerstattungsgesetz* (Brüg), the official name of *Wiedergutmachung,* an investigation into the final destination of the stolen goods was begun in the late 1950s, something Brüg insisted upon before paying compensation.

With the help of Liro index cards, the plundered 'clients' were divided into three categories. The first two were entitled to some compensation by virtue of the Brüg regulations; the third category was, with one exception, out of luck, because its members could not prove that they had been wartime residents of the areas specified by Brüg.

The first category could lay claim to items that had without any doubt gone to customers in the Federal German Republic or in Berlin (both East and West). The second category covered items that had originally gone to the territory to which the Brüg regulations applied, but had then been sold on and removed to some unknown destination. This category, too, was paid compensation in terms of the Brüg provisions.

For a number of the stolen works of art, a so-called *Führervorbehalt* (Führer reservation) was issued during the war by H. Posse or by one of his colleagues. This meant that the items concerned were provisionally reserved for the Führermuseum in Linz, even though they did not invariably end up there. In any case, no other Dienststelle could requisition them. At most a total of one dozen works of art handed in to Liro were actually claimed by the Linz museum, an indication that Liro did not have many true masterpieces.

The third category laid claim to items for which the chances of compensation were extremely slight, because almost all the buyers resided outside the territory covered by Brüg – in many cases in the Netherlands or in East Germany. These items accounted for roughly 12 per cent of all the works of art sold through Liro.

Approximately 75 per cent of these, or 8 per cent of all the items handed in to Liro, were sold at auctions by Mak van Waay.[27]

In general, we thus know very little about the final destination of the loot sold inside the Netherlands. That, at least, was the case until recently, because most of the wartime archives of Mak van Waay, taken over in 1974 by Sotheby's of London, had disappeared, and with them all the correspondence with Liro, the buying and selling slips and the acknowledgements of receipt of goods offered for sale.[28]

In the preface I referred to the sudden discovery of archives, and this is a case in point. Early in November 1998, I received a telephone call from Sotheby's with the good news that the records thought to have been lost had been found. They included the valuations Mak van Waay did for Liro and, as it now appears, also for the DSK, which, as is well known, deposited confiscated goods with Liro. The Amsterdam auction house also valued collections on loan from Jewish sources. The catalogues show further that Omnia Treuhand offered paintings and antiques for sale through Mak van Waay. From the recovered documents it is possible to tell what was sold, who the buyers were (even if their addresses are unknown), and what the various items fetched. The goods sold are in most cases described in detail, not only the paintings whose dimensions are listed, but also, for instance, a porcelain plate with 'two small cracks'. The name of Koffieberg figures on the list of suppliers, though it is not clear if he acted on his own behalf or for Liro, his employer.[29]

From other sources it emerged, even before the recovery of the Mak van Waay records, that twelve auctions of goods sent in to Liro were held between 14 April 1942 and July 1944, fetching a total of 460,931 guilders. The auction house collected 55,552.52 guilders in commission.

The contacts between Mak van Waay and Liro were initiated by K.V. K. Mulisch, a Liro executive who had been a client of Mak van Waay in Rokin, Amsterdam even before the war.[30] As mentioned above, Liro sent goods for auction as early as 14 April 1942, that is even before the surrender of goods ordered by the Second Liro Decree. These were the possessions of Jewish emigrants covered by the so-called *Auswanderer Durchschleusungsverfahren* (emigrants' processing procedure) that had been handed over to the Liro emigration section by the Zentralstelle für jüdische Auswanderung (Central Office for Jewish Emigration).[31] From the sales records of the auction held on 14 April 1942, it appears that at that time seventeenth-century masters constituted the main sales items.[32]

Jewish Art on Loan to Museums

Even during the early months of the war, Dutch museums were inspected for works of art on loan to them by foreigners. In principle, no national Dutch art treasures were confiscated. Apparently the Reichskommissar had used his personal influence to leave national museum property untouched.[33] However, when it came to enemy property or, at a later stage, to Jewish property, things were naturally quite different.

Almost immediately following the proclamation of the Decree on Enemy Property (24 June 1940), the Rijksmuseum in Amsterdam was instructed to specify all 'moveable property' covered by the enemy property decree and loaned to the museum by Jews. Two sculptures certainly seemed to be covered by the decree, but in three cases (including a self-portrait by Rembrandt owned by the Rathenau heirs) there was some doubt, because it was not clear whether or not the lenders had changed their 'German nationality . . . for another'.[34]

Seyss-Inquart showed great interest in Rembrandt's self-portrait from the outset. As early as the summer of 1940, Mühlmann, acting on behalf of the Reichskommissar, informed the Rijksmuseum that the self-portrait, on loan to them since 1925, had to be returned to German territory in terms of the *Reichssperrliste* (blocked list). The acting permanent secretary of the Ministry for Education, Science and Culture (Departement van Opvoeding, Wetenschap en Cultuurbescherming, the OWC) – which was responsible for the Rijksmuseum – consulted the state prosecutor on the matter, and was advised to hand the portrait over to Mühlmann because the decision of the Reichskommissar, 'though expressed in very friendly terms, nevertheless represents an order by the highest occupation authority'.[35]

Looting by confiscation of enemy property began on a small scale. However, things changed drastically with the Second Liro Decree, which called for the surrender of collections of any kind, including works of art. An exception was still made for works on loan – they had merely to be registered with Liro. On 26 September 1942, Liro knew about nine loans from Jewish owners.[36]

The cultural property of Jews from such neutral counties as Sweden and Switzerland had also to be registered with Liro, as the Reichskommissar made known on 17 June 1942,[37] but this measure had no further repercussions for the owners.

As usual, the Sonderauftrag Linz (special Linz commission), followed by the Dienststelle Mühlmann, had first choice. What they rejected was in principle destined for Liro, but the possibility was left open that the museums holding the loans could buy them at the assessed value – on condition, of course, that the Germans themselves were not interested in them.[38]

Works on loan were registered through the OWC in The Hague. Detailed lists were carefully compiled of all institutions holding works on loan. The directors of all museums and libraries were sent a letter by Professor Dr J. C. van Dam, permanent secretary of the OWC, with a request for registration by return

> of objects that, by virtue of the provisions of the Decree by the Reichskommissar No. 58/1942 concerning Jewish property, have to be surrendered to the bank of Lippmann, Rosenthal & Co., but that are at present on loan to the institution under your control, together with a short description of the importance of each one.

It was essential, Van Dam continued, to determine where the objects on loan by Jewish owners were located, so that attempts could be made to retain them as Dutch cultural property.[39]

One day earlier, Van Dam had written a letter to Wimmer in which he remarked, in connection with the Second Liro Decree, that the Netherlands was *wiederum* (once again) likely to suffer a painful cultural loss. Once again a number of art, art historical and scientific collections were in danger of being lost to the Netherlands.[40]

Van Dam's *wiederum* was fully justified. The Ministry of Economic Affairs had voiced grave concerns about the export of paintings to Germany. During the second half of 1942, canvases to the value of eleven million Reichsmarks had crossed the frontier, and clearance of another one million guilders had just been requisitioned for the purchase of works of art. It was furthermore pointed out that the removal of art treasures was 'increasingly damaging to Dutch cultural interests'. Van Dam's help was needed to cut the flow of exports, but in the event his attempts proved to be vain: Seyss-Inquart insisted on keeping the grant of export licences for works of art in his own hands.[41]

Van Dam had suggested that Liro, the organization responsible for implementing *Verordnung* 58/1942 and hence in charge of the sales, be prevented until further notice from selling works of art without prior consultation with the Dutch authorities. The Netherlands must be given first refusal on works of art of national importance, and above all on all works on loan to various Dutch museums. In the event, however, the permanent secretary was unable to stop the removal from the Netherlands of any painting on which Mühlmann and his men had set their sights.

One of the Jewish collections on loan that had caught Mühlmann's eye was Dr Alphons Jaffé's collection of paintings in De Lakenhal, the Leiden municipal museum. Dr Jaffé himself lived in London. He had loaned his collection of just under ninety nineteenth-century masters to De Lakenhal for greater safety, much as the widow Larsen-Menzel had done in 1939. In 1941, part of these two collections was taken under the 'protection' of the Dienststelle Mühlmann. Some of the canvases joined Hitler's and Göring's collections. To this day, twenty-nine of the paintings have not been retraced.

The funds needed for purchases on behalf of the Ministry of Education, Science and Culture had to come from the 500,000 guilders Van Dam tried to extract from the Ministry of Finance. The permanent secretary, a collaborator but a man of some culture, pleaded with the Germans to do no more than register the works concerned for the time being, and meanwhile to leave them where they were. Large-scale transfers necessarily meant poor storage conditions and hence damage to cultural property.[42]

Van Dam's appeal seems to have been partly successful, for when the order came in 1942 to turn cultural property on loan to museums into cash, the museums were given the chance of buying them at the assessed value. Needless to say, there were some restrictions, not least when it came to objects earmarked for 'authorized German agencies'. If the museums did not avail themselves within the stipulated period of time of the opportunity offered to them, the works or art were due to be sold by auction.

Purchases by Dutch Museums from Liro

Dutch museums, too, showed interest in paintings surrendered to Liro. Dr D. Hannema (Museum Boymans), M. D. Henkel (Rijksmuseum, Amsterdam) and Dr J. G. van Gelder (Rijksbureau voor Kunsthistorische Documentatie) called on Liro on behalf of Dutch museums, in order to inspect and possibly to purchase works of art. According to Dr Hannema, they were not very enthusiastic about what was on offer:

Nothing very special there. A few works are of interest to us, however. We shall no doubt be told how to proceed.

There is one painting that strikes us as being right for the Leeuwarden Museum, and a few other pieces that may be considered for the Municipal Museum in Amsterdam, including the Isaac Israels painting *De Munttoren*.

The best pieces have already gone, of course. E. Plietzsch had some forty works transported to The Hague for, among others, the 'stelle Mühlmann'.[43]

As mentioned earlier, it was forbidden to buy paintings by Jewish artists or portraits of Jews by 'Aryan' painters, and special regulations applied to these works.[44]

The Rijksmuseum was interested in fifteen paintings, including several canvases by Jozef and Isaäc Israëls, two Jewish painters whose works could not be sold. The same was true of the work *De Munttoren* chosen for Leeuwarden. Van Dam authorized the director of the Rijksmuseum in writing to take steps with Liro to buy the works for a sum of up to about 17,000 guilders, to be paid out of the budget for the 'purchase of objects of cultural importance formerly in Jewish possession for Dutch state collections of history and art'. Subsequently the works in question may be made over to other interested museums at the purchase price. The purchase price must then be remitted to Giro Account No. 1 for credit to the State Treasury, giving the date and number of this letter, and specifying 'minimization of objections: Art. 228 b'.[45]

The sum of half a million guilders for the acquisition of works of art of Jewish provenance put at the disposal of the museums in December 1942 by the Ministry of Finance following Van Dam's appeal was almost entirely paid out. The Birnbaum (later also called Bingham) and Isaac Goudsmit collections were bought for 26,025 and 26,128 guilders respectively. R. May's collection was bought by the Rijksmuseum for 329,460 guilders. A few works went to the Amsterdam Stedelijk Museum (48,615 guilders) and the Museum for Asian Art (34,800 guilders), both in Amsterdam and nowadays housed in the Rijksmuseum. The Stedelijk Museum also bought the collection of D. C. Paraira (3,700 guilders) and two paintings by J. van den Bergh-Dantzig for 960 guilders. I. Hartog's collection went to the Hague Municipal Museum for 28,170 guilders.[46]

Not all collections on loan were bought. The lists submitted to the OWC by the various museums contain names not mentioned on the purchasing lists accounting for the 500,000 guilders set aside by the Ministry of Finance.[47]

Items from the Hartog collection appeared to have been mentioned earlier in a catalogue issued by the auction house of Van Merle & Bignell in The Hague. This caused Hannema to complain to the OWK that these paintings were being sold without the knowledge of Dutch museums. He thought it more correct to offer paintings of national importance to Dutch museums at the assessed value, 'as seems likely to be done in Amsterdam as well'. Hannema asked for a ruling. The department then approached Plutzar of the German Hauptabteilung Wissenschaft, Volksbildung und Kulturpflege (Central Department of Science, National Education and Culture), adding that they would gladly act as intermediaries in the matter.[48]

Liro took a direct interest in the registration of works of art on loan, because Sarphatistraat suspected that not all loans were being reported. In a letter to the Netherlands Ministry for Education, Science and Culture, the robber bank maintained that it was desirable to hold an enquiry 'in order to make certain that all collections and works of art belonging to Jews and housed in museums, etc., have actually been registered with us.'

Liro asked the ministry in The Hague to issue a circular urging all the institutions concerned to register Jewish works of art in Sarphatistraat even at this late stage. The ministry was not keen to comply and took its time over the matter. Not until June 1943, six months after the Liro request was received, did it write back to say that it saw no reasons for sending a circular to the museums.

Liro, which had meanwhile discovered that a collection of porcelain in the Hague Municipal Museum had not, in fact, been registered with them, urged that the ministry reconsider its decision.[49]

The Rijksmuseum

The Amsterdam Rijksmuseum also held works of art on loan from the Amsterdam Portuguese-Israelitic Community, from the Netherlands-Israelitic Central Synagogue and from the Netherlands-Portuguese-Israelitic Community in The Hague.[50] The Portuguese-Israelitic Community had also placed some five cases with valuable possessions (including its most precious books and ritual objects) in a safe deposit at the Kas-Vereeniging N.V. in Amsterdam. None of these items was to escape the vigilant eye of the ERR.[51]

In February 1941, the leaders of the Portuguese-Israelitic Community placed five cases of valuable objects on loan with the Rijksmuseum. In September 1945 the museum returned them 'in good order.[52] In this particular case, the deliberate attempt to keep the objects out of the hands of the Germans was certainly successful.

From a list compiled in July 1943, it appears that the Rijksmuseum had thirty works of art of Jewish provenance under its care, including works by Willem Arnold Witsen (estimated value 150 guilders), a George Hendrik Breitner (30 guilders), three works by Jan Sluyters (not assessed) and one Jacob Maris (40 guilders).[53] From the figures we can tell that no masterpieces were involved, although the assessed value was not stated in several cases. Whether this was done deliberately to keep the Germans in the dark is not known, nor do we know if attempts were made to keep the names of artists off this list in order to save their work from confiscation.

There are, however, numerous indications that this was precisely what happened. Thus a tapestry that Karl S. Warburg had sent in for safekeeping is not mentioned on the list. The Germans confiscated it all the same, but only after discovering the loan receipt in Warburg's safe deposit at the Westerse Bank.[54]

The ruse of taking works of art to safety by means of a 'donation' was well known, but it is difficult to establish how often it was used. It would appear that the property of W. A. van Leer was one such case. In September 1942, he donated seven cases of glassware and paintings to the Rijksmuseum, with the clear intention of recovering everything in better days. In handing the articles over, the donor stipulated that the donation must not be disclosed for two years 'under any circumstances'.[55]

The collection of Robert May, one of the partners of Lippmann, Rosenthal & Co., Nieuwe Spiegelstraat, was undoubtedly the most valuable to come to the attention of the Germans. May was forced to surrender his collection, consisting of silver, porcelain, tapestries and paintings, to the Rijksmuseum in Amsterdam. Why a member of the old Liro board, of all people, had to surrender his collection to a place other than Sarphatistraat, unlike thousands of his fellow victims, cannot be made out from the documents. Were there perhaps inadequate storage facilities for his collection (assessed at over 400,000 guilders)?[56] Or was it because the Liro board did not know what to do in his case? At one point, there was even a state of 'suspended animation': Liro was allowed to take charge of the collection but not to turn it into money.[57] Alfred Flesche, the *Verwalter* of Liro, Nieuwe Spiegelstraat, who was able to protect May throughout the occupation, probably played some part in the unusual disposal of May's collection.[58]

Even before the introduction of the Second Liro Decree, two auctions were held by Frederik Müller (on 14 October 1941 and on 2 December 1941) at which May family property was sold. This came from the estate of Paul May and his wife Rosa Fuld, who had committed suicide on 15 May 1940. The estate was treated as enemy property, because the heiress, Ellen Marx-May, had fled the country, whereupon her share of the estate had been placed under German administration. The October auction fetched 234,285.77 guilders; the December auction 204,458.28 guilders. Paul May's famous collection of books did not, however, go under the hammer. It disappeared to Germany, but was returned almost complete after the war, to be sold at auction by Laube of Zürich. This auction of the May estate, which included works by Goya, Chardin and d'Hondecoeter, attracted considerable attention. The directors of the Rijksmuseum informed one of the prospective buyers who had certain reservations that 'he could buy works of art at these auctions without any qualms'. A member of the May family had even told the directors that he would be glad if many of the items were bought by Dutch people. In that case the paintings would remain in the Netherlands, which would greatly simplify their return to the rightful owners. This account was confirmed by several sources. Robert May, the brother of the deceased Paul May, also urged his acquaintances to bid at the auctions, seeing that the 'larger the proceeds the better for settling up later'. B. F. M. Mensing, managing director of Frederik Müller & Co., also let Robert May know 'that he would find it most convenient and advantageous if I did not refuse any invitations to auction the items. Mr May tended to think that the proceeds would be greatest if I conducted the sales, which, he believed, would be in his best interest.'[59]

The Germans barely laid hands on non-Jewish art in Dutch museums. Doing so did not fit in with their belief that the Netherlands was destined to become part of the German Reich. In these circumstances it did not matter greatly if a painting was shown in Amsterdam or, say, in Dresden. On the contrary, keeping paintings in

Amsterdam helped a balanced distribution of works of art inside the Reich. All this does not alter the fact that the Germans could, of course, always resort to 'temporary loans', a tactic they used several times with the Rijksmuseum. Needless to say, the directors were none too happy, but could do little more than delay completion of the loan formalities for as long as possible.

Incidentally, not a single canvas loaned to German institutions remained in Germany for long. In April 1945, fifteen paintings were admittedly still on loan in Germany, but after the Liberation all of them were returned to the Rijksmuseum. An overview of the entire war period even leads one to conclude that, thanks to the Germans and their *Verordnungen*, the Rijksmuseum was enriched by 'several fine new acquisitions'.[60]

−10−

The Looting of Household Effects: the M-Aktion

In the Netherlands, Rosenberg's organization was responsible, not only for the looting of libraries but also for the theft of household effects, the so-called M-Aktion (the *Möbel*, or furniture, campaign), launched officially on 1 January 1942 on the initiative of Alfred Rosenberg, Hitler's Reichsminister für die besetzten Ostgebiete (Reich Minister for the Occupied Eastern Territories). Rosenberg's Ostministerium provided the civil administration for the occupied Soviet territories. During their invasion immeasurable damage was inflicted on the inhabitants, while the German officials had to work under deplorable conditions. There was a shortage of everything, not least of office and household furniture. Reichsleiter Rosenberg thought he could solve the problem in a relatively simple way – by exporting confiscated household effects from the West to the East. Many houses belonging to Jews who had fled stood empty, especially in Paris and surroundings. In December 1941, Rosenberg disclosed his plan to Hitler, who approved it at once.

The implementation of the M-Aktion was delegated to the ERR, which, as we have said, had been busy since the summer of 1940 with the large-scale looting of libraries and art collections in the Netherlands, Belgium and particularly in France. The Reich ministry and the ERR became the two main pillars of Rosenberg's personal power base.

When the ERR proved unable to do its job properly, the Dienststelle Westen des Reichsministeriums für die besetzten Ostgebiete (Western Headquarters of the Reich Ministry for the Occupied Eastern Territories) was entrusted with the task. In particular, the Dienststelle Westen took a hand in emptying the homes of Jews, whose systematic deportation was begun in the summer of 1942. In the Netherlands, unlike France, the Dienststelle Westen operated under the name of Einsatzstab Reichleiter Rosenberg – Hauptarbeitsgruppe Niederlande (ERR – Central Task Force Netherlands), led by Albert Schmidt-Stähler. From the summer of 1942, more and more furniture transports were diverted from the eastern territories to Germany, which had come increasingly to feel the weight of the Allied air raids.

The term M-Aktion was not only a misnomer but was deliberately misleading: in practice not only furniture but all household effects were looted – or 'pulsed' as it was called at the time. The term 'pulse' was a reference to the furniture removers A. Puls, who carted off most Jewish household effects in Amsterdam. To some extent the M-Aktion overlapped the thefts based on the Second Liro Decree.[1]

The staff of the ERR were sworn to strict secrecy and were not allowed to talk about their work even after their discharge. Breaches of this prohibition were treated as treason and punished accordingly. Moreover, a declaration that all ERR staff had to sign stated that they realized that all goods removed from Jewish homes were the property of the Third Reich, and that misappropriation of such goods would be treated as theft.[2] The fact that they were made to sign this declaration suggests that ERR staff kept considerable amounts of the loot for themselves.

The confiscation of household effects in the Netherlands was heralded by an announcement by the Zentralstelle für jüdische Auswanderung in the *Joodsche Weekblad* of 20 March 1942. It stated:

> Every Jew occupying his own or rented accommodation must under Section 3 of the decree by the Generalkommissar des Sicherheitswesens of 15 September 1941 obtain written permission from the Jewish Council in Amsterdam before removing furniture, fittings, household effects and other possessions. Any breach of this order will be treated as an omission to ask permission for their removal and will be severely punished.

This proclamation may be considered a removal ban, which had, in fact, never been promulgated in so many words. All the decree stated was that a permit was needed for 'the temporary or permanent change of address or the normal place of residence of Jews'.

But ban or not, the intention was perfectly clear. Jews, who had learned from what had already been inflicted on them, feared rightly that the Germans were about to strip them of their household effects as well. As far as possible, they therefore tried to save their possessions by entrusting them to non-Jewish acquaintances and friends. Some of these were never to return the articles they had been asked to look after.

The notice published on 20 March 1942 became the prelude to the systematic ransacking of Jewish homes. In July 1942, with the start of the deportations, the household-effects plundering machine, too, began to go into in top gear. Just over a year later, in September 1943, its job had been largely done.

Rosenberg's plunder team did its work on the basis of inventory records compiled by a special unit, the Hausraterfassungsstelle (Household Effects Registration Bureau), in the homes of deported Jews.[3] On 1 March 1942, the ERR was officially put in charge of the clearance of Jewish homes, to the dismay of several other German agencies that had also set their greedy sights on the loot. As a result, Seyss-Inquart was put under pressure from all sides to strip the ERR of its monopoly. The Reichskommissar was of course loath to burn his fingers by interfering in the

Führererlass, and so Rosenberg's team was able to continue its work unhampered. Those items in which the ERR was not interested were handed over to Liro. The ERR owed Liro some sort of compensation for the loot they had collected from the deserted Jewish homes. That debt amounted to the assessed value of the loot less a discount of 5 per cent. These payments by the ERR were credited to a special Liro account, the *Sonderkonto H.R.II*, as were the proceeds from items the ERR had scorned and had left for Liro to collect.

The looting was organized down to the last detail. In Amsterdam, the Zentralstelle für jüdische Auswanderung, responsible for the deportations to the East, played a crucial role in the process. In 1941, it had close links to the Sicherheitspolizei. Kriminalrat Willy Lages, commander of the Aussendienststelle Amsterdam der Sicherheitspolizei (Amsterdam Outpost of the SD), was put in overall charge, while the everyday administration of the Zentralstelle was placed in the hands of F. H. aus der Fünten. The Hausraterfassungsstelle was a special section of the Zentralstelle; it employed some eighty men, most of them Dutch, and was headed by Hauptsturmführer K. Wörlein.

The 'inventory teams' were made up of so-called columns of about twenty men each. When a Jewish family was removed from its home, two members of a column usually went along to register the household effects. A Liro official was present as well, to confiscate valuable items and to take them straight to the robber bank. These items were generally easy to transport, and consisted mainly of cash, shares, objets d'art and ornaments.

The front-door key was handed in to the Zentralstelle after the inventory had been compiled, to be fetched at some later stage by the ERR to enable it to remove the contents. For the rest, once the residents had been deported, the houses were sealed up by the Hausraterfassung and not opened up again until the ERR found time to ransack them.

Through storage depots in the port of Amsterdam the loot made its way to Germany in barges. The firm of Puls saw to the transport from home to port.[4]

The inventories list the (greatly reduced) values of the household effects. One copy of the inventory went to Liro, one to the Zentralstelle and one to the ERR. Present at the removal were one representative each of the Hausraterfassung, the Dutch police and the ERR, to make certain that the goods listed on the inventory were still there. In most cases, nothing was found to be missing and the total value of the household effects was noted on the inventory. A list of all the goods removed was also compiled. If items of value were discovered during the compilation of the inventory they were taken straight to Liro – in most cases even before the removal of the rest of the effects.

From the middle of 1942 (by which time the Second Liro Decree was in force), the procedure described above was widely used. This continued until February/March

1943, when the Hausraterfassung ceased attending house clearances and no list of the goods removed were compiled any longer. At about the same time the flow of valuable objects dried up, having sharply declined since the autumn of 1942. It may be assumed that the ERR had, increasingly since that autumn and from February/March 1943 in practically all cases, confiscated whatever objets d'art, silver and jewellery they discovered in the homes of deported Jews.

Schmidt-Stähler, who succeeded August Schirmer as head of the ERR Hauptarbeitsgruppe Niederlande in April 1941, declared at a discussion with the Liro board that, by virtue of the *Führererlass* of 1 March 1942 (on the tasks of the ERR), but above all by virtue of a secret *Verordnung* issued by Seyss-Inquart on 16 June 1942, he was responsible for ensuring that

> all furnishings, including household effects and cultural property (paintings, carpets, objets d'art, etc.) released through the resettlement and evacuation of Jews, will be put at the disposal of the Reich Ministry for the Occupied Eastern Territories as laid down in the *Führererlass* of 1 March 1942.[5]

At least 29,000 Jewish homes were cleared in this way, and as early as August 1943 most of the household effects of 25,000 of them had been taken to Germany. Some of the furniture remained in Amsterdam. Chairs and tables of better quality were handed over to the Wehrmacht; those of lesser quality were sold to a Dutch buyer.[6]

The average value of each set of household effects was 2,700 guilders. Hence, if we can take it that there were some 29,000 'pulsed' homes, household effects with a total value of about 78 million guilders were stolen. After the war, some 13,000 survivors were paid compensation totalling about 62 million guilders. In the remaining cases the lawful owners had been murdered in concentration camps or could not be traced.[7]

Although quantities and figures are not even approximately known, what is certain is that staff of the Hausraterfassung, Liro, the ERR and Puls pilfered like magpies. In short, there was a band of thieves within a band of robbers. In particular, money, gold and small, easily secreted valuables disappeared without a trace.

A number of homes, generally of the better type, were allocated to evacuees by the municipal authorities (these evacuees were non-Jews who were removed from their houses by the Germans for strategic purposes). The best were sold or rented out to NSB members or Germans; the worst remained empty.[8]

Needless to say, there were Jews who tried to keep at least some of their effects out of the robbers' clutches. But the Germans were prepared for that, and sent investigation teams into the storerooms and depots of all Dutch forwarding and removal agents. From their point of view, the campaign was a great success: they managed to recover numerous paintings, objets d'art, silver and porcelain. A large part of that loot was sold by auction at The Hague for approximately 120,000 guilders. The rest – clothes, linen, and household effects – went to Berlin.[9] The proceeds make it clear that the quantity of the objets d'art recovered was appreciably greater than their quality.

Items that did not fall into the paintings and carpet division, into the *Ramschlager* (jumble depot), or the gold, silver and jewellery section, went to Liro for storage in a special department generally referred to as 'Koffieberg', so called after its chief. It comprised an assorted collection of objects such as piggy banks, mortgage deeds, postage stamps, private letters, in short 'all the motley objects you might find in a drawer when clearing a house'.[10]

From the inventories we can see that literally everything was confiscated and that all Jewish homes were combed and cleared from top to bottom. An enormous quantity of disparate objects poured into Sarphatistraat. The 'Koffieberg' department had the job of sorting it all and of handing valuable objects accompanied by a delivery note over to the right quarter, where they could be processed further. IOUs went to the claims department, insurance policies to the policy department, money orders to the banking department, and mortgage deeds and conveyances to the Niederländische Grundstücksverwaltung (Dutch Property Administration).[11]

As part of the M-Aktion, a large quantity of books from Jewish homes also fell into the hands of the ERR. In Amsterdam, a sorting centre for these books was opened at the beginning of January 1943 at 116 Rokin (to which address the accounts department had also moved from Keizersgracht). From the Rokin address the goods were taken to the port for shipping to Germany. The M-Aktion had their own offices at 796 Prinsengracht.

In the summer of 1943, the Reichskommissar ordered the liquidation of Jewish congregations and seminaries, as a result of which the ERR received a further stream of books and other property. Until the summer of 1942, books were sent to Berlin or to Frankfurt am Main. The ERR sections Erfassung und Sichtung (Registration and Inspection), also known as the Buchleitstelle (Book Control Centre), and the Zentralbibliothek der Hohen Schule der NSDAP (Central Library of the NSDAP Academy) had their headquarters in the German capital. Frankfurt was the headquarters of the Institut zur Erforschung der Judenfrage (Institute for the Study of the Jewish Question). In the autumn of 1942, the Berlin Central Library was evacuated and transferred to the Grand Hotel, Annenheim, in Carinthia, Austria. Shortly before, a depot had been opened in Tanzenberg monastery near Sankt Veit an der Glan, also in Carinthia. Because of the increasingly concentrated Allied air attacks, the Buchleitstelle, too, had to be moved from Berlin. It went to Ratibor (Racibórz) in Poland. When the Russians captured Ratibor, they came upon millions of books, most of them still unpacked.

Sheet music was first taken to the Amt Musik (Music Office) in Berlin, but later, again under pressure of Allied bombardment, moved to Leipzig and later still to

Langenau Castle near Hirschberg in the Riesengebirge. Books earmarked for the RSHA went without exception to Amt VII (Weltanschauliche Forschung und Auswertung, Referat VII A 1, Philosophical Research and Evaluation, Section VII A 1) in Berlin. Later, they too were taken to safety in various places in East Germany and in the Protectorate of Bohemia and Moravia. Part of the Berlin RSHA library was set on fire by Allied bombs.[12]

The book collection of the Jewish Historical Museum in Amsterdam fell into the hands of the ERR in late April 1943.[13] For the rest, a great many books confiscated in the homes of deported Jews in the course of the M-Aktion proved of no interest to the Hohe Schule and were therefore sold as scrap paper to Van Gelder & Co. in Wormer. Many of them were modern prayer books.[14]

The records of the Hausraterfassung were stored in a central card-index system. Every Jew was assigned one index card or more. The filing system was arranged by Hausraterfassungsnummer (H.R. number), every Jew having a number and a sub-number for the individual items surrendered, for instance H.R. No.7384/1, 7384/2 or 7384/3.

The goods were kept in the following divisions, or rather depots: a) Carpets; b) Paintings; c) Antiques, Furniture and Bronze; d) Gold, Silver and Jewellery, and e) *Ramsch*, that is, goods of little value not covered by Article 10 of the Second Liro Decree.

The depot chiefs kept a *Lagerbuch* (store book) in which all incoming goods were recorded by store serial number and date, and also by the H.R. number of the central record system, but not the name of the Jewish owner. There was also a description of the objects concerned. Upon being sold, the name of the buyer, the date of the sale and the price of the goods were noted. In the store book the assessed value was noted as well (except for *Ramsch* articles).

Liro's fire and theft insurance policies were based on these values. No store book was kept in the largest 'shop' (silver, jewellery and gold), which meant that no assessment was recorded. Precious stones and precious metals were not valued until they were sold. This was bound to cause Liro difficulties – in cases of fire or theft, it would prove nearly impossible to determine the losses. The central filing system, if it was kept up to date, could of course help to show what was in the storeroom, but without a valuation that information was of little use.[15]

Liro's store records have been lost, but the filing system is intact. All the goods handed in are recorded on about 13,000 index cards. The accounts section, covering Liro's receipt of, and proceeds from, goods surrendered have also survived the war.[16]

Practically all the *Ramsch* was bought by N. V. Adoc, a firm registered in Amsterdam-Wenen and owned by Herman Olij, who had been in the business since the end of 1941, mainly under the name of 'Dr Bosch'. Thanks to his excellent connections with the occupying power, Olij had been able to procure a German passport in the name of Bosch. This document gave him greater freedom of movement in occupied Europe.

Before goods were sold to this pseudo-doctor, Liro employees were given the opportunity of buying articles at bargain prices. The only condition was that they purchase them for personal use and not for trading purposes.

Ramsch goods to a total value of 71,708.83 guilders were sold to Herman Olij's Adoc. Olij operated not only in Amsterdam, but also in Berlin, Brussels, Paris and Cracow; in addition to Adoc he also ran several other businesses.

A glance at Liro's invoice number 172, April 1942, shows that practically everything was grist to Olij's mill – the invoice covers such diverse objects as clocks, mirrors, candlesticks, pots, bowls, jars, dolls, shells, a bust of Goethe, commemorative plates, a 'stone hen', '1 vase (broken)', miniature steam engines, a fleece, '1 small rake', '1 table tennis bat', a wooden dog, a piggy bank, a radio valve, '1 brick', and an egg cup. Another invoice, dated 20 September 1943, was for paintings alone, the prices ranging from three to 200 guilders. The bulk, however, fetched from ten to fifty guilders.[17] The sale of *Ramsch* brought in 39,130 guilders in 1942; from 1 January 1943 to 30 September 1943, *Ramsch* to the tune of 144,646 guilders left the Liro storerooms.[18]

In this household-goods robbery sector, the Henneicke Column of the Hausraterfassung, so called after its head, W. C. A. Henneicke, was particularly notorious. The Column was not set up by the Germans but they condoned its activities. It was not only interested in movable property but also, and primarily, hunted down Jews, for whom it was paid a premium ('head-money'). The payments ranged from five to about fifteen guilders per Jew. The victims were taken to the Hollandsche Schouwburg in Plantage Middenlaan, Amsterdam, whence they were usually transported to Westerbork.

All valuables were confiscated and registered, although it is not, of course, possible to tell how much went under the counter. A report dated 19 August 1943 – to take a random case – records the apprehension of a Jewish couple and of their two children aged fifteen and ten. They had been hidden in the West End of Amsterdam by an 'Aryan woman'. The woman had been unaware that they were Jews and was therefore not arrested. The entire family was 'committed' to the Schouwburg, an Amsterdam theatre converted into a Jewish music hall; their cash and valuables were handed over to the Amsterdam SD outpost. The Henneicke Column made at least 3,400 arrests in less than six months.[19] After the war, five of these 'Jew hunters' were sentenced to death. Henneicke himself was executed by an Amsterdam resistance group in December 1944.[20]

–11–

Sperrstempel, Emigration and Tax

Sperrstempel and Emigration

Not all Jews had done their 'duty' to surrender all their diamonds, trinkets and gold in accordance with the Second Liro Decree. Jewellery was relatively easy to hide. The Germans realized that, of course, and did all they could to root out and confiscate these items. The great efforts they made to lay their hands on what they considered to be 'black' Jewish possessions were fuelled above all by the severe shortage of foreign currency the Reich had had to contend with from the beginning of the war.

It was probably in the autumn of 1942 that The Hague received instructions to issue 'exemptions until further notice from labour service outside the Netherlands'. Labour service was no more than a euphemism for deportation, and 'exemptions until further notice' could only be obtained by the surrender of hard foreign currency, jewellery, diamonds and gold in fixed quantities.

Kriminalrat (the lowest rank in the upper officer class of the Criminal Police) Willy Lages declared after the war that the conditions for issuing such exemptions had been conveyed to him by Dr W. Harster, Commander of the Security Police and the SD, in person. As far as is known, these conditions were never put into writing. After the war, Harster mentioned his talk with Lages during an interrogation. He had indeed spoken to the Kriminalrat about new instructions from Berlin

> which made it possible to grant Jews, in return for their surrender to the German authorities of valuable jewellery, shares and foreign currency, a measure of favourable treatment by the German authorities. As far as I remember the value of the surrendered items had to be about twenty thousand Swiss francs per person. This privilege was thus confined to prosperous Jews . . . At the same time I drew Lages's attention to the fact that the initiative in this matter must not be seen to come from the Security Police and that all valuables handed in by Jews under this agreement must be used for the implementation of Hermann Göring's four-year plan, that is, for the purchase abroad of raw materials needed for Germany's conduct of the war. The polished diamonds (jewellery) surrendered by Jews were exchanged in Switzerland for the rough diamonds the German war industry needed so badly.

In exchange for their 'black' property, Jews were issued with a so-called *Sperrstempel* (deferment stamp), which spared them from deportation (at least temporarily) and which – as was hinted – might even pave the way for emigration. In any case, the threatened deportation was temporarily blocked (*gesperrt*). The exemptions were never permanent but only valid 'until further notice'.

This temporary deferment from deportation was a variant of the earlier issue of emigration stamps against hard foreign currency. Emigration matters were handled by the Reichssicherheitshauptamt in Berlin.

The so-called *Sperrstempel* were issued against payments ranging from 20,000 guilders per person (until 10 June 1943) to 30,000 guilders per person (after 10 June 1943). Children under fifteen were generally *gesperrt* automatically with their parents. The increase in the price reflected the increase in the price of diamonds. The stamps could not be bought with guilders but had to be paid for in precious stones, precious metals or hard foreign currency. If payment was made in gold, then one kilogram or the equivalent in gold coins had to be handed over.

The stamps were numbered, their numbers ranging from 10,000 (for, among others, foreign Jews) to 120,000. The last category was reserved for Jews able to surrender diamonds or other valuables. The surrender of the requisite items began in August 1942. The last holders of a 120,000 stamp were picked up during a raid on 29 September 1943, and sent to the *Vorzugslager* (preferential camp) of Bergen-Belsen, where most of them perished before the year was out.[1]

The proceeds from the emigration stamps went straight to the RSHA in Berlin, which dealt with emigration questions, but on special instruction, they could be diverted to the Four-Year Plan or the Reichsbank. The proceeds from the *Sperrstempel* went to the Zentralstelle für jüdische Auswanderung and from there to a normal Dutch bank whence they were taken to Germany at regular intervals by representatives of the Four-Year Plan. The accounts of this trade in human beings were kept 'scrupulously', as Harster explained after the war: 'Over the years, the accounts and the treatment of the valuables were examined repeatedly and approved unreservedly by the Chief Audit Office.'[2]

Probably to avoid giving the impression that the German police could be 'bought', the Nazis used intermediaries for these transactions. For the same reason, the deals were kept out of the public eye. In the autumn of 1942, the British press and radio did, however, get wind of the 'trade in human beings for foreign currency', and news about the affair also began to filter through to Switzerland.[3] On 25 November 1942, the Swiss *Tagesanzeiger* reported that:

> Under the official designation of 'Trade in Human Beings', the British government has issued the following statement:
>
> 'For several months now the British government has been receiving proof that the enemy is doing a considerable trade in permits to emigrate from the occupied countries, and from Holland in particular.'

Sperrstempel: *Emigration and Tax*

The paper went on to point out that the US government had issued similar reports, mentioning that up to $7,500 per person was being paid.

The probable result of these reports was to make the Germans proceed even more cautiously. The subject had meanwhile also alarmed the German Ministry of Foreign Affairs, which was worried that the news had leaked out through broadcasts from Britain, including one broadcast by Radio Oranje on 24 November 1942. Besides being afraid that the German Security Police might gain the reputation of being corrupt, provided enough money was on offer, the German authorities were also seriously worried that their country's international standing was being impaired. In particular, foreign countries might gain the impression that Germany's supply of foreign currency was so severely depleted that the Reich was forced to resort to objectionable practices.[4]

The Dutch government, too, was worried about the news from Switzerland, but its concern was purely bureaucratic and legalistic. It failed to show any sympathy for the desperate situation of Dutch Jewry. On the contrary, according to the Dutch government-in-exile, these Jews were in breach of Section A6, which prohibited all dealings with the enemy unless special permission had been obtained beforehand. In a letter to Her Majesty's ambassador, J. J. B. Bosch Ridder van Rosenthal, a ministry spokesman wrote:

> I cannot share your view that it makes no difference whether the Gestapo obtains money by such transactions or whether the fortunes of Jews were confiscated after their transportation to the East, since in the first case foreign currency is released to the enemy, which does not happen in the second case.[5]

According to the historians L. de Jong and J. Presser, the chief intermediaries between Jews and German agencies in the purchase of *Sperrstempel* were J. J. Weissman and E. A. P. Puttkammer. Both historians take a negative view of Weissman, while their opinion of Puttkammer is less harsh. Yet the inclusion of a name on the Puttkammer list could no more save Jews from deportation to the East than could inclusion on the Weissman list.[6]

Puttkammer acted as intermediary between, on the one hand, the Devisenschutzkommando and the Befehlshaber der Sicherheitspolizei und des SD, Abteilung IV b 4 (two bodies concerned, inter alia, with tracing surrendered Jewish possessions), and the Jews on the other. The surrendered jewellery and cash (hard currency such as Swiss francs, dollars and Swedish crowns) were worth a considerable amount – Jews paid a fortune for the temporary stay of deportation orders. A glance at the archives shows that diamonds, pearls, diadems, bracelets, necklaces, cash, and pure gold were some of the items they handed over. Every item was accompanied with a short description and a note giving its assessed value, together with the reason for its surrender:

> ... 1 ring with diamonds currently valued at ca. 25,000 guilders, 1 pendant and 1 diamond pin, 3,000 guilders for temporary revocation of labour service and *Sperre* in Westerbork [dated 26 June 1943].

> ... 1 diamond wrist watch currently valued at ca. 11,000 guilders, 1 lady's diamond and sapphire ring, 7,000 guilders, 1 blue diamond pendant, 12,000 guilders ... for temporary deferment from labour service and release from the Schouwburg [dated 6 July 1943].

> ... You are requested to exempt this Jewish couple, at present in Westerbork, from transportation to Germany and to confine them to Westerbork. In return they have offered 10,000 guilders in ready cash; 2 diamond eardrops set in gold; one gold ring with diamonds; one white gold collar with 20 small diamonds; one white gold ring with 3 diamonds; one white gold ring with 17 diamonds; one solitaire. The estimated current value of this jewellery is 30,000 guilders. The cash and the jewellery have been deposited with me ... [dated 20 April 1943].

These are but a few random samples. All in all, the Germans seem to have considered this system of handing in valuables and currency a convenient method of confiscation. Moreover, they wanted to have their cake and eat it, as we can see from a letter Puttkammer wrote to one of his 'clients', who, through his intervention, had handed in several pieces of jewellery to the Zentralstelle für jüdische Auswanderung. They were valued at 230,000 guilders and were used to obtain a *Sperrstempel* from the 120,000 series. However, the Zentralstelle had the jewelley revalued and arrived at an estimate of no more than 124,500 guilders. 'In this connection,' Puttkammer wrote to the *Sperrstempel* candidates, '... I would ask you to be so kind as to let me know if you are able to hand over other items of jewellery so that the 210,000 guilders required for your *Sperre* can be reached.'[7]

Erich August Puttkammer was a German subject who had been naturalized in the Netherlands in 1939. He worked as deputy manager in the German division of the Rotterdamsche Bankvereeniging (Robaver) in Amsterdam, nowadays part of the ABN-AMRO concern. Towards the end of 1940 he was approached by the board of his bank with a request to mediate on behalf of one of their Jewish clients threatened with deportation to Germany. Thanks to his background, Puttkammer was thought to be particularly suited to handling German agencies.

For the rest, Jews found their way to Puttkammer without prompting because, as he himself explained, he had paid 'flight capital' from German Jews into secret Robaver accounts. As a result he had been able to keep a large part of their assets out of the hands of the Nazis. A number of his Jewish clients, who were aware of his contacts with the Devisenschutkommando, asked him with for help with emigration permits. Puttkammer then made contact with the heads of the Devisenschutzkommando, and pleaded for preferential treatment for the bank's clients.

Puttkammer was soon so overwhelmed with work that the board of the bank allowed him and a secretary to devote all their time to these cases.

Sperrstempel: *Emigration and Tax*

In the beginning, the petitioners were still offered a chance of emigrating to a neutral country (generally in South America). To avail themselves of this opportunity, they did not have to surrender foreign currency but had to leave all their property behind. Early in 1943, the Security Police started to demand 30,000 guilders per head in foreign currency. In exchange, applicants received a 'Puttkammer stamp', also called a '120,000 stamp'. The 30,000 guilders had preferably to be remitted in diamonds or gold.

All exemptions were granted until further notice, as we have seen. According to his own testimony, Puttkammer intervened in 400 to 500 cases, handing the surrendered valuables and money over to Hauptsturmführer K. Wörlein of the Zentralstelle für jüdische Auswanderung.[8] In other words, he handled assets amounting to at least one and a half million guilders. After the war, the Centrale Vermogens Opsporingsdiens (the Central Property Recovery Service, the CVO) put the amount at about ten million guilders, on the assumption that the estimated values of the items handed in had been kept deliberately low. In many cases, Puttkammer's 'clients' used non-Jewish intermediaries who wanted to remain anonymous.

Puttkammer took no fee, but he did draw the attention of petitioners to a fund into which they could pay 'voluntary' contributions – 'no more than a maximum of 300 guilders per case' – to meet his expenses. How these transactions were accounted for to Robaver – ultimately Puttkammer's employers – is not known (if indeed they ever were). Puttkammer himself stated that he never dipped into the fund personally. No books were kept. Puttkammer declared that he was very doubtful if the Germans were likely to fulfil their obligations to the stamp applicants, but he failed to say whether or not he actually realized that the stamps named after him offered no guarantee whatsoever.[9]

Puttkammer's role remains mysterious and it is an open question why Robaver collaborated in operations that, as they ought to have known, invariably came to a bad end. After the war, Puttkammer was unconditionally acquitted of all charges for lack of evidence. He returned to Robaver, the only large bank that, as the former Resistance newspaper, *Het Parool* (19 July 1945) remarked bitterly, had 'with all sorts of excuses, refused credits to the National Assistance Fund for help to people in hiding'. The fact that Puttkammer had put many millions of guilders into the enemy's hands was not held against him either.

When it is remembered that Jews were prohibited by Section A6 from buying emigration permits, astonishment is the only reaction.

After the war, Puttkammer made efforts to obtain reparations for the duped Jews. There is confusion about the value of the surrendered jewellery, since the estimates (given by the press at the time of his trial) varied from 400,000 guilders to ten million guilders. According to *Het Vrije Volk*, 8,754,676 guilders of that total accounted for jewellery, including precious metals and precious stones; 15 kilograms of pure gold; 1,000 American gold dollars; 600 ten-guilder gold coins and large quantities of precious stones, the value of which could not be established. These figures have been taken from the CVO.[10]

The press estimate of ten million guilders does not seem to be exaggerated and is, if anything, likely to be on the low side. From a document published by the Ministry of Justice, in which not all the transactions have been entered, it appears that the amounts that went to the Germans, thanks to Puttkammer's exertions, are close to those given by *Het Vrije Volk*. Puttkammer, it seems, accepted not only cut but also uncut diamonds; in addition the list mentions gold, 'scrap gold', a painting (possibly a Van Gogh) and a camera.[11]

A lawyer who served as intermediary between his Jewish clients and Puttkammer has argued that Puttkammer must have known that the 120,000 stamps were of no use whatsoever. However, other witnesses testified on Puttkammer's behalf.

The testimony by the valuer H. J. C. Jansen raises more questions than it answers. Like Puttkammer, he declared that he took no fees for his work. Puttkammer had consulted him some forty times and his valuations had run to a total of one million guilders (an average of 25,000 guilders per valuation), but for lack of bookkeeping entries there is no corroboration of that figure. He himself claimed that he advised Jews several times not to surrender their money or valuables against *Sperrstempel*, 'the less so as Puttkammer told him several times that he too considered them "futile"'.

Testimony for and against Puttkammer can be drawn at will from his court records. He continued to stress that the Amsterdamsche Bank acted in much the same spirit as he had done by supplying the Germans with industrial diamonds against a *Sperre* for their Jewish 'diamond-clientele'.[12] I have been unable to discover any concrete evidence confirming or refuting Puttkammer's claim.

After the war, a host of contradictory evidence was produced, with all the accused trying to paint the best possible picture of their actions. Quite often attempts were made to discredit colleagues, the better to present one's own role in a favourable light. In most cases, the aim was a milder sentence or if at all possible an acquittal. The dossiers, especially in the case of such controversial figures as Puttkammer, are an archival minefield in which the historian can make serious errors of judgment, no matter how conscientious his analysis may be.[13]

The jewellery and gold handed over have probably disappeared for good, so that with few exceptions physical restitution must be considered impossible. Puttkammer assumed that the items concerned were originally taken to Germany (possibly to the Reichssicherheitshauptamt), and then vanished without a trace.[14] In almost all cases, the description of the valuables handed in was so perfunctory that the original owners could not possibly prove their claim to them – a description such as 'a bracelet with three diamonds' is wholly inadequate.

Sperrstempel: *Emigration and Tax*

Other notorious 'mediators' were N. J. Ros and P. C. Docter, two characters from the Amsterdam underworld who charged a commission of 10 per cent for their services. After the war, a Special Court of Justice found that 293 Jews had handed over goods to the value of 8,790,000 guilders to Docter, plus a commission of 879.00 guilders. After the war, a significant part of the money could be repaid to the parties concerned through the Nederlandse Beheersinstituut (Netherlands State Property Administration). Docter and Ros took their fees in cash, jewels, precious stones, gold, and sometimes in shares. They accepted anything of value, but they rarely fulfilled their promise to obtain a *Sperrstempel* or exit visa from the Sicherheitspolizei. Ros also made use of Puttkammer's services.[15]

No less notorious was one Walter Büchi, a Swiss businessman resident in Amsterdam who mediated between prosperous Jewish families who were keen to emigrate to Switzerland and the Sicherheitspolizei. Thus he relieved the Esso and Meijer families of about 200,000 guilders in exchange for an exit visa to Switzerland. In Germany, that is, on the way to Switzerland, the families were dragged out of the train and packed off to a concentration camp, where almost all of them perished.

The two families were arrested in Germany rather than at some Dutch railway station, which would have been simpler, because the chances of anyone witnessing the scene in Germany were minimal. The SD was anxious to mislead the outside world into believing that emigration to neutral Switzerland was a real possibility, and it would have looked suspicious or strange if the agency issuing the exit visa was the one that also arrested the visa holders.

A Gestapo officer's answer when asked by the arrested families why they could not return to the Netherlands instead of being packed off to the East was revealing: 'Büchi must be allowed to continue his work.' After all, this trade in human flesh yielded considerable sums of money. Together with the SD, Büchi stage-managed the 'emigration' to perfection.

Quite a few other Jews ended up in concentrations camps rather than in Switzerland thanks to Büchi's 'mediation'. As a tool of the SD, Büchi pocketed large sums of money – in most cases more than the 10 per cent 'commission' he ostensibly charged for his work. The difference between the amount the SD demanded for a stamp and the sum his victims handed over went straight into the wallet of this Amsterdammer from Switzerland.

Büchi took pitiless advantage of the situation. Thus he claimed on various occasions that the price of diamonds in Switzerland had suddenly tumbled and that the proffered sum was therefore insufficient. In all such cases, the families concerned had to pay up again, some more than once.

Jews who believed that they could obtain a 'safety guarantee' by making payment for their visas dependent on their safe arrival in Switzerland, nevertheless remained dependent on Büchi's intervention. The transfer of jewels or foreign currency to a Swiss bank was made by Büchi in person, and during the transfer phase his 'clients' could do little more than hope that he would indeed do what he had promised.

In a letter from the Schweizerische Bankgesellschaft in Zurich, addressed to Büchi, Stadionkade, Amsterdam, the bank declared that it would pay Büchi 25,000 Swiss francs once Anna Linz-Esslinger had confirmed her arrival on neutral territory. The letter was dated 24 October 1942. Anna Linz-Esslinger died in Auschwitz on 26 February 1943. The available material does not make clear what happened to the 25,000 Swiss francs. In all probability, Büchi managed to lay his hands on them, for his file shows that he had mastered the art of wheedling powers of attorney out of his clients and hence of pocketing sums of money to which he was not entitled.[16] It also seems to be self-evident, for why would he have smuggled valuables to Switzerland unless he was sure that he could to lay his hands on them later? Nor did the valuables remain in the bank – the name of Anna Linz-Esslinger does not at any rate appear on the lists of fugitive Jewish capital in Switzerland published on 23 July and 29 October 1997.

We know of some 1,200 cases of Jews who surrendered diamonds, jewellery and other valuable items to obtain a *Sperrstempel* and hence deferment from deportation.[17]

Finally, the Dutch tax agency interfered in the affairs of emigrating Jews. Formally, the Dutch tax authorities were fully within their rights, and yet many people must wonder whether they could not have been more magnanimous in their dealings with a group of people of which one could have told, even at that time, that their situation was fraught with danger.

Liro and Tax

The tax authorities could not have failed to realize that Jewish assets had been concentrated on the premises of Liro, Sarphatistraat. Beyond that, they took a keen interest in 'Israelites wishing to move their residence abroad'. It was especially for this group – according to a letter from the fiscal authorities – that the Zentralstelle für jüdische Auswanderung had been set up in Amsterdam. The letter explained that Jews had to go through a number of formalities there. Among other things, it had to be established that there were no objections from a fiscal point of view to their departure. To that end, an application for a 'clearance certificate' for emigration from the Netherlands was to be handed in. Before issuing the certificate, the Zentralstelle forwarded the application to the relevant tax office for scrutiny and confirmation. The application had to be accompanied by a letter to the official in charge, informing him what if any enquiries he was expected to make. The inland revenue had its own representative in the Zentralstelle in the person of C. J. W. van Dintel.[18]

Van Dintel voiced doubts about the fiscal ethics of 'some of the emigrants', who seemed quite indifferent to paying their taxes. That was certainly the case when their assets had been deposited with Liro, many of them 'refusing their collaboration' in instructing Liro to pay their taxes out of their Liro accounts. During an interview, the Liro board let it be known that the robber bank set great store by having the 'emigrants' themselves give instruction to make the taxes over to the receiver of revenue, although if they refused Liro was willing to do the job for them upon production of duplicate tax assessments and an explanation of their special circumstances. However, Van Dintel felt that such cases had to be kept to a minimum and hence made the following suggestion:

> The Receiver of Revenue will first try to compel the emigrant to settle his debt by an injunction, by confiscation of his remaining assets or by instructing Lippman, Rosenthal & Co. to do so. If no satisfaction can be obtained, then he must bring the case before me through the Inspector, submitting copies of tax assessments and details of the case with a request for payment by Lippmann, Rosenthal & Co.[19]

Jewish emigration remained limited in number and occurred mainly in 1940 and 1941.[20] After the promulgation of the First Liro Decree, tax debts could only be settled through a Liro account. Liro proved to be slow in making payments, however, and the robber bank was not the only recalcitrant debtor. The collector of taxes in Amsterdam complained that the *Verwalter* too lagged behind with their payments. Moreover, the Niederländische Grundstücksverwaltung (Netherlands Estate Administration), Omnia and the VVRA – all of them administrators of Jewish assets – were loath to part with money when it came to settling tax debts. The Devisenschutzkommando generally refused to hand over any part of the money it had confiscated. Another source of worry for the fiscal authorities was the unpaid tax of diamond merchants. Their case was, however, treated more sympathetically because 'their diamonds having been sequestrated, these tax payers cannot possibly meet their tax obligations. Only by confiscating their furniture can the debt be settled, but this is something I consider particularly harsh in the given circumstances.'

Even so, the confiscation of the furniture of Liro account holders who did not pay their taxes could not be avoided in the long run. To that end, the tax authorities made contact with Liro, which, however, let it be known that such a measure was 'inadmissible by virtue of the decision of the competent German bodies'. The tax authorities had obviously overlooked the fact that, as part of the M-Aktion, Liro and the ERR were busily confiscating Jewish furniture and household equipment, and that they were loath to have the tax authorities interfere with these activities.

It seemed essential to enter into consultations with the German authorities to discover how the Treasury was to recover its money.[21]

And that is what happened. The acting permanent secretary of the Ministry of Finance wrote a letter to the Hauptabteilung Finanzen (Central Finance Section) of the Reichskommissariat, asking how taxes owed by Jews – inasmuch as such taxes were to be paid out of the assets they had been forced to deposit with Liro – were best to be collected.

> In the middle of November 1942, the outstanding private tax bill of Amsterdam Jews (income and property tax, personal tax and inheritance tax) came to 10,647,000 guilders. Since there is no Jewish working class and since small Jewish businessmen can in general be taxed for no more than small sums, I believe that at least 6,000,000 guilders of this amount must be met out of credits lodged with Lippmann, Rosenthal & Co. In arriving at this figure, I have borne in mind the possibility that Jews will meet further tax bills out of their remaining resources.

The Ministry of Finance thus demanded six million guilders from Liro out of accounts held by Amsterdam Jews. But not all Dutch Jews lived in Amsterdam. According to the computation presented by the acting permanent secretary of the Ministry to the Hauptabteilung Finanzen, 79,497 Jews (80,000 in round figures) lived in the capital, and a total of 140,000 Jews lived in the Netherlands as a whole. In view of these figures, the permanent secretary believed that the total amount of personal taxes to be paid out of Liro funds should be put at '140/80 × f.6,000,000 = 10,500,000 guilders'. That amount had, however, to be increased to allow for assessments 'levied after the middle of November'. On the other hand, the definite assessments of Jews for the income tax year 1942 were likely to be lower, and hence the permanent secretary thought it reasonable to reduce the estimated tax debt from 10.5 to ten million guilders.[22] But Liro argued that it could in no way be expected to settle the tax debt of Dutch Jewry. In 1943, the bank offered to make a one-off payment of eight million guilders to the tax authorities as part of an overall settlement.[23]

Conclusion

The State of Affairs at the Liberation

When the Dutch authorities prepared a first inventory in the summer of 1945, it appeared that Liro had fully earned its name of 'robber bank'.

Effects surrendered:

Cash and/or bank giro payments	Hfl.	55,000,000.00
Shares (at the official rate on randomly chosen dates, on average several months after surrender)	Hfl.	300,000,000.00
Insurance policies (estimated surrender value)	Hfl.	25,100,000.00
Reassigned claims (estimated)	Hfl.	39,685,000.00
Gold, silver, jewellery, art ('with a very low resale estimate').	Hfl.	6,041,500.00
Total	Hfl.	425,826,500.00

Effects still held on 25 May 1945:

Cash and accounts	Hfl.	2,857,179.53
Treasury bills	Hfl.	3,000,000.00
Shares: home	Hfl.	14,021,019.38
Shares: abroad	Hfl.	82,613.20
Shares (remainder of the 300 million surrendered)	Hfl.	58,178,190.00
Sundry debtors	Hfl.	815,613.46
Unsurrendered policies	Hfl.	33,800.00
Works of art, etc.	Hfl.	36,750.00
Reassigned, unsettled claims	Hfl.	10,782,479.29
Total	Hfl.	89,807,644.86

Handed over by Liro to:

VVRA	Hfl.	234,388,000.00
Deutsche Revisions und Treuhand	Hfl.	19,998,200.00
Repayments to 'mixed marriages' and yellow star exemptions	Hfl.	20,293,875.00
Repayments to persons mistakenly forced to surrender their assets	Hfl.	2,067,950.00
The German Supreme Court	Hfl.	603,228.00
Total	Hfl.	277,351,253.00
Grand total of effects still held and handed over by Liro	Hfl.	367,158,897.86

The assets left with Liro and those handed over to the VVRA and others (89,807,644.86 and 277,351,253.00 guilders respectively) came to a total of 367,158,897.86 guilders. Since 425,826,500.00 guilders had been received during the occupation, a difference of some 60,000,000.00 remained to be accounted for, and to that end the *Sammelkonto* had first to be unravelled.[1] However, apart from the *Sammelkonto*, large sums of money and parcels of shares had been made over by Liro to VVRA, without proper bookkeeping records. That, too, had to be disentangled before the final figure could be determined. A similarly chaotic situation prevailed in the VVRA, though we do know that the VVRA held shares to the tune of 63,902,800.00 guilders on 25 May 1945.[2] In addition, some Jewish property had also ended up in the hands of, among others, the Devisenschutzkommando, the Security Police, the ERR, the Dienststelle Mühlmann and the RSHA.

We know roughly which assets could be recovered after the war. Immovable property naturally caused the fewest problems, although matters could be complicated even here, for instance when the property had been sold on to second, third and even later buyers. It was reasonable to assume that the first buyer had acted in bad faith – if he had kept the immovable property after the war (and on top of that was a German or an NSB member) the return of the property to its legitimate owner offered few problems in principle. But if the property had been sold on once or several times, matters were more complicated, certainly if one of the later owners could prove that he had acted in good faith.

Businessmen often found that their concerns had been plundered of all their contents. The machinery or other capital assets had vanished or been left in a deplorable state; the supplies had disappeared and the raw materials had been removed. Administrators of associations and foundations encountered a similar situation. No provision for compensation of any kind could be made.

Conclusion

The amounts paid for *Sperrstempel,* in foreign currency, precious stones and precious metals, seemed to have largely vanished, and the surrendered Jewish shares were scattered all over the country (and parts of the world), although a sizeable portion had remained with the VVRA and with Liro.

The surrendered insurance policies had to be reactivated, that is, their purchase by the Germans in collaboration with the insurance companies had to be revoked.

Nearly all collections of valuables and works of art handed over in accordance with the Second Liro Decree seemed to have vanished. Jewellery, gold, silver, precious metals, art, postage stamps, antiques, sculptures and paintings of any value had been packed off to Germany and sold, or placed at the disposal of institutions and sometimes of private individuals. Anything that the Germans were not interested in had been sold by Dutch auction houses or through other channels. Nearly everything in this category had vanished for good. Much the same was true of the household effects and furniture carried off to Germany or further east.

The looting can be summed up in the following figures, but these figures must not be considered as conclusive – the stipulations and qualifications mentioned in the relevant chapters apply to all categories.

The Looting of Jewish Property 1940–45

Loot	Amount in millions of guilders
Shares	300–400
Bank deposits, giro balances and cash	26–55
Insurance policies	25
Claims	38
Mortgages	22
Building land	150
Agricultural property	17
Businesses (liquidated)	6.5
Businesses (Aryanized)	75^3
Art, gold, etc.	6^4
Household effects	78
Puttkammer stamps, etc.	10
Non-profit-making associations and foundations	10
Devisenschutzkommando, SD, SP	10^5
Total (lowest estimate in round figures)	774
Total (highest estimate in round figures)	903

Both estimates are certainly incomplete and too low. Bearing in mind what has been said among other things about the Aryanization of businesses, it is reasonable to assume, on the basis of the available data, that the Germans robbed Dutch Jewry of *at least* 1,000 million guilders (at the then going rate).

The Selling-off of Dutch Cultural Property

Large depredations of Dutch cultural possessions were the result of sham or 'indirect' sales. Countless works of art were bought by German art agents and disappeared over the German border for good. In some cases, pressure was exerted on the prospective vendors, but much more often Dutch art dealers and private individuals were anxious to profit from the boom in the art market created by the war. All of them did good business and were paid in guilders, albeit in guilders bought with unredeemable Reichsmarks. The Reichsbank in Berlin refused to honour its own banknotes, especially after 1 April 1941, when the currency border with Germany was abolished and the Dutch market was fair game for German buyers.

After the war, the Nederlandsche Bank was swamped with about 4,000 million practically worthless Reichsmarks, mostly accumulated through what may be called 'technical' or 'indirect' robbery. In practice, the sales and hence the profits of the art trade meant a proportionately great loss for the Nederlandsche Bank, and hence for the Dutch state. Ultimately, huge profits were being made on the back of Dutch citizens.

All trade with the occupying power was banned by the Dutch government-in-exile under emergency decree A6, but at the time of its promulgation (in June 1940) the Dutch government had no means of enforcing the decree. Nor was that the purpose of A6; it was more of a big stick, a threat that all such transactions would be revoked after the war.

The Allied Declaration of 3 January 1943 must be viewed in much the same light. During the war, both measures were necessarily little more than warnings against any dealings with the invaders, but later these warnings were followed by action: the transactions were declared null and void. This subject will be dealt with in a subsequent volume.

Discrepancies

Not only Jews, but the Dutch people as a whole suffered badly from the German occupation and the rapacity that went with it. If we consider the 26,000 million guilders the Netherlands claimed at the Paris Reparations Conference, we obtain

Conclusion

no more than a vague idea of the damage inflicted by the Nazis on the Netherlands, although this figure gives a good indication of its impact nevertheless.

The claim for 26,000 million guilders had deliberately been set high by the Dutch government for safety's sake. It covered all forms of damage the country had suffered, and was therefore not confined to the theft of machinery, rolling stock and other means of transport, metals, raw materials, cultural property, securities, canal boats, church bells, clothing, cattle and the like. The material loss inflicted by the robbery of Dutch Jewry came to at least 1,000 million guilders at the then prevailing values. That is a very large sum, considering that the pre-war Jewish population of the Netherlands was about 140,000 souls, in a total population of 8.5 million people.

A simple comparison conveys some impression of the differences in the damage inflicted. The comparison is not altogether accurate because the total damage (that is, not through looting alone) is being compared with the damage suffered by Dutch Jews, which can be blamed almost entirely on Nazi looting practices. However, it does provide an excellent comparison of the material damage inflicted, and demonstrates conclusively how disproportionately Dutch Jews suffered during the Second World War even in material respects. Whereas the average Dutchman suffered damages of about 3,058 guilders, every one of his Jewish fellow citizens lost on average at least 7,142 guilders.

If we confine the comparison to damage by looting, we see that the Netherlands as a whole lost 3.64 billion guilders, of which more than 1 billion came from the Jewish population. In other words, some 1.6 per cent of the population suffered about one third of the total losses. These figures refer to the mainland Netherlands only. The differences in the damage suffered are therefore vast and were due primarily to the fact that Jews had to surrender all their possessions. Admittedly, the average Dutch citizen did not escape occasional orders to surrender his possessions, but compared with what was imposed on his Jewish fellow citizens, these impositions were relatively mild. Only the Gypsies suffered a fate comparable to that of the Jews. We have no precise figures, but they too had to hand over all their property to the Nazis because, like the Jews, they were the victims of Nazi racism.

The looting of Dutch Jewry was brutal and direct, although to avoid unrest it was camouflaged whenever possible. The aim was the total confiscation of Jewish property. All other Netherlanders, with the exception of the Gypsies, were spared these systematic depredations.

The Tactics of the Looting Process

For the looting of Jewish property a special, more or less logical 'legal' system was devised and declared applicable to all Jewish possessions. In using it, the German authorities kept the Hague Convention respecting the laws and customs of war on land in mind, if only as a matter of form. If any mistakes were made – which happened repeatedly in the case of mixed marriages – the parties forced to surrender their property had it duly restored to them.

In promulgating their various looting decrees the Germans tried to leave as little as possible to chance. Even so, additions, corrections and fresh stipulations had to be introduced repeatedly. Any loopholes left by a decree were quickly closed with as many extra clauses as were deemed necessary. In this context, it was characteristic that anyone who thought he was not liable to surrender his property could raise objections. Hitler's looting empire was a strictly structured and bureaucratic world, in which confiscations were not left to chance or whim – at least not in the Netherlands.

Decrees probably also played a major role in guiding the officials and agencies doing the robbers' work. Their world was structured accordingly, and it is an open question whether the expropriation of a section of the population on so large a scale could have been carried out had not this impersonal, bureaucratic and administrative machinery provided a front behind which they could shelter. It is likely that the camouflage methods used also facilitated the work of the executive staff. The practices of such regular bands of robbers as the Henneicke Column are left out of consideration here. No one apparently felt any need to gloss over their openly criminal activities.

The German decrees (*Verordnungen*) were directed against

- businesses;
- non-profit-making associations and foundations;
- individuals.

This distinction was always and consistently taken into account. *Verordnungen* were not allowed to overlap and cause administrative problems.

The Germans suspected that not all Jews heeded the order to hand in their possessions. Not only the Devisenschutzkommando but the Security Police, too, went in search of any possessions Jews tried to keep back. To that end, these organizations used special informers (*Vertrauensmänner* or *V-männer*).

One way of recovering 'black money', or what the Germans considered as such, was to sell *Sperrstempel*, providing deferment from transportation. The Germans' downright perverse approach was reflected in the release of 'diamond Jews' from Westerbork, described in my preface, once it had become clear that these men had failed to hand over significant quantities of diamonds. After their temporary release, they were once more, and this time thoroughly, stripped of their stones and 'put on transport', without reprieve.

Conclusion

When it came to the confiscation of 'enemy property', it was invariably the Jews who were the victims. While the 'enemy property' of non-Jews was nearly always placed under administrative control, Jewish property was turned into cash for the Germans.

Even works of art on loan to museums did not escape their attention, and had to be surrendered to Liro, or at least registered there. This was but a minor aspect, but it does show how carefully considered and systematic the German looting process was. The Nazis could fall back on the vast experience they had had in their own country ever since Hitler came to power in 1933.

Little can be said with certainty about property Jews handed over for safe-keeping during the war and which was not returned to them after the Liberation, despite all promises to do so. There were few written agreements, and the many murdered Jews could not, of course, claim back what goods they had entrusted to others. Survivors knocked on closed doors in many cases – the number of those whose claims were disputed is not even approximately known. What and how much was misappropriated in this way cannot even be guessed at for lack of reliable data.

Traceability

The participation of Dutch citizens and institutions in the sale of stolen Jewish property was indefensible even by the standards of the time. The common excuse that the property at least remained in the Netherlands and could therefore be recovered fairly easily after the war is in most cases spurious.

The purchases by Dutch museums from Liro are more defensible, because these institutions were undoubtedly Dutch in essence and the purchases were made for the museums themselves, with no intention to sell them on. After the war, these properties could indeed be retraced and restored to their legitimate owners without too much detective work. Unfortunately, however, that process did prove unduly slow in a number of cases, thus raising doubts about the good intentions of the institutions concerned.

The argument that museum acquisitions are easily traceable may be defended on the grounds that they facilitated post-war recovery. Things were quite different, however, with the banks and the Amsterdam Stock Exchange Association, which put forward the same argument repeatedly and vigorously. For a short period of the war they may be given the benefit of the doubt. However, the 'dumping days', the extra commission of 1 per cent offered by Rebholz for the purchase of American shares, the possibility of specifying stolen securities of Jewish provenance and the use of front men who helped to keep the real buyers of the securities out of the picture, strongly suggest that quite other motives were at work.

To Close

After the war, the Dutch government was left with the immense task of restoring property to its legitimate owners. The country was in chaos, and the accounts and archives of Liro, the VVRA and other German looting agencies, which could have shown where things had gone to, were in a state of confusion, or had disappeared or been destroyed.

Of the 107,000 or so deported Jews, only some 5,200 returned from the death camps, robbed of their possessions, of most of their families, spouses, friends and acquaintances. There were scarcely any reception arrangements, and often little interest in what they had gone through. In the opinion of many of them the restoration of their rights was not handled satisfactorily, so much so that the subject has become a source of argument and indeed of great agitation and moral indignation towards the end of the millennium, a good fifty years later.

The historian is able to place the period from 1940 to 1945, the years in which this large-scale looting occurred, into a historical framework and hence shed some light on it. However, explaining it *in full* – and that applies first and foremost to its impact on the victims, on those compelled to surrender all their possessions – is beyond his powers.

Notes

Introduction

1. There are no general accounts of the German looting in the Netherlands during the Second World War. In his standard work. *Het Koninkrijk der Nederlanden in de Tweede Wereldoorlog* (14 volumes), Dr Louise de Jong did of course dwell on the subject. The same is true of Dr J. Presser's *Ondergang. De vervolging en verdelging van het Nederlandse Jodendom 1940–1945* (2 volumes) (English translation: *Ashes in the Wind*) and Abel J. Herzberg's 'Kroniek der jodenvervolging' in *Onderdrukking en Verzet. Nederland in oorlogstijd.* Aspects of the looting are, moreover, mentioned in the literature: in his *Een Eeuw Vol Effecten. Historische schets van de Vereniging voor de Effectenhandel op de Amsterdamsche Effectenbeurs 1876–1976*, Professor J. de Vries has devoted an important chapter to the trade in stolen shares of Jewish provenance. Gerard Aalders has contributed a paper entitled 'Plundering of Jewish assets during the Second World War' to *Spoils of War* (1996).

    There exists a number of publications focusing attention on the looting of cultural goods, including particularly Peter Manasse, *Verdwenen archieven en bibliotheken. De verrichtingen van de Einsatzstab Rosenberg gedurende de Tweede Wereldoorlog* and A. Venema, *Kunsthandel in Nederland 1940–1945*.
2. *Verslag over het jaar 1948*. For 1997 exchange rates, see the table on page 283.
3. Washington National Records Center (WNRC), Record Group (RG) 84, The Hague Embassy file, box 3, 'Looted Art in Occupied Territories, Neutral Countries and Latin America, August 1945' and National Archives, Records of the United States Occupation Headquarters WWII, Ardelia Hall Collection, RG 260, box 12, 'Looted Art in Occupied Territories, Neutral Countries and Latin America', 5 May 1945. The Washington National Records Center in Suitland, Maryland has since been closed. The archive has been transferred to the National Archives in College Park, Washington.
4. National Archives (NA), Records of the United States Occupation Headquarters WWII, Ardelia Hall Collection, RG 260, box 182, 'Trial Address. Plunder of art treasures'.
5. Algemeen Rijksarchief (ARA), 2.06.40, ministerie van Economische Zaken, Bureau Herstelbetalingen 1945–52, box 80, note 19 I/PI, 13 June 1949 and *Verslag over het jaar 1948*, pp. 86 ff.

Nazi Looting

6. Sayer and Botting, *Nazi Gold*.
7. Literature on this subject is scanty and in any case incomplete. However, since about 1995 most European countries have started investigations of the looting and of post-war restitution. These investigations were a direct consequence of the world-wide interest, from the summer of 1995 onwards, in the fate of Jewish 'flight capital' in Switzerland.
8. Bullock, *Hitler and Stalin*, p. 336.
9. For the Convention on War on Land, see Staatsblad 1900, no. 163 and Staatsblad 1910, no. 170. Cf. the Avalon Project at Yale Law School, 1998.
10. Quoted from Van Konijnenburg, *Roof Restitutie Reparatie*, p. 56.
11. Van Konijnenburg, *Roof Restitutie Reparatie*, p. 206.
12. Sijes, *Vervolging van Zigeuners*, pp. 106–22 and passim.
13. According to Section 3, Article 1 of the Decree of 3 June 1940, the inventory was to cover practically all fields: 'In terms of their professional authority, the commissioners-general have the right to demand information of any kind from all Netherlands authorities, departments, and institutions, both public and private, and to issue the necessary instructions to them.'

Chapter 1: The Many Guises of Robbery

1. The classification (and in part the description) of the various looting methods are, unless otherwise specified, taken from *Roof Restitutie Reparatie*, a publication by the Netherlands Ministry of Economic Affairs. For detailed accounts of the looting, see also De Jong, *Het Koninkrijk der Nederlanden in de Tweede Wereldoorlog,* vols. 1–14, Presser, *Ashes in the Wind* and Herzberg, 'Kroniek der jodenvervolging' in *Onderdrukking en Verzet. Nederland in oorlogstijd.*
2. For 'indirect robbery' ('technical looting') see Nederlands Instituut voor Oorlogsdocumentatie (hereafter referred to as Niod), Bregstein archive, box 1, folder 1 f, note on technical looting; box 4, folder c, appendix I, Indirect Robbery, and box 5, folder 1105 W, letter no. 965/G 283, dated 3 September 1951 from Minister of Finance P. Lieftinck to members of the Ministerial Council of Economic Affairs; Paape (ed.), *Studies over Nederland in oorlogstijd.* For foreign bonds and the complex manipulations involved, see A. J. van der Leeuw. 'De handel in Duitse effecten tijdens de bezetting', pp. 100–16, and Trip, *De Duitsche bezetting van Nederland.*
3. Royal Decree of 10 May, 1940. *Staatsblad* (Government Gazette) 484.
4. The exchange rate was 75.36 guilders for 100 Reichsmarks. Before May 1940, 100 Reichsmarks bought approximately 15 guilders. Source: Ministry of Justice, depot 70, box no. 2, no. 7, bank dossier.

Notes

5. Trip, *Duitsche bezetting*, p. 41.
6. According to Trip, *Duitsche bezetting*, pp. 17 ff, the Wehrmacht received 477 million guilders in 1945 (June to December); 1,124 million guilders in 1942; 1,181 million guilders and 1,328 million guilders in 1943; 1,757 million guilders in 1944; while a further 489 million guilders was transferred in 1945. The total occupation cost thus came to 6,356 million guilders. For the quotation, see p. 17.
7. For the legality of using the civil administration, see Paape (ed.), *Studies over Nederland in Oorlogstijd*, J. C. H. de Pater, 'Doel van de Duitse civiele bestuur in Nederland', pp. 39–47, and A. E. Cohen, 'Opmerkingen over de notitie van de dr. de Pater over het doel van het Duitse civiele bestuur in Nederland', pp. 48–59; see also Jansma, *Het bezettingsrecht in de practijk van de Tweede Wereldoorlog*, Proposition X: 'A civil authority in occupied territory must be considered unlawful in all circumstances.'
8. The other three commissioners-general were Dr Friedrich Wimmer (Generalkommissar für Verwaltung und Justiz – Administration and Justice); H. A. Rauter (Generalkommissar für das Sicherheitswesen – Security) and Fritz Schmidt (Generalkommissar zur besonderen Verwendung – General Purposes), who was succeeded after his death in June 1943 by W. F. A. Ritterbusch. In addition, Seyss-Inquart appointed a *Beauftragter* (administrator) for the eleven provinces and for Amsterdam and Rotterdam. The commissioners-general held wide powers, enabling them to wield complete control over their respective sectors.
9. The 'Convention Respecting the Laws and Customs of War on Land' adopted at the Second Peace Conference in The Hague in 1907 was signed by Germany and the Netherlands among other countries. The rights of occupying powers are specified in Section III: 'Military Authority over the Territory of the Hostile State', which comprises fifteen articles (42–56). For the complete text of the Convention, see the Avalon Project at Yale Law School on the Internet. See also *Staatsblad* 1910, no. 73.
10. Trip, *Duitsche bezetting*, pp. 19–20.
11. For the organization of the Foreign Currency Department, see archive of the ministerie van Justitie (Ministry of Justice), depot 70, box 2, no.107, bank dossier.
12. Archive of ministerie van Buitenlandse Zaken (Ministry of Foreign Affairs), Bern Embassy archive, 1945–55, inventory no. 813, letter from the Minister of Finance to the President of the Council of Ministers, undated. The nominal value was 187,765,590 guilders, made up of guilders, dollars, pounds sterling, and Swiss, Belgian and French francs. For foreign bonds, see Van der Leeuw, 'De handel in Duitse effecten' in Paape (ed.), *Studies over Nederland in Oorlogstijd*.

Hjalmar Schacht was President of the Reichsbank in the period from 1933 to 1939 as well as Germany's Minister of Economic Affairs.

13. Ministry of Finance, Directorate-General for Internal Revenue, verbal transcripts 1936–1975, 39/09/19/24 107, 'De Duitsche Deviezenmaatregelen, de Nederlandsch-Duitsche Clearing- en Transferregelingen, voor zoverre van belang voor aanslagregeling I.B. en V. B'.
14. Niod, Auslandbonds dossier I. The Reichskommissar was able to 'buy' Dr F. Mannheimer's collection because the curator of the bankrupt Mannheimer estate (the banker Mannheimer had died in 1939) was faced with the threat of having the collection confiscated. In these circumstances, 'selling' seemed the best solution. After the war, the collection was returned to the Netherlands almost intact (see Leistra, *Recuperatie in Nederland 1945–1946*). For the Mannheimer Collection, see also: Venema, *Kunsthandel in Nederland*, pp. 172–85 and 489–93.
15. *Verslag over de jaren 1945 en 1946*, p. 56.
16. NA, RG 59, Decimal Files 1945–49, box 4183, Miedl folder report no. 4, Miedl Case. Account of the German Activities on the Art Market in Holland
17. Trip, *Duitsche bezetting*, p. 5.
18. De Jong, *Koninkrijk*, vol. 7, pp. 215–35.
19. Niod, 'Notities voor het Geschiedwerk', no. 116.
20. De Jong, *Koninkrijk*, vol. 7, p. 227.
21. This account is taken from Van Konijnenburg, *Roof Restitutie Reparatie*, p. 81. For 'Winterhulp', see, inter alia, De Jong, *Koninkrijk*, vol. 4, part 2, pp. 681–6 and pp. 849–54, and 6, part I, pp. 489–96.
22. Niod, Doc I, 'Dagboek van prof. mr. A. M. de Jong.'
23. *De Prinsestad*, 14 October 1950.
24. The total collection came to 30 million guilders. Of that sum, more than 26 million was paid out in 1940–1; 6.2 million in 1941–2; 9.6 million in 1941–2 and 10.6 million in 1942–3. No figures for 1943–4 are available. After Mad Tuesday (September 1944) little more was heard of the organization. The figures are taken from De Jong, *Koninkrijk*, vol. 6, part 1, p. 494.
25. Van Konijnenburg, *Roof Restitutie Reparatie*, p. 82. Oddly enough, *Het Parool* of 27 September 1945 mentions that according to the audit office 12 million guilders were credited to the private accounts of some 1,700 NSB members. After the war, the money was apparently confiscated and shared out among, inter alia, the Bio Holiday Resort and the Salvation Army, which had been forced to deposit their funds in Winterhulp on its foundation in 1940.
26. For an overview of stolen property, see De Jong, *Koninkrijk*, vol. 7, part 1, pp. 1–270 and vol. 10b, pp. 70–97.
27. For an overview of labour service (*Arbeitseinsatz*) in all its aspects, see Seijes, *Arbeidsinzet*.

28. Hayes, *Industry*, pp. 355–68. See also Borkin, *Crime and Punishment*, and OMGUS, *Ermittlungen gegen I. G. Farben*, passim.
29. Niod, Doc II, 'Vorderingen door geallieerden'.
30. De Jong, *Koninkrijk*, vol. 4, p. 815, note; for Amsterdam, Heerlen and Bussum, see Niod, Doc II, 'Zoengeld'.
31. Ministry of Finance, Directorate-General Inland Revenue, verbal transcripts 1936–75, inventory no. 47–02–25/197 258, 'Nota Zoengelden'.
32. Niod, GKzbV, Neuordnung auf dem Gebiete der nichtwirtschaftlichen Personenvereinigungen und Stiftungen in den Niederlanden, 20 October 1941. See also De Jong, *Koninkrijk*, vol. 5, part 1, pp. 418–23.
33. Archive of ministerie van Buitenlandse Zaken, 313.212, Paris Embassy, GA 1952–64, box 4, 'Derde bespreking van de "Rebholz"-subcommissie', 21 January 1955.
34. Niod, Doc II, 'Verenigingen – opheffing'.
35. Ministerie van Financiën, Bewindvoering archive, rubric 1450 LVVS, 'Verslag Betreffende de Vermögensverwaltungs- und Renten-Anstalt', 9 February 1953. The report indicates that the liquidation of non-profit-making associations and foundations and of Masonic lodges fetched about 8,500,000 guilders: ARA, 2.09.10.02 Centraal Archief Bijzondere Rechtpleging (CABR), box 31, folder 70, 'Verslag van beheerders' (ultimo 1945). In *Koninkrijk*, vol. 5, p. 421, De Jong claims that more than 10.2 million guilders came from the liquidation of Jewish property. For the Jewish share, see 'Non-profit-making Associations and Foundations' in Chapter 5.
36. For 'Aryanization', see 'Aryanization' in Chapter 5. The figure of 50 million guilders is taken from De Jong, *Koninkrijk*, vol. 4, p. 379. See also Aalders, *Three Ways of German Economic Penetration*; Niod, archive 44, FiWi, Feindvermögen, folder IIA. A report ('Arbeitsgebiet Feindvermögen') dated 31 March 1943 indicates that 384 mergers were being negotiated at the time.
37. Ministerie van Justitie, CABR, von Karger dossier; Aalders, *Three Ways of German Economic Penetration* and Ulshöfer, *Einflussnahme auf Wirtschaftsunternehmungen*, pp. 140–2.
38. The collaboration of the Dutch financial world will be discussed in connection with the First Liro Decree (the sale of confiscated securities).

   For a detailed discussion of 'collaboration', see Gerhard Hirschfeld, *Fremdherrschaft und Kollaboration*. In this particular context, 'collaboration' is treated as a form of voluntary cooperation and not as the result of coercion. Clearly, not all forms of collaboration the German authorities could enforce by virtue of their position can be treated as collaboration. German 'requests' or orders could not, of course, be turned down without the threat of serious repercussions. The borderline is not easy to identify.
39. Ministerie van Justitie, depot 70, box no. 2, no. 7, bank dossier.

40. Ministerie van Justitie, depot 70, box no. 2, no. 7, bank dossier.
41. Letter from Shell to the author, 23 November 1993, and *Koninklijke Olie*, pp. 105–27.
42. Niod, archive 44, FiWi Feindvermögen, folder II A, report by 'Abteilung Feindvermögen,' 30 May 1944.
43. Letter from Philips to the author, 23 November 1993, and Blanken, *Geschiedenis van het Philips Electronics N.V.*, pp. 151–9 and 213–19.
44. Letter from Unilever to the author, 10 January 1944.
45. Niod, Fin. Div., *RWM, Feindvermögen*, vol. 41, *Zusammengefasster Bericht über die Kapitalverflechtung mit Holland und Belgien seit der Besatzung in Mai 1940*.
46. For a detailed discussion of the role of the Dresdner Bank, see OMGUS, *Ermittlungen gegen die Dresdner Bank;* for the song about Rasche, see p. vii.
47. Niod, N 157/1, Dresdner Bank, extract from 'Report on Dresdner Bank Investigation' by Office of Military Government for Germany (U.S.), section IV, *The Dresdner Bank in the Netherlands*.
48. Niod, NID 14333, N 90/1 folder, Office of Chief of Counsel for War Crimes, APO 696 A, US Army. Staff Evidence Analysis, 30 January 1945.
49. Niod, Fin. Div., RWM Collection, *Feindvermögen*, vol. 42. Apart from the HTW, the following banks are named: Handel-Maatschappij H. Albert de Bary & Co. (Deutsche Bank), N. V. Hollandsche Koopmansbank N. V. (Berliner Handels Gesellschaft), Continentale Handelsbank N.V. (Kali-Syndikat), Wodan Handelsmij N.V. (Dego), Theodor Gilissen, Rhodius Koenigs Handel Mij. N.V. (Delbrück. Schickler & Co. and Rebholz Effectenkantoor, formerly Fa. Leeser). The data on significant German capital participation are taken from Hamburger Stiftung für Sozial- und Wirtschaftsgeschichte (HSSW), OMGUS, Finad, RG 260, box 226, folder 14. The HSSW owns a large collection of papers in the banking and industry sectors, the originals of which can be found in the National Archives of the Washington National Records Center (Washington DC).
50. Niod, Fin. Div., *RWM, Feindvermögen*, vol. 41, *Zusammengefasster Bericht über die Kapitalverflechtung mit Holland und Belgien seit der Besatzung in Mai 1940*.
51. Niod, Fin. Div., Reichswirtschaftsministerium (RWM) Collection, *Feindvermögen*, vol. 41, *Zusammengefasster Bericht über die Kapitalverflechtung mit Holland und Belgien seit der Besatzung in Mai 1940*.
52. De Jong, *Koninkrijk*, vol. 10a, pp. 575, 579, 580 and vol. 10b, pp. 1,147–8.
53. Niod, Doc II, 'Arnhem, Plundering, Bericht van de Rijksrecherche, Arnhem, nr. 11/45, 12 December 1945' and *idem*, 'Proces-verbaal van J. Bijker, 31 March 1949'.
54. Niod, Bregstein archive, box 11, folder A1, Memorandum Concerning Netherlands Aspects of Looted Securities.

55. ARA, 2.09.16, Nederlands Beheers Instituut (NBI), box 600, *Vermerk Devisenschutzkommando Niederlande betreffend Niederländische Bank, Filiale Arnhem*, 5 December 1944. A total of 27,641,298 guilders is mentioned. Part of this amount consisted of converted Reichsmarks, whose value was far less than normal.
56. The estimate of 150 million, taken from the *Volkskrant* of 23 May 1950, seems to be too high.
57. For the post-war restoration of legal rights, see Aalders, Gerard, *Berooid. De beroofde joden en het Nederlandse restitutiebeleid sinds 1945*, Amsterdam, 2001.
58. The theft of monetary gold in the Netherlands is only touched upon here. For a fuller treatment of this subject, see Aalders, Gerard, *Eksters. De Nazi-roof van 146 duizend kilo goud bij De Nederlandsche Bank*, Amsterdam, 2002.
59. For a general survey of the theft of gold in Europe, see Werner Rings, *Raubgold aus Deutschland, Die 'Golddrehscheibe' Schweiz im Zweiten Weltkrieg;* cf. Arthur L. Smith Jr., *Hitler's Gold. The Story of the Nazi War Loot*, and Trepp, *Bankgeschäfte mit dem Feind.*
60. De Vries, *Nederlandsche Bank*, p. 378.
61. Ministerie van Financiën, Bewindvoering archive, rubric 1514, Gestolen Goud, 'Memorandum explaining why all the gold which during the German occupation was removed from the Netherlands to Germany, was unlawfully removed', and Aalders, 'Looting or Spoils of War? The removal of monetary gold from the Netherlands', lecture on the occasion of the symposium *Economia de Guerra e o Ouro Nazi – War Economy and Nazi Gold*, Lisbon, 27 February 1998.
62. Ministerie van Financiën, Bewindvoering archive, rubric 1514, Gestolen Goud, 'Adjudication by the Tripartite Commission for the Restitution of Monetary Gold on a claim submitted by the Royal Netherlands Government for the Restitution of 145,650 kgs of fine gold', 9 June 1958.
63. Ministerie van Financiën, Bewindvoering archive, rubric 1514, Gestolen Goud: 'Tijdens de Duitse bezetting werden de volgende hoeveelheden goud naar Duitsland gevoerd', and 'Adjudication by the Tripartite Commission for the Restitution of Monetary Gold on a claim submitted by the Royal Netherlands Government for the Restitution of 145,650 kgs of fine gold', 9 June 1958.
64. De Vries, *Nederlandsche Bank*, pp. 363, 368–70 and 378.
65. Ministerie van Financiën, Binnenlands geldwezen archive, 'Explanation of the circumstances under which the gold of the Netherlands was delivered up to Germany during the German occupation of the Netherlands'. In 1946, one kg of gold was worth about 2,970 guilders.
66. Ministerie van Financiën, Bewindvoering archive, rubric 1514, 'Bericht über die bisherige Tätigkeit auf dem Gebiet des Devisenschutzes und der

Devisenfahndung seit dem Einrücken in das besetzte Niederländische Gebiet bis zum 30. Juni, 1940', dated 1 July 1940.
67. ARA, 2.09.16, NBI, box 60, 'Monatsbericht für den Monat Mai 1941', dated 3 June 1941, and 'Erfolgsübersicht I für die Zeit vom 17. Mai 1940 bis zum 30. April 1941', dated 19 May 1941. The monetary gold included United States coins worth approximately 1 million RM and Dutch coins worth more than 4 million RM; the United States bank notes came to more than 1.5 million RM and foreign securities to almost 2 million RM. Ministerie van Financiën, Domestic Payments, letter from the Devisenschutzkommando to the Nederlandsche Bank, 16 March 1942.
68. ARA, NBI, box 600, 'Korte beschrijving van de taak en de werkwijze van het Devisenschutzkommando Niederlande'; ministerie van Justitie, CABR, O. K. Gerbig dossier, inventory no. 109, 'Verhoorrapport van 8 februari 1946', and Niod, Doc II, Liro, box 215, folder A. no.173, 'Betr.: Devisenschutzkommando', 13 August 1942, note by O. Witscher.
69. 'Denkschrift Hitlers über die Aufgaben eines Vierjahresplan' in *Vierteljahreshefte für Zeitgeschichte*, 1955, pp. 204–10.
70. *Proceedings of the International Military Tribunal Sitting at Nuremberg*, vol. 1, p. 1,053, and Milward, *Die Deutsche Kriegswirtschaft 1939–1945*.
71. Niod. Doc I, A. J. Bühler dossier. 'Onderhoud met Albert Bühler', report by L. de Jong and A. E. Cohen, 19 April 1949.
72. Niod, Doc I, A. J. Bühler dossier. Deposition no. 206 B, recorded by A. Olthof, 17 July 1946. Bühler justified his own position as follows: 'I am a German, of course, and so have a sense of duty'. He claimed that he had been proposed for membership of the NSDAP on the recommendation of others; he had not wanted to refuse, because non-members could not get anywhere. It should be borne in mind that this declaration was made after the war when Bühler was anxious to portray himself in the most favourable light possible.
73. Niod, Doc I, A. J. Bühler dossier, 'Exposé über meine Geschäftsführung als Beauftragter für die Niederl. Bank unter besonderer Berücksichtigung der Stellung des Bankiers Otto Rebholz', 25 August 1946.
74. Niod, Doc I, A. J. Bühler dossier, 'Onderhoud met Albert Bühler', report by L. de Jong and A. E. Cohen, 19 April 1949.
75. Niod, Doc I, Otto Rebholz, folder 6. Declaration made in May 1947.

Chapter 2: The Looting of Cultural Property

1. Letter to the author from B. Woelderink, director of the Royal House Archive, 21 October 1997.

Notes

2. After the war, the Inter-Allied Declaration Against Acts of Dispossession Committed in Territories Under Enemy Occupation or Control, 5 January 1943, proved to be of paramount importance in matters of post-war restitution. It will be referred to several times in the course of this book. On 7 August 1956, the UNESCO Convention and Protocol for the Protection of Cultural Property in the Event of an Armed Conflict came into force. It is also known as the The Hague Convention and Protocol of 1954.

   On 24 April 1942 there followed the UNESCO Convention on the Means of Prohibiting and Preventing the Illicit Import, Export and Transfer of Ownership of Cultural Property.

   During the 20th General Conference of UNESCO, held from 24 October to 28 November 1978, the Statutes of the Intergovernmental Committee for Promoting the Return of Cultural Property to its Countries of Origin in Case of Illicit Appropriation was adopted by Resolution 4/7.6/5.

   The latest measure in the field of cultural protection so far is the UNIDROIT Convention on Stolen or Illegally Exported Cultural Objects.
3. Quoted from Kaye, 'Laws in Force at the Dawn of World War II', p. 101.
4. Kaye, 'Laws in Force at the Dawn of World War II', pp. 101–2.
5. Niod, Doc II, 'Roof Kunstschatten', folder H (Linz), letter from Hitler, Obersalzberg, 26 June 1939.
6. Niod, Doc. II, 'Roof Kunstschatten', folder H (Linz), letter from Posse to Bormann, 15 January 1941. The file also contains lists of purchases, names of painters and amounts paid.

   For Hitler and the Linz Museum, see NA, RG 260, Records of United States Occupation Headquarters WWII, Ardelia Hall Collection, box 33, Detailed Interrogation Report No. 1, Subject: Heinrich Hoffmann, 1 July 1945; and Niod, archive 281, no title. The document contains a survey of works of art, amounts and dealers from the beginning of 1942 to 1944. It begins with the first *Sonderkonto* account and ends with the seventh.
7. Niod, Doc II, 'Roof Kunstschatten', folder G. Consolidated Interrogation Report No. 4, 15 December 1945. 'Linz, Hitler's Museum and Library.'
8. NA, RG 260, Records of United States Occupation Headquarters WWII, Ardelia Hall Collection, box 260, H. Hoffmann Interrogation, 20 June 1945. 'Hoffmann's role as adviser to Hitler.'
9. NA, RG 59, General Records of the Department of State, Decimal Files 1945–1949, box 4183, Miedl folder, Miedl Case, 'Account of German activities on the Art Market in Holland'.
10. NA, RG 260, Records of United States Occupation Headquarters WWII, Ardelia Hall Collection, box 450, Rosenberg, 'Consolidated Interrogation Report, No. 2, 15 September 1945, The Goering Collection', and Ministry of Justice, CABR, J. Dik, jr. dossier: 'Onderzoek naar de handel in kunstschatten

die Dik Jr., zowel alleen als in samenwerking met anderen heft gedreven met onze bezetters', and *idem*, 'Getuige verhoor van Dr. B. Lohse'.
11. Washington National Record Center, RF 84, The Hague Embassy file, box 3, *Looted Art in Occupied Territories, Neutral Countries and Latin America*, August 1945 and NA Washington, Records of the United States Occupation Headquarters WWII, Ardelia Hall Collection, RG 260, box 12, 'Looted Art in Occupied Territories, Neutral Countries and Latin America', 5 May 1945.
12. Aalders, 'By Diplomatic Pouch: Art Smuggling by the Nazis'.
13. NA, Records of the United States Occupation Headquarters WWII, Ardelia Hall Collection, RG 260, box 12, 'Looted Art in Occupied Territories, Neutral Countries and Latin America', 5 May 1945.
14. NA, RG 260, Records of United States Occupation Headquarters WWII, Ardelia Hall Collection, box 180, Interrogation of Alfred Rosenberg, 30 August 1946.
15. For 'Sonderstab Musik', see Wim de Vries, *Sonderstab Musik*. The book has been translated into English and German.
16. Petropoulos, *Art as Politics*, pp. 124–39.
17. NA, RG 260, Records of United States Occupation Headquarters WWII, Ardelia Hall Collection, box 180, Interrogation of Alfred Rosenberg, 30 August 1946.
18. Petropoulos, *Art as Politics*, pp. 124–39; the Kümmel quotation is taken from Friemuth, *Die geraubte Kunst*, p. 16.
19. Flanner, *Men and Monuments*, p. 237, and NA, RG 260, Records of United States Occupation Headquarters WWII, Ardelia Hall Collection, box 182, 'Trial Address. Plunder of Art Treasures'.
20. Niod, archive 281, 'Stellungnahme des Einsatzstabes Reichsleiter Rosenberg zum Einspruch der französischen Regierung (Generalkommissariat für Judenfragen) vom 25. Juli 1941 gegen die Beschlagnahme von Kunstschätzen aus jüdischem Besitz'. The *Führerentscheidungen* (Führer decisions) referred to will be discussed below.
21. Petropoulos, *Art as Politics*, pp. 127–8, and *Nazi Conspiracy and Aggression*, vol. III, p. 184 (Rosenberg Interrogation).
22. Quoted from Niod, 'Notities voor het Geschiedwerk', no. 118. *Entziehung öffentlicher und privater Bibliotheken in den besetzten Westgebieten und ihre Verbringung nach Deutschland.* Supplement 'Aktenvermerk über die Rechtsgrundlagen für die Arbeit des Einsatzstabes Reichsleiter Rosenberg', 11 January 1941, signed by Dr Berger.
23. Quoted from Niod, 'Notities voor het Geschiedwerk', no. 118. *Entziehung öffentlicher und privater Bibliotheken in den besetzten Westgebieten und ihre Verbringung nach Deutschland.* Supplement 'Aktenvermerk über die Rechtsgrundlagen für die Arbeit des Einsatzstabes Reichsleiter Rosenberg', 11 January 1941, signed by Dr Berger.

Notes

24. *Nazi Conspiracy and Aggression*. Supplement B, pp. 1,332–6.
25. *Nazi Conspiracy and Aggression,* Supplement B, pp.1,333–7, and Niod, 'Notities voor het Geschiedwerk ' no. 118. *Entziehung öffentlicher und privater Bibliotheken in den besetzten Westgebieten und ihre Verbringung nach Deutschland.*
26. Central State Archive of the High Organs of Government and Administration in the Ukraine (Tsentral'nyi derzhavnyi arkhiv vyshchykh orhaniv vlady i upravlinnia UkrXny). Catalogue number 3676.
27. Petropoulos, *Art as Politics*, pp. 129–39; *Nazi Conspiracy and Aggrestiob*, suppl. B, pp. 1,333–7; Kurtz, *Nazi Contraband*, pp. 22–7; and Niod, archive 281, 'Gedächtnisniederschrift über die Besprechung am 3. März 1960 mit Herrn Professor Dr. Ernst Grumach', by A. J. de Leeuw. The comment 'ungeheure Rivalität' comes from Grumach.
28. NA, RG 260, Records of United States Occupation Headquarters WWII, Ardelia Hall Collection, box 182, 'Trial Address. Plunder of Art Treasures'.
29. Niod, 'Notities voor het Geschiedwerk', no. 118. *Entziehung öffentlicher und privater Bibliotheken in den besetzten Westgebieten und ihre Verbringung nach Deutschland; idem* Niod, Doc II, Einsatzstab Rosenberg, 'Resumé van enkele punten uit de bespreking van 21 januari 1960 in Bonn met de heren Koppe, Dr. Heinrich, Dr. Andrae en Dr. Hoffmann', by A. J. van der Leeuw, and Manasse, *Verdwenen archieven en bibliotheken*, pp. 63–7.
30. Niod, archive 264, Chief Counsel War Crimes, Nuremberg, N 81/1. Letter from Rosenberg to Hitler, 16 April 1943, and Intermediary Report, 16 April 1943.
31. Manasse, *Verdwenen archieven en bibliotheken*, pp. 35–60. For Ets Haim, see also *Ets Haim-Livraria Montezinos*; for the International Archive of the Women's Movement, see Annette Mevis, *Women's Archives Recovered*; for the Ashkenazi archive and small Jewish archives, see Vlessing, *Recovering Looted Archives*. See also Niod, 'Notities voor het Geschiedswerk', no. 118, *Entziehung öffentlicher und privater Bibliotheken in den besetzten Westgebieten und ihre Verbringung nach Deutschland* by A. J. van der Leeuw.
32. For these two agencies, see 'The Dienststelle Mühlmann' in this chapter.
33. Petropoulos, *Art as Politics*, pp. 139–41; NA RG 260, Records of United States Occupation Headquarters WWII, Ardelia Hall Collection, box 450, Rosenberg, 'Consolidated Interrogation Report. No. 2, 15 September 1945. The Goering Collection'.
34. NA, RG 260, Records of United States Occupation Headquarters WWII, Ardelia Hall Collection, box 435, 'Dr. Kai Mühlmann'.
35. See Kröller-Müller elsewhere in this chapter.
36. Hoover Institution on War, Revolution and Peace, Göring collection, box 1. Letter from Hofer to Göring, 26 September 1941.
37. NA, RG 260, Records of United States Occupation Headquarters WWII, Ardelia Hall Collection, box 182, 'Report on the activities of the Einsatzstab

of the Bureau of the Reichsleiter Rosenberg in the Occupied Western Territories and The Netherlands. Working Group Netherlands'; Manasse, *Verdwenen archieven en bibliotheken*, pp. 41–2; and *Nazi Conspiracy and Aggression*, pp. 203–9. For Masonic archives, see also Kwaadgras, *The Fate of a Special Collection*.

38. Manasse, *Verdwenen archieven en bibliotheken*, p. 42.
39. *Nazi Conspiracy and Aggression*, pp. 206–9.
40. Manasse, *Verdwenen archieven en bibliotheken,* pp. 54–8; Hoogewoud, *The Nazi Looting of Books*. For the Bibliotheca Rosenthaliana, see Fuks, *Vijf en twintig jaar Bibliotheca Rosenthaliana*, and De la Fontaine Verwey, 'De Bibliotheca Rosenthaliana tijdens de bezetting', and NA, RG 260, Records of United States Occupation Headquarters WWII, Ardelia Hall Collection, box 180, folder 'Interrogation of War Criminals', 'Special Interrogation of Seyss-Inquart by *mr.* H. S. Leonard at Nurnberg on the evening of 21 August 1946 in the presence of defence attorney Dr. Sennbauer', and ministerie van OWC, Ancient Art and Natural Protection Division, inventory no. 31.4 (re: 'Die Art des Eigentümers').
41. Brummel, L., 'Tien jaren Koninklijke Bibliotheek (1938–1947)', p. 7.
42. Central State Archive of the High Organs of Government and Administration of the Ukraine (Tsentral'nyi derzhavnyi arkhiv vyshchykh orhaniv vlady i upravlinnia UkrXny). Catalogue number 3676, description (folder) no. 1, 1941–44. HQ of Rosenberg for Occupied Eastern Territories. Inventory no. 205, 'Sonderstab für Bibliotheksausbau Holland'.
43. Brummel, 'Tien jaren Koninklijke Bibliotheek (1938–1947)', pp. 8–9.
44. Letter to the author from Dr A. T. Bouwman, conservator of Western manuscripts in the University of Leiden, dated 2 October 1997 (with copies of the relevant documents).
45. Letter dated 24 September 1941 from Dr T. P. Sevensma, librarian of the University of Leiden, to his colleague in Groningen State University. A copy of the letter was made available to me by courtesy of Groningen State University.
46. According to copies of documents made available to me by Groningen State University on 20 December 1997.
47. Kernkamp, *Economisch-Historische Aspecten van de Literatuurproductie*, p. 5.
48. Central State Archive of the High Organs of Government and Administration in the Ukraine (Tsentral'nyi derzhavnyi arkhiv vyshchykh orhaniv vlady i upravlinnia UkrXny). Catalogue number 3676, description (folder) no. 1, 1941–44. HQ of Rosenberg for Occupied Eastern Territories. Inventory no. 205. 'Sonderstab für Bibliotheksausbau Holland.' The following 'acquisitions' are recorded, but without mention of their origin:

Encyclopedia Britannica 1–32 + 3
English Catalogue of Books
English Studies 1–22
Journal of the Anthropological Institute of Great Britain 1–47
Acta Sanctorum 1643 ff
Analecta Bollandiana 1–58
Studia catholica 1–12
Archief voor Nederlandsche Kerkgeschiedenis 1–39
Revue ecclésiastique de Liège 1905–33
Ons geestelijk erf 1–14
Tauler, Gheestelijke Sermonen, Antwerp 1657
De Katholieke encyclopedie, 1933 ff
Bibliografie van de moderne Vlaamse literatuur 1893–1930
Bibliotheekleven 1–25
Rijksgeschiedkundige Publicatiën 1–83 and 1–29 (Kl Series)
Oud Holland 1–57
Bijdragen voor vaderlandsche geschiedenis en oudheidkunde 1936–41
Brugmans, Geschiedenis van Nederland 1–8 (1935–8)
Onze Eeuw 1–24
Geschiedenis van Vlaanderen 1–5
Sipma. Oudfriesche Oorkonden 1–3
Bijdragen en mededeelingen van het Genootschap te Utrecht 1–62
Bibliothekecae Academia Lugduno-Batavae. Catalogue 1–47
Codex diplomaticus neerlandicus Neophilologus 1–26
E. Verwijs and J. Verdam, Middelnederlandsch woordenboek II EDE 1885–1941
Dijkstra, Friesch Woordenboek 1–4
Doormkaat, Wörterbuch der ostfriesischen Sprache 1–3
Kalff, Geschiedenis der Nederlandsche letterkunde 1–7
Tijdschrift voor wijsbegeerte 1–26
Kantstudien 1–39
Petermanns Mitteilungen 1–70, 72–84
Jahrbücher d. Landeskunde der Herzogtümer Schleswig-Holstein 1858–69
Zeitschrift d. Gesellschaft f.f. Geschichte der Herzogtümer Schleswig-Holstein
Zeitschrift für deutsche Philologie 1–46
Biologisches Zentralblatt 1–56
Internationales Archiv für Ethnographie 1–24
Bibliografisches Bulletin der schweizerischen Landesbibliothek 1918–41
Brockelmann, Geschichte der arabischen Literatur 1–3
De Vaux, Les Penseurs d'Islam 1–5. 1921

Revue celtique 1–12, 14–16, 19–51
Revue belge de philologie et d'histoire 2–18
Revue d'histoire de la guerre mondiale . . . 1–15.1923

49. All the libraries and archives mentioned in the document have been contacted by me. The Haarlem Municipal Library replied that the requested titles, such as those appearing in the Kiev document, were no longer kept in the library. A search of the archive of the bishopric of Haarlem also proved unproductive. It should however be mentioned that the size of that archive (or what has remained of it) is small. In the Catharijne Convent Museum in Utrecht, which has been in charge of the library of the Bisschoppelijk Museum, Haarlem since 1976, nothing was known about sold or exchanged books either. This emerged from a letter dated 16 July 1998 from the Catharijne Convent Museum in Utrecht, where the Episcopal collection has been housed since 1976.

    Enquiries in the Fries Genootschap and in the Rotterdam, Nijmegen and Utrecht libraries were unsuccessful.

50. Hoogewoud, *The Nazi Looting of Books*, p. 163.
51. Niod, archive 103, Departement van Volksvoorlichting en Kunsten, afdeling Boekwezen, dossier 167, correspondence. For antiquarian bookshops during the war, see also Buynsters, *Het Nederlandse antiquariaat*.
52. Niod, archive 281, 'Vermerk für II a. Betr. Jüdische Besitzernamen auf Büchern', 13 February 1944.
53. Ministerie van OCW, Afdeling Oude Kunst en Natuurbescherming, inventory no. 31.4. Various documents and correspondence about the Wasmann and Schmitz collections.
54. Ministerie van OCW, Afdeling Oude Kunst en Natuurbescherming, inventory no. 31.4. Documents about the Wasmann and Schmitz collections.
55. For an outline of the life of K. Mühlmann, see Petropoulos, *The Importance of the Second Rank: The Case of the Art Plunderer Kajetan Mühlmann.*
56. Niod, 'Notities voor het Geschiedwerk', no. 121, *Die Bestimmung der vom deutschen Reich entzogenen und von der Dienststelle Mühlmann übernommen Kunstgegenstände; idem*, archive 281, 'Dealers in Holland' (with a detailed list of Dutch art dealers), and Leistra, 'A short history of art loss and art recovery in the Netherlands'.
57. Niod, 'Notities voor het Geschiedwerk', no. 121, *Die Bestimmung der vom deutschen Reich entzogenen und von der Dienststelle Mühlmann übernommen Kunstgegenstände.*
58. NA, RG 239, American Commission for the Protection and Salvation of Artistic and Historic Monuments in War Areas, box 25, 350/77/01/02, 'Private collections Netherlands', and *idem*, RG 260, Records of United States Occupation Headquarters WWII, Ardelia Hall Collection, box 435, 'Joseph Mühlmann', and *idem*, box 435, 'Dr. Kai Mühlmann'.

Notes

59. Provinciaal Archief Noord-Holland, Rijksmuseum Amsterdam, entry 476, inventory no. 2458. Letter from OWC to Director of Rijksmuseum, Amsterdam, 4 July 1940, and reply by Rijksmuseum two days later, on 6 July 1940.
60. Niod, 'Notities voor het Geschiedwerk', no. 121, *Die Bestimmung der vom deutschen Reich entzogenen und von der Dienststelle Mühlmann übernommen Kunstgegenstände*; Niod, archive 281, 'List of paintings acquired from The Hague through Understate's Secretary Muehlmann by order of Dr. Posse 20 and 27.XII.40'.
61. Niod, Doc II, 'Roof Kunstschatten', folder H (Linz), 'Selection of acquisitions in the months December 1940–March 1941. Dienststelle Mühlmann, The Hague'.
62. Niod, archive 281, 'Feindvermögen (jüdische Kunsthandlungen)'.
63. Niod, 'Notities voor het Geschiedwerk', no. 121, *Die Bestimmung der vom deutschen Reich entzogenen und von der Dienststelle Mühlmann übernommen Kunstgegenstände;* Leistra, 'A short history of art loss and art recovery in the Netherlands'; Petropoulos, *Art as Politics,* p. 141.

    A survey of Dutch art collections can be found in NA, RG 239, American Commission for the Protection and Salvation of Artistic and Historic Monuments in War Areas, box 25, 350/77/01/02, 'Private collections Netherlands'. The list includes over 140 private collections, with their addresses and in many cases a brief description of the nature of the collection. The list covers all art forms. However, a comparison with the names given in Venema, *Kunsthandel in Nederland*, p. 12, shows that the list is not complete.

    See VO 7, the decree governing the treatment of enemy property (*Feindvermögen*) issued on 27 June 1940. Works of art could be confiscated, inter alia, by virtue of Article 2.2, covering 'natural persons who are subjects of enemy states or who reside or stay in the territory of an enemy state'. Works of art and other possessions of Dutch refugees were thus liable to confiscation.
64. Niod, Doc II, 'Roof Kunstschatten', box 422, folder F, Report by Plietzsch to Mühlmann, 12 September 1940.
65. Niod, archive 281, 'Aktenvermerk über eine Besprechung zwischen Staatssekretär Dr. Mühlmann, Dr. Plietzsch und Herrn von Stechow am 1.10.1943 im Haag'.
66. Niod, Doc II, 'Roof Kunstschatten', box 422, folder F. Report by Plietzsch to Mühlmann, 12 September 1940.
67. Niod, 'Notities voor het Geschiedwerk', no. 121, *Die Bestimmung der vom deutschen Reich entzogenen und von der Dienststelle Mühlmann übernommen Kunstgegenstände*; *idem*, archive 281, 'Einkäufe von Gauleitern Programme F. Linz u.Wien' signed by Dr. K. Mühlmann; Leistra, 'A short history of art loss and art recovery in the Netherlands'; Petropoulos, *Art as Politics*, p. 141, and NA, RG 239, American Commission for the Protection and Salvation of

Artistic Monuments in War Areas, box 9, 350/76/35/06, Report on Joseph Mühlmann.

68. NA, RG 59, Decimal Files 1945–1949, box 4183, Miedl folder, report no. 4, Miedl Case. Account of the German Activities on the Art Market in Holland. For the Mühlmann quotation, see ministerie van Financiën, Centraal Archief Bijzondere Rechtspleging (CABR), J. Dik, jr. dossier: 'De kunsthandel in Nederland', compiled by Douwes Bros., art dealers in Rokin, Amsterdam. From the accompanying letter to A. H. van der Veen, public prosecutor of the Special Court of Justice in Amsterdam, it appears that the 'exposé' of the structure and development of the Dutch art trade was written on the instructions of the 'judicial authorities'.

69. Niod, Doc II, 'Roof Kunstschatten', box 422, folder F. Report by Plietzsch to Mühlmann, 12 September 1940.

70. Niod, Doc II, 'Roof Kunstschatten', box 422, folder G. Consolidated Interrogation Report No. 4, 'Linz: Hitler's Museum and Library, 15 December 1945'.

71. Ministerie van Justitie, Centraal Archief Bijzondere Rechtspleging, J. Dik, jr. dossier: 'De kunsthandel in Nederland', compiled by Douwes Bros., art dealers in Rokin, Amsterdam.

72. NA, American Commission for the Protection and Salvation of Artistic and Historic Monuments in War Areas, RG 239, box 47, 350/77/01/02 'Netherlands Art Treasures since the German Occupation'.

73. Ministerie van Justitie, Centraal Archief Bijzondere Rechtspleging, J. Dik, jr. dossier; 'De kunsthandel in Nederland', compiled by Douwes Bros., art dealers in Rokin, Amsterdam.

74. NA, RG 331, Allied Operation and Occupation Headquarters, World War II, box 328, 290/7/27/6, 'Removal of works of art from the Netherlands during the German Occupation' and National Archives, RG 260, Records of United States Occupation Headquarters WWII, Ardelia Hall Collection, box 450, Rosenberg, 'Consolidated Interrogation Report No. 2, 15 September 1945, The Goering Collection'.

For a list of firms and auction houses that did business with the Germans, see Venema, *Kunsthandel in Nederland*, pp. 267–356; for the quotation see NA, RG 260, Records of the United States Occupation Headquarters WWII, box 12, 'Looted Art in Occupied Territories, Neutral Countries and Latin America', 5 May 1945 (my italics).

75. See Chapter 3, The Allies and the Loot.

76. NA, American Commission for the Protection and Salvation of Artistic and Historic Monuments in War Areas, RG 239, box 47, 350/77/01/02 'Netherlands Art Treasures since the German Occupation'.

77. Centraal Museum Utrecht archive, 'Catalogus Veiling door Van Marle & Bignell', 1 September 1942 (with notes on buyers and prices in the margins),

and Niod, Doc II, 'Roof Kunstschatten', box 422, folder G, Consolidated Interrogation Report No. 4, 'Linz, Hitler's Museum and Library', 15 December 1945.
78. Centraal Museum Utrecht archive. List of paintings on loan, letter from A. Chabot and G. Rog, 12 June 1942; letter from Centraal Museum to the mayor of Utrecht, 13 June 1942, and his reply, 7 July 1942; 'Catalogus Veiling door Van Marle & Bignell', 1 September 1942 (with notes on buyers and prices in the margins).
79. Niod, Doc II, 'Roof Kunstschatten', box 422, folder G, Consolidated Interrogation Report No. 4, 'Linz, Hitler's Museum and Library', 15 December 1945; ministerie van Justitie, Centraal Archief Bijzondere Rechtspleging, J. Dik, jr. dossier: 'Memorandum betreffende den verkoop van Rembrandts Pauwen uit het bruikleen van J. J. M. Chabot aan het Rijksmuseum', 13 April 1943, and *idem*, letter from SNK (A. B. de Vries) to Bureau Collaboratie, 4 February 1946.
80. Niod, Doc I, F.I. Govaerts and *idem*, W.M.A. Weitjens. See also Niod, Doc II, 'Roof Kunstschatten', box 422, folder G, Consolidated Interrogation Report No. 4, 'Linz, Hitler's Museum and Library', 15 December 1945; ministerie van Justitie, Centraal Archief Bijzondere Rechtspleging, J. Dik, jr. dossier: 'Memorandum betreffende den verkoop van Rembrandts Pauwen uit het bruikleen van J. J. M. Chabot aan het Rijksmuseum', 13 April 1943, and *idem*, letter from SNK (A. B. de Vries) to Bureau Collaboratie, 4 February 1946.
81. Article 1.1: 'The property of persons or associations that have promoted, promote, or of whom it may be assumed that they will in future promote, activities against the German people or the German Reich can be confiscated completely or in part.'
82. Niod, Doc II, 'Roof Kunstschatten', folder H (Linz), in which the paintings taken to Munich are listed; *idem*, 'Notities voor het Geschiedwerk' no. 126. 'Die Sammlung Lugt'; *idem*, archive 281, 'Sammlung Lugt, Den Haag', note by K. Mühlmann; NA, RG 260, Occupation Headquarters, U.S., World War II, Ardelia Hall Collection, box 435, Report on Joseph Mühlmann; Nicholas, *The Rape of Europe*, pp. 82 and 103.
83. Niod, archive 281, 'Notitie betreffende een bespreking met Dr. Erhard Göpel', 13 November 1960.
84. Niod, archive 281, 'Memorandum van C.A. J. Brans betreffende de collectie schilderijen van den heer Lugt en steun aan het Rijksbureau voor kunsthistorische en ikonografische documentatie'.
85. They emigrated to the United States and Americanized their name.
86. Niod, Doc II, 'Roof Kunstschatten', folder H (Linz), 'Partial List of Purchases for Linz made in Holland'. The list mentions an Isenbrandt, a Cranach the Elder, a Van Goyen and a J. Elsner. See also NA, RG 260, Records of United States Occupation Headquarters WWII, Ardelia Hall Collection, box 178,

H. Hoffmann Interrogation, 'Hoffmann's Role as Adviser to Hitler', and WNRC, RG 84, The Hague Embassy, confidential file, box no. 3, 'Looted Art in Occupied Territories, Neutral Countries and Latin America', August 1945. The information about the Gutmann Collection is taken from Anne Webber's documentary 'Making a Killing'. Anne Webber kindly sent me additional information by e-mail on 17 January 1999.
87. A large collection of cuttings about the fate of the Koenigs Collection can be found in the Niod collection of cuttings: KB I, 11753. See also Elen, *Missing Old Master Drawings from the Franz Koenigs Collection*.
88. NA, RG 59, Decimal Files 1945–49, box 4183, Miedl folder, report No. 3. However, an added 'correction' states that Koenigs received the amount he had asked for, and that 'the money was paid in guilders on the spot'. Miedl is said to have had a financial interest (74 per cent) in Lisser & Rosencranz: ministerie van Financiën, Stichting Nederlands Kunstbezit 1945–51, box 71, inventory No. 187, 'Miedl's present assets in Europe'.
89. Nicholas, *The Rape of Europe*, pp. 100–1, and NA, RG 260, Records of United States Occupation Headquarters WWII, Ardelia Hall Collection, box 435, 'Joseph Mühlmann'. For another of Göring's exchanges, see Venema, *Kunsthandel in Nederland*, pp. 76–7.
90. Niod, Doc II, 'Roof Kunstschatten', folder H (Linz); Venema *Kunsthandel in Nederland*, pp. 258–66; and Nicholas, *The Rape of Europe*, pp. 108–9.
91. NA, RG 59, Decimal Files 1945–49, box 4183, Miedl folder, report No. 3.
92. Niod, cuttings archive, KB I, 8150, Dr A. B. de Vries.
93. Ministerie van Justitie, CABR, J. Dik, jr. dossier, and Niod, Doc II, 'Roof Kunstschatten', folder G.
94. NA, RG 260, Records of United States Occupation Headquarters WWII, Ardelia Hall Collection, box 450, Rosenberg, 'Consolidated Interrogation Report', no. 2, 15 September 1945, 'The Goering Collection'; *idem*, box 180, folder 'Interrogation of War Criminals'. Interrogation of Herrmann Goering, 30 August 1946, and NA, RG 331, Allied Operation and Occupation Headquarters, World War II, box 328, 290/7/27/6 'Removal of Works of Art from the Netherlands during the German Occupation'.
95. For literature on Goudstikker, see Den Hollander, *De Zaak Goudstikker*; Venema, *Kunsthandel in Nederland*, pp. 120–72; and Ageeth Scherphuis, 'Een heer in de kunsthandel' in *Vrij Nederland*, 10 November 1990.

See also Niod, Doc II, NV Kunsthandel J. Goudstikker, 'Overzicht van de gebeurtenissen in de periode van 31 december 1939 tot april 1952' by A. E. D. von Saher.
96. NA, RG 260, Records of United States Occupation Headquarters WWII, Ardelia Hall Collection, box 180, 'Special Interrogation of Seyss-Inquart', 31 August 1946.

Notes

97. Den Hollander, *De Zaak Goudstikker*, pp. 52–7; for the 'pledge', see Provinciaal Archief Noord Holland, 'Inventory of the archives of the Rijksmuseum in Amsterdam, 1807–1945', inventory no. 2120; NA, RG 260, 390/44/43, box 629, Records of the US Occupation Headquarters WWII, Interrogation and Reports Pertaining to Financial Matters 45–46: 'Interrogation 28 Sept. 1945 – Walter Andreas Hofer' by Eldon J. Cassoday.
98. NA, RG 59, General Records of the Department of State, Decimal Files 1945–9, box 4183, folder: Miedl reports 2,3 and 4. Miedl case report no. 2: 'Identification and Description of the Pictures Deposited by Alois Miedl in the Free Port of Bilbao'; Miedl case report No. 3: 'Introduction' and Miedl case report No. 4: 'Account of German Activities on the Art Market in Holland'. For the annulment of the transactions see Chapter 3, The Allies and the Loot.
99. NA, Records of the United States Occupation Headquarters WWII, Ardelia Hall Collection, RG 260, box 12, 'Looted Art in Occupied Territories, Neutral Countries and Latin America', 5 May 1945.
100. NA, RG 59, General Records of the Department of State, Decimal Files 1945–49, box 4183, folder: Miedl reports 2, 3 and 4. Miedl case report no. 3: 'Introduction' and Miedl case report no 4: 'Account of German Activities on the Art Market in Holland'.
101. Petropoulos, *Art as Politics*, pp. 3–16 and passim. For the original layout of Karinhall see a photograph in Wilamowitz-Moellendorff's *Carin Göring*. The name of Carin (von Fock) is often spelled as Karin – hence 'Karinhall' and 'Carinhall'.
102. NA, RG 260, Records of the United States Occupation Headquarters WWII, Ardelia Hall Collection, box 32, 'Treatment of works of art in Germany'.
103. NA, RG 260, Records of the United States Occupation Headquarters WWII, Ardelia Hall Collection, box 450, Rosenberg, 'Consolidated Interrogation Report, No.2, 15 September 1945, The Goering Collection', and *idem*, box 180, folder 'Interrogation of War Criminals', 'Special Interrogation of Seyss-Inquart by H. S. Leonard at Nurnberg on the evening of 31 August in the presence of defence attorney Dr. Sennbauer', and *idem*, box 180, Interrogation of Alfred Rosenberg on 30 August 1946.
104. Petropoulos, *Art as Politics*, pp. 3–16 and passim.
105. Petropoulos, *Art as Politics*, p. 187.
106. Petropoulos, *Art as Politics*, pp. 181–98, and *idem*, 'For Germany and Themselves: the Motivation behind the Nazi Leaders Plundering and Collecting of Art' in *Spoils of War*, International Newsletter No. 4, August 1997.
107. NA, RG 260, Records of the United States Occupation Headquarters WWII, Ardelia Hall Collection, box 435, 'The total seizure of art objects through the Third Reich during the war', and *idem*, box 178, 'H. Hoffmann Interrogation, 26 June 1945. Hoffmann's role as adviser to Hitler', and *idem*, box 33,

'Detailed Interrogation Report No. 1, Subject: Heinrich Hoffmann', 1 July 1945. Hoffmann mentioned 6, 8, 12 and 20 Pfennig postage stamps, issued in 1941. The examiner did not consider Hoffmann a reliable witness: 'The interrogation of Hoffmann is a thankless task. He is an alcoholic and has all the weaknesses that go with that vice. His memory is bad and he changes his story from day to day, according to what he thinks will please his interrogators most . . . He curses and praises Hitler alternately. Above all, his chief concern is the future of his material possessions. He appeared more upset about the theft of his linen than by the unfavourable reports about his immediate family.'

108. Niod, Doc II, 'Roof Kunstschatten', box 422, folder G, Consolidated Interrogation Report No. 4, 'Linz: Hitler's Museum and Library, 15 December 1945'.
109. NA, RG 260, Records of the United States Occupation Headquarters WWII, Ardelia Hall Collection, box 180, 'Interrogation of Hermann Goering', 30 August 1946.
110. NA, RG 260, Records of the United States Occupation Headquarters WWII, Ardelia Hall Collection, box 450. OSS files. Art Looting Investigation Unit. Consolidated Investigation Report No. 2, 15 September 1945, 'The Goering Collection'.
111. NA, RG 260, Records of the United States Occupation Headquarters WWII, Ardelia Hall Collection, box 450. OSS files. Art Looting Investigation Unit. Consolidated Investigation Report No. 2, 15 September 1945, 'The Goering Collection'.
112. NA, RG 260, Records of the United States Occupation Headquarters WWII, Ardelia Hall Collection, box 450. OSS files. Art Looting Investigation Unit. Consolidated Investigation Report No. 2, 15 September 1945, 'The Goering Collection'.
113. NA, RG 260, Records of the United States Occupation Headquarters WWII, Ardelia Hall Collection, box 450. OSS files. Art Looting Investigation Unit. Consolidated Investigation Report No. 2, 15 September 1945, 'The Goering Collection'.
114. Hoover Institution on War, Revolution and Peace, Göring Collection, box 1. Letter from Göring to Fischböck, 21 November 1940.

Chapter 3: The Allies and the Loot

1. Published in *Staatsblad van het Koninkrijk der Nederlanden uitgegeven te Londen*, 1940–43, Series A-D.

Notes

2. For the background to the emergency legislation, see J. C. E. van den Brandhof, *De besluitwetgeving van de kabinetten De Geer en Gerbrandy*.
3. There were a Corvo-London, a Corvo-Batavia and a Corvo-Curaçao.
4. NA, RG 56, General Records Department of the Treasury, box 47, entry 66A816, folder FTC History Foreign Funds Control, and *idem* RG 56, General Records Department of the Treasury, subject files 450/80/19/7, box 20, 'Report for Rains and Schwarz'; RG 60, Department of Justice, Antitrust Division Economic Warfare Section, subject files, box 130, 230/31/03/02, 'Netherlands, Money and Banking, Division of Research and Statistics, Board of Governors of the Federal Reserve System, July 1944' (preliminary draft); Dickens, 'Foreign Long-Term Investments in the United States 1937–1939', and 'Census of Foreign Owned Assets in the United States'.
5. Quoted from Meijers, *Het Voorstel van L.V.V.S.*, pp. 2–3.
6. Quoted from Meijers, *Het Voorstel van L.V.V.S.*, p. 4. For the original text of the *Inter-Allied Declaration Against Acts of Dispossession Committed in Territories Under Enemy Occupation or Control*, see FRUS, vol. 1, 1943, *General*, pp. 443–4.
7. FRUS 1944, vol. II, pp. 218–20.
8. Published in *Staatsblad van het Koninkrijk der Nederlanden uitgegeven te Londen*, 1944, Series E. The main compiler was Professor J. Eggens.
9. *Staatsblad van het Koninkrijk der Nederlanden*, 1945, Series E.
10. Published in *Staatsblad van het Koninkrijk der Nederlanden uitgegeven te Londen*, 1944, Series E.
11. Published in *Staatsblad van het Koninkrijk der Nederlanden uitgegeven te Londen*, 1944, Series E.

Chapter 4: The Destination of the Loot

1. Lööw, *Swedish Policy Towards Suspected War Criminals*.
2. Hamburger Stiftung für Sozial- und Wirtschaftsgeschichte (HSSW), NA, RG 84 (Davos), copy of original in the National Archives, Washington. As far as I know, these data have been neither confirmed nor denied. The phenomenon of registration under a different name is well known and often referred to as 'cloaking'.

 The true property relations are camouflaged before the authorities for all sorts of reasons, depending on place, time and circumstances. The subject is discussed at length in Aalders and Wiebes, *The Art of Cloaking Ownership*.

The truth of the stories about Davos is difficult to check for lack of literature. What is certain is that such camouflage was never revealed or else glossed over by the authorities.
3. WNRC, RG 407, Foreign Occupied Area Reports, box 043, 'Memorandum for the Director of the Finance Division from the individuals', External Assets Branch, 8 February 1946. The material deals with personal enrichment by the Nazi leaders and is largely taken from this document. The document does not claim to be complete seeing that the investigation was still in progress. See also NA, RG 59, Safehaven subject files 1945–47, box 03, Safehaven special subjects folder, 'Insurance'. The rumours about hidden treasure have acquired fresh momentum since the spate of reports about so-called Nazi gold in the autumn of 1995.
4. Niod, KB II, no. 755, Toplitzmeer, 'goudschat nazi's'.
5. Niod, KB I, 2627, Hermann Göring. For Argentina, see NA, RG 260, Records of the United States Occupation Headquarters WWII, Ardelia Hall Collection, box 12, 'Looted art in occupied territories', 5 May 1945.
6. Heydecker and Leeb, *Opmars naar de galg*, p. 51. The book mentions Can$132, £25,935, eight million French francs, three million Algerian and Moroccan francs, one million Reichsmarks, one million Egyptian pounds, two Argentinian pesos, half a Japanese yen and 7,500 Palestine pounds.

Chapter 5: The Looting of Jewish Property

1. Joseph Walk (ed.), *Das Sonderrecht für die Juden im NS-Staat*. The quotation is from W. Maser, *Der Sturm auf die Republik,* 1981, p. 469.
2. Bullock, *Hitler and Stalin*, p. 170.
3. Joseph Walk (ed.), *Das Sonderrecht für die Juden im NS-Staat*. The authors do not claim to present a complete survey. For the anti-Semitic policies of the Third Reich, see also Adam, *Judenpolitk im Dritten Reich;* Blau, *Das Ausnahmerecht für die Juden in Deutschland 1933–1945;* and Benz, *Die Juden in Deutschland. Leben unter nationalsozialistischer Herrschaft.*
4. Joseph Walk (ed.), *Das Sonderrecht für die Juden im NS-Staat*, pp. 36, 255, 262 and 357; Blau, *Das Ausnahmerecht für die Juden*, pp. 22–3, 53, 56–61 and 99–102.; and Niod, 'Notities voor het Geschiedwerk', no. 146. A. J. van der Leeuw, *Der Griff des Reiches nach dem Judenvermögen.*
5. NA, RG 56, General Records Department of the Treasury, box 47, entry 66A816, folder FTC History Foreign Funds Control, and *idem* RG 60, Department of Justice, Antitrust Division Economic Warfare Section, subject files, box 130,

Notes

230/31/03/02, Netherlands, Money and Banking, Division of Research and Statistics, Board of Governors of the Federal Reserve System, July 1944 (preliminary draft).

6. My computations are expressly confined to looting in the Netherlands. I am greatly indebted to Dr Helen B. Junz for letting me see her *Final Draft for Comment. Report on the Wealth Position of the Jewish Population in Nazi-Occupied Countries and Germany and Austria* (3 February 1999 version). Dr Junz stresses that her data are not definitive and that no absolute conclusions should be drawn from them. There are a number of uncertain factors, and not all the necessary data for the investigation are extant, at least as far as one can tell at the present. Even so, she claims that her report can be justified. The methods of calculation and investigation used are set out in some detail.

7. The Netherlands Statistics Bureau puts the wealth of private individuals in 1939 at 12.4 billion guilders, which, according to the same source (*Zeventig jaren statistiek in tijdreeksen*, p. 138), amounts to 1,423 guilders per person. If we put the number of Jews at 140,000, then we find that their average wealth amounted to 14,300 guilders each. In his *Vermogensverhoudingen in Nederland*, p.110, Wilterdink puts the overall wealth at 17.6 billion guilders. The difference of 5.2 billion between his figure and that of the Netherlands Statistics Bureau is due to the inclusion of possessions below the registration limit. If we adopt Wilterdink's figure, the average of 1,423 guilders per person is increased to about 2,020 guilders; that of Jews from 14,300 to 20,299 guilders. The Junz report estimates that on the eve of the Second World War approximately 400 million guilders owned by Jews were held abroad.

8. Ministerie van Financiën, Generaal Directoraat Belastingen, Verbaalarchief 1936–75, inventory no. 45–08–27/143 222, 'Maatregelen met betrekking tot in verband met den oorlog gemaakte winsten en behaalde voordeelen'.

9. The decree (*Erlass*) was published in the *Reichsgesetzblatt*, Teil I, p. 778. It can also be found (in German and in Dutch) in the *Verordnungsblatt für die besetzten niederländischen Gebiete 1940*. All decrees mentioned in this book can be found in this *Verordnungsblatt*, which was published from 1940 to 1945. The various volumes can be found in Niod.

10. Niod, 'Inleiding bij inventaris en regestenlijst van Doc II, Lippmann, Rosenthal & Co.' by A. J. van der Leeuw. Many examples of rules and regulations can be found in Doc II, Lippmann, Rosenthal & Co, box 215, folder I, 'Directie-Correspondentie', August 1941–July 1943, and folders B 1 and B2, 'Afdeling inspectie, interne circulaires'.

11. Article 43 of the War on Land Convention reads: 'The authority of the legitimate power having actually passed into the hands of the occupant, the latter shall take all steps in his power to re-establish and insure, as far as possible, public order and safety, while respecting, *unless absolutely prevented* [my

italics], the laws in force in the country.' Germany was a co-signatory to the Convention.
12. Niod, Doc II, Liro.
13. Article 2 of VO 6/1941 laid down that '(1) For the purposes of this decree, a person is considered to be wholly or partly of Jewish blood who has at least one full-blooded Jewish grandparent. (2) A grandparent will be considered a full-blooded Jew if he or she was or is a member of the Jewish religious community.'
14. The 'G' for 'gemengdbloedigen' (persons of mixed blood) was based on 'Besluit Aanmeldingsplicht II', *Nederlandsche Staatscourant* of 3 February 1941, no. 23 by the Permanent Secretary of the Department of the Interior (altered to 'Besluit Aanmeldingsplicht III' of 19 February 1941, *Nederlandsche Staatscourant*, 19 February 1941, no. 35).

    The largest number of Jews (87,026) lived in North Holland province; the smallest number (174) in Zeeland. Source: *Statistische Gegevens van de Joden in Nederland*, vol. 1.
15. Ministerie van Financiën, Bewindvoering archive, rubric 1450, LVVS, 'Verslag betreffende de Verwaltungs- und Rentenanstalt met bijgevoegde balans per 25 Mei 1945', and Niod, Doc II, Lippmann, Rosenthal & Co., Sarphatistraat, box 218, folder H, 'Onderzoek inzake Lippmann, Rosenthal & Co., Sarphatistraat, Amsterdam'. Interrogation of Friedrich Fromm and A. J. Bühler, 17 January 1947.
16. Enemy countries were the United Kingdom and France with their overseas possessions, colonies, protectorates, mandated territories and dominions, Egypt, Sudan, Iraq and Monaco. Enemies, according to article 2 of VO 26/1940 were (amongst others) enemy states including their territorial divisions and 'natural persons being subjects of enemy states or residing in the territory of an enemy state'.
17. Niod, archive 281, 'Verslag inzake Beheer, Sammelverwaltung Feindlicher Hausgeräte', March 1946.
18. Niod, archive 44, FiWi Feindvermögen, folder II A, report by the 'Abteilung Feindvermögen', 30 May 1944.
19. Lindner, 'Das Reichskommissariat für die Behandlung feindlichen Vermögens im Zweiten Weltkrieg', pp. 161–7.
20. Berkley, *Overzicht*, pp. 21–7.
21. Niod, archive 182b, Archief Commissaris Niet Commerciële Vereenigingen en Stichtingen 1941–4, box 1, folder 2i. The names of the two associations referred to are taken from 'Rapport over de maand oktober 1943, district 5'.
22. Introduction to the inventory of archive 182b (Niod), Archief Commissaris Niet Commerciële Vereenigingen en Stichtingen 1941–4. The Jewish share is unknown. (A list prepared by the Jewish Council dated 11 February 1942 gives

116 Jewish organizations active in the social sphere, twenty-one of which had been dissolved. See Amsterdams Gemeentearchief, 'Joodse Vereenigingen op sociaal gebied' 0.032.)
23. Berkley, *Overzicht*, pp. 21–7.
24. ARA 2.09.10.02, CABR, box 175, letter from Seyss-Inquart to Wimmer, Fischböck, Rauter et al., 25 November 1941, 'Zur Behandlung der Judenfrage'.
25. Niod, archive 182 b, Archief Commissaris Niet Commerciële Vereenigingen en Stichtingen 1941–4, box 2, folder 3f, 'Rapport over Oktober 1943'.
26. Niod, Bregstein archive, box 20, folder 1075 ('Rechtsherstel'), 'De liquidatie van het Joodsch onroerend goederenbezit', and ARA, 2.09.16 NBI, inventory no. 74, 'Joodsche commissie voor Herstel', March 1946.
27. Niod, archive 182, folder 33 j, 'Exposé' and folder 5c.
28. ARA, 2.09.10.02 (CABR), box 31, folder 70, 'Verslag van beheerders', end of 1945.
29. De Jong, *Koninkrijk*, vol. V, part 1, p. 421.
30. VO 26/1940 issued on 24 June 1940 covered the *Feindvermögen* of Jewish Netherlanders living abroad.
31. For the liquidation of Jewish concerns, see Niod, Bregstein archive, box 20, folder 1075, Rechtsherstel, 'De liquidatie van het joodsch onroerend goederenbezit'; *idem*, 'De geleidelijke beknotting der vermogenspositie haar juridische grondslagen'; Niod, Doc II, no. 1213, 'De behandeling van aan joden toebehorende vermogenswaarden tijdens en na de oorlog'; Niod, HSSPF, 65 A, 'Betrifft "Entwicklung und Stand der Arisierungsfrage in den besetzten niederländischen Gebieten"'; ministerie van Financiën, Bewindvoering archive, rubric 1450 LVVS, 'Bijlage IIa behorende bij Agendapunt II, Vergadering van 8 mei 1946'; *idem*, 'Verslag betreffende de Vermögensverwaltungs und Rentenanstalt (V.V.R.A.)'; Niod, Doc II, Lippmann, Rosenthal & Co., Sarphatistraat, box 218, folder H, 'Onderzoek inzake Lippman, Rosenthal & Co., Sarphatistraat, Amsterdam'. Interrogation of Friedrich Fromm, Rudolf Schönthür and A. J. Bühler, 17 January 1947, and *idem*, letter from the Wirtschaftsprüfstelle to J. Keyser and S. Hekster, 28 April 1942; the other named documents bearing on the subject will also be found here. Ministerie van Justitie, CABR, inventory no. 81379, Liro, box 1, 'Verhoor van Friedrich Fromm, 6 January 1947'; De Jong, *Koninkrijk*, vol. 5, pp. 583–604, and *idem*, vol. 7, pp. 419–34 (for the deportation plans, see pp. 592 and 1017–18); Herzberg, 'Kroniek der Jodenvervolging' in *Onderdrukking en Verzet*, pp. 69–76; Van der Leeuw, 'Reichskommissariat und Judenvermögen in den Niederlanden' in *Studies over Nederland in oorlogstijd*; Stephan H. Lindner, 'Das Reichskommissariat für die Behandlung feindlichen Vermögens im Zweiten Weltkrieg', and Aalders, 'Three ways of German economic penetration in the Netherlands'.

32. Niod, 'Zusammenfassende Darstellung der Entwicklung bezüglich Hortung des jüdischen Vermögens', 21 June 1941; Niod, archive 264, N. 90/1, folder B, letter from Seyss-Inquart to Bormann, 'Ariseringsraport', 27 January 1941. Cf. De Jong, *Koninkrijk*, vol. 5, part 1, pp. 586, 589 and 591–601, and Aalders, 'Three ways of German economic penetration in the Netherlands'.
33. Ministerie van Financiën, Bewindvoering archive, rubric 1450 LVVS, 'Verslag betreffende de Vermögensverwaltung und Rentenanstalt (V.V.R.A.)'.
34. De Jong, *Koninkrijk*, vol. 5, part 1, pp. 597–8; ministerie van Financiën, Bewindvoering archive, rubric 1450 LVVS, 'Bijlage IIa behorende bij Agendapunt II, Vergadering van 8 mei 1946'; *idem*, 'Verslag betreffende de Vermögensverwaltungs und Rentenanstalt (V.V.R.A.)', 9 February 1953; *idem*, 'Verslag betreffende de Vermögensverwaltungs und Rentenanstalt (V.V.R.A.) met bijgevoegde balans per 25 mei 1945'; Niod, Doc II, 1213, 'De behandeling van aan joden toebehorende vermogenswaarden tijdens en na de oorlog' (quotation). A. J. van der Leeuw, a former Niod staff member from whom the above quotation is taken, has estimated (probably in about 1960) the value of Jewish immovable property at from 150 to 300 million guilders. See also Niod, 'Notities voor het Geschiedwerk', no. 84.
35. NA, RG 331, Allied Operation and Occupation Headquarters, World War II, box 328, 290/7/27/6, 'Removal of works of art from the Netherlands during the German occupation'.
36. See Chapter 11, *Sperrstempel*, emigration and taxes.
37. For 'diamond Jews' see Presser, *Ashes in the Wind*, pp. 371–4; De Jong, *Koninkrijk*, vol. 6, pp. 298–301, and *idem*, vol. 7, pp. 421–2. For *Aktion Bozenhardt*, see Niod, 'Notities voor het Geschiedwerk', no. 119: *Die Aktion Bozenhardt & Co.* by A. J. van der Leeuw, and Niod, archive 281, 'Aktennotiz über eine Besprechung mit Herrn Arthur Bozenhardt in Hamburg am 29.3.1961'.
38. Niod, 'Notities voor het Geschiedwerk' no. 124, 'Das "Hanemann-geschenk"', by A. J. van der Leeuw.
39. Niod, 'Notities voor het Geschiedwerk' no 112, 'Der Entziehungsvorgang bei der sog. Sperrdiamanten-Aktion und die im Individualfall vorliegenden Beweisunterlagen', and De Jong, *Koninkrijk*, vol 6, part 1, p. 299.
40. Niod, Bregstein archive, box 20, folder 1075/ Rechtherstel, 'De liquidatie van het joods onroerend goederenbezit', and De Jong, *Koninkrijk*, vol. 5, part 1, pp. 604–5.
41. Ministerie van Financiën, Bewindvoering archive, rubric 1450, LVVS, 'Verslag betreffende de Verwaltungs- und Rentenanstalt met bijgevoegde balans per 25 mei'. The buildings of (Jewish) non-profit-making associations and foundations had already been seized under VO 41/1941 of 28 February 1941.

42. Niod, Doc II-1213, 'De behandeling van aan joden toebehorende vermogenswaarden tijdens en na de oorlog'. De Jong, *Koninkrijk*, vol. 5, part 1, p. 605 gives 200 million guilders for building plots and 27 million for mortgages; cf. Niod, Doc II, no. 556, Niederländische Grundstücksverwaltung, folder 4, Exposé no. 25, which lists 25,000 and 16,000 building plots respectively, based on a series of documents, and estimates that 6,000 mortgages were involved.
43. Niod, Doc II, no. 556, Niederländische Grundstücksverwaltung, folder 4, Exposé no. 25, and Niod, Bregstein archive, box 20, folder 1075/Rechtsherstel, 'De liquidatie van het joods onroerend goederenbezit'.
44. Niod, Doc II, Algemeen Nederlandsch Beheer van Onroerende Goederen, 'Notulen van de vergadering van beheerders, makelaars en procuratiehouders van de A.N.B.O.-kantoren gehouden op 29 maart 1943'.
45. Niod, Bregstein archive, box 20, folder 1075/Rechtsherstel, 'De liquidatie van het joods onroerend goederenbezit'.
46. Niod, Bregstein archive, box 20, folder 1075/Rechsherstel, 'De liquidatie van het joods onroerend goederenbezit', and Niod, Doc II, Landelijke Hypotheekbank N.V., 'Nota betreffende de toepassing van Hoofdstuk VII A juncto Hoofdstuk III van Besluit E 100 . . . op hypotheken, gevestigd na het onvrijwillig bezitsverlies van het onderpand door den oorspronkelijken eigenaar.'
47. Niod, Bregstein archive, box 20, folder 1075/Rechtsherstel, 'De liquidatie van het joods onroerend goederenbezit', and Niod, 'Notitie voor het Geschiedwerk', no. 123, 'Gründung, Ziel und Tätigkeit der Landelijke Hypotheekbank N.V.'.
48. De Jong, *Koninkrijk*, vol. 7, part 1, pp. 426–7.

Chapter 6: The Robber Bank in Sarphatistraat, Amsterdam: Lippmann, Rosenthal & Co. (Liro)

1. Ministerie van Financiën, Bewindvoering archive, rubric 1450, LVVS. 'Eindverslag van Beheerders-Vereffenaars Betreffende Liquidatie van Verwaltung (L.V.V.S.) aan het Nederlandse Beheersinstituut te 's-Gravenhage', 24 April 1958; Niod, archive 48, box 3, folder 5b, 'Generalkommissariat für Finanz und Wirtschaft, Hauptabteilung Wirtschaft', 'Bericht' signed by von Karger; *idem*, 'Eröffnungsbericht gemäss Ziffer V 1 der Richtlinien für die Verwaltung von anmeldepflichtigen Unternehmungen', n.d.
2. Ministerie van Justitie, CABR, Alfred Flesche dossier, inventory no. 423, I. 'Processen Verbaal van 12 september 1947; 26 juni 1947 en 2 januari 1946.'

Flesche became administrator by virtue of Article 13 of the decree covering the treatment of enemy property, 27 June 1940:

'(1) In the case of legal persons, associations, institutions governed by private law, assets earmarked for special purposes, and private companies (enterprises) having their headquarters or a branch in occupied Netherlands territory, administrators may be appointed to safeguard and maintain the assets of any enterprise predominantly under direct or indirect enemy influence. The same applies to enterprises without management capable of representing the enterprise legally or of which it may be assumed that the management cannot provide adequate guarantees that the enterprise will heed the interests of the Reichskommissar in the occupied Netherlands territories.

'(2) In case of doubt, the Commissioner General for Finance and Economic Affairs will decide whether or not the conditions specified under (1) apply.

'(3) The cost of the administration will be borne by the enterprise.'

A further reason, no less important according to Flesche, was that the bank controlled a capital of three million guilders from Russia, the true owners of which were not known. In theory, this might have been 'enemy property' and for that reason it had to be 'safeguarded for the present'.

For Flesche's letter of appointment, see ministerie van Justitie, CABR, inventory no. 81379 Liro, box 4. Letter from the Generalkommissariat für Finanz und Wirtschaft, 8 July 1940.

3. Niod, Doc I, Alfred Flesche, 'Korte inhoud uit dossier ten name van Flesche'.
4. Ministerie van Justitie, CABR, Gerbig dossier, inventory no.109. Letter from Devisenschutzkommando to Zentralstelle für jüdische Auswanderung, 2 October 1942.
5. Jews were persons defined by Article 4 of VO 189/1940. The (additional) sources of the two so-called Lippmann-Rosenthal *Verordnungen*, apart from the *Verordnungsblatt*, are taken – unless stated otherwise – from Berkeley, *Overzicht van het ontstaan*, pp. 32–3, and Niod, Bregstein archive, box 20, folder 1075, 'De geleidelijke beknotting der vermogenspositie. Haar juridische grondslagen'. For the First Liro Decree, see also Niod, Doc II, Lippmann, Rosenthal & Co., Sarphatistraat, box 217, folder D, various circulars, etc. 'Op wie de Verordening van toepassing is.' The document was sent to the Jewish Council as elucidation of the First Liro Decree, and *idem*, 'Toelichting op de artikelen 1–4 der Verordening van den Rijkscommissaris'.

For the change of the name of Sarphatistraat to Muiderschans, see Straatnaamwijzigingen, *Gemeenteblad* (Amsterdam) 1942, section 3, Ia, serial nos. 18 and 539. Here, too, the name 'Sarphatistraat' continued to be used.
6. Boas, 'De misleidingstactieken van de nazi's bij de liquidatie van de Europese joden'.

Notes

7. Ministerie van Financiën, Bewindvoering archive, rubric 1450, LVVS. 'Eindverslag van Beheerders-Vereffenaars Betreffende Liquidatie van Verwaltung (L.V.V.S.) aan het Nederlandse Beheersinstituut te 's-Gravenhage', 24 April 1958, and Niod, Doc II, Liro, box 218, folder H.
8. De Jong, *Koninkrijk*, vol. 5, part 1, pp. 591–2.
9. Ministerie van Financiën, Bewindvoering archive, rubric 1450, LVVS. 'Eindverslag van Beheerders-Vereffenaars Betreffende Liquidatie van Verwaltung (L.V.V.S.) aan het Nederlandse Beheersinstituut te 's-Gravenhage', 24 April 1958.
10. Niod, Doc II, Lippmann, Rosenthal & Co., Sarphatistraat, box 217, folder D, various circulars, etc. 'Einige Daten über die Entstehung und Entwicklung der Warenabteilung', 1 November 1943.
11. Ministerie van Financiën, Bewindvoering archive, rubric 1450, LVVS. 'Eindverslag van Beheerders-Vereffenaars Betreffende Liquidatie van Verwaltung (L.V.V.S.) aan het Nederlandse Beheersinstituut te 's-Gravenhage', 24 April 1958.
12. Niod, Doc II, Lippmann, Rosenthal & Co., Sarphatistraat, box 217, folder D, various circulars, etc. 'Einige Daten über die Entstehung und Entwicklung der Warenabteilung', 1 November 1943.
13. Niod, Doc II, Lippmann, Rosenthal & Co., Sarphatistraat, box 215, folder 'Directie-correspondentie I', August 1941–July 1943, letter from Liro to Generalkommissar für Finanz und Wirtschaft, 23 November 1942, and *idem*, letter from Liro to Zentralstelle für jüdische Auswanderung, 11 June 1943 (quotation).
14. Niod, Doc II, Lippmann, Rosenthal & Co., Sarphatistraat, box 217, folder D, various circulars, etc. 'Goederenontvangst', 15 June 1943.
15. Niod, 'Notities voor het Geschiedwerk', no. 116.
16. Ministerie van Financiën, Bewindvoering archive, rubric 1450, LVVS. 'Eindverslag van Beheerders-Vereffenaars Betreffende Liquidatie van Verwaltung (L.V.V.S.) aan het Nederlandse Beheersinstituut te 's-Gravenhage', 24 April 1958, and Niod, Doc II, Liro, box 218, folder H, Interrogation of J. van Blanken and Interrogation of J. Scheltens.
17. Niod, Doc II, Lippmann, Rosenthal & Co., Sarphatistraat, box 215, folder 'Directie-correspondentie I', August 1941–July 1943, letter from Liro to Generalkommissar für Finanz und Wirtschaft, 23 November 1942, and *idem*, letter from Liro to Zentralstelle für jüdische Auswanderung, 11 June 1943 (quotation).
18. Niod, Doc II, Liro, box 216, folder B1, no. 73. 'Forms of address'.
19. Niod, archive 48, box 3, folder 5b, Generalkommissariat für Finanz und Wirtschaft, Hauptabteilung Wirtschaft, 'Eröffnungsbericht gemäss Ziffer V I der Richtlinien für die Verwaltung von anmeldepflichtigen Unternehmungen',

n.d. However, a letter to the Wirtschaftsprüfstelle dated 4 August 1941 states that the building was rented for 25,000 guilders a year, Niod, archive 97, A. Flesche Collection, folder I, B.
20. Niod, archive 48, box 3, folder 5b, Generalkommissar für Finanz und Wirtschaft, Hauptabteilung Wirtschaft, 'Eröffnungsbericht gemäss Ziffer V I der Rechtlinien für die Verwaltung von anmeldepflichtigen Unternehmungen', n.d.
21. Niod, archive 97, A. Flesche Collection, letter from Generalkommissar für Finanz und Wirtschaft to Flesche, 7 July 1941.
22. Niod, Doc I, Alfred Flesche, 'Korte inhoud uit dossier ten name van Flesche'.
23. Niod, archive 97, A. Flesche Collection, 2 boxes, and ministerie van Justitie, CABR, inventory no. 81379, Liro, box 1, 'Vereinbarung zwischen den Unterzeichneten Herren A. Flesche . . . und O. Witscher . . .', 15 August 1943.
24. Niod, 'Inleiding op de Inventaris en regentenlijst van archief 97', A. Flesche Collection, by A. J. van der Leeuw.
25. Ministerie van Justitie, CABR, Lippmann, Rosenthal & Co. dossier, inventory no. 81379, and *idem*, von Karger dossier.
26. Ministerie van Justitie, CABR, Lippmann, Rosenthal & Co. dossier (inventory no. 81379).
27. Niod, Doc II, Lippmann, Rosenthal & Co., Sarphatistraat, box 217, folder D, 'Vergleichende Übersicht per 31.12. 1941, 31.12.42, 30.9.43 und 31.10.43', and *idem*, 'Kurze Organisationsübersicht der Firma Lippmannn, Rosenthal & Co., Sarphatistraat', 31 December 1942, and ministerie van Justitie, CABR, Lippmann, Rosenthal & Co. dossier, inventory no. 81379, box 1, 'Personeelsledenlijst'.
28. Ministerie van Justitie, CABR, Henneicke dossier, 'Arbeidsovereenkomst', 30 June 1942.
29. Unless stated otherwise, the data on the internal Liro organization are taken from Niod, Doc II, Lippmann, Rosenthal & Co., Sarphatistraat, box 217, folder D, various circulars and organizational schemas; Gefolgschaft Lippmann, Rosenthal & Co., Sarphatistraat, Muiderschans 47–55, Amsterdam (C). 'Vergleichende Übersicht per 31.12.1941, 31.12.42, 30.9.43 und 31.10.43', and *idem*, 'Kurze Organisationsübersicht der Firma Lippmann, Rosenthal & Co., Sarphatistraat', 31 December 1942.

The various reports show little difference in the number of staff. The general picture is not significantly affected.
30. Ministerie van Justitie, CABR, Koffieberg dossier, and *idem*, Lippmann, Rosenthal & Co. dossier (inventory no. 81379).
31. Ministerie van Justitie, CABR, Koffieberg dossier, and *idem*, Lippmann, Rosenthal & Co. dossier (inventory no. 81379). When questioned about emigration, von Karger could not recall more than three names after the war:

Notes

Cohen (from the Bonneterie concern), the Stokvis family, and Busch. Ministerie van Justitie, CABR, von Karger dossier, and Niod, Doc II, Lippmann, Rosenthal & Co., Sarphatistraat, box 217, folder D, various circulars, etc. 'Einige Daten über die Entstehung und Entwicklung der Warenabteilung', 1 November 1943. From the sales ledger (14–15 April 1942) of the auctioneers Mak van Waay it appears that paintings by seventeenth-century masters were sold for 66,815 guilders. Sotheby's archive, Mak van Waay archive (for this archive, see also in Chapter 9, The Liro Sale of Cultural Property).

32. Niod, archive 264, N 90/1, folder A, letter from Dr Holz (with 'Anlage' by Seyss-Inquart) to Liro, 16 October 1942.
33. Niod, Doc II, Lippmann, Rosenthal & Co., Sarphatistraat, box 217, folder D, various circulars, etc. 'Notiz über eine Besprechung mit Herrn Mulisch über die von uns abgeschlossenen Versicherungen am 4. März 1943.' CABR, inventory no. 81379, box 1 at the ministerie van Justitie, contains a detailed survey of the various insurance policies and valuations, premium assessments, terms, etc. Paintings were apparently insured on the basis of valuations by Mak van Waay.
34. Niod, Doc II, Lippmann, Rosenthal & Co., Sarphatistraat, box 217, folder D, 'Aktennotiz Nr. 130. Betr.: onze loopende verzekeringen', 24 September 1943, signed Witscher.
35. Niod, Doc II, Lippmann, Rosenthal & Co., Sarphatistraat, box 217, folder D, initialled note, undated, beginning with: 'Durch Dr. von Karger wurde mir im Namen von Herrn Flesche an Hand nachstehende theoretischer Beispiele die Frage gestellt: Wer bemerkt Veruntreuungen und wie und wann?'
36. Niod, Doc II, Lippmann, Rosenthal & Co., Sarphatistraat, box 217, folder C, 'No. 73. Betr.: het openen van safeloketten, 22 mei 1943'.
37. Niod, archive 97, A. Flesche Collection, box 1, letter to O. Witscher, 4 May 1943, and ministerie van Justitie, CABR, Olij dossier, inventory no. 24811.
38. Niod, Doc II, Lippmann, Rosenthal & Co, Sarphatistraat, box 218, folder H, 'Verhoor van R. H. K. von Blaschke en K.V. K Mulisch', 28 January 1946.
39. Niod, Doc II, Liro, box 217, folder d, 'Liste derjenigen Wertsachen, die am 22.11. 43 in der Wohnung des Baron v. Stechow in Berlin, Bismarckstr. 102/III sichergestellt wurden und aus der Fa. L.R. u. Co stammen'.
40. Ministerie van Justitie, CABR, Koffieberg dossier.
41. Ministerie van Justitie, CABR, Koffieberg dossier, and *idem*, Lippmann, Rosenthal & Co., inventory no. 81379.
42. Ministerie van Financiën, Bewindvoering archive, rubric 1450, LVVS 'Eindverslag van Beheerders-Vereffenaars Betreffende Liquidatie van Verwaltung (L.V.V.S) aan het Nederlandse Beheerinstituut te 's-Gravenhage', 24 April 1958.

43. Ministerie van Financiën, Bewindvoering archive, rubric 1450, LVVS 'Eindverslag van Beheerders-Vereffenaars Betreffende Liquidatie van Verwaltung (L.V.V.S) aan het Nederlandse Beheerinstituut te 's-Gravenhage', 24 April 1958.
    For the letter of 21 November 1942, see ministerie van Justitie, CABR, inventory no. 81379, Liro, box 1, 'Künftige Behandlung der von Ihnen erfassten jüdischen Vermögenswerte'.
44. Niod, archive 97, A. Flesche Collection, box 1, 'Bericht über das erste Quartal 1943', 16 April 1943.
45. Niod, Doc II, Lippmann, Rosenthal & Co., Sarphatistraat, box 217, folder D, various circulars, etc. 'Aktennotiz', 15 December 1943.
46. Niod, Doc II, Lippmann, Rosenthal & Co., Sarphatistraat, box 215, folder 'Directie-correspondentie I', August 1941–July 1943, letter from Reichskommissar to Liro, 21 November 1942.
47. Niod, archive 97, A. Flesche Collection, box 1, 'Jahresbericht 1942 der Prüfungsabteilung'.
48. Niod, Doc II, Lippmann, Rosenthal & Co., Sarphatistraat, box 215, 'Afdeling Inspectie II, Interne circulaires', no. 240, 24 December 1942. 'Betr.: Uitbetaling van gelden aan joden'. The quotation from the *Joodsche Weekblad* was taken from this circular.
49. Niod, Doc II, Lippmann, Rosenthal & Co., Sarphatistraat, box 215, folder 'Directie-correspondentie I', August 1941–July 1943, letter from Generalkommissar für Finanz und Wirtschaft re 'Künftige Behandlung der von Ihnen erfassten jüdischen Vermögenswerte', 10 December 1942, and *idem*, letter from Reichskommissariat (general section) to Provinciale Utrechtsche Electriciteits Mij., 22 February 1943.
50. Niod, Doc II, Liro, box 218, folder H, Interrogation of J. M. Goudsmit.
51. Niod, Doc II, Lippmann, Rosenthal & Co., Sarphatistraat, box 215, folder 'Directie-correspondentie I', August 1941–July 1943, letter from Generalkommissar für Finanz und Wirtschaft to Liro, 'Behandlung des Vermögens des jüdischen Eheteiles in Mischehen', 24 January 1943, and *idem*, letter from Liro,'Zu dem Schreiben des Herrn Generalkommissar für Finanz und Wirtschaft, Generalreferent, vom 24.1.43 . . . betr. Behandlung des Vermögens des jüdischen Eheteiles in Mischehen'. This folder lists numerous supplementary rules and regulations covering 'mixed marriages'. They have not been detailed above.
52. Niod, Doc II, Lippmann, Rosenthal & Co., Sarphatistraat, box 215, folder 'Directie-correspondentie I', August 1941–July 1943, circular from Liro to the Nederlandsche Advocatenvereeniging, The Hague; the Nederlandsch Instituut voor Accountants, Amsterdam, and Nederl. Mij. tot bevordering van Geneeskunst, Amsterdam, 17 September 1941.

Notes

Chapter 7: The First Liro Decree in Practice

1. Niod, Doc II, Lippmann, Rosenthal & Co., Sarphatistraat, box 218, folder H, 'Verhoren' (K. van den Berg) and Interrogation of R. H. K von Blasche and K.V. K. Mulisch, January 1946 (quotation).
2. Niod, Doc II, Lippmann, Rosenthal & Co., Sarphatistraat, box 217, folder D, various circulars, etc. 'Op wie de Verordening van toepassing is.'
3. Niod, Doc II, Lippmann, Rosenthal & Co., Sarphatistraat, box 215, 'Afdeling Inspectie II, Interne circulaires No. 271', 8 February 1943, 'Betr. Postcheque en girodienst' and *idem*, box 217, folder c, Aktennotiz no.147.
4. ARA, 2.09.48, Raad voor het Rechtsherstel, inventory no. 2057, letter from Liro to Broederschap van Notarissen in Nederland, 19 September 1941.
5. Niod, Doc II, Lippmann, Rosenthal & Co., Sarphatistraat, box 215, 'Afdeling Inspectie II, Interne circulaires, No. 292', 13 March 1943, 'Betr.: verplichting van banken tot inlevering van joodsch vijandelijk vermogen'.
6. Niod, archive 48, box 3, folder 5b, Generalkommissar für Finanz und Wirtschaft, 'Eröffnungsbericht gemäss Ziffer V I der Richtlinien für die Verwaltung von anmeldepflichtigen Unternehmungen', n.d.
7. De Jong. *Koninkrijk*, vol. 1, part 1, p. 609.
8. See also figures in Conclusion, The Looting of Jewish Property 1940–45.
9. Niod, Bregstein archive, box 20, folder 1075, 'Welk bedrag werd aan effecten ingeleverd?' The lawyer Marcel Bregstein played a very active part in *Rechtsherstel* on behalf of the Dutch government.
10. Niod, Doc II-1213, 'De behandeling van aan joden toebehorende vermogensvoorwaarden tijdens en na de oorlog', and ministerie van Financiën, Bewindvoering archive, rubric 1450, LVVS, 'Eindverslag LVVS', 24 April 1958.
11. Ministerie van Buitelandse Zaken, DVE 1945–84, inventory no. 180, letter from 'beheerders/vereffenaars LVVS' to Rinnooy-Kan, ministerie van Financiën, 30 September 1953.
12. The parcels were processed using an impractical procedure that ended in chaos within a short time. The numbered parcels were marked 'L' or 'P' and recorded under their 'L' and 'P' numbers together with the date of arrival in the so-called cellar book, which owed its name to Cellar III, where the incoming parcels were temporarily stored.

    Next, the parcels were entered, one by one, in the so-called receipt book of the depot department and marked with a 'D'. At the same time, they were recoded on personal index cards. Then the appended specified lists were checked against the receipt book. After that the parcels, marked with 'L' or 'P' number, the deposit number and a series number (under which they had been registered in the receipt book), were placed in the Cellar II safe deposits. For the convenience of the Cellar administration, the parcels were moved again and, after having been recorded on share cards, finally stored under their respective deposit numbers in Cellar I.

Although the parcels were thus recorded once more (this time on share cards), they remained in their original state and were stored unopened under the appropriate deposit number. The share-card system of the depot section was, however, retained. But this process was of very short duration since the backlog quickly became so unmanageable that the Liro board was forced to put a stop to it: Niod, Bregstein archive, box 20, folder 1075, 'Welk bedrag werd aan effecten ingeleverd?'

13. Niod, archive 48, box 3, folder 5B, Generalkommissariat für Finanz und Wirtschaft, Hauptabteilung Wirtschaft, 'Eröffnungsbericht'.
14. Niod, 'Notities voor het Geschiedwerk': 'Entziehung und Verbringung nach Deutschland der beim "Bankhause" Lippmann, Rosenthal & Co., Sarphatistraat abgelieferten Wertpapiere' by A. J. van der Leeuw.
15. Niod, Bregstein archive, box 20, folder 1075, 'Welk bedrag werd aan effecten ingeleverd?'
16. Van Lennep, 'Effectenbeurs en Rechtsherstel' in *De Gids*, October 1952, no. 10. The view outlined by Van Lennep (camouflaged sale), which was also upheld by Carel F. Overhoff, president of the Stock Exchange Union, is not, however, consistent, as we shall see in the further course of this chapter.
17. Vereniging voor de Effectenhandel archive, 'Notulen Raad van Bijstand 1951', December 1947.
18. De Jong, *Koninkrijk*, vol. 5, part I, p. 611.
19. Tammes, *Rechtsherstel en praktijk inzake effecten*, p. 11.
20. *De handel in effecten gedurende de jaren 1940–1945*, p. 7. This brochure (compiled by the VvdE) was presented in November 1951 to the members of the First and Second Chambers of the States-General, to enable them to form an opinion about the trade in Jewish securities during the German occupation.
21. De Vries, *Een eeuw vol effecten*, p. 192.
22. *De handel in effecten gedurende de jaren 1940–1945*, p. 9.
23. *Nederlandsche Jurisprudentie*, no. 271, 12 January 1942.
24. Quoted from Meijers, *Het Voorstel van LVVS*, pp. 2–3.
25. Vereniging voor de Effectenhandel archive, 'Notulen Raad van Bijstand': 'Enige vragen inzake de handel in effecten tijdens de bezettingsjaren', 13 May 1950. The answers can be found in the minutes of the meeting on 20 July, 'Bespreking naar aanleiding van enige vragen inzake den handel in effecten tijdens de bezettingsjaren'.
26. Ministerie van Justitie, CABR, Rebholz dossier, no. 649/001, 19 December 1950.
27. Ministerie van Justitie, CABR, Rebholz dossier, 'Opdracht' (instructions) to an expert committee (on the Rebholz affair). For a report of the collapse of

Notes

Kerkhoven & Co., see Meihuizen, *Goed fout,* pp. 30–7 and passim; see also *De Vlam,* 6 November 1948, *Het Vrije Volk,* 5 September 1949 and *Het Parool,* 22 October 1948, amongst other sources. In Overhoff's *Herinneringen,* based on Niod (Doc I, C. F. Overhoff) the Kerkhoven collapse was not mentioned for understandable reasons. His recollections of the Stock Exchange and of Liro activities have a pronounced apologetic tone.

28. Vereniging voor de Effectenhandel archive, 'Notulen Raad van Bestuur', 1951, December 1947, letter from C. F. Overhoff to Raad van Rechtsherstel, Afdeling Effectenregistratie.
29. Niod, Doc II, Liro, box 218, Interrogation of H. A. Eysten, 8 October 1998.
30. Vereniging voor de Effectenhandel archive, 'Notulen Raad van Bestuur', 1951, December 1947, letter from Carel Overhoff to the Raad van Rechtsherstel, Afdeling Effectenregistratie. Author's italics.
31. Niod, Doc I, C. F. Overhoff. Overhoff wrote his 'Oorlogsherinneringen' (War Reminiscences) on behalf of the Netherlands Institute for War Documentation and was paid a fee of 200 guilders a month for them. The duration of Overhoff's activities – six months – was agreed in advance. A 'declaration' marked the contents as 'secret'. Cf. *idem,* letter from N. W. Posthumus, then director of the Netherlands Institute for War Documentation, to C. F. Overhoff, 22 December 1948.
32. De Vries, *Een eeuw vol effecten,* p. 203, mentions 110 to 115 million guilders; De Jong, *Koninkrijk,* vol. 12, part 1, gives a total of 146 million guilders; A. J. van der Leeuw mentions 'at least' 145 million guilders, Niod, archive 281, 'Rapport inzage het optreden van dr. A. J. Bühler en O. Rebholz tijdens de Duitse bezetting'.
33. Niod, Bregstein archive, box 9. Unsigned and undated declaration by Rebholz. Niod, Doc 11–1213, 'De behandeling van aan joden toebehorende vermogensvoorwaarden tijdens en na de oorlog'. A. J van der Leeuw, the author of the article, puts the value of the shares sold at ca. 234 million guilders.
34. De Vries, *Een eeuw vol effecten,* p. 193.
35. ARA, 2.19.042.56. Archive of the Commissie tot Bescherming der Aanspraken der Gedepossedeerden (1946–57), inventory no. 30. 'Depositorekening'.
36. Niod, archive 48, box 3, folder 5 B, Generalkommissariat für Finanz und Wirtschaft, Hauptabteilung Wirtschaft, 'Eröffnungsbericht'.
37. Vereniging voor de Effectenhandel, copy of letter from C. F. Overhoff to J. C. M. Smits, 8 November 1951. Overhoff quotes an 'Aktennotiz' by Bühler (dated 2 August 1943), which he acquired after the war.
38. Niod, archive 281, 'Rapport inzage het optreden van dr. A. J. Bühler en O. Rebholz tijdens de Duitse bezetting'.
39. De Vries, *Een eeuw vol effecten,* p. 195.

40. *De Telegraaf*, 6 March 1942 and *Amsterdamsch Effectenblad*, 3, 4, 5 and 6 March. For the statement by J.H. Wijnand, the editor, see 'Buitenlandse Zaken, Ambassade Bern, 1945–1951' inventory no. 729. Translation of a 'declaration' by Wijnand, at the time financial editor of *De Telegraaf*. The declaration was originally handed in to the Raad voor het Rechtsherstel, Afdeling Effectenregistratie.
41. Buitenlandse Zaken, Ambassade Bern 1945–51, inventory no. 729: 'Bericht: Über die Angelegenheiten des Handels in Royal Dutch Aktien, die am 6. März 1942 an der Börse durch Lippmann, Rosenthal & Co., Sarphatistraat . . . verkauft wurden (sogenannter Schleudertag von Hali)', and archive of the Vereniging voor de Effectenhandel, no. 1987 B I, dossier 26 B (Otto Rebholz). W. Willems, 'Note on the trade in Koninklijke Petroleum shares on 6 March 1942 and on the so-called "dumping days"'.
42. Niod, Doc II, Liro, box 218, Interrogation of Otto Rebholz on 9, 16 and 17 October 1947.
43. Vereniging voor de Effectenhandel, 'Notulen Raad van Bijstand 1943–1944, 'Overzicht van den voorzitter (. . .)', 16 December 1943. For black market stock-exchange quotations, see De Vries, *Een eeuw vol effecten*, p. 188.
44. Niod, Doc II, Liro, box 218, Interrogation of Otto Rebholz on 9, 16 and 17 October 1947.
45. Niod, Doc II, Liro, box 218, Interrogation of Otto Rebholz on 9, 16 and 17 October 1947.
46. Niod, Doc II, Liro, box 218, Interrogation of Liro employee H. A. Eysten on 5 October 1946; Interrogation of Otto Rebholz on 9, 16 and 17 October 1947, and *idem*, Bregstein archive, box 9, unsigned and undated statement by Rebholz.
47. Niod, Doc I, Rebholz dossier, 'Rapport Van Oven'.
48. Not to be confused with the other two 'Konto Quartos' in which Rebholz participated in the spring of 1941 and in both of which the Handelsmaatschappij H. Albert de Bary & Co. N.V. and Rhodius Koenigs Handelsmaatschappij N.V. were involved. In one case, Wodan Handelsmaatscappij N.V. was also involved, in the second its place was taken by Hugo Kaufmann & Co.'s Bank N.V.: ministerie van Justitie, Rebholz dossier, no. 649/001.
49. Niod, Doc II, Liro, box 218, Interrogation of Liro employee H. A. Eysten, 5 October 1946; Interrogation of Otto Rebholz on 9, 16 and 17 October 1947; Niod, Doc I, Rebholz 'Rapport Van Oven', and ministerie van Justitie, Bewindvoering archive, the collection commonly referred to as the 'Boek' (documents, minutes, reports, interrogations, etc.), first so called by Hans Hazemeijer, documentalist at the Ministry.
50. ARA, 2.09.15, Afdeling Effectenregistratie van de Raad voor Rechtsherstel, inventory no. 48 'Doeleinden van de effectenregistratie'.

51. In addition to Rebholz and Liro, the Twentsche Bank, Oyens & Zonen, Hope & Co., and the Hollandsche Koopmansbank are also said to have been issued with general licences: archive of the Gerechtelijke Diensten, Amsterdam, box 2, folder II, office no.14638/268–I-54 F, O. Rebholz dossier, 'Verweerschrift van de verdediging in de zaak van het Openbaar Ministerie tegen Otto Rebholz', 27 July 1950.
52. *Rechtsherstel* 1950–1951, pp. 400–1, no. 114. Raad voor Rechtsherstel, Afdeling Effectenregistratie, 2 June 1950.
53. Archive of the Gerechtelijke Diensten, Amsterdam, box 2, office no. 14638/268–I-54 F, O. Rebholz dossier, 'Verweerschrift van de verdediging in de zaak van het Openbaar Ministerie tegen Otto Rebholz', 27 July 1950.
54. According to the membership list of the VvdE (Bedrijfsgroep Effectenhandel) issued in November 1943. Information from Amsterdam Stock Exchange given by telephone on 29 January 1999.
55. Archive of Gerechtelijke Diensten, Amsterdam, box 2, folder II, office no. 14638/268–I-54 F, O. Rebholz dossier. 'Productie 1.' List of VvdE members who bought American share certificates from Rebholz's Bankierskantoor. Also mentioned are the three licence numbers under which the shares were sold. (A. 59500, 38430 and 466995); in addition, the paper states which firms were given an extra discount ('uitkeering').

    The Incasso Bank merged with the Amsterdamsche Bank in 1948. In 1964, the year of the largest bank mergers, the Algemene Bank Nederland (ABN) was formed by a merger of the Nederlandsche Handel-Maatschappij and the Twentsche Bank, while the Amsterdamsche Bank and the Rotterdamsche Bank continued to trade as the Amsterdam-Rotterdam Bank (AMRO). In 1989, the Nederlandsche Middenstandbank merged with the Postbank, to be called NMB-Postbank until 1991, thereafter continuing as ING (after a merger with National Nederlanden). In 1991 ABN and Amro decided to join forces as ABN-AMRO.
56. Vereniging voor de Effectenhandel, 'Notulen van de Raad van Bijstand': 'Definitief voorstel van de Vereniging voor de Effectenhandel (Bedrijfsgroep Effectenhandel) inzake zwarte leden'. (Expulsion was based on the emergency decree governing the restoration of legal rights, the Besluit Herstel Rechtsverkeer.)
57. Archive of the Gerechtelijke Diensten, Amsterdam, box 2, folder II, office no. 14638/268–I-54 F, O. Rebholz dossier. 'Productie 1. Lijst van Leden van de Vereniging voor den effectenhandel die bij Rebholz' Bankierskantoor Certificaten van Amerikaansche Shares hebben gekocht'.
58. Niod, Bregstein archive, box 9, unsigned and undated declaration by Rebholz, and ARA, 2.19.042.56, archive of the Commissie tot Bescherming der Aanspraken der Gedepossedeerden (1946–1957), inventory no. 70, 'Pleitnota Polak/de Haan v.d. Werff'. The circulars and other documents are appended.

59. Archive of the Gerechtelijke Diensten, Amsterdam, box 2, folder II, office no.14638/268/ I-54 F, O. Rebholz dossier. 'Productie 3b. Aantekening betreffende het onderhoud tusschen de Heeren O. Rebholz en C. F. Overhoff ten kantore der Vereniging op 18 Mei 1943. Eenig exemplaar opgemakt door Overhoff.'
60. Niod, Archive 281, 'Rapport inzage het optreden van Dr. A. J. Bühler en O. Rebholz tijdens de Duitse bezetting' by A. J. van der Leeuw.
61. Vereniging voor de Effectenhandel archive, Notulen van de Raad van Bijstand, 8 October 1951, 'Aantekening. Verhandeling van certificaten van Amerikaanse aandelen tijdens de bezetting'. The note covers Overhoff's interrogation before the Judicial Division of the Raad voor het Rechtsherstel.
62. ARA, 2.19.042.56, archive of the Commissie tot Bescherming der Aanspraken der Gedepossedeerden (1946–1957), inventory no. 70, 'Pleitnota Polak/de Haan/v.d. Werff'. From the documents Rebholz handed over to the prosecution, it appears that Overhoff received commissions from Rebholz in December 1943, and again in January and February 1944: Niod, Bregstein archive, box 9, unsigned and undated statement by Rebholz. The circulars and documents with statements by Rebholz are appended.
63. Ministerie van Financiën, Bewindvoering archive, 'Pleidooi inzake Beheersinstituut tegen Rebholz en Rebholz-Schröter', 25 January 1955.
64. ARA, 2.09.15, Afdeling Effectenregistratie van de Raad voor het Rechtsherstel, inventory no. 233, copy of letter from Rebholz, address illegible, 24 July 1948.
65. ARA, 2.09.15, Afdeling Effectenregistratie van de Raad voor het Rechtsherstel, inventory no. 48 'Doeleinden van de effectenregistratie', and Vereniging voor de Effectenhandel, 'Notulen Raad van Bijstand', 1951, letter from Overhoff to Raad voor het Rechtsherstel, Afdeling Effectenregistratie, December 1947.
66. ARA, 2.19.042.56, archive of Commissie tot Bescherming der Aanspraken der Gedepossedeerden (1946–1957), inventory no. 70, 'Pleitnota Polak/de Haan/v.d. Werff', and Vereniging voor de Effectenhandel archive, 'Notulen van de Raad van Bijstand, 8 October 1951, 'Verhandeling van certificaten van Amerikaanse aandelen tijdens de bezetting', and Niod, archive 281, 'Rapport inzage het optreden van dr. A. J. Bühler en O. Rebholz tijdens de Duitse bezetting' by A. J. van der Leeuw. For Overhoff's endorsement 'not of Jewish origin', see 'Verklaring voor Raad voor het Rechtsherstel, Afdeling Rechtspraak', Amsterdam, 28 April 1952, in *Rechtsherstel*, 1952, 52/204.
67. *Rechtsherstel*, 1952, 52/204 and 52/205.
68. ARA, 2.09.15, Afdeling Effectenregistratie van de Raad voor Rechtsherstel, inventory no. 48, 'Doeleinden van de effectenregistratie'; Meihuizen, *'Goed fout'*, p. 47; De Vries, *Een eeuw vol effecten*, pp. 194–5; and *De Vlam*, 6 November 1948, 'De beurs op stelten'.

Notes

69. Niod, archive 281, 'Rapport inzage het optreden van dr. A. J. Bühler en O. Rebholz tijdens de Duitse bezetting', by A. J. van der Leeuw.
70. Niod, Doc II, Liro, box 218, folder H, 'Verhoor van M. G. Hali'.
71. Afdeling Effectenregistratie van de Raad voor Rechtsherstel, inventory no. 48 'Doeleinden van de effectenregistratie', and Niod, Bregstein archive, box 20, folder 1075, 'Welk belang werd aan effecten ingeleverd?'
72. ARA, 2.19.042.56, Archive of the Commissie tot Bescherming der Aanspraken der Gedepossedeerden (1946–1957), inventory no. 67, correspondence between Liro and D. W. Brandt, 5 January 1944, and between Brandt and Overhoff, 29 November 1943, 18 December 1943 and 6 January 1944.
73. ARA, 2.19.042.56, Archive of the Commissie tot Bescherming der Aanspraken der Gedepossedeerden (1946–1957), inventory no. 70, 'Pleitnota Polak/de Haan v.d.Werff', with various enclosures.
74. Niod, Doc II, Liro, box 218, Interrogation of Aufenacker, and Niod, Bregstein archive, box 20, folder 1075, 'Welk bedrag werd aan effecten ingeleverd?'; ministerie van Financiën, Bewindvoering archive, rubric 1450, LVVS, letter from T. J. Hoogland to Economische Recherche en Opsporingsdienst; and ARA, 2.09.15. Raad voor het Rechtsherstel 1945–71, Afdeling Effectenregistratie, inventory no. 249. Example of the transfer of shares to a different name. Instead of the full name, only the initials are given here; Niod, ARA, 2.19.042.56, archive of the Commissie tot Bescherming der Aanspraken van Gedepossedeerden (1946–57), inventory no. 70, 'Pleitnota' 4 April 1950.
75. Niod, archive 281, 'Rapport inzage het optreden van dr. A. J. Bühler en O. Rebholz tijdend de Duitse bezetting', by A. J. van der Leeuw.
76. The sale of Portuguese government bonds by Liro, Nieuwe Spiegelstraat, was not covered by the First Liro Decree (these bonds were not specifically Jewish property).
77. Niod, ministerie van Financiën, Bewindvoering archive, 'Rapport van Oven' and archive of the Gerechtelijke Diensten, Amsterdam, box 2, folder III, office no. 14638/268–I-54 F, O. Rebholz dossier, reports nos.1, 2,and 3 'on the realization of securities in Switzerland and accounts to 11 May 1943'; and *idem*, 'Rapport inzage het optreden van dr. A. J. Bühler en O. Rebholz tijdens de Duitse bezetting' by A. J. van der Leeuw.
78. Ministerie van Financiën, Bewindvoering archive, rubric 1450, LVVS, 'Eindverslag LVVS', 24 April 1958.
79. Niod, 'Notities voor het Geschiedwerk', *Entziehung und Verbringung nach Deutschland der beim 'Bankhause' Lippmann, Rosenthal & Co., Sarphatistraat abgelieferten Wertpapiere* by A. J. van der Leeuw; ministerie van Financiën, archive of the Commissie Rechtsherstel Buitenlandse Effecten, 'Memorandum', 30 September 1952.

80. Niod, Doc I, Rebholz, Civil Security Interrogation Center, 'Interrogation of Otto Rebholz', 5 December 1945, and Niod, Bregstein archive, box 9, untitled note by W. P. Bakhoven, judge advocate general of the Special Court in Amsterdam, 14 February 1947, and *idem*, attached to the above, unsigned and undated statement by Rebholz, and ministerie van Financiën, Bewindvoering archive, 'Boek'.
81. See Conclusion: The State of Affairs at the Liberation.
82. Ministerie van Financiën, Bewindvoering archive, rubric 1450, LVVS, 'Eindverslag LVVS', 24 April 1958.
83. ARA, 2.09.48, Raad voor het Rechtsherstel, inventory no. 2058, 'Eindrapport van P. Woortmann aan de directie der Firma Lippmann, Rosenthal & Co., Sarphatistraat, betreffende de ontvreemding van effecten ten nadele van de Derde Afdeeling en de vermissing van effecten', 10 December 1942.
84. Ministerie van Justitie, DGBR, Rebholz dossier, letter from De Pont to A. A. L. F. van Dullemen, Amsterdam Court of Justice, 22 December 1950, and *idem*, 'Dagvaarding', 2 February 1955.
85. Ministerie van Justitie, Rebholz dossier, no. 649/001, letter from Van Dullemen to Minister of Justice, 23 December 1950. Van Dullemen's italics.
86. Ministerie van Justitie, CABR, Rebholz dossier, inventory no. 284 II, letter from Ter Meulen and Vleming to chief counsel, Amsterdam Special Court, 30 December 1949.
87. Gerechtelijke Diensten archive, Amsterdam, box 3, folder 43, office no. 14638/268 I-54. F, O. Rebholz dossier, 'Request ex art. 241', and ministerie van Justitie, CABR, Rebholz, inventory no. 284 II, letter from public prosecutor to judge advocate general, 28 November 1953.
88. Ministerie van Justitie, CABR, Rebholz dossier, letter from De Pont to A. A. L. F. van Dullemen, judge advocate general, Amsterdam Court of Justice, 22 December 1950.
89. ARA, 2.19.042. 56, archive of Commissie tot Bescherming der Aanspraken van Gedepossedeerden (1946–57), inventory no. 14, 'Het revisieproces over het regelmatig beursverkeer'. The document also contains the minutes of the meeting of Amsterdam bankers and the VvdE. It was drawn up by F. Dellschow, managing director of the Handelstrust West.
90. ARA, 2.19.042.56, archive of Commissie tot Bescherming der Aanspraken van Gedepossedeerden (1946–57), inventory no.19, 'Conferentie met de ministers van Financiën en van Justitie', 24 February 1953, and *idem*, 'Pleitnotitie', 4 April 1950 and *Rechtsherstel*, no. 146, 5 December 1951.
91. ARA, 2.19.042.56, archive of Commissie tot Bescherming der Aanspraken van Gedepossedeerden (1946–57), inventory no. 19, 'Conferentie van ministers van Financiën en van Justitie', 24 February 1953, together with letter from Rotterdamsche Bank giving reasons for the 'share exchange'.

92. *Rechtsherstel*, 51/101, 2 July 1957, p. 274.
93. ARA, 2.19.042.56, archive of Commissie tot Bescherming der Aanspraken van Gedepossedeerden (1946–57), inventory no. 24, 'Recapitulatie: cert. v. aand. De Twentsche Bank, opgemaakt door Beheerders-vereffenaars LVVS'; *idem*, Prof. E. M. Meijers en H. Sanders to the securities registration department of the Raad voor het Rechtsherstel, 26 March 1952, and *idem*, 29 March 1952; *idem*, judge advocate to share registration department of the Raad voor Rechtsherstel, March 1952; *idem*, inventory no. 24, list of share certificates, Twentsche Bank (including date of sale, date of delivery, rates, and beneficiaries). Cf. *Rechtsherstel*, January 1949, no. 55, p. 208.
94. Niod, N156/1, folder A, 'Directe aankoopen, dus buiten de beurs om, gedurende de oorlogsjaren door de N.V. Handels Trust West van het bij Lippmann, Rosenthal, Sarphatistraat ingeleverde Joodsch effecten Bezit'. The actual total was between seven and eight million guilders. The list gives the names of companies, dates, nominal values and rates.
95. Niod, N156/1 'Resumé Handelstrust West, Keizersgracht 569'. Interrogation of C. Brandes, the director, of the deputy managers, and of the administrators by C. L. Buenting of the Vooronderzoek Collaboratie Bureau, 18 March 1946.
96. Niod, Bregstein archive, box 8, folder A XI, dossier 2026/9–V-18–70345/47. Monker was a notorious collaborator and was tried and sentenced after the war.
97. Ministerie van Financiën, Bewindvoering archive, rubric 1450, LVVS, 'Eindverslage LVVS', 24 April 1958. The value of the unlisted securities has been taken from 'Bericht no. 4' by W. Willems & Cie, sharebrokers, 1 April 1950. (Aalders archive, inventory no. L.3042.)

Chapter 8: The Second Liro Decree in Practice

1. Niod, Doc II, Lippmann, Rosenthal & Co. Sarphatistraat, box 217, folder D, 'Toelichting op de bepalingen van de VO 58/1942, 21 mei 1942, betreffende de behandeling van joodse vermogenswaarden'. Debt-register entries are 'national debts' – nominative claims on the Netherlands state. The (fixed) interest rates were rather low: 2.5 per cent or 3.5 per cent. Debt-register entries could not be repaid.
2. Niod, Doc II, Lippmann, Rosenthal & Co. Sarphatistraat, box 217, folder D, 'Toelichting op de bepalingen van de VO 58/1942, 21 mei 1942, betreffende de behandeling van joodse vermogenswaarden'.

3. Article 11 laid down that collections of all kinds, as specified in Article 10, namely works of art, etc., had to be surrendered by all Jews (as defined by VO 189/1940). However, if a Jew was married to a non-Jew, the surrender of the collections, works of art, etc. mentioned in Article 10 did not apply to

> the Jewish spouse inasmuch as there was any issue from the marriage that could not be considered to be Jewish in terms of the definitions given above, namely
>
> 1. the Jewish wife in case of childless marriages.
> 2. The provisions specified in paragraph 1, no. 1, apply even if the marriage has been dissolved.
> 3. The provisions specified in paragraphs 1 and 2 do not apply to marriages contracted after 9 May 1940.

4. Niod, Doc II, Lippmann, Rosenthal & Co. Sarphatistraat, box 217, folder D, 'Toelichting op de bepalingen van de VO 58/1942, 21 mei 1942, betreffende de behandeling van joodse vermogenswaarden'.
5. Niod, Doc II, Lippmann, Rosenthal & Co. Sarphatistraat, box 217, folder D, 'Toelichting op de bepalingen van de VO 58/1942, 21 mei 1942, betreffende de behandeling van joodse vermogenswaarden'.
6. For dental fillings made of precious metal, see Niod, Doc II, Lippmann, Rosenthal & Co. Sarphatistraat, box 215, Afdeling Inspectie II, 'Interne circulaires, Circulaire 227', 2 November 1942, 'Tandartsenijkundige behandeling van joden'.
7. NA, RG 260, OMGUS/Finad, 'SS-loot investigation of, inter alia, interrogations, correspondence Reichsbank-Berlin Pawn Shops', 1948.
8. Niod, Doc I, Carel F. Overhoff, folder B. The letters were sent to the appropriate commercial sectors (commercial banks and stockbrokers) as internal circulars; and *idem*, Doc II, Liro, box 216, folder B, circular 202 from Bühler, 13 March 1943; ARA, 2.09.48 Raad voor het Rechtsherstel, inventory no. 2061, letters from Liro to the Amsterdamsche Bank (22 June 1944) and the Incasso Bank (23 August 1944). The second letter is a reply to the letter from the Incasso Bank dated 18 August 1944.
9. Ministerie van Justitie, CABR, Van Rossum dossier (both quotations); Niod, Doc II, no. 1213, 'De behandeling van aan joden toebehorende vermogenswaarden tijdens en na de oorlog', and ministerie van Financiën, Bewindvoering archive, 'Eindrapport LVVS'.
10. Ministerie van Justitie, CABR, Lippmann, Rosenthal & Co. dossier, inventory no. 81379.
11. Niod, Doc II, Lippmann, Rosenthal & Co. Sarphatistraat, box 215, Afdeling Inspectie II, 'Interne circulaires, Circulaire 180', 24 August 1943, 'Vorderingen van ariërs op geëvacueerde of verdwenen joden'.

Notes

12. Ministerie van Justitie, CABR, Lippmann, Rosenthal & Co., box 81379, Procès-verbal, dossier no. 81379.
13. Supplement to the *Nederlandsche Staatscourant* of Monday, 5 October 1942, no. 193.
14. Niod, Doc II, Liro, box 218, Phöbus balance sheet, 30 September 1943.
15. Ministerie van Justitie, CABR, Lippmann, Rosenthal & Co., box 81379, Procès-verbal, dossier no. 81379.
16. Ministerie van Justitie, CABR, Van Rossum dossier (both quotations); Niod, Doc II, no. 1213, 'De behandeling van aan joden toebehorenden vermogenswaarden tijdens en na de oorlog'; and ministerie van Financiën, Bewindvoering archive, 'Eindrapport LVVS'.
17. Niod, Doc II, Liro, box 219, folder H3. Interrogation of D. Streefkerk, divisional head of Amstleven, 7 November 1946; undated report and circulars from the Insurance Group.
18. Niod, Doc II, Liro, box 219, folder H3, undated report.
19. Niod, Doc II, Liro, box 219, folder H3, undated report.

Chapter 9: The Looting of Cultural Property from Jews

1. Ministerie van Financiën. Bewindvoering archive, rubric 1450 LVVS, 'Verklaring van Th. J. Hoogland'. Hoogland worked for Liro during the war. The validity of his claims cannot be verified (he was anxious to blacken his superiors in order to play down his own part), but the fact that there were 'loans' to German officials is confirmed by Presser, *Ashes in the Wind*, pp. 361–2. For Rauter's *Woman Seated*, see Niod, Doc II, Lippmann, Rosenthal & Co. Sarphatistraat, box 217, folder D, 'Zu Ihrer Nr. 32 über angebliches Fehlen von Bildern aus B.N. Bestanden', 1 April 1943, and *idem*, 'List' in which the sale price of 300 guilders is given as the price at which this painting was sold. In the next column the 'maximum value' is also given as 300 guilders. This list usually reveals marked differences between the 'maximum value' and the selling price.
2. Niod, 'Notities voor het Geschiedwerk', no. 116. In addendum III, however, a 'total of 60' is mentioned.
3. Niod, Doc II, Lippmann, Rosenthal & Co. Sarphatistraat, box 218. folder F, 'Rechnung für Galerie für alte Kunst' with accompanying letter, dated 23 December 1942; *idem*, folder H, 'Getuigenverhoor in de zaak contra Lippmann Rosenthal, verhoor van M. S. Maes [widow of S. J. Mak van Waay]'; and *idem*,

box 219, folder H2, von Karger dossier; Niod, archive 181, Expert opinion & documentation, Reinheld folder; Niod, archive 281, 'Gekocht door dr. Mühlmann' ; 'Lijst van de door Lippmann verkochte schilderijen aan Muehlmann', and 'collectie Lippmann, Rosenthal & Co., Amsterdam'. Ministerie van Justitie, CABR, Mak van Waay dossier, procès-verbaux, and *idem*, Lippmann, Rosenthal & Co. dossier, inventory no. 81379, 'Proces-verbaal van verhoor van K. V. K. Mulisch'.

4. ARA, Stichting Nederlands Kunstbezit (1930) 1945–51 (1983), inventory no. 715, box 182. The dossier includes an alphabetic list of the names of people 'liable to surrender [their paintings]' together with a (presumably) fairly complete list of surrendered paintings and the names and addresses of their owners, the names of the artists, and a very brief description of the works, their assessed value, their sale price and the names of the buyers.

   According to a letter from Witscher to Flesche dated 17 July 1943, 2,359 paintings were still being held in the Liro storerooms at the time; Niod, Flesche archive, box 1 B4.

5. Niod, Doc II, Lippmann, Rosenthal & Co. Sarphatistraat, box 217, folder D, various circulars, etc. 'Einige Daten über die Entstehung und Entwicklung der Warenabteilung', 1 November 1943, and *idem*, box 218, folder H, 'Lippmann, Rosenthal & Co., Sarphatistraat, Amsterdam, Amsterdamsche Bank te Assen', and ministerie van Justitie, CABR, inventory no. 81379, Liro box 3, 'Verhoor van E. E. Wiegel', 30 November 1946.

6. Niod, 'Notities voor het Geschiedwerk', no. 116, 'Entziehung und Verbringung nach Deutschland der beim Bankhauses Lippmann, Rosenthal & Co. Sarphatistraat abgelieferten Vermögensgegenstände'.

7. Niod, archive 281, 'Notitie inzake L.V.V.S.-claim', January 1961, and *idem*, ministerie van Justitie, CABR, Mak van Waay dossier.

8. Ministerie van Justitie, CABR, Lippmann dossier, inventory no. 81379.

9. Niod, archive 281, 'Notitie inzake L.V.V.S.-claim', January 1961, and *idem*, ministerie van Justitie, CABR, Mak van Waay and Lippmann dossier and Rosenthal & Co. dossier, inventory no. 81379.

10. Niod, archive 281, 'Verkoop van collecties sieraden, tafelzilver en kuntsvoorwerpen door Liro-Sarphatistraat'.

11. Ministerie van Justitie, CABR, 'Proces Verbaal van verhoor van Paul Woortman', 1 July 1946.

12. Niod, Doc II, Lippmann, Rosenthal & Co. Sarphatistraat, box 219, folder H 2, 'Verhoor van Von Karger', 8 August 1947.

13. Niod, 'Notities voor het Geschiedwerk', no. 116.

14. Niod, Doc II, Lippmann, Rosenthal & Co. Sarphatistraat, box 217, folder D, 'Richtlinien für die Firma Lippmann, Rosenthal & Co., Sarphatistr., Amsterdam, 16.10.1942', and *idem*, archive 97, A. Flesche Collection, box 1, folder

Notes

IV, 'Monatsbericht über Juni 1943', and Niod, 'Notities voor het Geschiedwerk', no. 116. Ministerie van Justitie, CABR, inventory no. 813791, Liro, box 1, 'Richtlijnen voor de firma Lippmann, Rosenthal & Co.', undated.
15. De Jong, *Koninkrijk,* vol. 7, part 1, p. 55.
16. Niod, Doc II, Lippmann, Rosenthal & Co. Sarphatistraat, box 217, map D, 'Richtlinien für die Firma Lippmann, Rosenthal & Co., Sarphatistr., Amsterdam, 16.10.1942', *idem,* archive 97, A. Flesche Collection, box 1, folder IV, 'Monatsbericht über Juni 1943', Niod, 'Notities voor het Geschiedwerk', no. 116. Ministerie van Justitie, CABR, inventory no. 813791, Liro, box 1, 'Richtlijnen voor de firma Lippmann, Rosenthal & Co.', undated.
17. Petropoulos, *Art as Politics,* p. 320 and passim.
18. Niod, Doc II, Lippmann, Rosenthal & Co. Sarphatistraat, box 217, folder D, 'Richtlinien für die Firma Lippmann, Rosenthal & Co. Sarphatistr., Amsterdam, 16.10.1942', and *idem,* box 219, folder H2, von Karger dossier, and Niod, 'Notities voor het Geschiedwerk', no. 116. For Schmidt-Stahler, see Petropoulos, *Art as Politics,* p. 140.
19. Niod, archive 97, A. Flesche Collection, box 1, folder IV, 'Monatsbericht über Juni 1943', 7 July 1943.
20. Niod, 'Notities voor het Geschiedwerk', no. 116.
21. Leeuw, A. J. van der, 'Die Käufe des Generalkommissars z.b.V. Fritz Schmidt' in A. H. Paape, *Studies over Nederland in oorlogstijd,* The Hague 1972. Cf. p. 188 above.
22. Niod, archive 97, A. Flesche Collection, box 1, 'Bericht über das erste Quartal 1943', 16 April 1943.
23. Niod, archive 281, 'Aktenvermerk über eine Besprechung zwischen Staatssekretär Dr. Mühlmann, Dr. Plietzsch und Herrn von Stechow am 1.10.1943 im Haag'; Niod, Doc II, Lippmann, Rosenthal & Co. Sarphatistraat, box 215, 'Directie-correspondentie I' folder, August 1941–July 1943, *Führererlass,* 1 March 1942, and Niod, Doc II, Lippmann, Rosenthal & Co. Sarphatistraat, box 215, 'Directie-correspondentie I' folder, August 1941–July 1943, letter from Seyss-Inquart to Generalkommissar für Finanz und Wirtschaft, 26 March 1942.
24. Niod, archive 281, 'Aktenvermerk über eine Besprechung zwischen Staatssekretär Dr. Mühlmann, Dr. Plietzsch und Herrn von Stechow am 1.10.1943 im Haag', and Niod, Doc II, Lippmann, Rosenthal & Co. Sarphatistraat, box 215, 'Directie- correspondentie I' folder, August 1941–July 1943, *Führererlass,* 1 March 1942.
25. Niod, 'Notities voor het Geschiedwerk', no. 116.
26. ARA, 2.06.68. Commissariaat-Generaal voor de Nederlands Economische Belangen in Duitsland, 1945–50, box no. 60. Liro lists of stolen ornaments, watches, gold objects, etc. The dossier runs to 224 folio pages.

27. Niod, 'Notities voor het Geschiedwerk', no. 116
28. Letter from Sotheby's to author, 31 January 1997.

    During the war, S. J. Mak van Maay's auctions were run by his Maatschappij voor Kunst- en Antiekveilingen N. V. The company was wound up in 1953, but as early as July 1944, H. S. Nienhuis took over from Mak van Waay and continued the business under the name of 'Kunstveilingen S. J. Mak van Waay'. In 1967, Nienhuis changed the name of his auction house to 'Kunstveilingen Mak van Waay N. V.', which was taken over by Sotheby's in 1974. During a conversation with John van Schaik, managing director of Sotheby's, on 11 March 1999, the question arose whether Sotheby's could be held responsible in any way for the activities of Mak van Waay and Nienhuis (or their companies) during the war. It appears that they could not. A report of the investigation was placed at my disposal.
29. Sotheby archive, Mak van Waay archive, catalogues, lists of vendors and valuations.
30. Ministerie van Justitie, CABR, Mak van Waay dossier, various procès-verbaux.
31. See 'The Structure of Liro' in Chapter 6.
32. Sotheby's archive, Mak van Waay archive, sales ledger entries for the auction held on 14 and 15 April 1942.
33. NA, RG 260, Records of United States Occupation Headquarters WWII, Ardelia Hall Collection, box 180, 'Special Interrogation of Seyss-Inquart', 31 August 1946.
34. Provinciaal Archief Noord-Holland, 'Inventaris van de Rijksarchieven te Amsterdam, 1807–1945', letter from director-general of the Rijksmuseum to permanent secretary, acting head of the Departement van Onderwijs, Wetenschap en Cultuurbescherming (OWC), dated 6 July 1940.
35. Provinciaal Archief Noord-Holland, 'Inventaris van de Rijksarchieven te Amsterdam, 1807–1945', letter from the state prosecutor to the acting permanent secretary of the Departement van Onderwijs, 26 September 1940, and ministerie van OCW, Afdeling Oude Kunst en Natuurbehoud, inventory no.145.1, letter from Rijksmuseum to permanent secretary of the OWC, 19 September 1940 and accompanying correspondence.
36. Niod, Doc II, Lippmann, Rosenthal & Co. Sarphatistraat, box 217, folder D, 'Werte, die aus jüdischer Besitze in Museen und Firmen hinterlegt sind. Gemäss Stand 26/9'42'.
37. Niod, Doc II, Lippmann, Rosenthal & Co. Sarphatistraat, box 215, 'Directiecorrespondentie I' folder, August 1941–July 1943, letter from Reichskommissariaat (Dr Rothe) to Stadsbank van Lening, 17 June 1942.
38. Provinciaal Archief Noord-Holland, 'Inventaris van de Rijksarchieven te Amsterdam, 1807–1945', letter from Departement van Opvoeding, Wetenschap en Cultuurbescherming to Rijksmuseum, Amsterdam, 4 November 1942.

Notes

39. Niod, Doc II, box 217, 'Werte die aus jüdischem Besitze in Museen und Firmen hinterlegt sind. Gemäss Stand 26/9 '42', and ministerie van OWC, Afdeling Oude Kunst en Natuurbehoud, inventory no. 120.01, letter dated 2 June 1942 to museums and libraries.
40. Ministerie van OWC, Afdeling Oude Kunst en Natuurbehoud, inventory no. 120.1, letter from OWC to Wimmer, 1 June 1941.
41. Ministerie van OWC, Afdeling Oude Kunst en Natuurbehoud, inventory no. 145.1, letter from ministerie van Economische Zaken to Van Dam, 17 February 1945, and *idem*, reply by Van Dam, 19 February 1941. The letter from the ministerie van Economische Zaken was accompanied by an extensive list of exported paintings. The list also contained the names of buyers, sellers, subjects and (in many cases) the value. The major part of the 'exports' (more than 500 paintings) came from Goudstikker's business, then run by Miedl; the canvases went to Schantung Handsels A. G. Berlin (one of Miedl's companies) and the Reich Chancellery in Berlin. The second most important exporter was Katz & Co. in Dieren.
42. Ministerie van OWC, Afdeling Oude Kunst en Natuurbehoud, inventory no. 120.1, letter from OWC to Wimmer, 1 June 1942, and Provinciaal-Archief Noord-Holland, 'Inventaris van de Rijksarchieven te Amsterdam, 1807–1945', 'Nota OWC betreffende kunbstvoorwerpen uit Joodsch Bezit', 17 November 1945. One painting from the collection of R. May (Thomas de Keizer's *Portrait of Pieter Post*) in which Mühlmann was interested had to be handed over by return on 28 January 1943 to 'the bearer of this letter'. *Idem*, letter from Liro to the board of the Rijksmuseum. The Centraal Museum in Utrecht was able to purchase several paintings and thus keep them out of German hands and return them to their owners (including R. May, S. Kool and Mrs Gompertsz-Josephus Jitta) after the war: Centraal Museum Utrecht archive, 'Rapport betreffende het Joodsche bezit in het Centraal Museum tijdens de Duitsche bezetting', 1 August 1945. For the Jaffé Collection, see Niod, archive 281 and Cees van Hoore, ' "Sicher Gestellt". Waar is de schilderijverzameling van Dr Alphons Jaffé?' in *Vitrine*, no. 1, 1991, and *idem*, 'De "verzwegen" kunstroof bij de Lakenhal' in *Leids Dagblad*, 9 May 1990. For Van Dam as a 'high-class' collaborator, see Knegtmans et al., *Collaborateurs van niveau*.
43. Ministerie van OCW, Afdeling Oude Kunst en Natuurbehoud, inventory no.120.1, letter from Plutzar to Van Dam, OWC, 16 October 1942.; letter from Van Dam to (listed) museums, 4 November 1942; 'Minuut' no. 857/1942 K. W., 3 December 1942 and 'Minuut', 1 December 1942.
44. Provinciaal Archief Noord-Holland, 'Inventaris van de Rijksarchieven te Amsterdam, 1807–1945', letter from OWC to Rijksmuseum, 1 June 1943, and note by OWC issued on instruction by the Reichskommissar, 'Betreffende:

werken van Joodsche kunstenaars of Joodsche personen voorstellend', 4 October 1943.
45. Ministerie van OWC, Afdeling Oude Kunst en Natuurbehoud, inventory no. 120.1, letter from Rijksmuseum, Amsterdam to OWC, 1 December 1942, with an appended list of works of art of Jewish provenance. The Rijksmuseum was interested in works by James Ensor, Jozef Israëls (two canvases), C. Rochussen, C. Jegher (two canvases), Cardon, J. Bosboom, P. de Josselin de Jong, Isaac Israëls, W. Witsen, D. Ovens, W. de Zwart, A. Hanneman and Therèse Schwartze. For approval of the purchases, see *idem*, letter from OWC to Rijksmuseum, 1 June 1943.
46. Ministerie van OWC, Afdeling Oude Kunst en Natuurbehoud, inventory no. 120.1, 'Betreffende vorderingen op L.V.V.S', 20 October 1951, and archive of Stedelijke Museum, Amsterdam, Van den Bergh-Van Danzig Collection. Various documents make it clear that the OWC also authorized the purchase of the collections of Mevrouw Nathasius (95,000 guilders), Fuld (13,000 guilders) and Gompertz-Jitta (1,800 guilders). Aalders archive, inventory no. L.3249/43, note, 17 November 1945.
47. Ministerie van OWC, Afdeling Oude Kunst en Natuurbehoud, inventory no. 120.1 and 120.2. Mentioned inter alia are the following collections: Zander (Rijksmuseum van Oudheden, Leiden); Voorzanger, Franken and Reens (Museum Boymans); Kool (Utrecht); Cohen Tervaerts-Israëls and Van Dam (Museum van Oudheden voor Provincie en stad Groningen), Hartogs-Hijman (Rijksmuseumn voor Volkskunde, Arnhem); Van der Horst, Gosschalk, Menko Warendorf, Van Veen, Stokvis, Vles and Kochmann (Gemeentemuseum Den Haag).
48. Ministerie van OWC, Afdeling Oude Kunst en Natuurbehoud, inventory no. 120.1, 'Minuut Betreffende Kunstwerken in Joodsch bezit', 2 December 1942, and *idem*, letter from Hannema to J. K. van Haagen.
49. Ministerie van OWC, Afdeling Oude Kunst en Natuurbehoud, inventory no. 120.2, letters from Liro to OWC, 5 January 1943 and 4 September 1943. The letter of 5 January shows that Liro had received registrations from the Rijksmuseum, the Stedelijk Museum, the Allard Pierson Museum, the Museum voor Aziatische Kunst and the Handelsmuseum der Ver. Koloniaal Instituut (all in Amsterdam), and also from the Centraal Museum in Utrecht and the Rijksmuseum voor Oudheden in Leiden.
50. Provinciaal Archief Noord-Holland, 'Inventaris van de Rijksarchieven te Amsterdam, 1807–1945', list of works of art on loan to OWC, 6 June 1942.
51. Ministerie van OWC, Afdeling Oude Kunst en Natuurbehoud, inventory no. 31.4.
52. Provinciaal Archief Noord-Holland, Rijksmuseum Amsterdam, entry 476, inventory no. 2112. The lists of contents of the five cases have also been recovered.

Notes

53. Provinciaal Archief Noord-Holland, 'Inventaris van de Rijksarchieven te Amsterdam, 1807–1945', 'Kunstwerken uit joods bezit', July 1943. It is not known whether the list is complete.
54. Provinciaal Archief Noord-Holland, 'Inventaris van de Rijksarchieven te Amsterdam, 1807–1945', letter from Rijksmuseum to the financial counsellor at the Netherlands Embassy in London, 21 April 1948.
55 Provinciaal Archief Noord-Holland, 'Inventaris van de Rijksarchieven te Amsterdam, 1807–1945', letter from W. A. van Leer to Rijksmuseum, 27 September 1941, and accompanying note by the Rijksmuseum.
56. Provinciaal Archief Noord-Holland, 'Inventaris van de Rijksarchieven te Amsterdam, 1807–1945'. Various documents concerning the Robert May Collection.
57. Ministerie van Justitie, CABR, Alfred Flesche dossier, inventory no. 423 II, letter from Liro, Sarphatistraat to Flesche, 23 October 1942.
58. For Flesche's role as *Verwalter* see Chapter 7, Introduction.
59. Ministerie van Justitie, CABR, Frederik Muller & Co. dossier. See also Buijnsters, *Het Nederlandse antiquariaat*, pp. 28–9, and Venema, *Kunsthandel*, p. 614.
60. Baruch, *Het Rijksmuseum in Oorlogstijd*, pp. 56–62.

Chapter 10: The Looting of Household Effects: the M-Aktion

1. Niod, 'Notities voor het Geschiedwerk', no. 118. *Entziehung öffentlicher und privater Bibliotheken in den besetzten Westgebieten und ihre Verbringung nach Deutschland*; Niod, Doc II, 215C, Einsatzstab Rosenberg, 'Structuur Einsatzstab Reichsleiter Rosenberg, Niederlande', and *idem*, 'De historische documentatie voor de door het Cadsu behandelde claims' by A. J. van der Leeuw.
2. Niod, Doc II, Einsatzstab Rosenberg, 'Verklaring'.
3. Berkley, *Overzicht*, pp. 53–4; Presser, *Ashes in the Wind*, pp. 360–1; Niod, Bregstein archive, box 20, folder 1075, Rechtsherstel, 'De geleidelijke beknotting der vermogensdisposities. Haar juridische grondslagen.'
4. De Jong, *Koninkrijk*, vol. 6, pp. 335–9, and Niod, Doc II, Lippmann, Rosenthal & Co. Sarphatistraat, box 217, folder D, various circulars, etc. 'Zweiter Aktenvermerk über die Organisation der Hausraterfassung', 18 April 1942, and ministerie van Justitie, CABR, Willy Lages and F. H. aus der Fünten dossier.
5. Niod, 'Notities voor het Geschiedwerk', no. 138, 'Beschlagnahme von Gebrauchssilber in den Niederlanden durch den Einsatzstab Reichsleiter Rosenberg im Zuge der "M-Aktion"'; and ministerie van Justitie, CABR, P. C. Docter dossier (64632).

6. De Jong, *Koninkrijk*, vol. 6, part 1, pp. 335–9.
7. Niod, Doc II, no.1213, 'De behandeling van aan joden toebehorende vermogenswaarden tijdens en na de oorlog'.
8. De Jong, *Koninkrijk*, vol. 6, part 1, pp. 335–9.
9. Niod, Doc II, 215C, Einsatzstab Rosenberg, 'Structuur: Einsatzstab Reichsleiter Rosenberg, Niederlande'.
10. Niod, Doc II, Lippmann, Rosenthal & Co. Sarphatistraat, box 217, folder D, various circulars, etc. 'Nr. 52, Betr. Die Administration in der H.R. Abteilung/ Unterabteilung Dokumente I (de Munnik)'.
11. Niod, Doc II, Lippmann, Rosenthal & Co. Sarphatistraat, box 217, folder D, various circulars, etc. 'Nr. 52, Betr. Die Administration in der H.R. Abteilung/ Unterabteilung Dokumente I (de Munnik)'.
12. Niod, 'Notities voor het Geschiedwerk', no. 118. *Entziehung öffentlicher und privater Bibliotheken in den besetzten Westgebieten und ihre Verbringung nach Deutschland*, and Niod, Doc II, 215C, Einsatzstab Rosenberg. 'Structuur: Einsatzstab Reichsleiter Rosenberg, Niederlande'; this document lists various storage depots, office addresses and German destinations.
13. Leistra, *Recuperatie in Nederland*, and Van Voolen, *The Jewish Historical Museum*.
14. Hoogewood, *The Nazi Looting of Books*.
15. Niod, Doc II, Lippmann, Rosenthal & Co. Sarphatistraat, box 217, folder D, various circulars, etc. 'Nr. 53. Betr. Die Administration in der H.R. Abteilung'; *idem*, box 219, folder H2, 'Verhoor van von Karger'; *idem*, box 217, folder D, 'Richtlijnen voor de administratie en controle der afdeeling goederen', 12 May 1943, and ministerie van Justitie, CABR, Olij dossier, inventory no. 24811.
16. Niod, 'Notities voor het Geschiedwerk', no. 116.
17. Ministerie van Justitie, CABR, Olij dossier, inventory no. 24811.
18. Niod, Doc II, Lippmann, Rosenthal & Co. Sarphatistraat, box 217, folder D, various circulars, etc. 'Einige Daten über die Entstehung und Entwicklung der Warenabteilung, 1 November 1943'.
19. Ministerie van Justitie, CABR, W. C. H. Henneicke dossier.
20. Belinfante, *Bijltesdag*, p. 454 and De Jong, *Koninkrijk*, vol. 12, p. 583. The term 'Jew hunter' was coined by Belinfante.

Chapter 11: *Sperrstempel*, Emigration and Income Tax

1. Niod, 'Notities voor het Geschiedwerk', no. 112, 'Der Entziehungsvorgang bei der sog. Sperrdiamanten-Aktion und die im Individualfall vorliegenden

Beweisunterlassungen'; *idem*, Doc I, P. C. Docter, procès-verbaux, Interrogation of Willy Lages, Interrogation of Harster (quotation); *idem*, Doc I, N. J. Ros; *idem*, archive 77–85, Höhere SS- und Polizeiführer, folders 233f, 233g, 234 a, b and c on the allocation of various *Sperrstempel*. Cf. B. Karlsberg, *Beschleunigung durch Besondere Verfahren;* see also De Jong, *Koninkrijk*, vol. 6, part 1, pp. 279–80 and 298–9; Presser, *Ashes in the Wind*, pp. 522–3.

2. Niod, Archive 281, letter from W. Harster to Bundesministerium von Finanzen, 25 August 1958.
3. Niod, Doc I, Walter Büchi, deposition by W. Büchi, 8 November 1945.
4. Auschwitz Museum Archive, D.PF-3/RSHA/159a, inventory no. 158972, 'Betrifft Ausreisegegenehmigung für Juden', 27 November 1942, and letter from Vertreter des Auswärtigen Amtes, The Hague (Otto Bene) to Auswärtiges Amt, Berlin, 30 November 1942. For the typed copy of the report transmitted by Radio Oranje on 24 November 1942, see ARA, ministerie van Buitenlandse Zaken, Ambassade Bern, inventory no. 2.05.49.
5. ARA, ministerie van Buitenlandse Zaken, Ambassade Bern, inventory no. 2.05–49, 223, letter to Bosch Ridder van Rosenthal, Bern, 25 September 1942. The broadcast on 24 November 1942 also pointed out that Dutch law 'prohibits all actions likely to be to the enemy's direct or indirect advantage'.
6. De Jong, *Koninkrijk*, vol. 6, part 1, pp. 279–80, and Presser, *Ashes in the Wind*, pp. 522–3.
7. Niod, archive 181 H, box 1, folder 2a. For further examples, see the remaining folders in boxes 1 and 2.
8. To the Politieke Opsporingsdienst (Political Investigation Department, or POD), he mentioned a hundred cases. Originally, these were exclusively clients of the Rotterdamsche Bankvereeniging, but later many others joined them as well. Ministerie van Justitie, CABR, Puttkammmer dossier, undated 'Proces Verbaal POD', and Niod, KB 1, Erich Puttkammer.
9. Ministerie van Justitie, CABR, Puttkammmer dossier, 'Proces Verbaal van verhoor inzake E. A. P. Putkammer'; Interrogation of E.A.P. Puttkammer, 21 May 1945; deposition by Puttkammer, 24 May 1945, and deposition by Carolina Hoogland (Puttkammer's secretary).
10. Niod, KB 1, Erich Puttkammer. The figures mentioned cannot be found in Niod's CVO archive. The CVO archive is however incomplete.
11. Ministerie van Justitie, CABR, Ros dossier (inventory no. 76878).
12. Ministerie van Justitie, CABR, Puttkammer dossier, 'Proces Verbaal van verhoor inzake E.A. P. Puttkammer', Interrogation of A. W. Kymmel, Interrogation of W.S.W. de Beer and Interrogation of H. J. C. Janssen and passim, and deposition by Puttkammer, 24 May, 1945. Like Robaver, the Amsterdamsche Bank is now part of ABN-AMRO.

13. See Gerard Aalders, 'Het archief over de oorlog is een mijnenveld' in *De Volkskrant*, 4 May 1994.
14. Niod, archive 181 H, box 2, folder g, letter from Puttkammer to the Ministry of Finance in Bonn, 2 March 1953.
15. Niod, Doc I, N. J. Ros, and Doc I, P. C. Docter; ministerie van Justitie, CABR, N. J. Ros dossier.
16. Niod, Doc I, Walter Büchi.
17. Niod, archive 281, 'Sieraden, diamant etc. ingeleverd ter verkrijging van uitstel van deportatie' (note for Brüg).
18. Ministerie van Financiën, Directoraat-Generaal der Belastingen, Verbaalarchief 1936–1975, inventory no. 41–10–21/202 163, letter to the 'Heeren Directeurs der directe belastingen, invoerrechten en accijnzen der registratie en domeinen van 's Rijks belastingen', 21 October 1941.
19. Ministerie van Financiën, Directoraat-Generaal der Belastingen, Verbaalarchief 1936–1975, inventory no 42–01–27/194 170, letter from C. J. W. van Dintel, Zentralstelle für jüdische Auswanderung, Amsterdam, to Afdeling Rijksbelastingen aan Departement van Financiën, Afdeling Organisatie van den Belastingsdienst, The Hague, 24 December 1941.
20. De Jong, *Koninkrijk*, vol. 5, part 1, pp. 1,008–9.
21. Ministerie van Financiën, Directoraat-Generaal der Belastingen, Verbaalarchief 1936–1975, inventory no. 43–03–12/48 192, 'Brief van de ontvanger der Direkte Belastingen, Amsterdam, aan de Inspecteur van Belastingen, Amsterdam, 4 November 1942'.
22. Ministerie van Financiën, Directoraat-Generaal der Belastingen, Verbaalarchief 1936–1975, inventory no. 42–012–02/106 188, 'Brief van de waarnemend secretaris-generaal van het Departement van Financiën aan de Hauptabteilung Finanzen van het Rijkscommissariaat, 2 december 1942'.
23. Ministerie van Financiën, Directoraat-Generaal der Belastingen, Verbaalarchief 1936–1975, inventory no. 43–07–09/19 196, 'Pauschregelung. Zahlung des Bankhauses Lippmann, Rosenthal & Co. zur Begleichung jüdischer Steuerschulden'.

Conclusion

1. Ministerie van Justitie, CABR, Lippmann, Rosenthal & Co., inventory no. 81379, and ministerie van Financië, Bewindvoering archive, rubric 1450, LVVS, letter from board of Liro to minister van Financiën, 24 August 1945. The fact that the market value of gold, ornaments and silver in particular had been kept very low is stressed.

Notes

2. ARA, 2.09.48, Raad vor het Rechtsherstel, inventory no. 2001, 'Effectenbezit van de V.V.R.A.', as of 25 May 1945.
3. These are quite unreliable estimates; the true value is probably many times greater. For 'Aryanized' concerns an estimate of 150 to 200 million guilders seems realistic: Niod, Doc II-1213, 'De behandeling van aan joden toebehorende vermogensvoorwaarden tijdens en na de oorlog'. The unsigned document was drawn up by A. J. van der Leeuw.
4. These, too, are estimates that are unreliable in most cases. The amount is probably many times greater.
5. Very doubtful estimate.

Exchange Rates and Price Index

Exchange Rates in Guilders*

Year	1 US dollar	1 pound sterling	100 DM	100 Swed. Crowns	100 Swiss francs
1938	1.8393	8.545	73.75	44.00	41.475
1939	1.8788	7.4350	75.45	44.78	42.15
1940	1.88375	10.691	75.36	44.925	42.235
1941	1.88375		75.31	44.85	43.67
1942	1.25			44.85	43.67
1943				44.85	43.67
1944				44.85	43.67
1945	2.65	10.69		63.25	61.625
1946	2.65	10.69		73.81	61.625
1947	2.65	10.69		73.81	61.625
1948	2.6488	10.69	79.59	73.81	61.625
1949	3.80	10.64	79.59	73.46	86.90
1950	3.80	10.64	90.48	73.46	86.90

* *Source*: Nederlandsche Bank

Price Index**

One Dutch guilder (fl) in 1997 was worth in the years below:

1939	fl. 14.45
1940	fl. 11.52
1941	fl. 10.14
1942	fl 9.59
1943	fl 9.59
1944	fl 9.03
1945	fl 7.74
1946	fl 7.05
1947	fl 6.43
1948	fl 6.43
1949	fl 5.91
1950	fl 5.28

The figures have been rounded off to the nearest cent and should be treated with the utmost circumspection. They provide no more than a rule of thumb and one, moreover, that can only be used for comparisons in the consumption field. For the purchase of, for instance, raw materials or securities or for investments, other criteria must be applied. (See *95 jaar in Statistiek en Tijdreeksen*, published by the Dutch Central Office for Statistics.)

The sequence 1939 to 1950 has been chosen somewhat arbitrarily. The reason why 1939 was taken as the starting point is mainly because part of the damages were calculated after the war according to 1939 prices and not 1940 prices. A glance at the table will make it clear that this difference gives rise to considerable price differences. The cut-off point of 1950 has been chosen at random as well, chiefly in order to convey some idea of post-war values with those prevailing in 1997. Comparative figures for 2000 were not available at the time of publication.

** Source: *Consumentenprijsindex & koopkracht van de gulden, vanaf 1785*. The table was kindly provided by the Nederlandsche Bank.

The Main Anti-Jewish Property Decrees

1. *Verordnung* 26/1940, 27 June 1940 (enemy property, non-Jewish included).
2. *Verordnung* 41/1941, 28 February 1941 (non-profit-making associations and foundations).
3. *Verodnung* 48/1941, 12 March 1941 (Aryanization of businesses).
4. *Verordnung* 102/1941, 27 May 1941 (Jewish farmland).
5. *Verordnung* 148/1941, 8 August 1941 ('First Liro Decree').
6. *Verordnung* 154/1941, 11 August 1941 (real estate).
7. *Verordnung* 58/1942, 21 May 1942 ('Second Liro Decree').
8. *Verordnung* 37/1943, 19 April 1943 (mortgage repayments).
9. *Verordnung* 54/1943, 11 June 1943 (insurance policies).
10. *Verordnung* 89/1943, 25 September 1943 (claims other than mortgage dues).

Archives

Algemeen Rijksarchief
Algemene Zaken (ministerie van)
Amsterdams Gemeente Archief
Archiefdienst van de gerechtelijke Diensten, Amsterdam
Binnenlandse Zaken (ministerie van)
Binnenlandse Veiligheidsdienst
Buitenlandse Zaken (ministerie van)
Central State Archive of the Principle Organs of Government Power and Administration of the Ukraine (Tsental'nyi derzhavnnyi arkhiv vyshchykh orhanive valdy I uprvlinnia UkrXny)
Centraal Museum, Utrecht
Dienst der Domeinen, inspectie Haarlem
Economische Zaken (ministerie van)
Financiën (ministerie van)
Hamburger Stiftung für Sozial- und Wirtschaftsgeschichte
Hoover Institution on War, Revolution and Peace
Justitie (ministerie van)
National Archives, Washington, DC
Nederlandsche Bank
Nederlands Instituut voor Oorlogsdocumentatie
Nederlands Israëlitisch Kerkgenootschap
Nederlands Rode Kruis
Onderwijs, Cultuur en Wetenschap (OCW) (ministerie van)
Provinciaal Archief, Noord-Holland
Public Record Office, London
Rijksmuseum, Amsterdam
Rijksuniversiteit, Groningen
Rijksuniversiteit, Leiden
Riksarkivet, Stockholm
Riksbank, Stockholm
Sociale Zaken (ministerie van)
Sotheby's bedrijfsarchief (Mak van Waay)
Stedelijk Museum
Washington National Records Center

Bibliography

Aalders, Gerard. 'Schatgraven naar joods vluchtkapitaal' in *NRC Handelsblad*, 10 July 1996.
——. 'Jacht op nazi-goud nodeloos sensationeel' in *NRC Handelsblad*, 21 September 1996.
——. 'De Eksters van Europa', Groene Essay, in *De Groene Amsterdammer*, 2 October 1996.
——. 'By diplomatic pouch: art smuggling by the Nazis' in *Spoils of War. International News Letter*, no. 3, December 1996.
——. 'Plundering of Jewish assets during the Second World War' in *Spoils of War. International News Letter*, no. 3, December 1996.
——. 'Vluchtkapitaal en monetair goud' in *WP Jaarboek 1996*, Utrecht 1996.
——. 'Three ways of German economic penetration in the Netherlands' in *Die 'Neuordnung' Europas. NS-Wirtschaftspolitik in den besetzten Gebieten*. Edited by Rich J. Overy, Gerhard Otto, and Johannes Houwink ten Cate, Berlin 1997.
——. 'Nawoord' in Tom Bouwer, *Nazi Goud. De sinistere bankgeheimen van Zwitserland*, Amsterdam 1997.
——. 'Joodse miljardenclaims pure speculatie' in *Utrechts Nieuwsblad*, 22 February 1997.
——. 'Die Londoner Goldkonferenz, 2–4 Dezember 1997' in *1999. Zeitschrift für Sozialgeschichte des 20. und 21. Jahrhunderts*, 1, 1998, pp. 231–40.
——. 'Rechtsherstel joden heeft niet gefaald' in *NCR Handelsblad*, 25 November 1998.
Aalders, Gerard and Susanne Berger. 'Räddade av kalla kriget. Familjen Wallenbergs nazi-affärer i ny belysning' in *Dagens Nyheter*, 18 February 1997.
——. 'Verhuld in zaken. Hoe het Wallenberg-imperium oorlogsbuit heelde' in *NRC Handelsblad*, 19 April 1997.
——. 'Der Kalte Krieg als Rettung. Schwedens Nazi-Gold. Neue Einsichten in die Geschäftsbeziehungen der Familie Wallenberg zu Deutschland' in *1999. Zeitschrift für Sozialgeschichte des 20. und 21. Jahrhunderts*, 1, 1998, pp. 183–8.
Aalders, Gerard and Cees Wiebes, *Zaken doen tot elke prijs. De geheime economische collaboratie van nazi-Duitsland met de neutrale staten*, The Hague 1990. (English version: *The Art of Cloaking Ownership. The Secret Collaboration and Protection of the German War Industry by the Neutrals: the Case of Sweden*, Amsterdam 1996.)

Bibliography

Akinsha, Konstantin and Grigorii Koslov. *Stolen Treasure. The Hunt for the World's Lost Masterpieces*, London 1995.

Alford, Kenneth D. *The Spoils of World War II. The American Military Role in Stealing Europe's Treasures*, New York 1994.

Angst, Kenneth. *Der Zweite Weltkrieg und die Schweiz. Reden und Analysen*, Zürich 1997.

Balzi, Beat. *Treuhänder des Reichs. Die Schweiz und die Vermögen der Naziopfer: Eine Spurensuche*, Zürich 1997.

Barendregt, Jaap, *The Dutch Money Purge. The Monetary Consequences of German Occupation and Their Redress after Liberation 1940–1952*, Amsterdam 1993.

Barendregt, J. and T. Langenhuyzen. *Ondernemend in Risico. Nationale Nederlanden 1845–1995*, Amsterdam 1995.

Baruch, Jetje and Liesbeth van der Horst. *Het Rijksmuseum in oorlogstijd*, Amsterdam 1985.

Belinfante, A. D. *In plaats van bijltjesdag. De Geschiedenis van de Bijzondere Rechtspleging na de Tweede Wereldoorlog*, Assen 1978.

Benz, Wolfgang. *Die Juden in Deutschland 1933–1945. Leben und nationalsozialistische Herrschaft*, Munich 1988.

Berkley, K. P. L., *Overzicht van het ontstaan, de werkzaamheden en het streven van den Joodsche Raad voor Amsterdam*, Amsterdam 1945.

Biella, Friedrich, et al. *Die Wiedergutmachung nationalsozialistischen Unrechts durch die Bundesrepublik Deutschland. Das Bundesrückerstattungsgesetz*, vol. II, Munich 1981.

Blanken, I. J. *Geschiedenis van Philips Electronics N. V, Vol. IV (1935–1950). Onder Duits Beheer*, Zaltbommel 1997.

Blau, Bruno. *Das Ausnahmerecht für die Juden in Deutschland 1933–1945*, Düsseldorf 1955.

Blessin, Georg, *Wiedergutmachung*, Bad Godesberg 1960.

Blessin, Georg and Hans Wilden. *Bundesrückerstattungsgesetz, und elfte Verordnung über Ausgleichsleistungen nach dem Lastenausgleichsgesetz. Kommentar,* Munich and Berlin 1958.

Blom, J. C. H. *Crisis, Bezetting en Herstel. Tien Studien over Nederland 1939–1950*, Rotterdam 1989.

Boas, Jacob. 'De misleidingstactieken van de nazi's bij de liquidatie van de Europese joden' in Barnouw, N. D. J. et al., *Oorlogsdocumentatie '40–'45. Vijfde Jaarboek van het Rijksinstituut voor Oorlogsdocumentatie.*

Borkin, Joseph. *The Crime and Punishment of I. G. Farben*, New York 1978.

Bower, Tom. *Nazi Goud. De sinistere bankgeheimen van Zwitserland*, Amsterdam 1997.

Brandhof, J. C. E van den. *De besluitwetgeving van de kabinetten De Geer en Gerbrandy*, Deventer 1986.

Bibliography

Brouwer, S. *Beurs en Effectenhandel*, Amsterdam 1969.

Bruland, Bjarte et al. *Inndragning av jödisk eiendom i Norge under den 2. verdenkrig*, Oslo 1997.

Brummel, L. 'Tien jaren Koninklijke Bibliotheek (1938–1947)' in Brummel, L., ed. *Koninklike Bibliotheek. Gedenkboek 1798–1948. Uitgegeven met steun van de Vereniging Vrienden der Koninklijke Bibliotheek*, The Hague 1948.

Brunn, Walter et al. *Die Wiedergutmachung nationalsozialistischen Unrechts durch die Bundesrepublic Deutschland. Das Bundesentschädigungsgesetz*, vol. IV, part I, §§ 1 to 50 BEG, Munich 1981.

Bullock, Alan. *Hitler and Stalin. Parallel Lives*, London 1993.

Buijnsters, P. J. *Het Nederlandse Antiquariaat tijdens de Tweede Wereldoorlog*. Sixth Bert van Selm lecture, Amsterdam 1997.

Burgt, T. G. J. M. van de. *De 'Bank for International Settlements' te Bazel 1930–1948*, Amersfoort/Almere 1997.

Castelmur, Linus von. *Schweizerische-Allierte Finanzbeziehungen im Übergang vom Zweiten Weltkrieg zum Kalten Krieg. Die deutschen Guthaben in der Schweiz zwischen Zwangsliquidierung und Freigabe (1945–1952)*, Zürich 1997.

Chamberlain, Russel. *Loot! The Heritage of Plunder*, [n.p.] 1983.

Census of Foreign Owned Assets in the United States, Washington 1945 (published by the U.S. Treasury Department).

Clemens, Diane Shaver. *Yalta*, New York 1970.

Collins, Donald E. and Herbert P. Rothfeder. 'The Einsatzstab Reichsleiter Rosenberg and the Looting of Jewish and Masonic Libraries during World War II' in *Journal of Library History*, 18(1), Winter 1983, pp. 21–36.

De Duitsche Uitbuiting van Nederland, The Hague 1945.

De handel in effecten gedurende de jaren 1940–1945. Pamphlet for members of the First and Second Chambers of the States-General, November 1951.

Deuerlein, Ernst, ed. *Potsdam 1945, Quellen zur Konferenz der 'Grossen Drei'*, Munich 1963.

Dickens, Paul D. *United States Department of Commerce, Economic Series No. 11, Foreign Long-term Investments in the United States 1987–89*, Washington 1940.

Duynstee, F. J. F. M. and J. Bosmans. *Het kabinet Schermerhorn-Drees, 25 June 1945–3 juli 1946*, Assen/Amsterdam 1997.

Elen, Albert J. *Missing Old Master Drawings from the Franz Koenigs Collection Claimed by the State of the Netherlands*, The Hague 1989.

Elsner, Tobias von. *Alles verbrannt? Die verlorene Gemäldegalerie des Kaiser Friedrich Museums Magdeburg. Sammlungsverluste durch Kriegseinwirkungen und Folgeschäden*, Magdeburg 1995.

Feliciano, Hector. *Le Musée Disparu. Enquête sur le pillage des oeuvres d'art en France par les nazis*, Paris 1995.
——. *The Lost Museum. The Nazi Conspiracy to Steal the World's Greatest Work of Art*, New York 1997.
Fior, Michel. *Die Schweiz und das Gold der Reichsbank. Was wusste die Schweizerische Nationalbank?* Zürich 1997.
Fisch, Jörg. *Reparationen nach dem Zweiten Weltkrieg*, Munich 1982.
Flanner, Janet. *Men and Monuments. Intimate Portraits of the Major Masters and Events of Art in Our Time*, London 1957.
Fontaine Verwey, H. de la. 'De Bibliotheca Rosenthaliana tijdens de bezetting' in *Studia Rosenthaliana*, 4, 1980.
Friedman, Philip. 'The Fate of Jewish Books during the Nazi Era', in Steinbach, A. A., ed. *Jewish Book Annual*, 15, 1957–8, pp. 3–13.
Friemuth, Cay. *Die geraubte Kunst. Der dramatische Wettlauf um die Rettung der Kulturschätze nach dem Zweiten Weltkrieg*, Brunswick 1989.
FRUS. *Foreign Relations of the United States, Diplomatic Papers* 1944, vol. 2, General: Economic and Social Matters, Washington 1967.
——. *Foreign Relations of the United States, Diplomatic Papers*, 1943, vol. 1, General, Washington 1968.
Fuks, L. 'Vijf en twintig jaar Bibliotheca Rosenthaliana na de Tweede Wereldoorlog' in *Studia Rosenthaliana*, 5, 1971, pp. 159–77.

Gabriëls, H. *Koninklijke Olie: de eerste honderd jaar 1890–1990*, The Hague 1990.
Geljon, P. A. *Een zeer persoonlijk effectenhuis. Het Haagse Lissa & Kann 1800–1966*, Amsterdam 1998.
Giessler Hans et al. *Die Wiedergutmachung nationalsozialistischen Unrechts durch die Bundesrepublik Deutschland. Das Bundesentschädigungsgesetz*, vol. V, part II, §§ 51–171 BEG, Munich 1983.
Goldmann, Klaus and Günther Wermusch. *Vernichtet, Verschollen, Vermarktet. Kunstschätze im Visier von Politik und Geschäft*, Asendorf 1992.
Gordon, David L. and Royden Dangerfield. *The Hidden Weapon. A Popular Account of How Economic War Influenced Military and Political Strategy in World War II, with Consideration of Its Implications for Peace*, New York/ London [n.d.].
Grimstedt, Patricia Kennedy. *Archives of Russia Five Years After: 'Purveyors of Sensations' or 'Shadows Cast to the Past'?* IISG Research Papers, 1997.
——. 'Displaced Archives and Restitution Problems on the Eastern Front in the Aftermath of the Second World War' in *Contemporary European History*, 6(1), 1 March 1997, pp. 27–74.
Grossmann, Kurt R. *Die Ehrenschuld. Kurzgeschichte der Wiedergutmachung*, Frankfurt am Main 1967.

Bibliography

Hayes, Peter. *Industry and Ideology. I. G. Farben in the Nazi Era*, Cambridge 1987.

Hes, Max de. *Land loopt niet weg. Drie eeuwen joods sociaal-economisch leven in Hoogeveen*, Hoogeveen 1994.

Heyting, Lien. 'Kunstroof en Recuperatie' in *NCR Handelsblad*, 31 October 1997, 7 November 1997, 14 November 1997, 21 November 1997.

——. 'De dubbele agenda van A. B. de Vries' in *NCR Handelsblad*, 27 March 1998.

Herzberg, Abel J. 'Kroniek der jodenvervolging' in *Onderdrukking en Verzet. Nederland in oorlogstijd*, Amsterdam 1950.

Hilberg, Raul. *The Destruction of the European Jews*, (3 vols.), New York 1985.

Hirschfeld, Gerhard. *Fremdherrschaft und Kollaboration. Die Niederlande unter deutscher Besetzung 1940–1945*, Stuttgart 1984.

Hirschfeld, H. M. *Herinneringen uit de bezettingstijd*, Amsterdam/Brussels 1960.

'Hitlers Denkschrift zum Vierjahresplan 1936' in *Vierteljahresheft für Zeitgeschichte*, 1955, pp. 184–210.

Hollander, Pieter den. *De Zaak Goudstikker*, Amsterdam 1998.

Hoogewoud, F. J. 'The Nazi Looting of Books and its American "Antithesis". Selected Pictures from the Offenbach Archival Depot's Photographic History and in Supplement' in *Studia Rosenthaliana*, 26, pp.158–92, 1992.

——, ed. *The Return of Looted Collections (1946–1996). An Unfinished Chapter*, Amsterdam 1997.

Hoore, Cees van. 'De "verzwegen" kunstroof bij De Lakenhal' in *Leids Dagblad*, 9 May 1990, p. 38.

——. '"Sicher Gestellt". Waar is de schilderijenverzameling van Dr. Alphons-Jaffé?' in *Vitrine*, 1, 1991.

Houwink ten Cate, J. T. M. 'Het jongere deel' in Barnouw, N. D. J. et al., *Oorlogsdocumentatie'40–'45. Jaarboek van het Rijksinstituut voor Oorlogsdocumetatie*, Zutphen 1989.

Jaeger, Charles de. *The Linz File. Hitler's Plunder of Europe's Art*, Exeter 1981.

Jansma, T. J. *Het bezettingsrecht in de practijk van de Tweede Wereldoorlog*, Wageningen 1953 (dissertation).

Jong, L. de. *Het Koninkrijk der Nederlanden in de Tweede Wereldoorlog*, 14 vols., The Hague 1969–92.

Karlsberg, B. 'German federal compensation- and restitution-laws and Jewish victims in the Netherlands' in *Studia Rosenthaliana*, 2, pp. 194–244, 1968.

——. *Beschleunigung durch besondere Verfarhren, Sammelverfahren Belgien, Frankreich, Niederlande*, Munich 1981.

Kaye, Lawrence M. 'Laws in Force at the Dawn of World War II: International Conventions and National Laws' in Simpson, Elizabeth, ed., *The Spoils of War*, 1997.

Kernkamp, J. H. *Economisch-Historische Aspecten van de Literatuurproductie. Rede uitgesproken bij de aanvaarding van het ambt van hoogleraar aan de Nederlandsche Hoogeschool te Rotterdam op 3 Februari 1949*, The Hague 1949.

Kersten, J. W. 'Theorie en Praktijk van naoorlogs Rechtsherstel en Beheer' (unpublished manuscript, 1987).

Klemann, Hein A. M. 'De Nederlandse economie tijdens de Tweede Wereldoorlog' in *Tijdschrift voor Geschiedenis*, 1997, no. 1.

Knegtmans, Peter Jan, Paul Schulten and JaapVogel. *Collaborateurs van niveau. Opkomst en val van de hoogleraren Schrieke, Snijder en Van Dam*, Amsterdam 1996.

Koch, Peter Ferdinand. *Geheim-Depot Schweiz. Wie Banken am Holocaust verdienen*, Munich/Leipzig 1997.

Konijnenburg, E. van. *Roof Restitutie Reparatie*. Compiled for the Netherlands Ministry of Economic Affairs, The Hague 1947.

Kurtz, Michael J. *Nazi Contraband. American Policy on the Return of European Cultural Treasures, 1945–1955*, New York/London 1985.

Kwaadgras, E. P. 'The Fate of a Special Collection: Library, Archives and Museum of the Netherlands Freemasons' in Hoogewoud, F. J., ed., *The Return of Looted Collections (1946–1996). An Unfinished Chapter*, Amsterdam 1997.

Landsberger, L. 'De liquidatie der Duitsche vermogenswaarden in Zwitserland' in *Economisch Statistische Berichten*, no. 1555, 26 January 1947.

Lebor, Adam, *Hitler's Secret Bankers. How Switzerland Profited from Nazi Genocide*, London 1997.

Leeuw, A. J. van der. 'De handel in Duitse effecten tijdens de bezetting' in Paape, A. H., *Studies over Nederland in oorlogstijd,* The Hague 1972.

——. 'Der Griff des Reiches nach dem Judenvermögen' in Paape, A. H., *Studies over Nederland in oorlogstijd*, The Hague 1972.

—— 'Die Aktion Bozenhardt & Co.' in Paape, A. H., *Studies over Nederland in oorlogstijd*, The Hague 1972.

—— 'Die "Arisierung" eines jüdischen Betriebs in den Niederlanden' in Paape, A. H., *Studies over Nederland in oorlogstijd*, The Hague, 1972.

——. 'Die Käufe des Generalkommissars z.b. V. Fritz Schmidt' in Paape, A. H., *Studies over Nederland in oorlogstijd*, The Hague 1972.

——. 'Reichskommissariat und Judenvermögen in den Niederlanden' in Paape, A. H., *Studies over Nederland in oorlogstijd*, The Hague 1972.

Leistra, Josephine. 'A short history of art loss and art recovery in the Netherlands' in Simpson, Elizabeth, ed., *The Spoils of War. World War II and its Aftermath. The Loss, Reappearance and Recovery of Cultural Property*, New York 1997.

Bibliography

—— 'On the Recovery of Art. Recent Developments' in Hoogewoud, F. J., ed., *The Return of Looted Collections (1946–1966). An Unfinished Chapter*, Amsterdam 1997.

——. 'Recuperatie in Nederland 1945–1996. Schets van een niet afgesloten hoofdstuk' in Aalders, G. et al., *Achtste jaarboek van het Rijksinstituut voor Oorlogsdocumentie*, Zutphen 1997.

Lemmermaier, Doris and Dieter Opper. *Cultural Treasures Moved Because of War. A Cultural Legacy of the Second World War. Documentation and Research on Losses*, Bremen 1995.

Lennep, A. van. 'Effectenbeurs en Rechtsherstel' in *De Gids*, October 1952, No. 10.

Lijst van geslachtsnamen van personen van joodschen bloede, The Hague 1942.

Lindner, Stephan H. 'Das Reichskommissariat für die Behandlung feindlichen Vermögens im Zweiten Weltkrieg' in *Zeitschrift für Unternehmensgeschichte*. Edited by Pohl, Hans and Treue, Wilhelm. Supplement 67, 1991.

Lööw, Helène. 'Swedish Policy Towards Suspected War Criminals, 1945–87' in *Scandinavian Journal of History*, 14(2), 1989, pp. 135–53.

Lost Treasures of Europe. 427 Photographs, New York [n.d].

M-Aktion. Frankreich, Belgien, Holland und Luxemburg. 1940–1944. Frankfurt am Main 1958.

Manasse, Peter. *Verdwenen archieven en bibliotheken. De verrichtingen van de Einsatzstab Rosenberg gedurende de Tweede Wereldoorlog*, The Hague 1995.

——. 'Preservation of Historical Records and a Pro-active Approach to Collections' in Hoogewoud, F. J., ed., *The Return of Looted Collections (1946–1996). An Unfinished Chapter*, Amsterdam 1997.

Martin, James Stuart. *All Honorable Men*, Boston 1950.

Meihuizen, J. P. *'Goed fout.' Het criminele verleden van beursvoorzitter en verzetsman Carel F. Overhoff in de doofpot van historici*, Amsterdam 1995.

Meijers, E. M. 'Het voorstel van L.V.V.S. ann haar schuldeisers', Zwolle 1950 (brochure).

Memorandum van de Nederlandse Regering inzake de door Nederland van Duitschland te eischen schadevergoeding. Published on behalf of the Dutch Government, The Hague 1945.

Mevis, Annette. 'Women's Archives Recovered' in Hoogewoud, F. J., ed., *The Return of Looted Collections (1946–1966). An Unfinished Chapter*, Amsterdam 1997.

Milward, Alan A. *Die Deutsche Kriegswirtschaft 1939–1945*, Stuttgart 1966.

Mossé, Claude. *Ces messieurs de Berne 1939–1945*, Paris 1997.

Nazi Conspiracy and Aggression, 10 volumes, Washington DC 1946–9.

Nederlands Juristenblad (various years).

Bibliography

New, Mittya. *Switzerland Unwrapped. Exposing the Myths*, London/New York 1997.

Nicholas, Lynn H. *The Rape of Europa. The Fate of Europe's Treasures in the Third Reich and the Second World War*, New York 1994.

Nürnberg Trials. *International Military Trials Nürnberg,* 7 vols. 1946.

Old Master Paintings. An Illustrated Summary Catalogue, published by Rijksdienst Bildende Kunst, The Hague/Zwolle 1992.

OMGUS, *Ermittlungen gegen die Deutsche Bank*, Nördlingen 1985.

———. *Ermittlungen gegen die Dresdner Bank*, Nördlingen 1986.

———. *Ermittlungen gegen die I.G. Farben*, Nördlingen 1986.

Paape, A. H., ed. *Studies over Nederland in oorlogstijd,* vol. 1, The Hague 1972.

Petropoulos, Jonathan. 'The Importance of the Second Rank: The Case of the Art Plunderer Kajetan Mühlmann' in Bischof, G. and A. Pelinka, eds., *Austro Corporatism. Past, Present, Future. Contemporary Austrian Studies, Vol. 4.*, Chapel Hill 1995.

———. *Art as Politics in the Third Reich,* London 1996.

Poliakow, Leon and Josef Wulf. *Het Derde Rijk en de joden. Documenten en Getuigenissen,* Amsterdam 1956.

Presser, J. *Ondergang. De vervolging en verdelging van het Nederlandse jodendom 1940–1945*, (2 vols.), The Hague 1965; abridged English edition: *Ashes in the Wind*, London 1968.

Pross, Christian. *Wiedergutmachung. Der Kleinkrieg gegen die Opfer*, Frankfurt am Main 1988.

Rechtsherstel. Half-maandelijksch orgaan van den Raad voor Rechtsherstel (all volumes).

Rikhof, Frans. 'J. K. van der Haagen. Kunstbescherming in Nederland tijdens de Tweede Wereldoorlog' in Aalders, G. et al., *Negende Jaarboek van het Rijksinstituut voor Oorlog documentatie*, Zutphen 1998.

Rings, Werner. *Raubgold aus Deutschland. Die 'Golddrehscheibe' Schweiz im Zweiten Weltkrieg*, Zürich/Munich 1985.

Rosenberg, A.W. 'Ets Haim – Livraria Montezinos' in Hoogewoud, F. J., ed., *The Return of Looted Collections (1946–1996). An Unfinished Chapter*, Amsterdam 1997.

Roxan, David and Ken Wanstall. *The Jackdaw of Linz, The Story of Hitler's Art Thefts*, London 1964.

Rupierer, Hermann J. *The Cuno Government and Reparations 1922–1923. Politics and Economics*, The Hague/Boston/London 1979.

Bibliography

Sagi, Nana. *German Reparations. A History of the Negotiations*, Jerusalem 1980.

Sayer, Ian and Douglas Botting. *Nazi Gold, The Story of the World's Greatest Robbery – and its Aftermath*, London 1984.

Scherphuis, Ageeth. 'Een heer in de kunsthandel. Het korte gretige leven van Jacques Goudstikker' in *Vrij Nederland*, 10 November 1990.

Schie, A. J. van. 'Restitution of economic rights after 1945' in *Dutch-Jewish History*, Tel Aviv 1984.

Schwartz, Walter. *Die Wiedergutmachung nationalsozialistischen Unrechts durch die Bundesrepublik Deutschland, Rückerstattung nach den Gesetzen der Allierten Mächte*, vol. 1, Munich 1974.

Seydewith, Ruth and Max Seydewith. *Die Dame mit dem Hermelin. Der grösste Kunstraub aller Zeiten*, Berlin 1963.

Seyes, B. A. *De arbeidsinzet. De gedwongen arbeid van Nederlanders in Duitsland 1940–1945*, The Hague 1990.

Sijes, B. A. et al. *Vervolging van Zigeuners in Nederland 1940–1945*, The Hague 1979.

Simpson, Elizabeth, ed. *The Spoils of War. World War II and its Aftermath. The Loss, Reappearance, and Recovery of Cultural Poperty*, New York 1997.

Smith Jr., Arthur L. *Hitler's Gold. The Story of the Nazi War Loot*, Oxford/New York/Munich 1989.

Smyth, Craig Hugh. *Repatriation of Art from the Collecting Point in Munich after World War II. Background and Beginnings. With Reference Especially to the Netherlands*, Maarsen/The Hague 1986.

Spoils of War. International Newsletter (all issues).

Statistiek der Bevolking van joodschen bloede in Nederland, The Hague 1942.

Statistische gegevens van de joden in Nederland. Deel 1, Statistische Gegevens van de Joden in Amsterdam, waarin reeds opgenomen enkele voorlopige cijfers van de joden in Nederland, The Hague 1942.

Tammes, H. H. *Rechtsherstel en Praktijk inzake Effecten*, n.p. 1949.

Toelichtingen op de Besluiten Bezettingsmaatregelen, Herstel Rechtsverkeer en Vijandelijk Vermogen, The Hague 1947.

Trepp, Gian. *Bankgeschäfte mit dem Feind. Die Bank für Internationalen Zahlungsausgleich im Zweiten Weltkrieg. Von Hitlers Europabank zum Instrument des Marshallplanes*, Zürich 1993.

Trip, L. J. A. *De Duitsche bezetting van Nederland en de Financiële ontwikkeling van het land gedurende de jaren der bezetting*, The Hague 1946.

Uit Nederland Geroofde Goederen/Goods Looted from the Netherlands 1940– 1945, Register I, Machines en Werktuigen/Machines and Apparatus. Published by the Commissaris Generaal Recuperatie (CGR), Amsterdam 1946.

Ulshöfer, Otfried. *Die Einflussnahme auf Wirtschaftsunternehmungen in den besetzten nord-, west- und südosteuropäischen Ländern*, Tübingen 1958.

Venema, Adriaan. *Kunsthandel in Nederland, 1940–1945*, Amsterdam, 1986.
Verordnungsblatt für die besetzten Niederländischen Gebiete Jahr 1940 / Verordeningenblad voor het bezette Nederlandsche gebied, vols. 1940–5.
Verrijn Stuart, D. M. 'Enkele aspecten van de Duitse herstelbetalingen' in *Internationale Spectator*, 10(15), pp. 415–36.
Verslag over de jaren 1945 en 1946, ministerie van Economische Zaken, Commissariaat Generaal voor de Nederlandsche Economische Belangen in Duitsland, Amsterdam 1947.
Verslag over het jaar 1947, ministerie van Economische Zaken, Commissariaat Generaal voor de Nederlandsche Economische Belangen in Duitsland, Amsterdam 1948.
Verslag over het jaar 1948, ministerie van Economische Zaken, Commissariaat Generaal voor de Nederlandsche Economische Belangen in Duitsland, Amsterdam 1949.
Vincent, Isabel. *Hitler's Silent Partners. Swiss Banks, Nazi Gold, and the Pursuit of Justice*, New York 1997.
Vlessing, O. 'Recovering Looted Archives in Amsterdam' in Hoogewoud, F. J., ed., *The Return of Looted Collections (1946–1996). An Unfinished Chapter*, Amsterdam 1997.
Voolen, Edward van. 'The Jewish Historical Museum: A Partial Return of the Looted Collection' in Hoogewoud, F. J., ed., *The Return of Looted Collections (1946–1996). An Unfinished Chapter*, Amsterdam 1997.
De Vries, J. *Een Eeuw Vol Effecten. Historische schets van de Vereniging voor de Effectenhandel en de Amsterdamse Effectenbeurs, 1876–1976*, Amsterdam 1976.
——. *Geschiedenis van de Nederlandsche Bank. Vijfde deel. De Nederlandsche Bank van 1914 tot 1948. Trips tijdvak 1931–1948 onderbroken door de Tweede Wereldoorlog*, Amsterdam 1994.
Vries, Wim de. *Sonderstab Musik. Music Confiscations by the Einsatzstab Reichsleiter Rosenberg under the Nazi Occupation of Western Europe*, Amsterdam 1996.
——. *Sonderstab Musik. Organisierte Plünderungen in Westeuropa, 1940–1945*, Cologne 1998.

Walk, Joseph, ed. *Das Sonderrecht für die Juden im NS-Staat. Eine Sammlung der gesetzlichen Massnahmen und Richtlinien – Inhalt und Bedeutung*, Heidelberg/Karlsruhe 1981.
Weekblad voor Privaatrecht, Notaris-ambt en Registratie (various years).

Bibliography

Weis, George. 'Restitution through the ages', Noah Barou Memorial Lecture 1962, London 1962.
Werf, D. C. J. van der. *De bond, de banken en de beurzen*, Amsterdam 1988.
Wilamowitz-Moellendorf, Fanny, Gräfin von. *Carin Göring*, Berlin 1943.
Wilterdink, N. A. *Vermogensverhoudingen in Nederland. Ontwikkelingen sinds de negentiende eeuw*, Amsterdam 1983.

Zeventig jaren statistiek in tijdreeksen 1899–1969, The Hague 1970.
Ziegler, Jean. *Die Schweiz, das Gold und die Toten*, Munich 1997.

Index

ABN-AMRO 214
Adoc, N.V. 208–9
agricultural land 122–3
Algemeen Nederlands Beheer van Onroerende Goederen (General Netherlands Administration of Real Estate, ANBO) 123, 124
Algemene Kunstzijde Unie (General Rayon Union, AKU) 30, 31
Alien Property Custodian 104, 111
Alkmaar, Masonic Lodge 57
Allgemeine Elektrizitäts-Gesellschaft (AEG) 31
Alliance Française, The Hague 58
Allied Declaration (1943) 72, 87–8, 160, 165, 224
Allies
 air landings at Arnhem 11, 33–4
 air raids on Germany 25, 151, 191, 203, 207
 deception of through sham transactions 121
 discovery of hoards 2–3, 94
 and economic warfare 85
 liberation of Netherlands 25–6
American Civil War 44
American soldiers, stealing of buried gold 3
Amersfoort
 concentration camp 140
 Masonic Lodge 57
 see also Polak Collection
Amsterdam
 diamond industry 120
 expiation fines 26
 libraries looted by ERR 56, 58, 59
 looting of Jewish non-profit-making institutions 112
 statistics of Jews in 108
 tax bill of Jews 220
 see also under institutions etc.
Amsterdam Ashkenazi archive 56
Amsterdam Bankers' Association 171
Amsterdam Rubber 150, 158

Amsterdam Stedelijk Museum 198
Amsterdam Stock Exchange 13, 32, 40, 227
 and sale of securities 152–3, 155, 156, 157–9, 163–4, 166, 173
 and trade in American shares 159–63
Amsterdam University Library 59, 60
Amsterdamsch Effectenblad 158
Amsterdamsche Bank 34, 122, 131, 131–2, 162, 172, 216
Amsterdamsche Maatschappij van Levensverzekeringen (Amstleven, Amsterdam Life Insurance Company) 182–3
Amstmann, H. 29
Angerer, Josef 94
anti-Semitism 24
 legal measures 5, 81, 89, 99–101, 108, 132
antiques 64, 186, 189, 194, 208, 223
ants, Wasmann collection 62
Antwerp 120
Arcana (auction house), Hamburg 66–7
archives 1, 43, 53
 index records 192, 208
 looted by ERR in Netherlands 51, 52, 53–4, 55, 56, 57, 60, 192
 and provenance principle 60
 see also Treuhänder Archiv
Argentina 75, 94
arms industry
 German 24
 Swiss 35
Arnhem 11, 33–4, 37, 38
art works 1, 2, 47, 63, 77–8
 banning of Jews from disposing freely of 100
 confiscated by Liro 130, 176, 221
 confiscated as enemy property 63, 70–1, 111, 200
 confiscated in France 54–6
 Dutch art market 66–8
 Göring's ambitions to collect 42, 46
 hoards 2

– 301 –

Index

of Jewish provenance 49, 54–6
on loan to Dutch museums 195–7, 199–201, 227
looted in Poland 63
national collections 43
private collections 18, 56, 64–5, 68–75, 196
provenance principle 60
purchased by museums from Liro 197–8, 227
retracing of 193
seized by ERR 192
taken by Mühlmann 186
see also Dutch art market; paintings; sculpture
Aryanization 29, 62, 100, 114–19, 119–20, 124, 128, 156
of diamond industry 120–2
Asscher & Welcker (art dealers), London 82
Assen, Amsterdamsche Bank 131
assets
abroad 86, 180
recoverable after the war 222
associations and foundations 26–8, 111–14
Astra Romana Oil Company 31
auctions 57, 64, 66, 66–7, 110, 173, 186, 191, 200, 207, 223
Aufenacker, J.H.L. 166–7
Aurich State Archive 61
Auschwitz 6, 24, 71, 218
Auslandbonds 16–17, 29, 40
Austria
Berlin Central Library tranferred to 207
hoards of loot 2–3, 92–3, 93, 94
see also Linz

Baldung Grien, Hans 72
bank accounts
dormant 102, 104
Liro 132, 145, 147, 149
problems with tracing 103
and *Sammelkonto* 141–2
transferred to Liro 148
Bank der Deutschen Arbeit 32
Bank der Deutschen Luftfahrt (German Aviation Bank) 32
Bank of England 92
Bank voor Nederlandsche Arbeid 116
Bank voor West-Europeeschen Handel 116, 160

Bankierskantoor 18, 40–1, 160
banks
and abolition of currency border 13, 14–15, 224
banned from disposing of foreign currency 38
flight of Jewish capital to 101–4
hoards discovered in vaults 2
involved in Aryanization process 116
and *Kapitalverflechtung* 28–9, 29–30, 32–3
looting of gold from 35, 37
mortgage 125–6
purchase of *Amerikaantjes* 161–2
raiding of by German military 34
and securities 169–74
and transfer of accounts to Liro 148–9
see also under names of banks
Basel 74
Bazna, Eliezar 93
Bedrijfsgroep Levensverzekering (Life Insurance Group) 181–2
Belgium 15, 33, 47, 56, 168
Bellamy groups, libraries 58
Beltrand, Prof. Jacques 48
Berchtesgaden 94
Berghof, Obersalzberg 79
Berlin 42, 52, 151, 169, 190, 193
auctions 64, 66–7, 191
fall of 168
'purchasing' of art by museums and galleries 45
Von Stechow's home 140
see also under institutions, establishments, etc.
Berlin Central Library 207
Besluit Herstel Rechtsverkeer (Decree for the Restoration of the Rule of Law) 89
Besluit Rechtsverkeer in Oorlogstijd (A6) (Decree on Judicial Matters in Wartime) 85
Beth Hamidrash library 56
Beuningen, D.G. van 72
Bibles 28
Bibliotheca Rosenthaliana, Amsterdam 59, 60
bicycles 24, 33, 105, 109
Birnbaum (also called Bingham) collection 198
black market 19–20, 104, 122, 124, 134, 159, 167, 173
Blaschke, R. von 133, 168
Bloemendaal *see* Nienhuys Collection

Index

boats 24
Bohemia 54, 115, 208
Böhmker, H. 111–12, 191
Bol, Ferdinand 66
Bolle, Max 112–13
Bonn 45, 193
books 47, 200, 207–8
  see also libraries
bookshops 58, 59–62
Bordeaux, Rothschild collections 56
Bormann, Martin 45, 52, 73
Bormann, Dr O. 31
Botticelli, Sandro 71
Boymans Museum, Rotterdam 72, 197
Bozenhardt Bros 121
Brand, share auctions 166
Breda 168
Bregstein, Prof. M.H. 124
Breitner, George Hendrik 73, 199
Breslau 45, 61
Brethauer, F. 60
Bretton Woods, UN Monetary and Financial Conference (1944) 88
Britain *see* Great Britain; London
British Commonwealth 111
British Empire, looting in territories 1
British Museum, London 1, 2
Broek, A.A. ten 76
Brown Boveri 32
Brueghel, Pieter 64, 66, 73
Brüg regulations 193–4
Bruijn, Barthel 72
Brussels 47
Brussels Conference (1874) 44–5
Büchi, Walter 217–18
Bühler, Dr Anton 29–30, 40, 41–2, 133
  implementation of Liro Decrees 152, 154, 156, 157, 158, 161, 168, 171–2, 177–8
Bullock, Alan 5
bureaucracy, decrees against Dutch Jewry 106–7
businesses
  Aryanization 100, 124
  as enemy property 110–11
  Jewish 3, 114–19
  Kristallnacht 100
Busse & Co. 188, 189, 190
Bussum 26, 57

capital, flow after advent of Hitler 101–4
carpets 43, 63, 138, 140, 186, 187, 189, 190, 206
cattle 25
cemeteries, Jewish 111
Central Office for Jewish Emigration 108
Centrale Vermogens Opsporingsdiens (Central Property Recovery Service, CVO) 215
Cézanne, Paul 47
Chabot, A.B.C.D. 68
Chabot, J.J.M., and art collection 68–9
Chardin, Jean-Baptiste-Siméon 200
Chicago Art Institute 71
children, and *Sperrstempel* 212
Christmas campaign (1942) 20, 189
church authorities, searching of offices 53
citizenship, Nazi decrees on 100–1
claims
  registration and collection of 175, 178–80, 221
  of surviving Jews 227
clothing
  from M-Aktion clearances 207
  requisitioning of 25, 91
  searching of after death of Jews 176
  sold by Liro 188, 189
coins 187, 216
  collected by SS from concentration camps 176–7
collaboration 29–30, 133, 177
collections, Liro definition of 176
Cologne 41, 45, 66, 168, 186
Commerz Bank 32
communists 51, 53
  bookshops 58
compensation
  claimed by owners of looted valuables 193
  for looted household effects 206
  paid at the time for items surrendered 24
Compiègne, monument 52
concentration camps 4, 6, 24, 71, 100, 103, 129, 140, 177, 206, 217
  see also Westerbork transit camp
Corot, Jean-Baptiste-Camille 73
Cranach, Lucas (the Elder) 72, 73
Cuba 103
cultural property 43–5
  amount never recovered 91

Index

destination of looted items 91–2, 194
Dutch claim for stolen items 1
emotional value to owners 18
looting of Polish items 63
looting through the ages 11
repatriation of to Germany 49, 73
sham sales of Dutch items 224
sold by Liro 186–94
traceability 227
Utikal's report 50
valuation of by Liro 187–9
see also art works; paintings; sculpture
Curaçao 30–1
cutlery 176
Cuyp, Albert 66
Czechoslovakia 31

Dam, Dr J.C. van 196, 197, 197–8
Davos, Switzerland, as sanctuary for Nazis 91–2
De Bijenkorf (department store), Amsterdam 116, 118
De Lakenhal museum, Leiden 196
De Vijzel (auction house) 187
decrees (*Verordnungen* or VOs)
  abolition of currency border 13
  against non-profit-making institutions 26–7, 111–14
  against those harming German interests 26
  as basis for looting of Jews' property 3, 4, 5, 7, 105–9, 226
  on collections for charitable institutions 21
  for confiscation of money and property 23, 70
  control of Jewish businesses 114–19
  on enemy property 109–11
  foreign exchange 37
  Führererlass 57
  for restoration of property and rights 89
  on surrender or requisition 23–4
  see also Liro Decrees
Degas, Edgar 47, 71, 73
degenerate art (*entarte Kunst*) 47–8, 71, 73, 79, 190
Delbrück, Schickler & Co. 151
Delft, Masonic Lodge 57
Den Helder, Masonic Lodge 57
Denmark, German attack on 86, 101

dental fillings *see* teeth and fillings
department stores 116
deportation 136, 176, 179
  deferment from 120–1, 122, 212
  exemptions from 'labour service' 211
Deutsche Bank 29, 32
Deutsche Gold- und Silberscheideanstalt (Degussa, German Gold and Silver Refinery) 189, 190
Deutsche Golddiskontobank (Dego) (German Gold Discount Bank) 17, 18, 27, 41
Deutsche Revisions- und Treuhand AG (German Audit and Trustee Company, DRT) 109–11, 114, 142, 169, 222
Deutsche Verrechnungskasse 13
Deventer 34
Deventer, S. van 73
Devisenschutzkommando (Foreign Exchange Protection Commando, DSK) 13, 37–8, 57, 65, 105, 109, 128, 142, 167
  looting of property from Jews 187, 191, 192, 194, 213, 214, 219, 222, 226
Diamond Bourse, Weesperplein 130
Diamond Exchange 138
diamond industry
  Aryanization 120–2
  merchants 219
diamonds 34, 39
  retracing of 193
  sold by Liro 188, 190, 191
  and *Sperrstempel* 212, 213–14, 216, 226
Dienststelle Mühlmann 43, 56, 57, 62–6, 189, 190, 195, 196, 222
Dieppe, British raid on 151
Dietrich, SS-Trooper Sepp 93
Dik, Jan (Sr and Jr) 76
Dintel, C.J.W. van 219
Docter, P.C. 217
documentary evidence 4, 33
  disappearance of Jews' papers 103
  Liro index cards 193
  wartime archives of Mak van Waay 194
Dolle Dinsdag (5 September 1944) 25, 33, 134, 168
Dorotheum (auction house), Vienna 66, 66–7
Dou, Gerrit 63, 64, 66
drawings, collections 70, 71–2
Dresden art gallery 45

Index

Dresdner Bank 28–9, 30, 31–2, 33, 172, 173
Dullemen, A.A.L.F. 169, 170, 171
Dutch art market 45, 63, 64, 66–8, 73, 119, 186, 224
Dutch East Indies 67, 157
Dutch Economic and Historical Archive 56
Dutch government-in-exile 32, 68, 85–6, 86–7, 213
Dutch Ministry of Economic Affairs 2
Dutch Royal family 43, 64
Dutch Scientific Humanitarian Committe, library 56

Eastern Europe, looting by ERR 43
Ebert, Georg 52
Eckhart, Meister 59
Economic Warfare Department, archives 104
economics
  and Aryanization of businesses 115
  importance of in modern wars 85
  Kapitalverflechtung 28–33
  and slave labour 24–5
  see also Auslandbonds; banks; foreign currency; Four-Year Plan; occupation costs
Egmond, chronicle 61
Egypt 167
Eindhoven 31
Einsatzstab Reichsleiter Rosenberg (ERR) 43, 46, 48–9, 52, 112, 131, 190, 192, 222
  competition with Liro 189
  competition with RSHA 52–4, 56
  looting of art in France 43, 47, 48, 54–6, 56, 57, 81
  looting of art in Netherlands 48, 55, 56–8, 59–62, 192, 199
  M-Aktion confiscations 203–9, 219–20
Einthoven, L. 21
emigration
  permits 214–15
  and tax authorities 218–20
'enemy property' 39, 63, 76, 82, 109–11, 128, 195, 200, 227
  decree issued by Dutch government 89
England 64, 128, 151
equities 34, 109, 130, 153, 154
Esperanto Movement, library 58
Essen, J.C. van 160, 162
Esso, family 217
Everout, P. 123
Exaeten Castle 62
Excalibur 47
expiation (*Sühneleistung*) fines 26, 100

Fantin-Latour, Henri 73
Farben, I.G. (company) 24–5, 29
Feindvermögensverwaltung (Administration of Enemy Property) 56, 57, 65, 82
Final Solution 104
financial compensation *see* compensation
First World War 40, 51, 52, 66, 85
Fischböck, Hans 16, 28, 41, 82–3, 105, 110, 114, 115, 132, 133, 141, 142, 152, 158
fisheries sector, decree concerning Jewish property 122–3
Flesche, Alfred 128, 131, 132, 133, 134, 136, 139, 153, 200
flies, Schmitz's collection 62
Fock, Karin von 47
Fokker 32
foreign bonds 167, 172
  see also Auslandbonds
foreign currency
  abolition of currency border 12–15, 25, 42, 224
  Allied searches for 92
  First Liro Decree 38, 147, 161
  German measures to control 17–18, 37–8, 39–40, 101, 211
  Kapitalverflechtung 30
  looting of 2, 39, 217–18, 223
  and purchase of Lanz Collection 73–4
  Rebholz's provision of Germany with 41 shares 168
Foreign Currency Institute 161
Foreign Funds Control, archives 104
forgery, of British banknotes 92–3
foundations *see* associations and foundations
Four-Year Plan 39–40, 121, 122, 167, 168, 188, 189, 190, 212
France
  as investor in America 86
  looting by ERR in 43, 47, 48, 54–6, 56, 57, 81
  military occupation of 15

– 305 –

Index

and return of cultural property stolen by
    Grande Armée 44
selling of securities to 167
Utikal's report 50
see also Bordeaux; Compiègne; Paris
Frank, Hans 65
Frankfurt 2, 52, 59
Franz Ferdinand, Archduke of Austria, murder
    of 51
Freemasons 50, 51, 52, 53, 57, 192
    see also Masonic lodges
Fries Genootschap 60
Fromm, Friedrich 118
Führermuseum, Linz 18, 45, 47, 53, 63, 91,
    186, 190, 193
    assembling of paintings for 46, 63–4, 65, 68,
    70, 72, 80–1
Fuld, Edgar 128, 133, 135, 153
Fuld, Rosa 128, 200
Funk, Walther 28, 93
furniture 91, 110, 138
    antique or fine 43, 73, 130, 131, 186
    from M-Aktion Jewish house clearances 203,
    206, 208
    illegally taken by Liro employees 140, 141
    sold by Liro 186, 187, 189

Galerie Fischer, Lucerne, hoard of gold 67
Garmisch Partenkirchen 2–3
Gauguin, Paul 47
Gebroeders Gerzon (outfitters) 116
Gelder, J.G. van der 197
General State Archives, The Hague 192
Gennep 26
German army 25
German Communist Party 51
German Democratic Republic, Göring's buried
    treasure 94
German Federal Republic, reparations
    legislation 193
Germany
    Allied raids on 25, 151, 191, 203, 207
    art trade 47, 66, 196
    attempt to requisition Dutch workers 24
    hoards of loot 2–3, 94
    invasion and occupation of Netherlands 36,
    66, 85
    museums 79, 91

    particular needs and requisitions 25
    post-war reparation legislation 193
    proscription of Freemasonry 57
    selling of loot in 1, 47, 64–5, 223
    transporting of looted household goods to
    205
    war economy 30, 37, 41, 91
    see also Four-Year Plan
Gestapo 53, 65, 217
glassware 199
Goebbels, Joseph 49, 79, 80
Gogh, Vincent van *see* Van Gogh, Vincent
gold 1, 4, 34, 35–7, 38, 39, 100, 185, 221
    Allied investigations into hoards 2–3, 95
    collected by SS from concentration camps
    176–7
    confiscated by order of Second Liro 130,
    136, 176
    from M-Aktion house clearances 208
    sold by Liro 186, 187, 189, 190
    surrendered for deferment of deportation
    213, 216
    treasure dug up in Linz 93
Gold Declaration 88
Goldfalken 188, 189, 190
Goodman, Nick and Simon 71
Göpel, Dr Erhard 69, 70, 186
Göring, Hermann 18, 20, 28, 79, 92, 95
    administration of Four-Year Plan 39–40,
    93–4
    'arts fund' 80, 81–3
    assembling of his art collection 42, 45, 46,
    46–7, 65, 66, 72, 72–3, 74, 75, 79, 80,
    185, 196
    hidden treasure of 94
    interest in diamond industry 120, 121
    receiving of works of art looted by ERR
    48–9, 54–5, 56, 57
    and takeover of Kunsthandel J. Goudstikker
    75–6, 77, 78
Goudsmit, Isaac collection 198
Goudsmit, J.M. 143
Goudstikker, Jacques 75, 82
    see also Kunsthandel J. Goudstikker N.V.
Goudstikker-von Halban-Kurz, Desi 76, 77
Goya, Francisco di 66, 200
Goyen, Jan van 64, 77
Goyvaerts, F.I. 69

Index

Great Britain
   flight of Jewish capital to 101, 103, 104
   German property in 111
   intelligence service 35
   news leak about German 'trade in human beings' 212–13
   non-recoverable assets in 180
   see also British Commonwealth; British Empire; British Museum; London
Gritzbach, E. 47
Groenendijk, N.C.A.J. 187
Groesbeek 26
Groningen 57, 123
   University 60, 61
Grossouw, J.F. 172, 173
Grothe, Dr W. 60, 61
Guth, Oberzollinspektor 38–9
Gutmann, Friedrich and Louise, and Gutmann Collection 71
Gutmann, Fritz 75
Gypsies 6, 225

Haarlem, libraries and archives 60
Haberstock, Karl 71
The Hague 26, 32, 34, 57, 85, 142, 207
   see also under institutions etc.
Hague Convention 5, 12, 36, 45, 50, 226
Hague Municipal Museum 198, 199
Hali, M.G. 158, 166
Hamburg 37, 45, 66–7
Hamburger Collection, Laren 63
Handelsmaatschappij Albert de Bary & Co. 32, 64, 116
Handelstrust West (Commercial Trust West, HTW) 32, 172, 172–3
Handwerkersvriendenkring (Artists' Friendly Circle) 130
Hanemann, Carl 121–2
Hannema, Dr D. 72, 73, 197
Harster, Dr W. 211, 212
Hartog Collection, Wassenaar 63, 198
Hausraterfassung 205, 208
Heemaf 32
Heemstede 75
Heerlen 26
Heiliger, Max (fictitious name) 177
Heim im Holland 110
Heinemann, Dr 190

Hekster, S. 117
Helst, Bartholomeus van der 66
Henkel, M.D. 197
Henneicke, W.C. 135, 209
Hensson, P.L. 34
Hermann, Kurt 81
Het Parool 215
Het Vrije Volk 215–16
Heydrich, Reinhard 53–4, 54, 74, 92
Hilversum, Masonic Lodge 57
Himmler, Heinrich 80, 92, 94, 95, 189, 190
Hirsch, N.V. (outfitters) 116
Hirschfeld, Dr H.M. 28
Hitler, Adolf 28, 35, 41, 51, 52, 78, 79, 92, 93, 101, 226
   ambitions for the Netherlands 63, 105
   anti-Semitism 99
   collecting of art for Linz Führermuseum 18, 45, 46, 47, 53, 57, 64, 65, 66, 74, 76, 77, 80–1, 185, 196
   invoking of the law 5, 106
   and looting by ERR 48, 49, 54, 59
   love of art 78
   rapacity 2
   and Rosenberg's work 55, 203
   hoards, in southern Germany and Austria 2–3, 92–3, 93, 94
Hobbema, Meindert 68
Hofer, Andreas 46, 57, 74–5, 81, 82, 189
Hofer, Walter 77
Hoffmann, Heinrich 46, 80
Hoge Veluwe National Park *see* Kröller-Müller Museum
Hohe Schule der NSDAP (NSDAP Academy) 59, 62, 207, 208
Hollandsche Koopmansbank (HKB) 18
Hollandsche Sociëteit van Levensverzekeringen, N.V. 183
Holz, Dr 29
Homan, J. Linthorst 21
Hondecoeter, Melchior d' 200
Hoogendijk, D.A. (art dealer) 82
Hoogendijk, L. Proos 162
Hoogland, T.J. 185
household goods 6, 24, 58, 91, 105, 110, 130, 191
   looting of (M-Aktion) 203–9

Index

houses
  clearances 192, 204–5, 206
  confiscated by Wehrmacht 186
  decree controlling Jewish property 123, 124–5
  homes entrusted to another 3
  searches 33
Hunger Winter (1944–5) 25

Impressionist art 47, 73
Incasso Bank, N.V. 76, 162, 167, 172, 173, 178
Independent Order of Odd Fellows 58
industry
  and *Kapitalverflechtung* 28, 31
  strike against German recruitment of workers 24
  under German control 11–12, 14
informers 39
Institut zur Erforschung der Judenfrage (Institute for Research into the Jewish Question), Frankfurt 52
insurance policies, confiscated by Liro 136, 180–3, 221
International Archive of the Women's Movement 56
International Institute for Social History (IISG), Amsterdam 56, 58, 59
inventories, household effects 204, 205, 207
Israëls, Jozef and Isaäc 197
Italy, Dutch gold in 35

Jacob Stodel Fine Arts Company 119
Jaffé, Alphonse, collection of paintings 196
Jansen, H.J.C. 216
Japan, invasion of Dutch east Indies 157
jewellery 1, 4, 6, 93, 138, 140, 177, 185, 211, 221
  from M-Aktion house clearances 208
  sold by Liro 186, 187, 188, 189, 190, 191
  surrendered for deferment of deportation 213, 214, 215–16
jewels 92, 100, 190, 217–18
Jewish congregations and seminaries 56, 207
Jewish Council 111–13, 142–3
Jewish Historical Museum 208
Jewish Restitution Successor Organization 104
Jews
  active in black market 20
  Aryanization of business concerns of 29, 62
  associations and foundations 28
  'black' possessions of 211–12, 226
  confiscation of property of 38–9, 49–50, 65, 100–1, 132, 141–2
  deportations 136, 176, 179
  emigrants' possessions 194
  emotional value of cultural property 185
  estimate of material loss inflicted on 225
  Feindjuden 141, 142
  flight of 52
  of foreign nationality 141
  hunted down by Henneicke Column 209
  Kristallnacht 100
  laws and decrees against 5, 7, 99–101, 105–9, 122–6
  libraries and archives of 51, 56, 57, 59, 192
  Liro Decrees against 7, 38–9, 89, 128–31, 135–6, 147–73, 175–83
  looting of art collections of 54–6
  mixed marriages 131, 141, 142, 143–5, 222, 226
  Nazis' definition of 106–7
  non-profit-making institutions 111–14
  number returned from death camps 228
  registration of 107–8
  restoration of property and rights to 228
  securities stolen from 32, 100, 153–7, 164–5
  seen as Nazis' enemies 51–2, 53
  slave labour 24–5
  special expropriation measures against 6, 54
  transferring of capital abroad after advent of Hitler 101–4, 127
  transport of to extermination camps 100
  Utikal's report 50
  as victims of breaches of confidence 3–4
  see also Aryanization
Jong, Prof. A.M. de 29
Jong, Dr Louis de 4, 213
Joodsche Weekblad 142–3, 182, 204
Jüdische Unterstützungsstelle (Jewish Benefit Agency) 143
Junz, Helen B., and report on stolen Jewish capital 103–4
'just wars' 11

Kalb, Joseph 119
Kali Syndikat (potash syndicate) 81
Kaltenbrunner, Ernst 92, 95
Kapitalverflechtung 28–33, 166, 172–3

Index

Karger, Dr Walter von 132, 133, 134, 136, 189
Karinhall (Göring's country estate) 47, 79, 91
Kas-Vereeniging, N.V. 199
Katz, B., and fraud scandal 74
Katz, Nathan 74
Kenrath, Kreisleiter (District Officer) 34
Kerkhoven & Co. (stockbrokers), Amsterdam 155
Kernkamp, Dr J.H. 61
Keyzer, J. 117
Kieslinger, Dr Franz 63
Kirsten, Feliz 94
Knauth, Nachod & Kühne (Leipzig) 41, 168
Koenigs, Franz W. 71–2
Koenigs collection 45, 71–2
Koffieberg, J.P. 136, 137, 140–1, 194
Köhler, H. 191
Kol & Co. 18, 160
Koninklijk Nederlandsche Hoogovens (Royal Dutch Blast Furnaces) 30, 32
Koninklijke Bibliotheek (Royal Library), The Hague 59, 60
Koninklijke Olie *see* Shell
Konversionskasse für Deutsche Auslandsschulden (Conversion Bank for German Foreign Debts) 17
Kriminalpolizei (Kripo) 6
Kristallnacht 99, 100
Kröller-Müller, Helene and Müller, Anthony George 72
Kröller-Müller Museum, Hoge Veluwe National Park 57, 72, 72–3
Krüger, Berhard 92
Krup von Bohlen und Halbach, Alfred 80
Kümmel, Prof. Otto, report on Germany's cultural losses 49, 62
Kunsthandel J. Goudstikker, N.V. 68, 75–8

labour, requisitioning of 24–5
labour service 211
Lages, Willy 205, 211
Lake Toplitz, near Salzberg, hoard of treasures 92, 93
land, decrees to transfer Jewish property 100, 122–6
Landelijke Hypotheekbank (Rural Mortgage Bank) 125
Lange (auction house), Berlin 64, 66, 66–7
Lanz, Mrs 73, 74

Lanz, Otto 73
Lanz Collection 73–4
Laren *see* Hamburger Collection
Larson-Menzel, Mrs 196
Latin America 47
Laube (auction house), Zurich 200
League of Nations 51
Leer, W.A. van der 199
Leeser, F. 40
Leeuw, A.J. van der 119, 133, 165
Leeuwarden 26
  Museum 197
legacies 111
legal factors 3
  influence of Allied Declaration 87–8
  Nazi justification of crimes against Jews 100
  Nazi justifications for looting 5, 48, 77–8
  purchase of confiscated Jewish securities 165–6
  purchase of Goudstikker business 76
  registration of Jewish businesses 114
  theft of possessions of Nazis' 'enemies' 51, 70–1
  see also anti-Jewish laws; decrees
Leiden
  University Library 60, 60–1
  see also De Lakenhal museum
Leipzig 207
Lempert, Matthias (auction house) 66, 186, 189
Lenin, V.I., Swiss bank account 102
Liberation 4, 25–6, 169, 201
  inventory of effects surrendered to Liro 221–3
libraries 1, 43, 52, 53–4, 55, 208
  looted by ERR in Netherlands 56, 57, 58, 59–62, 192
  of Nazis' 'enemies' 51, 52, 57–8
Lieber Code 44–5
Liebknecht, Karl 51
Liechtenstein 171
Limburg 62
Lincoln, Abraham 44
Linz *see* Führermuseum
Linz-Esslinger, Anna 218
Lippmann, Rosenthal & Co. (Liro), Sarphatistraat 3, 4, 32, 38, 41, 105, 120, 122, 127–32, 228
  as accredited stockbroker 152–3
  administrative problems 143–5

– 309 –

Index

board of directors 132–3, 138
clientele 185
confiscating of art on loan to museums 195–7
and Dienststelle Mühlmann 63, 64
fire and theft insurances 138–9, 208
and First Liro Decree in Practice 147–73 passim
and funds from non-profit-making organizations 113–14
household goods handed to 205, 208–9
index cards 192, 193
internal fraud and theft 139–41, 192
inventory of effects surrendered to 221–3
and Jewish land proceeds 124, 125, 126
maintenance payments to Jews 142–3
and Mak van Way auction house 57
paintings purchased by Dutch museums from 197–9
and sale of cultural property 186–94
and sale of looted securities 157–9, 164, 169
Sammelkonto 109, 139, 141–2, 143, 152
and Second Liro Decree in Practice 175–83 passim
staff 135–6, 147
store records 208
structure 136–8
and the Treasury 218–20
Von Karger and Witscher 134–5
and VVRA 109, 117
see also Liro Decrees
Lippmann, Rosenthal & Co., Nieuwe Spiegelstraat 119, 127, 128, 135–6, 152, 153, 200
Liro Decrees 7, 38–9, 128–31, 135, 145
  First 147–73 passim 128, 161, 186
  Second 130, 136, 148–9, 149, 175–83 passim 187–8, 189, 192, 195–6, 223
Lisser & Rosencranz (Jewish bank) 72
livestock 24
Lohse, Dr Bruno 47
London 30, 82, 180, 194
  Dutch government-in-exile 32, 68, 85–6, 86–7
  see also British Museum
loot
  as term (*roof*) 4–5
  see also hoards

looting
  by compulsory charity 20–2
  by confiscation 23, 25, 36, 63, 70–1
  of cultural property 43–5
  Dutch authorities' definition of 5–6
  estimate of material loss to Dutch Jewry 225
  estimate of material loss to Netherlands 225
  euphemisms for 104–5
  by fining 26
  by forced surrender or by requisition 23–6
  forms of 4, 7, 12, 18–35
  by individuals 33–4
  legalizing of by Nazis 77–8
  by liquidation of associations and foundations 26–8
  in M-Aktion 203–9
  by purchase 18–20, 43
  scale of Liro activities 135, 150
  tactics 225–7
  through the centuries 11, 85
lotteries 22
Louvre 2
Lübeck 140, 191
Lucerne, Switzerland *see* Galerie Fischer
Lugt, Frits J. 70
Lugt Collection 63, 70–1
Luxembourg 15

M-Aktion 203–9
Maasdijk, H.C. van 125
Maastricht 38
machinery 1, 24, 25, 44, 91
Maes, Nicolaas 186
Maison de Bonneterie 116
Manet, Édouard 47
Mannheim 110
Mannheimer collection 18, 45–6
manuscripts 1, 43, 59–61
Maris, Jacob 199
marks
  Reichskreditkassenscheine 19
  and *Sperrmarken* 17
Marx-May, Ellen von 128, 200
Masonic Lodges 27, 56, 109
  see also Freemasons
Mauthausen 92
May, Paul 128, 200
May, Robert 128, 133, 153, 200

Index

Meermanno-Westreenianum, The Hague 60, 61
Meijer, family 217
Mein Kampf (Hitler) 80, 93
Melmer, Bruno 177
Mensing, Dr B. 68
Mensing, B.F.M. 200
Meppel 34, 37
merchandise
  estimated value 2
  looting by purchase 19–20
Merck, Finck & Co. 151
Merkel, O. 31
Merkers, Thuringia, mines near 2
metals 20, 23, 24
  see also gold; platinum; precious metals; silver
Metropolitan Museum of Art 1, 2
Metternich, Graf Wolff 54
Meulen, H. te 170–1, 171
Middle Ages, idea of 'just wars' 11
Miedl, Alois 46, 65, 68, 81, 93
  as customer of Nathan Katz 74
  and Koenigs Collection 72
  and Mannheimer collection 18
  and takeover of Kunsthandel J. Goudstikker 75–8
Mieris, Frans van 64
Milch, General Erhard 93
military decorations, German use of looted diamonds in 191
Ministry of Education, Science and Culture (OWC) 69, 195–6, 198–9
Mittenwald, hoard of gold 2–3
Modest, Dr W. 31
Mojert, Dr P. 29
Molotov-Ribbentrop pact (1939) 51
Monet, Claude 47
money
  accounting of 4
  cash confiscated by Liro 131, 138, 221
  collected by SS from concentration camps 176–7
  confiscated from Gypsies 6
  First Liro Decree 147–8
  found in Jews' houses 130
  looted from banks 34
  looted from non-profit-making organizations 113–14

Nazis' hidden hoards 95
  Second Liro Decree 176
  surrendered for permits 213, 214
  taken to safety by Jews 101–4
  see also foreign currency; marks
Monker, G.P.J. 173
Monowitz (near Auschwitz) 24
moral factors, purchase of confiscated Jewish securities 165–6
Moravia 54, 115, 208
Morgenthau, Henry 88
mortgages, Jewish 123, 125–6
Moscow
  as signatory of Allied Declaration 72
  Tretiakov Gallery 2
Mucke, Dr F.A. 34
Mühlmann, Josef 65
Mühlmann, Dr Katejan 18, 43, 47, 62–6, 70, 73, 80, 186, 190, 191, 192, 195
Mulisch, K.V.K. 133, 194
Müller, Frederik (auction house), Amsterdam 57, 66, 68, 200
Muller, G.M. 161
Müller-Lehning, Hans Werner 27, 28, 113
Munch, Edvard 79
Munich 93, 191
  auctions of Dutch art 66, 66–7
  Führerbau 46, 56
Munich Galerie für alte Kunst 186
Municipal Pawn Shop, Berlin 177
munitions 35
Munster 60
Museum for Asian Art 198
museums 43, 60, 62
  art collections 68
  cultural property loaned to 186, 195–7
  German 79, 91, 189, 190
  purchases of art from Liro 197–9, 227
  selling of art works from stores of 67

Napoleon 44, 48
Napoleonic Wars 49
National Giro Bank 148
National Socialism *see* Nazi ideology; NSB
Nazi ideology
  hereditary enemies of 50–2, 56–7, 57–8
  racial purity 6
  and Rosenberg's Hohe Schule 50–1

– 311 –

Index

Nazis
- dormant bank accounts in Switzerland 102
- ignoring of Hague Convention 5
- leading figures' love of art 78–80
- looting of occupied territories 1, 85
- political asylum 91–2
- scale of robbery by 3
- works of art sold to 64–5, 66, 70
- *see also* NSDAP; Third Reich

Nederlands Arbeidsfront (Dutch Labour Front) 27

Nederlandsch-Indische Aardoliemaatschappij (Dutch East Indies Mineral Oil Company) 31

Nederlandsch-Israelitic Seminary, library 56

Nederlandsche Bank 14, 19, 21–2, 28, 29, 34, 35, 36–7, 38, 40, 41–2, 167, 224

Nederlandsche Handelsmaatschappij 172, 173

Nederlandsche Unie (Netherlands Union) 21

Nederlandsche Volksdienst (Dutch people's Service) 113–14

Nederlandse Beheersinstituut (Netherlands Control Institute, NBI) 192

Nederlandse Clearinginstitut 12–13

Netherlands
- and abolition of currency border 12–15, 224
- *Auslandbonds* 17–18
- civil administration under Nazi control 11, 15
- claim against Third Reich at Reparation Conference 18–19, 224–5
- decrees and laws for looting of Jews' possessions 104–9
- emergency decrees issued from London 85–6, 89, 154
- ending of looting restrictions 11–12
- estimate of material loss through looting 225
- estimated value of articles looted from 2
- forms of looting 7, 18–35
- German invasion of 36, 66, 85
- Hitler's ambitions for 63, 105, 200
- as investor in America 86
- Jewish shares remaining in 173
- Junz report on stolen Jewish capital 103–4
- Liberation 4, 25–6, 169
- looting by ERR 48, 55, 56–8, 59–62
- looting by Mühlmann 43, 63–5
- looting of works of art 47, 55
- merging of economy with German Planned economy 28–33

- Nazis' rounding up of Gypsies 6
- paintings acquired by Hitler from 80
- participation of in sale of stolen Jewish property 227
- private art collections 18, 64–5
- robbery of through decrees imposed by Third Reich 12–16
- SS 41

Netherlands Administrative Institute 89

Netherlands Art-Collection Foundation 74

Netherlands Census Office 107, 108

Netherlands State Bureau for Art-Historical Documentation 70, 197

Netherlands State Institute for War Documentation 133, 165

neutral countries 88, 101, 163, 195
- *see also* Portugal; Spain; Sweden; Switzerland

New York *see* Metropolitan Museum of Art; Sotheby's

Niederländische Aktiengesellschaft für die Abwicklung von Unternehmungen (Netherlands Joint-Stock Company for the Liquidation of Businesses, NAGU) 115, 116, 118

Niederländische Grundstücksverwaltung (Netherlands Real Estate Administration, NGV) 109, 123, 124, 219

Nienhuis, H. 187

Nienhuys Collection, Bloemendaal 63

Nijmegen 38, 57
- Municipal Museum 60

Nolte, L. 31

non-profit-making institutions, decrees against 26–8, 111–14

Norway 15, 86, 101

NSB (Nationaal-socialistische Beweging, Dutch National Socialist Movement) 14, 21, 26, 41, 69, 123, 125, 151, 154, 158, 162, 187

NSDAP (German Nazi Party) 42, 46, 52, 53, 99–100, 133
- *see also* Nazi ideology; Nazis

Nubé, G.R. 169–70

Nuremberg
- hanging of top Nazis 95
- International Military Tribunals 2, 40, 48, 59

Nuremberg Laws 5, 99

Index

Obersalzberg *see* Berghof
objets d'art 131, 136, 185, 186, 187, 189, 190
   from M-Aktion clearances 206, 206–7
   illegally taken by Liro employees 140, 141
occupation costs 15–16, 16, 25, 36, 88
   claimed by Allies after Liberation 25–6
Olij, Hermann (Dr Bosch) 140, 208–9
Omnia Treuhand 64, 115, 116, 118, 187, 194, 219
Oranienburg concentration camp, forgery of British noted 92
Ostade, Adriaen van 63, 64, 66, 68, 186
Otto Wolff Konzern 41, 168
Overhoff, Carel F. 152–3, 154, 155, 156–7, 158, 159, 161, 162–3, 165, 166

paintings
   acquired for Hitler's Linz collection 46, 63–4, 65, 68, 70, 72
   by Jewish artists or portraits of Jews 197–8
   confiscated by Liro 131, 138, 186
   Dutch art market 66–7
   estimated value of items stolen from Netherlands 1, 2, 45
   illegally taken by Liro employees 140, 141
   items never recovered 91
   on loan to Dutch museums 195, 196, 199, 200–1
   looted from private collections 68–75, 76, 196
   M-Aktion clearances 206, 206–7, 208
   purchased by Dutch museums from Liro 197–9
   Rosenberg's report to Hitler on looting of 55
   Second Liro Decree 176
   smuggling of 47
   sold by Liro 186, 187, 189, 190, 194
   taken by leading Nazis 64–5, 70, 185, 189
Pannwitz, Caterina von, and Pannwitz Collection 74–5
Paraira, D.C. 198
Paris
   abandonment of libraries and archives 52
   black market in foreign currency 167
   buying of paintings for Hitler and Göring 47
   ERR 47, 81
   houses of Jews who had fled 203
   report estimating extent of Nazi looting 2
   Rothschild collections 56

Second Peace of (1815) 44
   see also Louvre; Reparation Conference
patents 111
pearls 130, 176, 188, 213
Peru 93
Pfeffer, Dr 29
Philips 30, 31, 111, 165
Phöbus, N.V. 180
Picasso, Pablo 47
Piek, Carel 21
Piero di Cosimo 66
pillage 33–4
Pissarro, Camille 73
platinum 100, 130, 176
Plietzsch, A. 73
Plietzsch, Dr Eduard 63, 64, 65, 189, 191, 197
Plutzar, Dr F. 62, 198
Polak Collection, Amersfoort 63
Poland 43, 54, 63, 100, 207
political material, search of archives 53
political parties, liquidation of 27
Pont, J.H. de 169, 170
porcelain 176, 187, 189, 199, 200, 206–7
   Göring's buried treasure 94
Portugal 2, 30, 35, 47, 91, 167
Portuguese-Israelitic Community 199
Portuguese-Israelitic Seminary Ets Haim 56
Posse, Dr Hans 31, 45, 46, 63–4, 71–2, 73, 74, 189, 190, 193
postage stamps 176, 177, 187, 191, 223
Potter, Paulus 66
Prague 115
precious metals 2, 91, 92, 100, 138, 185, 223
   sold by Liro 186, 187
   value of items surrendered for permits 215–16
   see also gold; silver
precious stones 1, 38, 130, 176, 185, 223
   sold by Liro 186, 187, 188, 191
   value of items surrendered for permits 215–16
   see also diamond industry; diamonds
Presser, J. 213
private property
   anti-Jewish measures for expropriation of 99, 100–1, 122–6, 129–31, 132, 175, 178
   confiscation of 23, 36
   Hague Convention 45, 50
   WOL stipulation on 23, 25

Index

property rights, of Dutch citizens during war 86
Prussian Mint 177
Puls (furniture removers) 204, 205
Puttkammer, E.A.P. 213–16

Quay, J.E. de 21

racial purity
  Nazi ideology 6, 51
  NSDAP programme 99–100
Radio Oranje 32, 85, 86–7, 154
radios 11, 24, 105, 109
Rahusen, H.P. 153
Ramschware (shoddy goods) 192, 208–9
Rasche, Dr Karl 31
Rathenau, Walter 51–2, 195
Rauter, Hanns 108–9, 185, 190
raw materials 25, 39, 40, 41, 91
real estate 111, 123
Rebholz, Otto 18, 27, 40–1, 42, 160, 227
  and implementation of Liro Decrees 158–9, 159, 160–1, 162, 162–3, 165, 167–8, 169, 170–1, 173
Reemstma (tobacco plant owner) 81
Reger, Hans 46
Regteren Altena, M. van 153, 154
Reich Ministry for Occupied Eastern Territories 203
Reichert & Co. 188
Reichsarchiv, Vienna 60
Reichsbank 2, 19, 35, 36, 37, 41, 42, 93, 167–8, 177, 191, 212, 224
Reichskreditgesellschaft, Berlin 168
Reichskristallnacht *see* Kristallnacht
Reichssicherheitshauptamt (Central Security Department of Reich, RSHA) 94–5, 168, 208, 212, 222
  competition with ERR 52–4, 56
Reinheldt (trader) 140, 186, 188, 189
Rembrandt Harmensz van Rijn 63, 64, 66, 68, 69, 74, 195
Renoir, Jean 47, 71, 73
rent, outstanding payments 179
Reparation Conference, Paris (1945) 18–19, 224–5
reparations
  for items surrendered in hope of emigration 215
  legislation in German Federal Republic 193

requisitions, stipulation of WOL Convention 12, 15
restitution 3, 4, 124
  clauses embodied in Treaty of Versailles 85
  impossibility of 216
  influence of Allied Declaration 87–8
  post-war legal decrees 88–9
  of property and rights 89, 228
Rheinmetall Borsig AG 32
Ribbentrop, Joachim von 80, 92, 94–5, 95
Rijksmuseum, Amsterdam 63, 69, 73, 77, 195, 197–8, 199–201
Rijnsburg *see* Spinoza House library
Rijnsche Handelsbank 116
ritual objects 1
  looted from Freemasons 57
robbery
  by purchase 75
  forms of 33
  indirect 7, 12–16, 19
  scale of 3, 178
Roermond 38, 62
Rog, G. 68, 69
Rohstoff-Handelsgesellschaft (Roges), The Hague 20
Romania 31
Roosevelt, President Franklin D. 86, 180
Ros, N.J. 217
Rosenberg, Dr Alfred 4, 43, 47–8, 48–9, 79, 81
  confiscating of abandoned art collections 54–6, 56–7
  justification for thefts from Nazis' 'enemies' 51, 57
  and NSDAP High School 49, 50–1, 52, 52–3
  see also Einsatzstab Reichsleiter Rosenberg (ERR)
Rosenberg, Paul, art collection 57
Rosenthal, J.J.B. Bosch Ridder van 213
Rosicrucians 27, 58
Rosier, J.P. 140
Rossum, J.T. van 181
Rotary Clubs 27, 58
Rothschild, family 52, 56
Rothschild collections 46, 55, 56
Rotterdam
  Masonic Lodge 57
  municipal library 60
Rotterdamsche Bank 34, 80, 162, 172, 173

– 314 –

Index

Rotterdamsche Bankvereeniging (Robaver) 214, 215
royal archives 43
Rubens, Peter Paul 63, 64, 72
Ruhbaum, Paul 60
Russia *see* St Petersburg
Ruysdael, Jacob van 63, 64, 66, 77

safe deposits
  Amsterdamsche Bank 131, 132
  contents treated as enemy property 111
  fraud at Liro 139
  inspection of 38–9
  and Second Liro Decree 177, 179
St Petersburg 72
Sarajevo, murder of Archduke Franz Ferdinand 51
Sarphati, Samuel 127
Schacht, Hjalmar 17
Schallenberg, Friedrich 34
Schellenberg, Walter 94–5, 95
Schendel, A. van 69
Schifferstein, F.H. 29
Schilling, G. 187, 188
Schirach, Baldur von 65
Schirmer, August 58, 206
Schmidt, General-Kommissar Fritz 188–9, 189, 191
Schmidt-Stähler, Albert 190, 191, 192, 203, 206
Schmitz, Hermann, and collection of flies 62
Schweizerische Bankgesellschaft, Zurich 218
Schwend, Friedrich 93
Schwerin Krosigk, L. von 157
sculptures 63, 73, 176, 223
Searle, Daniel C. 71
Second World War
  extent of looting by Germans 1
  German 'purchases' of cultural property 45
  outbreak of 99
  pillage 33
securities 4, 17, 29–30, 34, 94
  Allied searches for 91, 92
  First Liro Decree in practice 147–73 passim 131, 138
  from Jewish sources 32, 100, 153–73 passim
  looted from non-profit-making organizations 113
  in private safe deposits 38
  Second Liro Decree in practice 177
  see also shares
Seyss-Inquart, Dr Arthur 11, 15, 39, 79, 105, 127, 129, 196, 203–4
  at Nuremberg Tribunal 59
  and *Auslandbonds* 18
  and Bühler 41, 42
  interest in objets d'art 185
  issuing of decrees 7, 21, 23, 28, 37, 56, 57, 105, 106, 108, 112, 117, 118, 123, 206
  jurisdiction of enemy property 76, 195
  and Liro Decrees 143, 149
  and Mühlmann 18, 62–3, 65, 73
  presenting of looted paintings to Hitler 70
  and sale of looted securities 152, 157, 163, 165, 168
shares
  American 34, 159–63, 227
  collected by SS from concentration camps 177
  confiscated by Liro 131, 147, 150, 151–2, 164, 169, 173, 176, 221
  foreign currency 168
  Kapitalverflechtung 30, 32–3, 166
  looted from non-profit-making organizations 113
  outstanding claims abroad 179–80
  sold in neutral countries 30, 41
  taken to safety by Jews 101
  see also securities
sheet music 207–8
Shell (Koninklijke Olie) 30, 30–1, 111, 150, 158, 159, 165, 168, 172
shops 100, 116
  see also bookshops
Sicherheitsdienst (German Security Service, SD) 28, 42, 57, 109, 118, 134, 142, 167, 217
Sicherheitspolizei (German Security Police, SP) 6, 23, 34, 58, 59, 70, 108, 109, 118, 121, 205, 213, 215, 222, 226
Sicherstellung (safekeeping) 49, 63, 120
silver 1, 4, 100, 185, 221
  collected by SS from concentration camps 176–7
  confiscated by order of Second Liro 130, 136, 176
  M-Aktion clearances 206–7, 208

Index

in private safe deposits 38
  sold by Liro 186, 187, 189, 190
  surrendered to museums 200
Sittard 38
slave labour, I.G. Farben 24–5
Sluyters, Jan 199
smuggling
  of looted works of art 47
  post-war trade 34
social democrats 53
Societas Spinoza, library (The Hague) 58
Sotheby's
  London 194
  New York 71
South America 35, 91, 92, 93, 163, 167, 215
Soviet troops, seizure of drawings from Koenigs Collection 72
Soviet Union 16, 36, 51, 52
  occupied territories 203
  see also Moscow; Stalingrad
Spain 2, 30, 35, 47, 77, 91, 93
Spartacus League 51
Speer, Albert 45
Sperrstempel 122, 211–18, 223, 226
Spiegel, N.V. (mirror and picture-framing works) 117
Spinoza House library, Rijnsburg 56, 58
Spiritualists, library 58
SS (Schutzstaffel) 24, 93, 109
  see also Gestapo
Staatsarchiv, Munster 60
Stalingrad, fall of 124
Stechow-Kotzen, Thilo Carl, Baron von 134, 140, 187, 191–2
Steen, Jan 63, 64, 66, 77
Stern 92
Sternheim, D.A. 75
Stichting Winterhulp Nederland *see* Winterhulp
Stodel, Salomon and Bernhard *see* Jacob Stodel Fine Arts Company
Streefkerk, D. 182–3
Struycken, A.A.M. 169, 171
Supreme Court, Netherlands (Hoge Raad), ruling on Jewish equities 153, 154
Sweden 30, 35, 47, 91, 92
Switzerland 86, 217
  acceptance of tainted German gold 35, 35–6
  banks and banking organizations 2, 35, 93, 101, 102, 103
  dormant bank accounts 102
  and exit visa of Mrs Pannwitz 75
  Göring's hoard of funds in 93–4
  and Lanz Collection 74
  and Lugt 70, 71
  as market for 'degenerate art' 79, 190
  non-recoverable assets in 180
  as safe haven for Jews' capital 101–2, 103, 218
  as sanctuary for Nazis 91–2, 92
  selling of art in 47, 79
  selling of securities and shares in 30, 167, 168
  see also Galerie Fischer, Lucerne; Zurich
synagogues 100, 111, 112, 199

Tagesanzeiger 212–13
Tailor, Francis H. 1
tapestries 199, 200
tax authorities, and emigrating Jews 218–20
teeth and fillings, gold 176, 177
Telefunken 31
De Telegraaf 158, 173
Ten Cate Collection, Twente 65
Tenkink, Justice J.C. 21
testimonies 4, 216
textiles 24
theft
  difficulty in proving 3
  Dutch authorities' definition 6
  scale of 4
Theosophical Society library 58
Theresienstadt 71
Third Reich
  anti-Semitic laws and decrees 12, 99–101, 132
  arraignment of leaders 40
  claims against presented at Reparation Conference 18–20
  different attitudes towards possessions 93
  and fall of Stalingrad 124
  hoard of gold in soil of 2
  looted Jewish gold as property of 204
  rapacity of 1–2, 176
  see also Nazis
Thirty Years' War 49
Thyssen, Fritz 93–4
Tiel 34
Tintoretto 77

Index

Tonningen, M.M. Rost van 14, 21, 22, 36, 42, 159
trade, Germany and Netherlands 13
trade unionists 53
transport 1, 11, 24, 25, 44
Treaty of Locarno 52
Treaty of Versailles 49, 85
Tretiakov Gallery, Moscow 2
Treuhänder Archiv (fiduciary archive) 134
Trip, L.J.A. 14, 19, 28, 42, 153
Troost, Cornelis 64
Turkey 35, 93
Twentsche Bank 172, 173

Unilever 30, 30–1, 31, 158
United States of America (USA)
  assets and investments in 86, 180
  attempts to sell looted works of art to 47
  Economic Warfare Department 1
  entry into Second World War 70, 110
  flight of Jewish capital to 101, 103, 104, 180
  German property in 111
  Gold Declaration 88
  intelligence service 35
  Lugt's flight to 70, 71
  report on money and securities in Davos 91
  shares traded by Amsterdam Stock Exchange 159–62, 227
  Treasury archives 104
Utikal, Gerhard 49–50
Utrecht
  Centraal Museum 68
  Masonic Lodge 57
  University library 60

Valkenburg Monastery library 56
valuation
  by Liro of looted cultural property 187–9
  of cultural property 1–2, 43–4
  effects surrendered to Liro 221–3
  household effects 206
  items surrendered for deferment of deportation 215
  of looted Jewish property 223–4
Van Gelder & Co., Wormer 208
Van Gogh, Vincent 73, 79, 216
Van Marle & Bignell (auction house), The Hague 57, 68, 110, 198

Vattel, Empheric de, *The Law of Nations* (1758) 44
Velde, Esaias van de 186
Velde, Willem van de (the Younger) 68
Veltjens, Colonel Josef 20
Vereeniging voor de Effectenhandel (VvdE, Stock Exchange Union) 152–3, 171
  and trading of securities from Jewish sources 153–7, 157, 161, 162, 163, 164–5, 166
Vermeer, Jan 65, 74
Vermögensverwaltungs- und Rentenanstalt (Property Administration and Pensions Institute, VVRA) 38, 89, 109, 117–18, 118–19, 123, 124, 152, 168, 169, 173, 219, 222, 223, 228
Verordnungsblatt (*Verordnung* Gazette) 106
Vienna 45, 46, 60, 65, 66, 66–7
visas
  exchanged for paintings 74, 74–5
  Jews making payments for 217–18
Vleming, J. 170–1, 171
Volcker, Paul, and Volcker Committee 103
Vollmer, Dr 60
voluntary associations 27
Voss, Dr Hermann 46
Vries, Dr A.B. de 74
Vries, D.H. de 125
Vught concentration camp 109

Waay, Mak van, and auction house 57, 186, 187, 189, 194
Waffen-SS shooting competitions, prizes 190
War on Land Convention *see* WOL Convention
Warburg, Karl S. 199
Wasmann, E., and collection of ants 62
Wassenaar *see* Hartog Collection
watches 176, 177, 185, 188
Wehrmacht 12, 15, 20, 24, 25, 52–3, 69, 186, 192, 206
Weimar Republic 52
Weinmüller (auction house) 64, 66, 66–7
Weissman, J.J. 213
Weitjens, W.M.A. 69
Wellington, Arthur Wellesley, 1st duke of 44
Werkspoor, N.V. (Railway Track) 32
Westerbork transit camp 6, 109, 120, 121, 121–2, 131, 179, 209, 226
Westerse Bank 199

Index

Wiedergutmachung legislation *see* Brüg regulations
Wiesbaden museum 46
Wijnand, J.H. 158, 173
Willemsen, H.B. 172, 173
Wimmer, Dr F. 59, 196
Winterhulp (Dutch Winter Aid Foundation) 20–2, 27, 113–14
Wirtschaftsprüfstelle (Economic Investigation Bureau, WPS) 39, 109, 114, 115, 116, 117, 118, 189
Witscher, Otto 132, 133, 134–5, 136, 139, 142
Witsen, Willem Arnold 199
Wodan Handelsmaatschappij 18
Wohltat, H.C.H. 41
WOL Convention (Convention Respecting the Laws and Customs of War on Land) 5, 11, 85
    Nazis' deliberate misreading of 5, 12, 106
    on occupation costs 16, 36, 88
    on pillage 33
    on private property 23, 25
    and question of Jewish securities 153–5
    role of cultural property 44
    stipulations on requisitions 12, 15, 24
Wolf, Martin 187, 188
Wolff, SS-General Karl 93
World Jewish Congress 102, 103
Wörlein, K. 205, 215

Zaandam 57
Zentralstelle für jüdische Auswanderung (Central Office of Jewish Emigration) 131, 135, 194, 205, 212, 214, 215, 218–19
Zoological Museum, University of Berlin 62
Zurich 102, 200, 218